D1523500

Indoor Air Quality

Indoor Air Quality

Solutions and Strategies

Steve M. Hays, P.E., C.I.H.

Ronald V. Gobbell, AIA

Nicholas R. Ganick, P.E.

McGraw-Hill, Inc.

New York   San Francisco   Washington, D.C.   Auckland   Bogotá
Caracas   Lisbon   London   Madrid   Mexico City   Milan
Montreal   New Delhi   San Juan   Singapore
Sydney   Tokyo   Toronto

Library of Congress Cataloging-in-Publication Data

Hays, Steve M.
    Indoor air quality / Steve M. Hays, Ronald V. Gobbell, Nicholas R. Ganick.
        p.   cm.
    Includes bibliographical references and index.
    ISBN 0-07-027373-1
    1. Indoor air pollution.   2. Air—Purification.   I. Gobbell, Ronald V.
II. Ganick, Nicholas R.   III. Title.
TD883.1.H39   1995
628.5′3—dc20   94-25996
                                                      CIP

1 2 3 4 5 6 7 8 9 0 DOC/DOC 9 0 9 8 7 6 5 4

ISBN 0-07-027373-1

The sponsoring editor for this book was Robert W. Hauserman, the editing supervisor was Nancy Young, and the production supervisor was Pamela A. Pelton. This book was set in Century Schoolbook by McGraw-Hill's Professional Book Group composition unit.

Printed and bound by R. R. Donnelley & Sons Company.

This book is printed on acid-free paper.

Contents

Preface

With the emergence of indoor air quality (IAQ) as a significant issue in this decade, research on the subject has accelerated. There is no shortage of information that addresses individual aspects of IAQ, and we can expect this trend to continue as IAQ concerns continue, perhaps into the next century. Because we, the writers, make our living in architectural, engineering, and environmental consulting, we have made a point of following the articles, reports, books, and papers that have been written on IAQ issues. We have contributed to the stockpile, as well. What we have recognized is a need for a reference for the professional community of architects, engineers, industrial hygienists, and people who own, manage, maintain, and operate buildings that organizes a vast array of knowledge into a methodical, holistic approach to IAQ control. When we were given the opportunity to write this book, we knew the direction we would take.

The writers of this book are an architect, a certified industrial hygienist with a background in chemical engineering, and a mechanical engineer. We know from experience that IAQ is a complex issue and that each of these disciplines—architecture, industrial hygiene, and mechanical engineering—is a part of the puzzle. *Indoor Air Quality: Solutions and Strategies* is based on a philosophy of interrelated disciplines. Our work in the field of IAQ has combined the three disciplines synergistically. Our book comes from literature review, from experience in practice, and from consultations with our colleagues. It is important to note that much of the information available is still new, untested, and often conflicting. We have used our best judgment in presenting such information.

This book is written as an overview for professionals in the building industry. It is our intention to provide a foundation of IAQ analysis and control, showing relationships among the various disciplines which are fundamental to an understanding of IAQ issues and the practical applications of these disciplines to IAQ.

Indoor Air Quality: Solutions and Strategies offers a fundamental course in what we know about IAQ. Volumes are yet to be written based on knowledge that will be gained during the next decade. This text should be utilized for guidelines and general procedures, with the understanding that the information presented is based on and, in some instances, limited to current technical and scientific knowledge. There is no substitute for hiring a qualified IAQ consultant for specific situations.

Reference to a specific trade name or commercial product does not constitute the authors' endorsement, recommendation, or censure for use.

Steve M. Hays
Ronald V. Gobbell
Nicholas R. Ganick

Acknowledgments

The authors wish to acknowledge a few of the individuals whose efforts helped to make this book possible—or better.

We are grateful to Jeffrey Davidson of the Environmental Protection Agency for sharing information and ideas. In addition, we wish to thank Robert Axelrad of the EPA, who provided a wealth of resource materials for our research and examination.

To Eva Ewing, vice-president of Compass Environmental, Inc., we extend our sincere gratitude for a thorough, thoughtful, time-consuming review of portions of the manuscript.

We wish to thank those manufacturers' representatives who were willing to discuss their products candidly and to provide documentation and information in the interest of presenting the most current and accurate facts to the public. One of these individuals was William Freeman, manager of special projects in the floor division of Armstrong World Industries, whose cooperation and advice we deeply appreciate.

Our own staff at Gobbell Hays Partners, Inc. (GHP) never failed in their support of our efforts. To Harriet Cates, who provided painstaking research, we are deeply indebted. To those on our staff who worked with the authors on a variety of tasks and to those who worked on our other projects so that the book could happen, we thank you for your invaluable contribution.

Without reservation, our greatest appreciation is to Phyllis Gobbell, who coordinated the efforts of the authors and the GHP staff. She composed draft language for portions of the manuscript and guided the authors through the considerable effort required for the book. Her skills as a writer, coordinator, grammarian, editor, and taskmaster made this book a reality.

Indoor Air Quality

Introduction

1.1 The IAQ Problem

Indoor air quality (IAQ) is a complex issue, much more so than any single environmental issue. There are hundreds of pollutants that affect IAQ and thousands of sources. Research indicates that more than 900 different contaminants are present in indoor environments,[1] depending on the particular operations and activities which occur within the specific environments. The indoor environment in any building involves the interactions of a complex set of factors that are constantly changing.

A healthy indoor environment is one which promotes the comfort, health, and well-being of the building users. Temperature and humidity are controlled within a comfort zone. Normal concentrations of respiratory gases, such as carbon dioxide, are maintained. The air is free of significant levels of contaminants and odors. Also contributing to a sense of well-being are comfortable levels of lighting and sound, appropriate ergonomic conditions, and job satisfaction. These factors are not air quality issues in the strict sense but, nevertheless, affect occupants' perceptions of IAQ and, therefore, are important in a healthy indoor environment.

1.1.1 The nature of the problem

If needs for comfort, health, and well-being are not satisfied, building users may begin to complain of symptoms which are associated with poor IAQ. Headaches, burning and itching eyes, respiratory difficulties, skin irritation, nausea, and fatigue are some of the common complaints. These symptoms are often vague, but they generally seem worse after a day in the workplace and may altogether disappear when the occupant leaves the building. A number of symptoms may occur together, without a specific identifiable cause.

Sick building syndrome (SBS) is now a common term in the workplace—and the building owner's nightmare. SBS has been defined as the condition in which at least 20 percent of the building occupants display symptoms of illness for more than 2 weeks, and the source of these illnesses cannot be positively identified. Another term associated with unhealthy buildings is *building-related illness* (BRI), a condition in which the cause of the symptoms is known. BRI can be traced to a specific building source and is characterized by a distinguishable set of symptoms.[2]

A discussion of IAQ symptoms, SBS, and BRI is found in Chap. 2.

1.1.2 The magnitude of the problem

Beyond the concern for the health of the building users, which is a significant issue in itself, the economic considerations are monumental. The United States Environmental Protection Agency (EPA) has estimated that the United States spends over $1 billion in direct medical costs attributable to IAQ problems.[3] "Sick" buildings are costly for a number of reasons. Productivity is decreased and absenteeism rates are elevated. The EPA's latest estimate is $60 billion lost annually in decreased productivity brought about by poor IAQ.[3] This estimate is considered conservative because many workers continue to work even while experiencing symptoms that are related to poor IAQ, and many do not connect their symptoms with the air quality of the workplace. Compare the $60 billion figure to the national cost associated with lost productivity from non-IAQ-related major illnesses, an estimated $4.7 to $5.4 billion annually.[3]

Lost productivity is only a fraction of the cost of sick buildings. Vacant facilities may be the result of actual IAQ problems or perceived IAQ problems. Legal implications are an ever-increasing cause for concern. Building owners and managers are the primary defendants in the rising number of lawsuits related to IAQ, but many other professions are affected. In the case of Buckley vs. Kruger-Benson-Ziemer, a computer programmer filed a lawsuit against 9 named and 280 unnamed defendants, including the building's architects, mechanical contractors, heating and air-conditioning consulting engineers; manufacturers, sellers, installers of building air-conditioning equipment; even the manufacturers, distributors, sellers, and installers of carpeting, floor tiles, adhesives; and manufacturers, distributors, and sellers of chemicals used in office machinery.[4] The nation's first IAQ legal case, Call vs. Prudential, was settled out of court in Los Angeles in 1992 after 5 years of litigation.[5] The judge ruled that a building was like a product, and anyone in the chain of people associated with the leasing, design, and construction of the building would be liable for injuries suffered by the plaintiffs.[6] More than 20 federal agencies are involved in IAQ policy-making efforts, and Congress is currently considering two major IAQ bills that could lead to building design guidelines, indoor emission standards, and product labeling requirements. EPA and the World Health Organization (WHO) have estimated that 20 percent of buildings in the United States have serious IAQ problems, 40 percent have somewhat serious problems, and 40 percent have no serious problems.[7]

1.1.3 Reasons for IAQ problems

It is now common knowledge that the energy-efficient designs of the 1970s resulted in tighter building envelopes with improved insulation and low-energy-consuming ventilation, without operable windows, and that under these conditions, indoor pollutants were not sufficiently diluted with fresh air. A further discussion of the heating, ventilation, and air-conditioning systems (HVAC) operations and their impact on IAQ is found in Chap. 3.

Add to the tight building problem an increase in indoor pollutant sources. New building materials, products, and furnishings emit a significant number of potentially hazardous chemicals into the air. The operation of "high-tech" office equipment, which also require cleaning and service, adds another group of products that may be the source of contaminants. Operational activities such as the use of cleaning agents and pesticides contribute to the level of indoor pollutants, as well. The human factor is not to be underestimated as a contributor to the quality of the indoor environment. The presence of people, breathing and emitting body odors, affects IAQ. Human activities such as smoking significantly alter the indoor environment. Cosmetics and personal care products are sources of contaminants. The resulting situation is an increase in contaminants circulating through the indoor environment, with insufficient outside air introduced through the HVAC system to dilute the contaminants.

Sections 3.6, 4.2, and 4.3 include in-depth discussions of maintenance activities, building materials, and building operations, which affect a building's IAQ.

Another factor contributing to the IAQ issue is a change in a building's function, or the function of a space, without proper modifications in the HVAC systems. There has been an increase in commercial renovation during the last decade for a number of reasons. The "modern" office building is easier to renovate than its predecessor; therefore, renovation is often a more cost-effective solution than new construction. When changes in interior layout occur or new equipment that requires additional ventilation is introduced, corresponding changes in the mechanical systems often do not keep pace. Sections 3.3 and 4.4 address functional issues related to IAQ.

Certain other physical factors can relate to building occupants' perception of indoor air quality. Glare from artificial lighting and visual stress from the use of visual display terminals (VDTs) can cause headaches and eye irritation. Vibration and noise may contribute to dizziness, nausea, and general irritability. Ergonomic stressors, such as chairs that are the wrong height for the required task, may promote fatigue. Psychosocial factors, such as excessive workload and poor interpersonal relations, may cause headaches, irritability, and other symptoms that can be mistakenly attributed to poor IAQ. The fact that all these symptoms are similar to symptoms associated with IAQ problems complicates the issue. The symptoms may be incorrectly blamed on contaminated air; however, physical, ergonomic, and psychosocial stressors can, in fact, produce a heightened sensitivity to poor IAQ and, therefore, must be a consideration in the overall IAQ problem. Section 4.5 addresses these factors that affect IAQ perception.

1.2   Diagnosis and Remediation of IAQ Problems

Solutions to IAQ problems require a methodical approach. Figure 1.1 is a graphic illustration of the investigative procedure found to be most effective in practice. Existing building investigations may be required for two reasons: (1) A building assessment is requested to evaluate the potential for IAQ problems. This occurs generally in connection with the purchase or lease of a building, when the buyer or leasor requires an audit of the property. This may also occur as good general practice by building owners or managers who recognize the prudence in preventing problems. (2) Most commonly a building assessment is requested in response to specific complaints by occupants. The design of a new structure or renovation should be reviewed to avoid IAQ problems with occupancy. This is further discussed in Secs. 3.5 and 4.7.

The building assessment is an investigative process which uses three checklists: (1) a core checklist, with general information about the facility, (2) an HVAC checklist, with information regarding mechanical systems, and (3) an architectural components checklist, with information on architecture, construction, and operations. Sample checklists of each type are found in the Appendices. Sections 3.4 and 4.6 use the HVAC and architectural components checklists to discuss the questions that an IAQ investigator should ask when per-

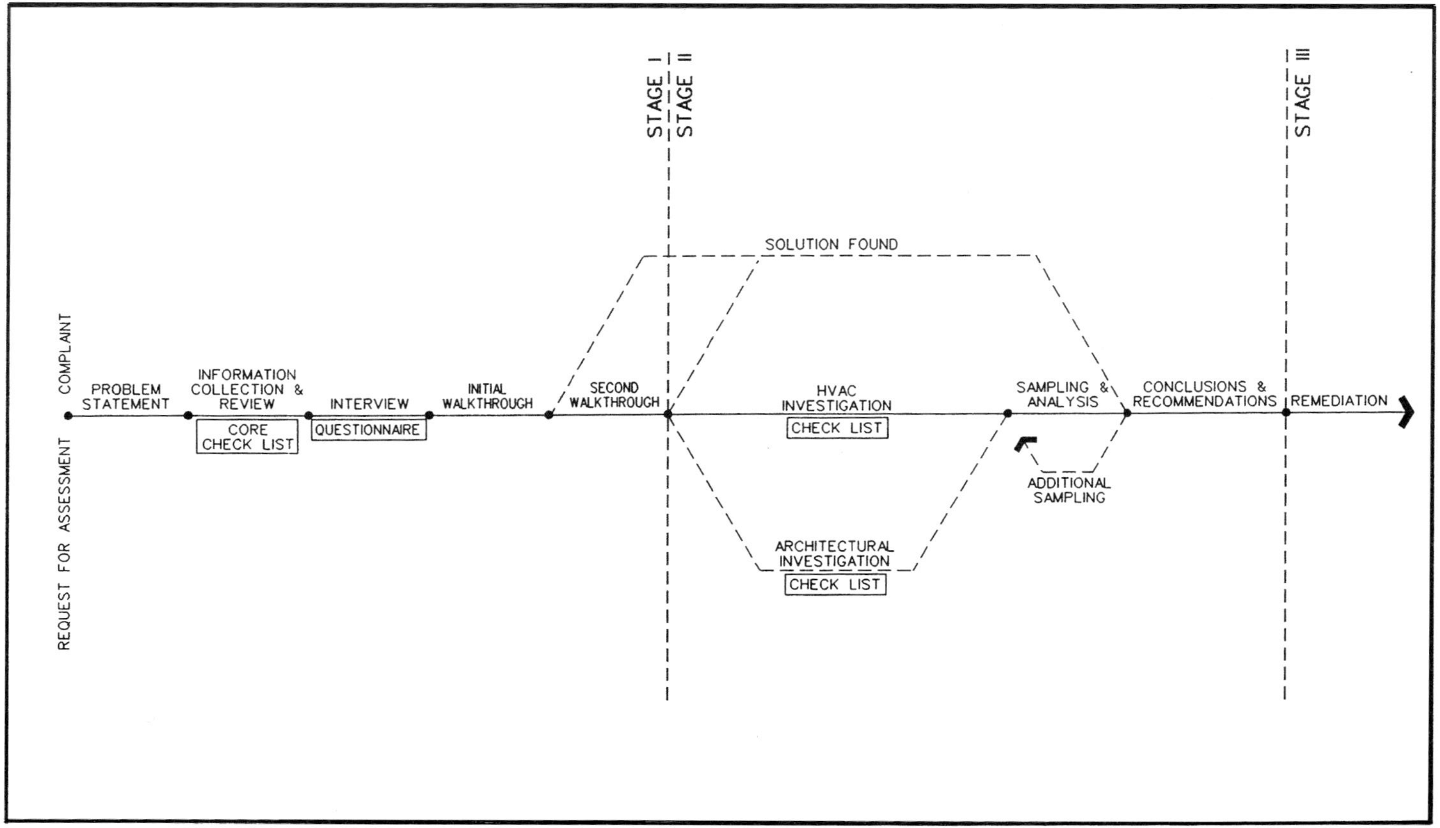

Figure 1.1 Diagnostic procedure. (*Used with permission of Gobbell Hays Partners, Inc., Nashville, Tenn.*)

forming a building assessment. Occupant interviews are discussed in Sec. 2.4. The information obtained from these checklists should allow the building investigator to reach certain conclusions about deficiencies or potential problems in the facility. These findings, along with recommendations, will make up the final report.

1.3   The Interdisciplinary Approach

Indoor air quality is a complex interaction of many constantly changing factors. These factors are discussed as they relate to industrial hygiene, mechanical engineering, achitecture, construction, and operations, along with practical advice for the understanding and control of IAQ problems.

Industrial hygiene investigations provide information that relates symptoms to indoor air contaminants and that identifies sources of the contaminants. Since sources may be architectural components of buildings, the architectural discipline is a critical adjunct to a complete investigation and to a comprehensive remediation design. HVAC systems may also be sources of contaminants and, if not sources, may distribute pollutants from sources to building occupants. The mechanical engineering discipline is appropriate to study HVAC systems and to design system modifications for remediation. In some cases, the HVAC system distribution mechanism may not be the source or the distribution mechanism, but it may be the most cost-effective way to solve a problem by changes in ventilation and/or air distribution. In summary, straightforward IAQ problems can often be identified and solved by knowledgeable practitioners in any of these three disciplines. The more complicated situations, however, are best addressed by an investigation team comprising all three disciplines. It is highly recommended that a team approach be used and that the disciplines engage in a coordinated and comprehensive investigative effort.

This book is not presented as an exhaustive thesis on industrial hygiene, mechanical engineering, or architecture or on the role in the IAQ topic played by any of these disciplines. The chapter on industrial hygiene is not written for industrial hygienists who are competent in investigating IAQ problems. It is written to acquaint architects, mechanical engineers, building managers, and others who are not industrial hygienists with the discipline of industrial hygiene and with the industrial hygiene approach to IAQ problems and solutions. The same applies to the chapters on mechanical engineering and architecture. Architects who are competent in IAQ investigations will find the mechanical engineering and industrial hygiene chapters useful. Mechanical engineers who understand IAQ issues from the perspective of that discipline will benefit from the chapters about archi-

tecture and industrial hygiene. The objective is to facilitate understanding among the three major disciplines involved in IAQ problem
definition and remediation and to facilitate team work that will provide the best and most cost-effective solutions for building owners,
managers, users, and maintenance and custodial personnel. The book
is structured to allow readers interested in IAQ to use the sections
which are beneficial to them and to omit topics which they already
understand without loss of textual cohesiveness.

1.4   References

1. Brooks, Bradford O., and David, William F., *Understanding Indoor Air Quality,* CRC Press, Boca Raton, FL, 1992, p. 19.
2. Hansen, Shirley, *Managing Indoor Air Quality,* The Fairmont Press, Lilburn, GA, 1991, pp. 1–2.
3. Hennessey, John F., III, "How to Solve Indoor Air Quality Problems," *Building Operating Management,* July 1992, p. 25.
4. Kirsch, Laurence S., "Liability for Indoor Air Pollution," *Indoor Air Pollution,* Lewis Publishers, Chelsea, MI, 1991, p. 10.
5. "California IAQ Lawsuits Increasing," *Occupational Health and Safety,* May 1992, p. 16.
6. Manko, Joseph, "Investing a Few $$ Can Avert IAQ Litigation," *Econ,* January 1993, p. 23.
7. Hennessey, p. 24.

2

Industrial Hygiene and Its Application to IAQ

2.1 Introduction

The major objective of this chapter is to provide a basic understanding of the industrial hygienist's role in diagnosing and correcting IAQ problems and controlling IAQ in general. The chapter discusses methodologies for applying industrial hygiene principles to IAQ problems in commercial facilities. The methodologies practiced by industrial hygienists for investigation and remediation of health and safety issues in industrial settings, when appropriately modified, are a vital component of the multidisciplinary approach to IAQ recommended for nonindustrial facilities.

This book is related to nonindustrial settings only. If exposure to a substance, or substances, reaches a regulated limit, the situation is considered a classic occupational exposure problem and is outside the scope of this chapter and of this book.

2.1.1 What industrial hygiene is

At this point in history, many professions have unclear identities to the general public and sometimes to the specific publics which they serve. This is because of the proliferation of new professions in recent times, concomitant with advances in knowledge and rapid changes in technology. A confounding issue is the application of the term *profession* to trades or businesses. A profession is "a vocation requiring knowledge of some department of learning or science."[1] Industrial hygiene is "that science and art devoted to the anticipation, recognition, evaluation, and control of those environmental factors or stresses arising in or from the workplace, which may cause sickness, impaired health and well-being, or significant discomfort among workers or among the citizens of the community."[2] In short, the industrial hygienist is a professional concerned with preventing health and safety problems in the workplace, any workplace, be it a factory, construction site, farm, or office. An Italian physician, Bernardino Ramazzini, is often credited with being the father of industrial hygiene because he discovered that a definite link exists between occupational exposures and health of workers. He was a seventeenth-century pioneer in environmental and occupational medicine.[3]

The industrial hygienist usually has a degree in chemical, mechanical, or environmental engineering; chemistry; biology; physics; or industrial hygiene. The American Board of Industrial Hygiene (ABIH) certifies individuals who meet its criteria for education and experience and who pass its examination regimen. Examination questions for those wishing certification in comprehensive practice cover the following rubrics: air pollution; analytical chemistry; engineering; heat, pressure, ergonomics and other physical factors; ionizing radiation; nonionizing radiation; noise and vibration; personal protective equipment; regulations, standards, and guidelines; sampling and instrumentation; and toxicology.[4] A person certified by ABIH is called a certified industrial hygienist (CIH).

Federal, state, and local regulations exist to protect the general public and workers from harmful exposures to hazardous substances and to protect the environment from pollutants. The United States Congress passed the Occupational Safety and Health Act (OSHAct) of 1970. The objective of this legislation is to "assure so far as possible every working man and woman in the nation safe and healthful working conditions and to preserve our human resources." This Act authorized the U.S. Department of Labor to promulgate and enforce occupational safety and health standards.[5] Industrial hygiene has gained importance and prominence in the corporate setting by assisting businesses in protecting their employees and in complying with applicable occupational and environmental regulations. The OSHAct also established a National Institute for Occupational Safety and Health (NIOSH) to conduct research on health effects of exposures in the workplace and thereby to determine safe levels of exposures to factors and stresses in the work environment.[5] This research is necessary and basic to the practice of industrial hygiene.

Industrial hygienists generally classify factors and stresses that cause discomfort or morbidity as chemical, physical, biological, or ergonomic. A chemical hazard may be toxic by inhalation, ingestion, or absorption through the skin or other body membranes. Physical agents include radiation, noise, vibration, pressure, and temperature. A biological hazard is any living organism that can cause disease in humans (e.g., virus, bacteria, fungus, and parasite). (Biological and chemical hazards often occur concurrently.) Ergonomic hazards include improper lifting and reaching and repeated body motions in an awkward position.[6] A fundamental consideration in any industrial hygiene problem is the route by which the harmful agent enters the body. Biological hazards (biohazards) can gain entry through inhalation, injection, ingestion, or by skin contact.[7] Chemical agents follow similar routes. Physical agents generally act on the body by means of the ambient environment proximate to the body, such as high temperatures in the workplace, or by imparting physical energy stresses to the body through vibration, noise, or various electromagnetic radiations. These physical factors can result in harmful biochemical changes and tissue and organ damage. Ergonomic insults result from the action and reaction of body forces on and to objects and forces in the work environment (e.g., lifting, reaching, pulling, pushing).

2.1.2   Terminology related to contaminants

Certain terms describing airborne contaminants are important in industrial hygiene, and their precise meanings must be comprehended if the discipline is to be properly understood, especially as it relates to IAQ. The following definitions are directly quoted from the Glossary of *Fundamentals of Industrial Hygiene.*[8]

Dusts.   Solid particles generated by handling, crushing, grinding, rapid impact, detonation, and decrepitation of organic or inorganic materials, such as rock, ore, metal, coal, wood, and grain. Dusts do not tend to flocculate, except under electrostatic forces; they do not diffuse in air but settle under the influence of gravity.

Gas.   A state of matter in which the material has very low density and viscosity; can expand and contract greatly in response to changes in temperature and pressure; easily diffuses into other gases; readily and uniformly distributes itself throughout any container. A gas can be changed to the liquid or solid state only by the combined effect of increased pressure and decreased temperature (below the critical temperature).

Vapors.   The gaseous form of substances that are normally in the solid or liquid state (at room temperature and pressure). The vapor can be changed back to the solid or liquid state either by increasing the pressure or decreasing the temperature alone. Vapors also diffuse. Evaporation is the process by which a liquid is changed into the vapor state and mixed with the surrounding air. Solvents with low boiling points will volatilize readily.

Aerosols.   Liquid droplets or solid particles, dispersed in air, that are of fine enough particle size (0.01 to 100 micrometers) to remain so dispersed for a period of time.

Fume.   Airborne particulate formed by the evaporation of solid materials, e.g., metal fume emitted during welding. Usually less than one micron in diameter.

Mists.   Suspended liquid droplets generated by condensation from the gaseous to the liquid state or by breaking up a liquid into a dispersed state, such as by splashing, foaming, or atomizing. Mist is formed when a finely divided liquid is suspended in air.

Smoke.   An air suspension (aerosol) of particles, originating from combustion or sublimation. Carbon or soot particles less than 0.1μ in size result from incomplete combustion of carbonaceous materials such as coal or oil. Smoke generally contains droplets as well as dry particles. Tobacco, for instance, produces a wet smoke composed of minute tarry droplets.

A definition of settled dust is given by Millette and Hays as "any material composed of particles small enough to pass through a one (1) mm screen and large enough to settle by virtue of their weight into a container from the ambient air."[9] This reference defines particulate as "a material composed of separate and distinct particles."[10]

Many terms of science and engineering will be used in this section. Definitions will generally not be given if the words are used consistent with commonly accepted meanings in these fields and, therefore, could be easily found in professional references. If, however, a term has a unique or different meaning in industrial hygiene, it may be defined in the text. For convenience of the reader, scientific terminology being applied to IAQ by industrial hygienists will be explained if it is considered essential to clarity.

2.2   Industrial Hygiene Methodology

2.2.1   Objectives

Industrial hygiene is based on four objectives: anticipation, recognition, evaluation, and control of hazards. Anticipating health and/or safety problems before they occur and acting to preclude the anticipated occurrences are the two things businesses and practitioners should most desire. Foreseeing hazardous situations is most readily done by examination of data collected previously under similar circumstances. These data may be available from the company involved and is often referred to as historical data. The Occupational Safety and Health Administration (OSHA) recognizes, under certain narrowly defined conditions, historical data as appropriate for predicting what will happen under the same occupational scenarios. If such relevant experience is not available directly, literature reviews are often helpful in anticipating risk from hazardous agents in the workplace. Absent historical data and relevant literature, predicting problems is based on knowledge of the relevant materials, the forces that will act on those materials, the activities of the people involved, and the environmental conditions (indoor and/or outdoor) under which these materials, forces, and people will converge. In this case, industrial hygiene studies are reduced to the fundamental components of science, engineering, and human behavior.

Prediction of hazards and risks from the event being studied is based on a review of the individual components that comprise the whole and on how all the pieces interact to form a whole. For example, the safety and health information on the individual chemicals used as reactants in a chemical process, the chemistry of the reaction, the process equipment in which the reaction occurs, the activities of the workers who operate the process, the environmental conditions in which these people work (temperature, humidity, air quality, noise, etc.), and the characteristics of the final product are all important to consider in defining hazards and evaluating risks. Anticipation can be straightforward in simple situations or extremely difficult in complex operations. The definition of industrial hygiene given in Sec. 2.1 referred to "science and art." These are appropriate descriptive nouns because in practice, at least in the more complicated instances, the science is supplemented by the art.

It is important to understand the terms *hazard* and *risk*. Though laypeople often use these as synonyms, they are not so in industrial hygiene, and the difference is important. A hazard is some thing or condition which has the capability of producing adverse health or safety consequences to humans. (The term can also be extended to plants and animals in the broader context of the environment.) The mere presence of the capability of harm is sufficient to classify a substance, action, or condition as a hazard or to describe such as hazardous. A chemical that is a known carcinogen is a hazard. Risk is a statement, either quantitative via statistical expression or qualitative via subjective expression, of the probability or likelihood that harm will actually occur. The chance of harm from many carcinogen hazards is low if the exposure to the hazardous substance is of low intensity and short duration (i.e., the risk is low). In the extreme, if the substance is separated from the human by a permanent and impenetrable barrier, the risk is virtually zero, even though the hazardous properties of the substance remain constant. As an additional example, an estimated 434,000 deaths per year in the United States are attributable to tobacco use, in particular cigarette smoking.[11] An individual who does not smoke or breathe environmental tobacco smoke avoids the risk, although the hazard of tobacco is the same to that individual and the smoker.

Risk, when used in this scientific context, requires even further delineation. Risk can relate to morbidity and/or mortality rates attendant with a quantifiable exposure to a substance or condition. This is an issue in the domain of the health sciences and is studied using animal toxicity and/or human epidemiology research. If a person is exposed to a given concentration of benzene in air for a given period of time, what is the probability that harm will result?

Risk can also relate to the potential for exposure to a harmful substance in the workplace. Given a work environment, what is the risk of exposure to a given hazardous substance for the workers in that environment? Benzene contained in a large, open vat, with no ventilation, presents a greater risk of exposure to benzene vapors than the same quantity of benzene contained in a closed-loop system. If an exposure does occur in either case, the risk of adverse health effects is a function of the amount of benzene vapor inhaled by the worker per unit of time (known as the dose rate) and the length of time of exposure. The risk of exposure and the risk of harm from exposure are the major factors in determining the total risk to a person from a hazardous substance in a certain set of circumstances.

Also important is the distinction between a health hazard and a safety hazard. *Health,* in the occupational context, is properly used in reference to the absence of diseases (mental and physical) which can be caused by exposure to workplace stresses (physical, chemical, emotional, biological, ergonomic). *Safety,* in the occupational context, is properly used in reference to preventing injury from specific events, usually manifested as a physical insult to the body (e.g., cuts, falls, explosions, fires).

If hazards exist and exposures occur, recognition of such is crucial. To recognize is "to perceive as existing or true."[12] In the industrial hygiene context, recognition is more than a sensory perception. It is also an intellectual understanding of how the sensory perceptions relate to health and safety and of what hazards exist. Recognition requires knowledge and comprehension of the work environment and the identification of known, or potential, chemical, physical, biological, and/or ergonomic stresses.[13] Ideally, perception of risk from a hazard occurs before injury or illness. Recognition is a necessary precursor to evaluation and control; however, it follows anticipation in real time and, in the worst case, may not happen until after harm befalls.

Evaluation is the decision-making process resulting in an opinion about the degree of health and/or safety hazard (or risk) that exists from recognized agents, stresses, or conditions.[14] Evaluation may require qualitative analyses if agents are unknown. After positive identification of the chemical, physical, and biological agents of concern, quantification is usually necessary to determine if risk is acceptable or if control measures are prudent. Rigorous quantification may not be necessary to conclude that control of a hazard is needed if (1) the risk is obviously unacceptable and violates good industrial hygiene practice (e.g., the open vat of benzene mentioned earlier), or (2) the exposure is so large that it can be perceived, or deduced, without analytical instrumentation (e.g., airborne cotton mill dust so dense that visibility is reduced to 3 ft).

Control is the final principle in the industrial hygiene creed. In general, there are four paramount approaches to hazard control: (1) elimination of the source (e.g., substitution of a nontoxic cleaning agent for a toxic one), (2) intercepting the hazardous substance before it reaches the worker (e.g., lead shielding to absorb x-rays and exhaust ventilation of organic solvent vapors before the vapors reach the workers' breathing zone), (3) altering the work environment to prevent worker contact with hazardous substances (e.g., automation of process lines to allow removal of workers from hot, noisy areas), and (4) providing workers with personal protective devices (e.g., dust respirators). The first is the most desirable from a worker protection perspective, but it may be economically unfeasible or technically impossible. The last approach is the least desirable form of control and is allowed by OSHA as a primary control strategy only if other approaches are not possible or feasible.

Evaluation may be done, as discussed previously, because a hazard has been recognized. Evaluation may also be done expressly to determine regulatory compliance or noncompliance. When exposures are quantified, the measured levels can be compared to regulatory standards, recommended standards, and/or the scientific and medical literature.

2.2.2 Sampling and analysis

When a situation or set of circumstances is recognized as deserving of evaluation, the industrial hygienist may choose a regimen that includes collection of samples and analysis of same. A sample is a small portion of something that is intended to represent the larger whole. The sample may be a portion of a substance, taken for identification of the material by laboratory analysis (e.g., a sample of an unlabeled and unidentified liquid located in an area that is being evaluated). Samples are also collected to determine if workers are inhaling or ingesting hazardous materials and, if they are, to quantify the exposure. The most routinely used sampling for characterizing chemical exposure is sampling air for the presence of contaminants, generally referred to as air sampling.

The objective of air sampling is to capture the material of concern from the air for analysis in the laboratory. If the substance to be sampled is an airborne particulate, air is drawn, via an electric air pump, through a filter sufficient to capture and retain the particles. If the material to be sampled is a gas or vapor, mixed with air or otherwise, the material is drawn, again via an electric pump, through a collection medium, called a sorbent, which absorbs or adsorbs the gas from the air. The filter or the sorbent is then submitted to the laboratory for analysis. Sampling for gases in air can also be done by filling a previously evacuated flask with the air to be analyzed. The sealed flask, called a grab sample, is submitted to the laboratory. This technique represents the sampled air at a given instant in time (it only takes a few seconds to fill the flask). Use of air pumps and collection media (Fig. 2.1) allows integrated sampling over a period of time (which could be minutes, hours, or days).

Air samples may be collected from a person's breathing zone and are, consequently, called personal samples. These are intended to represent the air which is being inhaled by that person. Samples may also be collected of the air in the general area being evaluated. This type of sampling is useful to estimate peoples' exposures as they move from one workspace to another.

Sampling and analysis procedures may be qualitative or quantitative. Qualitative procedures provide only the knowledge of whether a substance has been identified in the sample submitted to the laboratory (e.g., the sampled air analyzed positive for benzene, the flooring material analyzed positive for asbestos). Quantitative procedures identify the substance and allow a numerical expression of the amount of the substance contained in a given volume of air or within a given amount of some other material (e.g., the sampled air contains 5 mg/m^3 of benzene; the flooring material contains 45 percent chrysotile asbestos in the backing layer). Qualitative procedures may be faster

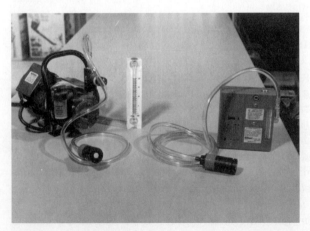

Figure 2.1 Air pumps and sample collection media. High-volume air-sampling pump with cassette, rotameter, and personal air-sampling pump with cassette. (*Used with permission of Gobbell Hays Partners, Inc., Nashville, Tenn.*)

and less expensive than quantitative and may be used to gain preliminary information when the mere presence of a substance is not known but is suspected. Qualitative information may be collected as a precursor to quantitative sampling. Quantitative information is usually needed to completely evaluate exposure.

The air sampling discussed thus far is referred to as active sampling because some force acts on the air during the collection process, usually a mechanical air pump driven by an electric motor. Passive sampling is the collection of the substance to be analyzed on the medium without the action of a sampling power source on the air. Passive dust fall sampling for asbestos is an example. A collection tin is placed in the area to be sampled, opened, and allowed to remain for a specified time period (usually weeks or months). The tin collects dust as it settles from the air. The laboratory can then analyze the contents of the tin and determine the number of asbestos structures which have settled from the air onto a unit of surface area per unit of time.

Descriptions to this point have been primarily related to sampling for elemental chemicals, particulates, or chemical compounds, as present in combination with other materials or in air. Airborne microbiological hazards, such as bacteria, fungi, and viruses, can also be sampled using active techniques. The air is drawn through a sampling device and is directed toward a culture medium (i.e., a medium on which captured microbes can live and multiply). The air is channeled onto the surface of the culture concoction such that the inertial forces acting on the microbes present in the airstream are enough to cause the microbes to stick to the culture on impact. The generic term for this device is *impaction sampler*. In the laboratory, the culture medium is maintained in a controlled environment specified to enhance the reproduction of the suspected organisms. If microorganisms were captured from the sampled air, this cultivation process allows the laboratory to identify and quantify them. Other things, in addition to air, suspected of containing microbes can be sampled in the field and cultured in the laboratory. Samples of dust, for example, can be collected with a wipe or swab. The laboratory will transfer the sampled material to an appropriate medium and attempt to culture any organisms of concern which may be present.

Sampling performed in the field, followed by analysis in the laboratory, provides useful data, reliable within the statistically described limitations of the sampling and analytical protocols, but it may take days or weeks before complete data are available. For situations where real-time measurements of chemical agents are needed, such as when health and/or safety may be immediately threatened, direct-reading instruments are available for many individual compounds and groups of compounds. When activated, an electronic instrument samples the air surrounding the device and displays the result via a digital read-out or a needle and dial. The data are usually in units of parts of vapor or gas per million parts of contaminated air (ppm). Colorimetric indicator tubes, also called detector tubes, are also available. These devices are simple and usually less expensive than direct-reading electronic instruments. A small measured quantity of air is drawn through the detector tube with a syringe. The tube contains an appropriate chemical which changes color when exposed to the substance being sampled. The amount of color change in the tube (i.e., the length of the stain) is used to estimate the airborne concentration of the substance of concern.[15]

Many physical agents, like temperature, pressure, and noise level, are always measured directly with instruments in the field. (*Field* is used to refer to the workplace, or other area, being studied and may be indoors or outdoors.)

Direct-reading instruments can be accurate for many chemical and physical stressors and may provide all the data necessary for proper evaluation. For accurate measurements of some things, however, these devices may need to be supplemented by sample collection and laboratory analysis. They are often used as a precursor to more expensive laboratory procedures. Table 2.1 contains questions to answer before taking air samples.

2.2.3   Standards

In the industrial hygiene evaluation process, sampling and analysis play an integral part. Laboratory analysis and/or direct-reading instruments can determine whether hazards are present and in what

TABLE 2.1   A Hierarchy of Questions to Answer Before Selecting Sampling and Analytical Techniques for the Presence of Chemical or Microbiological Agents in Air

1. Is the substance I wish to measure in the form of a solid particle, mist, gas, or vapor, or is it a microorganism?

2. Do I need personal air data, area air data, or both?

3. Do I need quantitative, qualitative, or qualitative and quantitative data?

4. Are conditions conducive to active sampling, or will passive sampling best suit the situation?

5. Do I need the precision and accuracy of laboratory generated data?

6. Do I have the time required to collect air samples and analyze them in a laboratory?

7. Are direct-reading instruments available to measure this substance in air, and will they provide sufficient accuracy and precision?

quantities. But how are these data used to assess the risks presented by the hazards? Comparison of exposure to recommended or regulated limits is an accepted assessment practice. Exposures that exceed such limits require control action. But what are these limits and who establishes them?

OSHA is the U.S. federal agency responsible for setting and enforcing health and safety standards in the workplace. OSHA publishes limits that are legally binding for employers who are covered by the OSHAct. There are three kinds of these limits:

1. *Permissible exposure limit (PEL).* The highest 8-h time-weighted average (TWA) airborne concentration of a substance to which a worker may be exposed.

2. *Ceiling limit (CL).* The airborne concentration above which a worker may not be exposed at any time during an 8-h shift.

The TWA is the average concentration weighted according to the time of exposure to various concentrations of a given substance. For example, if a worker was exposed to an airborne concentration C_1 for 4 h and a different concentration C_2 (because of a different work assignment) of the same substance for 4 h, the 8-h TWA would be

$$\frac{(C_1 \cdot 4h) + (C_2 \cdot 4h)}{8h}$$

It is necessary to comply with the PEL and the CL at all times. OSHA also publishes a legal standard called the action level (AL). This is an airborne concentration that is lower for a given substance than the PEL. Exposure may exceed the action level, but if it does so for more than a specified period of time (the time depends on the regulated substance), certain actions must be taken by the employer to attempt to preclude the concentration's reaching the PEL and to monitor the health of the employees (the actions required depend on the regulated substance). Not all substances which have a PEL have been assigned an AL by OSHA.

The degree to which OSHA considers a PEL to be protective of those exposed depends on the substance. The agency is allowed by the OSHAct to consider economic and technical feasibility in establishing standards. In the supporting arguments, documentation, and literature references for its various regulations, OSHA may comment on how protective a given standard is estimated to be. For example, the Proposed Rule for 29 CFR, Parts 1910 and 1926, as published in *Federal Register,* vol. 55, no. 140, Friday, July 20, 1990, says in its summary that "lowering the TWA (time-weighted average) PEL from

2 f/cc to 0.2 f/cc reduces the asbestos cancer mortality risk from life-time exposure from 64 deaths per 1,000 workers to 7 deaths per 1,000 workers."

The American Conference of Governmental Industrial Hygienists (ACGIH) is a professional society devoted to the administrative and technical aspects of occupational and environmental health.[16] ACGIH has published, and updates annually, recommended exposure standards. These standards are initially established, and reviewed annually, by a committee of knowledgeable professionals. These limits are intended for guidance only, since ACGIH is not an official government authority, and are called threshold limit values (TLVs) by the ACGIH. Some TLVs may be in conflict with regulated limits. TLVs are airborne concentrations of substances under which it is believed that nearly all workers may be repeatedly exposed day after day without adverse health effects.[17] Three categories of TLVs are specified by ACGIH:[18]

1. Threshold Limit Value-Time-Weighted Average (TLV-TWA)—the time-weighted average concentration for a normal 8-hour workday and a 40-hour workweek, to which nearly all workers may be repeatedly exposed, day after day, without adverse effect.

2. Threshold Limit Value-Short-Term Exposure Limit (TLV-STEL)—the concentration to which workers can be exposed continuously for a short period of time without suffering from 1) irritation, 2) chronic or irreversible tissue damage, or 3) narcosis of sufficient degree to increase the likelihood of accidental injury, impair self-rescue or materially reduce work efficiency, and provided that the daily TLV-TWA is not exceeded. It is not a separate independent exposure limit; rather, it supplements the time-weighted average (TWA) limit where there are recognized acute effects from a substance whose toxic effects are primarily of a chronic nature. STEL's are recommended only where toxic effects have been reported from high short-term exposures in either humans or animals.

3. Threshold Limit Value-Ceiling (TLV-C)—the concentration that should not be exceeded during any part of the working exposure.

Airborne concentrations are generally reported as parts of vapor or gas per million parts of contaminated air by volume, referred to in abbreviated form as parts per million (ppm) or as milligrams of substance per cubic meter of air (mg/m^3). Measurements of particles in air may also be reported as the number of particles per unit volume of air [e.g., airborne asbestos concentrations are reported, when analyzed by certain transmission electron microscopy (TEM) methods, as asbestos structures per cubic centimeter of air (s/cm^3)].

The ACGIH, in its threshold-limit values publication, also provides reference values for biological monitoring. Biological monitoring assesses exposure to workplace chemicals by measuring the amount of a chemical, or some other chemical to which the target chemical has been metabolized by the body, present in biological specimens (blood, urine, exhaled air) collected from the worker. Biological exposure indices (BEIs) are reference values intended as guidelines for the evaluation of potential health hazards in the practice of industrial hygiene. BEIs represent the levels of determinants which are most likely to be observed in specimens collected from a healthy worker who has been exposed to chemicals to the same extent as a worker with inhalation exposure to the TLV.[19] BEIs are reported in many different units of measure, depending on the chemical being sought, the biological specimen being examined, and the analytical procedure being used.

ACGIH also recommends TLVs for many physical agents, including heat, cold, noise, and laser radiation. Physical agents are not IAQ issues in the strict sense, but it will be demonstrated elsewhere in this book (see Sec. 4.5) that symptoms caused by physical agents can be mistakenly attributed to poor IAQ.

In 1968 the OSHA adopted the ACGIH's TLV list and promulgated these values as the nation's first PELs.[20] Because of the OSHA's PELs, industrial hygienists do evaluations of workplace conditions to document compliance with the PELs and with other aspects of applicable OSHA regulations. However, compliance with the OSHA regulations and/or the ACGIH recommendations does not ensure that no adverse health effects will occur in a given population. As discussed earlier, OSHA does not consider its PELs as completely protective of all people in all circumstances. ACGIH makes this statement about TLVs:[21]

> Because of wide variation in individual susceptibility, however, a small percentage of workers may experience discomfort from some substances at concentrations at or below the threshold limit; a smaller percentage may be affected more seriously by aggravation of a pre-existing condition or by development of an occupational illness. Smoking of tobacco is harmful for several reasons. Smoking may act to enhance the biological effects of chemicals encountered in the workplace and may reduce the body's defense mechanisms against toxic substances.
>
> Individuals may also be hypersusceptible or otherwise unusually responsive to some industrial chemicals because of genetic factors, age, personal habits (smoking, alcohol, or other drugs), medication, or previous exposures. Such workers may not be adequately protected from adverse health effects from certain chemicals at concentrations at or below the threshold limits.
>
> TLVs are based on the best available information from industrial experience, from experimental human and animal studies, and, when possible, from a combination of the three. The basis on which the values are established may differ from substance to substance; protection against impairment of health may be a guiding factor for some, whereas

reasonable freedom from irritation, narcosis, nuisance, or other forms of stress may form the basis for others.

The amount and nature of the information available for establishing a TLV varies from substance to substance; consequently, the precision of the estimated TLV is also subject to variation and the latest TLV *Documentation* should be consulted in order to assess the extent of the data available for a given substance.

These limits *are not* fine lines between safe and dangerous concentration nor are they a relative index of toxicity.

The ACGIH also believes that the best practice is to maintain concentrations of all atmospheric contaminants as low as is practical.[22]

Health effects research is the basis for PELs and TLVs. Research is done using animal toxicity and human epidemiological studies. The NIOSH publishes *Criteria Documents* that address chemical and physical stressors in the work environment. The ACGIH publishes periodically the *Documentation of the Threshold Limit Values and Biological Exposure Indices,*[23] which presents the scientific information and data upon which the TLVs and BEIs are based. Many other scientific references exist in the literature. The science upon which a regulated or recommended limit is based can be important to understand in invoking limits in certain situations.

It is also important to note that PELs and TLVs are set for healthy people in the workplace. Many IAQ studies are done in places where people are not in good health, such as hospitals and nursing homes; therefore, workplace standards may not be sufficiently protective.

Table 2.2 outlines how to look for chemical contaminants.

2.3   Indoor Air Quality and Industrial Hygiene

2.3.1   Terminology

The indoor environment has become much more complicated technically as building science and technology have become more complex. The overwhelming number of building products, systems, and furnishings with which building designers must contend leads to a bewildering array of possible stressors to the indoor environment. Building knowledge that is comprehensive and building management that is competent are more important than ever before. Because so many factors exist in today's buildings that can influence the environment for better or worse, indoor environmental management should be treated with due priority and commitment.

Indoor air quality is not a term that needs precise definition; dictionary entries for the three words are quite sufficient for conversational uses. Some words and phrases, however, are evolving into terms of art, and it is useful for practitioners to agree on their meanings. An understanding of IAQ jargon and of relevant industrial hygiene terms

TABLE 2.2   A Summary of Industrial Hygiene Methodology for a Known or Suspected Airborne Chemical Contaminant

A. Recognition

  1. Collect and review facts, data, and other pertinent information.
      a. Interview parties involved (workers, managers, medical professionals, etc.).
      b. Review available information, facts, and data (reports, workers' complaints/suggestions, engineering reports, regulatory reports, and/or citations, etc.).
      c. Observe the workplace (Are hazardous substances present? What activities are done around, with, and to those substances? To what is there exposure or risk of exposure?).
  2. Interpret the information which has been collected and reviewed.
      a. Correlate complaints, concerns, symptoms, observations, facts, data, and information.
      b. Deduce agents suspected of causing exposures.

B. Evaluation

  1. Perform sampling and analysis for suspected agents.
  2. Evaluate the analytical data in a statistically appropriate way.
  3. Interpret the analytical data in the context of the facts relevant to the times of sample collections.
  4. Compare exposure data to appropriate guidelines and regulatory standards.
  5. Develop conclusions about measured exposure levels and risk of future exposures.

C. Control

  1. Design and implement control measures, as dictated by the evaluation process.
  2. Conduct sampling and analysis on a frequency sufficient to validate the efficacy of the control measures.

and practices will lead in succeeding sections to an exploration of industrial hygiene methodology applied to IAQ problems. The goal is the practical application of industrial hygiene and health sciences, in concert with architecture, mechanical engineering, and building management, to answering whether the air quality is good or bad, to determining what to do about it if it is bad, and to designing new construction and/or renovation of existing construction to preclude indoor air of poor quality.

An unfortunate phrase that seems to be here to stay is sick building syndrome (SBS). The term seems more slanted to news media taste than scientific taste; nonetheless, it has a somewhat rigorous definition. SBS is a situation wherein 20 percent or more of a building's occupants develop various symptoms which endure for 2 weeks or more. The symptoms are generally headaches, nausea, dizziness, dry skin, itchy skin, sinus congestion, sore throats, nose irritation, or excessive fatigue.[24] The symptoms may occur singularly or in combinations in different individuals. There is usually evidence that the symptoms subside or disappear entirely when the occupants leave the building overnight or for the weekend.

A BRI is a medically verifiable illness that is attributable to a condition in the building[25] (e.g., the legionella species of bioaerosols which are found in cooling towers and which cause Legionnaires' disease). The cause of a BRI is known, but specific SBS causes may not be known.[25]

Multiple chemical sensitivity (MCS) is a condition in which a person is sensitive to a number of chemicals, all at very low concentrations.[26] Research indicates that the symptoms are not consistent with reported toxicological properties for the chemicals involved, at the exposure concentrations involved.[27] There is considerable debate in the medical community over whether MCS is really a physical illness or is psychosomatic in nature. It is important to understand the condition because the people who claim to be victims are resolute in believing that MCS is due to poor IAQ. The IAQ practitioner must recognize MCS as a possible IAQ consequence, the medical debate notwithstanding.

Selected definitions follow which are important in IAQ studies and which are also common in the industrial hygiene discipline. The IAQ usage of some of these may differ slightly from the corresponding definitions in general industrial hygiene. Most of these are taken from the United States EPA's *Building Air Quality: A Guide for Building Owners and Facility Managers.*[28]

Antimicrobial.   Agent that kills microbial growth. See *disinfectant, sanitizer,* and *sterilizer.*

Breathing zone.   Area of a room in which occupants breathe as they stand, sit, or lie down.

Disinfectant.   One of three groups of antimicrobials registered by EPA for public health uses. EPA considers an antimicrobial to be a disinfectant when it destroys or irreversibly inactivates infectious or other undesirable organisms, but not necessarily their spores. EPA registers three types of disinfectant products based upon submitted efficacy data: limited, general or broad spectrum, and hospital disinfectant.

Ergonomics.   Applied science that investigates the impact of people's physical environment on their health and comfort (e.g., determining the proper chair height for computer operators).

Hypersensitivity diseases.   Diseases characterized by allergic responses to animal antigens. The hypersensitivity diseases most clearly associated with IAQ are asthma, rhinitis, and hypersensitivity pneumonitis. Hypersensitivity pneumonitis is a rare but serious disease that involves progressive lung damage as long as there is exposure to the causative agent.

Off-gassing.   Release of gases, such as organic vapors, from a building material after the manufacturing process is complete.

Pollutant pathway.   Route of entry of an airborne contaminant from a source location into the occupant breathing zone through architectural or mechanical connections (e.g., through cracks in walls, vents, open windows).

Psychosocial factors.   Psychological, organizational, and personal stressors that could produce symptoms similar to poor IAQ.

Sanitizer.   One of three groups of antimicrobials registered by EPA for public health uses. EPA considers an antimicrobial to be a sanitizer when it reduces but does not necessarily eliminate all the microorganisms on a treated surface. To be a registered sanitizer, the test results for a product must show a reduction of at least 99.9 percent in the number of each test microorganism over the parallel control.

Soil gases.   Gases that enter a building from the surrounding ground (e.g., radon, volatile organics).

Sterilizer.   One of three groups of antimicrobials registered by EPA for public health uses. EPA considers an antimicrobial to be a sterilizer when it destroys or eliminates all forms of bacteria, fungi, viruses, and their spores. Because spores are considered the most difficult form of a microorganism to destroy, EPA considers the term *sporicide* to be synonymous with *sterilizer.*

Tracer gases.   Compounds, such as sulfur hexafluoride, which are used to identify suspected pollutant pathways and to quantify ventilation rates. Tracer gases may be detected qualitatively by their odor or quantitatively by air monitoring equipment.

Volatile organic compounds (VOCs).   Compounds that evaporate from the many housekeeping, maintenance, and building products made with organic chemicals. These compounds are released from products that are being used and that are in storage. In sufficient quantities, VOCs can cause eye, nose, and throat irritations, headaches, dizziness, visual disorders, and memory impairment; some are suspected of causing, or are known to cause, cancer in humans. At present, not much is known about what health effects occur at the levels of VOCs typically found in public and commercial buildings. (EPA has a much more complicated definition of VOCs in its regulations promulgated under the Clean Air Act, which addresses outdoor air pollution, such as that caused by industrial smokestacks and automobiles.)

Some terms warrant more discussion than a glossary-style definition. A principal concern in IAQ can be the presence of *microorgan-*

isms, which are life forms too small to be viewed by the unaided eye.[29] An *organism* is a living thing, ranging from humans to single-cell bacteria, consisting of various parts, each specializing in a different function.[30] *Biological* is an adjective that describes something pertaining to *biology,* which is the science of life or living matter in all its forms.[31] *Micro-* is a prefix used with other words to mean that what is described by the other word is too small to be seen by the unaided eye.[32] Micro- also has a more specific meaning of one millionth of something (e.g., a *micrometer* is one millionth of a meter, which can be written 1×10^{-6} m. Micro- is combined with many scientific terms which are relevant to IAQ). *Microbiological* is an adjective that describes something which pertains to *microbiology,* which is a branch of biology dealing with microorganisms. *Microbial* is the adjective derived from the noun *microbe,* which is generally used to mean a microorganism that is pathogenic.[33]

There are several kinds of microorganisms that can adversely affect IAQ. *Bacteria* are one-celled organisms which are members of the Protista, a biological classification.[34] *Fungi* may be unicellular or multicellular organisms which do not carry out photosynthesis. Mushrooms, yeasts, and molds are fungi.[35] Mildew describes the coatings or discolorations caused by fungi on objects when exposed to moisture.[36] *Viruses* are considered part of the microbial world, but they are really not organisms because they are not cells. A virus particle is a piece of genetic material protected by a surrounding protein coat. Viruses possess some of the properties of living forms and many are pathogenic in humans.[37]

Bio- is a prefix meaning life.[38] An *aerosol* is a dispersion in air of liquid droplets or solid particles, which range in size from 0.01 to 100 μm[39] and which can remain suspended in air for some period of time. A *bioaerosol,* then, is an aerosol of biological material, such as microorganisms or body fluids. A sneeze produces a very common and frequently encountered bioaerosol. *Biocontaminants* are contaminants which are either life forms (molds of the genera *Aspergillus*) or are derived from living things (rodent droppings).

A particulate aerosol contains particles of different sizes, especially if the aerosol is generated from dust. *Dust* was defined in Sec. 2.1. It is distinguishable technically from *debris,* which can be defined as pieces of material that can be identified as to probable source by visual assessment of their color, texture, or composition,[40] and from *dirt,* which is commonly used to mean any foul or filthy substance.[41] Laypeople often use dirt to include dust and debris, as well as mud, soil, and grime.

If an aerosol is composed of particles, a pertinent consideration is whether the particles are of a size that can be inhaled into the lungs, passing through the body's respiratory defenses against foreign objects.

Respirable particles are generally considered to be those less than 10 μm in diameter. (If the particles are elongated rather than generally spherical, 10 μm would refer to the longest dimension.) Air sampling of such aerosols can be done using a size-selective device to separate the particles of respirable size for analysis.[42]

2.3.2 Health effects

Understanding health effects associated with indoor contaminants is fundamental to diagnosing and solving IAQ problems. The remainder of this section presents data and text taken from *Introduction to Indoor Air Quality: A Reference Manual* and *Introduction to Indoor Air Quality: A Self-Paced Learning Module*. Data is reproduced here directly from these publications. Some minor textual changes have been made for clarity.

Factors affecting potential health risks from contaminants. The potential health effects that will result from exposure to indoor air contaminants depend on a variety of factors interacting with one another. These include factors related to the toxic substance, the dose, the environment, and the occupant (see Table 2.3).

Factors related to the toxic substance. *Toxicity* is the innate ability of a contaminant to cause injury to biological tissue. The toxicity posed by natural and synthetic chemicals varies depending on the contaminant's chemical and physical properties and how those properties interact with the human body.

Solubility is simply the ability of one substance to dissolve in another substance. Chemicals can be classified as those that are solu-

---

TABLE 2.3   Key Factors Affecting the Hazard Posed by Toxic Substances

Factors related to the toxic substance:	Factors related to the environment:
Chemical properties	Temperature
Physical properties	Humidity
Toxicity	Light and noise levels
	Pressure differences
Factors related to the dose:	Presence of other contaminants
Concentration	
Duration of exposure	Factors related to the occupant:
Route of entry	Genetics
	Sex
	Personal habits
	Diet
	Age
	Health status

SOURCE: *Introduction to Indoor Air Quality: A Self-Paced Learning Module*, EPA/400/3-91/002.

ble in polar solvents and those that are soluble in nonpolar solvents. From a health standpoint this difference is important. Chemicals which are polar in nature (such as table salt) will be more easily excreted from the body; chemicals which are nonpolar (such as PCBs and DDT) will not readily be excreted and will remain in the body for long periods of time.

Vapor pressure is a term that describes how readily liquids and solids vaporize or evaporate into the air. Vapor pressure is important because those chemicals having a high vapor pressure (for example, methylene chloride in paint strippers and toluene in paints) will be more likely to be inhaled than those with a low vapor pressure (for example, hydrocarbons in solid floor waxes).

Chemical structure is one of the most important characteristics of natural and synthetic chemicals which determines toxicity. The body has receptor molecules that recognize and react to chemicals as helpful to the body or as harmful intruders. For example, when a banana is eaten, the carbohydrates are recognized as helpful, and they are broken down and used for fuel in the body. On the other hand, the presence of harmful bacteria in the body initiates a different set of reactions aimed at destroying the intruders and ridding the body of them.

The body has the ability to discriminate among very subtle differences in chemical structure. For example, two chemicals that have exactly the same type and number of elements may have very different effects on the body simply because of the location of the elements in relation to the overall structure of the chemical.

Size and *shape* are important physical properties of particles. Submicron-sized particles are more likely to be inhaled deep into the respiratory tract. The toxicity of asbestos is thought to be due to both its size and needlelike shape.

Factors related to the dose. The body's response to toxic substances (contaminants) depends in large part on the dose. The dose is the total amount of contaminant that is received by the target tissues. It depends on the concentration, the duration of the exposure, and on the route of entry.

Concentration, exposure, and dose. Dose should not be confused with the terms *exposure* or *concentration*. Concentration is the amount of contaminant that is present in the air at a given time and place. Exposure characterizes the contact between the contaminant and the person (skin, eyes, respiratory tract). The exposure will depend on both the concentration of the contaminant in a space and the length of time the person is in contact with the contaminant in that space. Dose is the amount of contaminant that is actually absorbed by the body. In many studies and assessments of risk, concentration is used as a surrogate for exposure or dose because the actual exposure or dose is difficult, and sometimes impossible, to measure.

In general, as the concentration of contaminants in the air increases, the exposure, dose, and effects also increase. People who are exposed to identical concentrations of contaminants, however, can receive different doses. For example, the dose of ozone received by a person who is sitting in a park on a hot day in Los Angeles will be different from the dose received by a person who is jogging in the park. The jogger receives a greater dose of ozone than the person who is sitting because the jogger is breathing faster and more deeply, causing more ozone to be in contact with the cells of the respiratory tract.

Route of exposure. Contaminants can enter the body through ingestion, skin puncture, absorption through the skin, and inhalation. Except for inhalation, these routes of exposure are generally unimportant in residential or office indoor air quality problems. Inhalation is the most important route of exposure for airborne contaminants because chemicals are quickly and rapidly absorbed from the lungs into the bloodstream, where they can be carried to other parts of the body.

Absorption through the skin can be an important route of entry for certain organic substances. Some substances can be absorbed through hair follicles, and others dissolve in the fats and oils of the skin (for example, organic pesticides and solvent compounds). Ingestion could become an important route of entry if improper fumigation with pesticides results in contaminated food or dishes.

Dose-effect relationship. The relationship between the dose and its effect on the body is known as the dose-effect relationship, and it can be represented graphically (Fig. 2.2). Small doses (characterized by low concentrations, short exposure times, and low respiration rates) usually cause minimal or no observable effects. As the dose increases (higher concentrations, longer exposure times, higher respiration rates), progressively more severe effects occur, which may include death at the highest doses. It should be noted, however, that a group of individuals who receive an identical dose of contaminant might not respond uniformly because of human variability.

Attempts to relate health effects to exposure to air contaminants are rooted in dose-effect curves, and these curves are important tools in developing public policy for chemicals and other toxic agents in the environment. Two basic dose-effect curves are used to describe the relationship between effects and the dose.

Curve A in Fig. 2.2 shows that no matter how low the dose, an effect will occur. This curve is called the linear dose-effect curve, and it is used to described the carcinogenic effect of exposure to carcinogens such as asbestos and radiation.

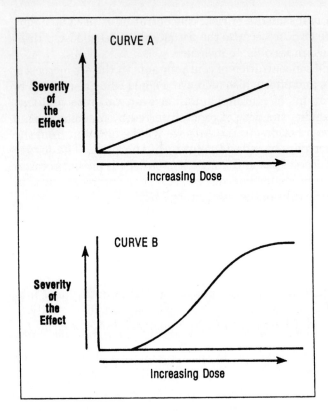

Figure 2.2 Dose-effect relationship. (*From* Introduction to Indoor Air Quality: A Self-Paced Learning Module, *EPA/400/3-91/002.*)

Curve B describes a contaminant that will not cause an effect below a certain dose. This curve shows that there is a threshold for the occurrence of effects. For example, the lowest-observed effect level for decreased hemoglobin production and central nervous system effects as a result of lead exposure in children is reported to be 0.1 to 0.2 μg of lead per milliliter of blood.[43] In adults, the lowest-observed-effect level (for decreased hemoglobin production) is in the range of 0.15 to 0.3 μg of lead per milliliter of blood.

In the standard-setting process, the dose-effect curve is important because it, along with exposure assessments, determines what levels of contaminants are assumed to pose potential health risks.

Factors related to the environment. Environmental factors such as temperature, humidity, light, and noise levels can have direct and indirect effects on the host. These factors can affect the host directly by causing discomfort (for example, eye strain or headache) or even dysfunction (such as hearing loss). These factors may also affect the susceptibility of the occupant to other environmental contaminants or factors.

Temperature, humidity, and light alter the chemical nature of some contaminants, which can make them more hazardous. In addition, high temperature and humidity can increase the rate of volatilization of organic chemicals such as formaldehyde. High humidity can foster the growth of microorganisms or increase the rate of chemical reactions which form acid aerosols. Reduced barometric pressure inside buildings relative to the outside pressure can increase the rate of entry of radon (and other soil gases) into the interior environment.

Factors related to the occupant. The development of health effects in an individual who is exposed to chemical, physical, and biological stressors also depends on factors including genetics, sex, personal habits, diet, age, and health status. Table 2.4 identifies some of the subpopulations with potentially greater susceptibility to indoor air contaminants.

Genetic variability can range from individuals who have no disease resistance from birth to those who are seemingly never ill. Most peo-

TABLE 2.4 Subpopulations at Greatest Risk from Exposure to Indoor Air Contaminants*

Subpopulation	Size of the subpopulation	Percent of population[†]
Newborns	3,731,000	1.5
Young children	18,128,000	7.5
Elderly	29,172,000	12.1
Heart patients	18,458,000	7.7
Persons with bronchitis	11,379,000	4.7
Persons with asthma	9,690,000	4.0
Persons with hay fever	21,702,000	9.0
Persons with emphysema	1,998,000	0.8
Smokers[‡]	46,772,500	26.5

*All subpopulations except smokers are based on 1986 data. Data for live births, children <5 years, and persons ≥65 years are based on U.S. Bureau of Census records. Data for persons with heart disease, bronchitis, asthma, hay fever, and emphysema are based on National Center for Health Statistics records.

[†]1986 national population of 241,078,000 was used for all categories except smokers.

[‡]Persons ≥17 years of age who smoked in 1986; *Smoking and Health: A National Status Report.* 1990. U.S. Department of Health and Human Services (DHHS). DHHS (CDC) 87-8396.

SOURCE: *Introduction to Indoor Air Quality: A Self-Paced Learning Module,* EPA/400/3-91/002.

ple fall in between these extremes, but even in this middle area there can be significant variation in response to contaminants, particularly at the low level of exposures that might be encountered in homes and offices. Men and women may also be affected differently by exposures to contaminants and other stressors because of their different chemical makeup. For example, men and women differ in the amount and distribution of body fat; this, in turn, may lead to a different distribution and accumulation of chemicals and subsequent toxic effects.

Personal habits such as smoking, alcohol intake, and other drug use can alter the body's ability to handle exposures to contaminants. Diet and psychological factors may also play an important role in determining the body's response to exposures. For example, individuals experiencing high stress levels may be more susceptible to the adverse effects of chemical exposure.[44] In addition, stress may result in symptoms such as skin rash and anxiety which can appear to be chemically related.

Age is an important factor that affects sensitivity to contaminants. Infants and children are more sensitive to chemical exposures than adults. Their brains are not fully developed until they are about 6 or 7 years of age, and they may experience irreversible changes in learning ability or behavior if exposed to lead and mercury compounds. They are also more sensitive because they have smaller body size, faster breathing rates, and immature immune and lung systems, and they are generally oral (mouth) breathers. Oral breathing circumvents some of the respiratory tract's defense mechanisms, resulting in larger doses to the remaining respiratory tract.

Older people may also be more sensitive to the effects of contaminant exposures because of the effects of aging on the immune system. The effects of aging and health status in response to chemicals were clearly illustrated during the serious air pollution episodes of the 1940s and 1950s. The people who were most affected and experienced the highest mortality were older people with preexisting heart and lung conditions.

In general, immunosuppressed individuals or those with chronic respiratory or cardiovascular diseases are more susceptible to the effects of indoor air contaminants, regardless of sex or age.

Fate of contaminants in the body.   After a contaminant enters the body, it may be absorbed into the bloodstream, excreted unchanged, or transported throughout the body. Once it reaches the body's tissues, it can be stored or can interact with the body to produce toxic effects.

Metabolism is the process by which a chemical is changed in the body through the action of enzymes to form a new chemical called a metabolite. Metabolism, which occurs primarily in the liver and kidneys, generally is not 100 percent efficient, so some of the original chemical will remain. One of the main purposes of metabolism is to detoxify harmful chemicals by converting them into less harmful chemicals which can easily be excreted. Sometimes, however, metabolites are formed which are more harmful than the original chemical.

After a chemical has been metabolized, it may have the same fate in the body as the original chemical. It may be excreted or stored in the blood or other parts of the body. Nonpolar compounds (PCBs, chlordane, DDT) are stored primarily in the fat; metals such as lead and cadmium may be stored in bone, and others can be stored in the blood.

The kidney is the most important excretory organ in the body, and it is able to excrete polar molecules such as alcohols, but it is less efficient with nonpolar molecules such as xylene. If a nonpolar metabolite is formed by the metabolism of a polar compound, the metabolite will be hard to excrete and may exert a toxic effect on the kidney. The original chemical or its metabolites can also be excreted through the feces, lungs, sweat, saliva, or breast milk.

The mechanisms by which toxic effects occur in the body have not been determined for all contaminants, and the process is not well understood for many conditions. However, it does appear that the initial step of chemical exposures involves the recognition of the toxic chemical by a specific molecule(s) known as the receptor. The chemical binds itself to the receptor, which initiates a chain reaction that may lead to an adverse health effect. As long as the receptor and the chemical are bound together, adverse effects can occur.

Over time, a balance is reached between bound and unbound receptors, and this balance can change as exposures increase or decrease. If a stored chemical is released, the potential for a toxic effect increases as the substance combines with receptors. For example, if a person who has been exposed to a nonpolar chemical such as PCBs loses weight, that chemical will be released into the bloodstream and adverse effects could result if the PCBs are not excreted.

The frequency of exposure also affects whether or not adverse effects occur. The body may be able to handle small exposures separated by long time periods during which the contaminant is metabolized and excreted. However, if the periods of time between exposures are shortened, adverse health effects may appear. For this reason, it is important to characterize exposures accurately.

Symptoms and classes of toxic substances. Symptoms do not always fit "textbook" patterns, and similar symptoms may be caused by different contaminants. In many instances reports of symptoms will include "low-level" complaints that are vague in nature and which could be attributed to any number of diseases or conditions. Very frequently, symptoms are characteristic of colds or the flu, or they are similar to symptoms accompanying stress and tension. Some examples of complaints include: "I feel tired and rundown." "I'm usually never sick, but now I have a lot of headaches." "I've been nauseated and have had a slight stomachache the last few months." "My nose always seems to be dry and my throat is scratchy."

Symptoms of different contaminants may also overlap. For example, formaldehyde can result in irritation of the upper respiratory tract and the eyes but so can cleaning chemicals, airborne pathogens, airborne allergens, and some solvents. In order to sort through potential sources and interpret data, one may need to obtain a careful symptom history along with information about when and where symptoms occur. In doing this, the investigator should also be aware of contaminants that may not result in overt symptoms.

Indoor air contaminants can be classified by their mechanisms of action in the body and resulting symptoms. These categories are typically used for toxic substances and include irritants, asphyxiants, narcotics and anesthetics, systemic toxicants, reproductive and developmental toxicants, and airborne pathogens and allergens. Physical stressors such as temperature, humidity, light, and noise can also affect health. Symptoms which are commonly associated with these categories are summarized in Table 2.5.

Irritants. Irritants (including pulmonary toxicants) are highly reactive substances which result in nonspecific tissue damage when in contact with the body, particularly the skin and mucous membranes. Irritants such as formaldehyde, sulfur dioxide, nitrogen dioxide, ozone, petroleum-based chemicals, soaps, detergents, bleach, and other cleaning agents have been associated with a wide range of health effects. In addition, irritation effects can result from fibers such as fiberglass and other insulating materials, volatile organics from fabric cleaners, paints, and pesticides, disinfectants, oven cleaners, glues, and epoxy resins.

Pulmonary toxicants. Acute and chronic exposure of the respiratory tract to irritants over a long period of time may be associated with increased susceptibility to bacterial infection, decreases in pulmonary function, changes in airway reactivity, and the development of lung diseases, including cancer.

Depending on particle size and the solubility of particles and gases, irritant contaminants can affect the upper or lower respiratory tract. Large particles and very soluble chemicals such as sulfur dioxide primarily affect the upper respiratory tract, while smaller particles and less soluble chemicals such as nitrogen dioxide and ozone affect primarily the middle and lower respiratory tract. Pulmonary toxicants also include airborne pathogens and allergens. Over time, pulmonary

TABLE 2.5 Typical Symptoms of Contaminant Classes and Physical Stressors

SYMPTOMS	Irritant (includes pulmonary toxicants)	Asphyxiant	Anesthetic/Narcotic	Systemic Toxicant	Airborne Pathogen/Allergen	Carcinogen*	Temperature	Humidity	Light/Noise
Eye Irritation, burning	✓								
Dry or sore throat	✓							✓	
Skin irritation, dryness or scaling	✓							✓	
Skin rash	✓						✓		
Tightness in the chest	✓				✓				
Runny nose	✓				✓				
Asthma (exacerbation of)	✓				✓				
Cough	✓				✓			✓	
Wheezing or other breathing problems	✓				✓				
Chest pain				✓					
Changes in rate and depth of breathing		✓	✓	✓			✓		
Changes in pulse rate		✓	✓	✓			✓		
Visual disturbances		✓	✓						✓ (noise)
Dizziness		✓	✓	✓			✓		
Fatigue		✓		✓					✓
Depression		✓		✓					✓
Clumsiness		✓	✓						
Drowsiness		✓	✓						
Headache			✓				✓		✓
Fever					✓				
Repeated throat infections					✓				
Sinus irritation or infection					✓				
Muscular pains					✓				
Change in heart rhythm				✓					
Tingling or numbness in extremities				✓					
Muscle twitching/convulsions				✓					
Nausea or vomiting				✓					
Abdominal pain				✓					✓ (noise)
Diarrhea				✓					
Loss of appetite									
Cold/flu symptoms					✓				
Cold extremities							✓		
Difficulty in sleeping					✓		✓		✓
Irritability							✓		✓
Backache/neckache							✓		✓
Eye strain									✓

*It is not possible to determine whether or not exposure to a carcinogen will result in a cancerous tumor based on symptoms because of the lag time between exposure and tumor development. However, carcinogens may also be classified as irritants, systemic toxicants, or anesthetic/narcotic, and may result in symptoms typical of these

SOURCE: *Introduction to Indoor Air Quality: A Self-Paced Learning Module*, EPA/400/3-91/002.

toxicants can contribute to the development of emphysema, bronchitis, pneumonitis, and changes in pulmonary function.

Asphyxiants. Asphyxiants are chemicals that interfere with the availability of oxygen for the tissues. A complete absence of oxygen in the blood (anoxia) will result in brain death in 3 to 5 min. Partial asphyxiation results in low levels of oxygen in the blood (hypoxia) and may result in brain damage or death, depending on the length of exposure. The normal oxygen level in the air is about 21 percent. Levels of oxygen in air below 19.5 percent are considered unsafe in the workplace, according to OSHA regulation 29 CFR 1910.94(d)(9).

There are two classes of asphyxiants, simple and chemical, that differ in their mode of action. Simple asphyxiants are physiologically inert gases that act by diluting or displacing oxygen in air below the level required for normal function. Simple asphyxiants include carbon dioxide, nitric oxide, nitrous oxide, and nitrogen.

Chemical asphyxiants react chemically with the body to prevent the uptake of oxygen by blood or interfere with the transport of oxygen from the lungs to the tissues. Chemical asphyxiants include carbon monoxide, hydrogen sulfide, hydrogen cyanide, and others. Of these, carbon monoxide is the most likely to be encountered in indoor investigations. (Typical sources in residential investigations include heating and cooking appliances and in some instances, the ambient air or emissions from automobiles in attached garages.)

Narcotics and anesthetics. Narcotics and anesthetics are chemicals that prevent the central nervous system from performing normally. Narcotic substances can result in symptoms that are similar to those caused by asphyxiants. Examples of narcotics and anesthetics include aliphatic ketones (methyl ethyl ketone, methyl isobutyl ketone, acetone), aliphatic alcohols (methanol, ethanol, isopropanol), and aromatic and substituted hydrocarbons (xylene, toluene, styrene, chlorobenzenes). Many of these chemicals are contained in paints, varnishes, pesticides, glues, and organic solvents that are commonly used in and around homes and in other nonindustrial settings.

Systemic toxicants. Systemic effects are those that occur after the distribution and absorption of the chemical at a site that is distant from the point of entry. The wide variety of ingredients in consumer products and in materials encountered in the nonindustrial environment can result in a range of systemic effects that is difficult to anticipate. Substances toxic to the liver (hepatotoxicants), kidney (nephrotoxicants), blood (hematopoietic toxicants), nervous system (neurotoxicants), and reproductive system can impair the functioning of these vital body systems.

Mutagens, carcinogens, developmental, and reproductive toxicants. Only a small fraction of the chemicals in commercial and consumer products have been tested for their potential as mutagens, carcinogens, and developmental or reproductive toxicants, and even less is known about mixtures of contaminants.

A mutagen is an agent that alters the genes or chromosomes of a living cell to cause mutations. Mutations can also occur spontaneously in the cell, and some are inherited. Cancer is thought to develop from a single cell that develops abnormally because of an alteration or mutation in the genetic material (DNA) which can occur spontaneously or after exposure to carcinogenic agents. Cancer usually develops years after exposure (7 to 40 years) to the agent.

Radon, asbestos, cigarette smoke, and formaldehyde are some of the agents in the indoor environment which have received attention for their carcinogenic potential. Symptoms of cancer typically do not occur until the tumor is already advanced.

Developmental toxicants are agents that cause some defect or malformation in the fetus; some defects may be so serious during the embryonic stage that a spontaneous abortion occurs. The fetus is most susceptible to the effects of developmental toxicants during the first 3 months of growth because this is a time of rapid cell growth and when organ systems begin to differentiate. Adverse effects, however, can occur throughout gestation.

Known human fetal toxicants include lead, alcohol, ionizing radiation, organic mercury, and some cancer-fighting drugs. Many more chemicals such as benzene, 2,4-D, nitrogen dioxide, PCBs, tetrachloroethylene, xylene, benzo(a)pyrene, phthalates, and others have been shown to be developmental toxicants in animal studies, but their effects on humans is not known.[45]

Reproductive toxicants are agents that can result in menstrual disorders in women and decreased fertility in men and women. These agents typically are encountered through occupational exposures.

Pathogens and allergens. Exposure to pathogens and allergens can result in a broad range of effects from mild irritation to life-threatening fevers and debilitating illness. These agents of illness can be particularly difficult to identify and relate to symptoms.

Airborne pathogens are infectious disease-producing agents such as viruses, fungi, and bacteria that are disseminated through the air. Common diseases that are spread by aeropathogens include influenza (virus), adenovirus and coxsackie respiratory diseases (virus), and coccidioidomycosis (fungus); other important diseases include Legionnaires' disease (bacterium), Pontiac fever (bacterium), and hypersensitivity pneumonitis (a variety of agents).

Allergens are substances that cause an allergic reaction in susceptible individuals. The allergic individual produces large amounts of an antibody when exposed to an allergen to which the individual is sensitive. When an antigen-antibody reaction takes place, histamine and other substances are released. Effects include dilation of blood vessels, mucus secretion, contraction of the bronchioles, and cellular inflammation.

Physical stressors. Physical stressors such as temperature, humidity, light levels, and noise can result in a variety of symptoms which usually produce discomfort. More severe symptoms and dysfunction, however, can result if physical stressors are not corrected within reasonable periods of time.

Symptoms, contaminants, and sources. The previous discussion classified indoor air contaminants and stressors according to broad classes and health effects which might typically be associated with those classes. The complexity of symptom patterns can complicate the task of relating symptoms to contaminants, but a knowledge of the sources of contaminants and general symptoms for different classes of contaminants can facilitate the investigation of indoor air quality problems. Table 2.5 helps identify which specific symptoms could be caused by various contaminant classes that are most likely causing the problem. Table 2.6 identifies specific contaminants that are associated with each contaminant class identified above, and Table 2.7 provides information on common sources of those contaminants. This information should help the investigator identify potential sources in the building that may be causing particular problems.

Particulates. Particulates which can be released into the indoor environment include inorganic fibers, metals, and a variety of organic materials. Particulates in the inhalable range (10-μm aerodynamic diameter or less) are potentially hazardous to health.

Lead exposure can affect both adults and children, but children (and fetuses) are at greater risk because of their smaller body size, breathing patterns, and the way lead is metabolized in their bodies. Health effects include damage to the kidneys, nervous system, red blood cells, and potential increases in high blood pressure. Lead exposure may also result in decreased coordination and mental abilities. The effects of lead exposure can be reversed if treatment begins in a timely fashion and continues for the prescribed course of therapy; however, if treatment is delayed or stopped prematurely, permanent brain damage can result.

Exposure to lead can occur via air, water, and food. Food is the largest contributor to the daily intake of lead for most people, but water and air can be important routes of exposure.

TABLE 2.6   Health Effects of Selected Contaminants*

Contaminant	Contaminant classification†						
	I	A	A/N	ST	P/A	C	Comments
VOCs	x	x	x	x		x	Many of these contaminants are neuro/behavioral toxicants, hepatotoxicants, and cardiac sensitizers.
Formaldehyde	x					x	May induce allergic responses.
Pesticides	x			x		x	Many of these contaminants are neurotoxicants, hepatotoxicants, reproductive toxicants, and sensitizers.
Lead				x			Neurotoxic and behavioral effects which may not be reversible.
Carbon monoxide		x					Increased frequency and severity of angina in patients; decreased work capacity in healthy adult males; headaches, decreased alertness, flu-like symptoms in healthy adults; exacerbation of cardiopulmonary dysfunction in compromised patient.
Carbon dioxide		x					Can also act as respiratory stimulant; increased respiration and decreased ability to perform strenuous tasks in humans; changes in blood pH and pCO_2; calcification of kidneys and structural changes in lungs of guinea pigs.
Nitrogen dioxide	x						Decreased pulmonary function in asthmatics; effects on pulmonary function in children, perhaps adults; synergistic effects with other contaminants in animals and children; increased susceptibility to infection in animals; animal studies indicate decreased immune capability, changes in anatomy and function of the lungs.
Sulfur dioxide	x						Decreased lung function in asthmatics and normal exercising males; animal studies show decreased lung function.
Biological contaminants (bacteria, viruses, molds, fungi, pollen, animal and human dander, insects and arachnid excreta)	x					x	Infectious diseases; allergic reactions; toxic effects

TABLE 2.6   Health Effects of Selected Contaminants* (Continued)

Contaminant	Contaminant classification†						Comments
	I	A	A/N	ST	P/A	C	
Environmental tobacco smoke	x					x	Irritation of mucous membranes, cardiovascular stress, chronic and acute pulmonary effects in children.
Polycyclic aromatic hydrocarbons	x					x	Some are irritants and can result in cardiovascular effects.
Asbestos		x				x	Asbestosis at occupational exposures, mesothelioma.
Radon						x	

*These are effects which have been associated or are thought to be associated with the individual contaminants based on toxicology or epidemiology studies. The concentration required for manifestation of the effect depends on a variety of factors. For some contaminants, there is scientific disagreement about various effect levels, and for other contaminants, there is insufficient data to determine effect levels.

†Classification codes: I = irritant, A = asphyxiant, A/N = anesthetic/narcotic, ST = systemic toxicant, P/A = pathogen/allergen, C = carcinogen.

SOURCE: *Introduction to Indoor Air Quality: A Self-Paced Learning Module,* EPA/400/3-91/002.

Asbestos is a naturally occurring mineral that can separate into long flexible fibers which are microscopic in size. Exposure to asbestos fibers does not result in immediate symptoms, but cancer and other effects can develop years after the exposure occurs. Mesothelioma, which is a cancer of the lining of the lung or abdomen, is considered to be a marker disease (specific to a contaminant) for asbestos exposure. Exposure to asbestos fibers can also result in other lung cancers and asbestosis. High levels of exposure are required to produce asbestosis, but much lower exposures can result in asbestos-related cancers. Smoking significantly increases the risk of developing cancer from asbestos exposure. EPA has classified asbestos as a "Known Human Carcinogen."

Radioactive contaminants. *Radon* is a naturally occurring radioactive gas which does not result in immediate symptoms. It is estimated that about 15 percent of the lung cancer cases in the United States are due to indoor radon exposures.[46] Smokers are at a much higher risk than nonsmokers of developing either asbestos-induced or radon-induced lung cancer. Radon is classified as a "Known Human Carcinogen" by EPA.

Combustion contaminants. There are many possible sources of combustion contaminants in residential and commercial buildings. These sources can release contaminants which can result in health effects

TABLE 2.7   Potential Sources of Selected Indoor Air Contaminants

Contaminant	Sources	
VOCs	Perfumes, hairsprays Furniture polish Cleaning solvents Hobby and craft supplies Pesticides Carpet dyes and fibers Glues, adhesives, sealants	Paints, stains, varnishes, strippers Wood preservatives Dry cleaned clothes, moth repellents Air fresheners Stored fuels and automotive products Contaminated water Plastics
Formaldehyde	Particleboard, interior-grade plywood Cabinetry, furniture	Urea formaldehyde foam insulation Carpet, fabrics
Pesticides	Insecticides (including termiticides) Rodenticides	Fungicides, disinfectants Herbicides (from outdoor use)
Lead	Lead-based paint	Exterior dust and soil
Carbon monoxide, carbon dioxide, nitrogen dioxide	Improperly operating gas or oil furnace/hot water heater, fireplace, wood stove	Unvented gas heater/kerosene heater Tobacco products, gas cookstove Vehicle exhaust
Sulfur dioxide	Combustion of sulfur-containing fuels (primarily, kerosene heaters)	
RSP (respirable particulates)	Fireplace, woodstove Unvented gas heater	Tobacco products Unvented kerosene heater
PAHs (polycyclic aromatic hydrocarbons)	Fireplace, woodstove Unvented kerosene heater	Tobacco products
ETS (environmental tobacco smoke)	Tobacco products	
Biological contaminants	Plants, animals, birds, humans Pillows, bedding, house dust Wet or damp materials	Standing water Humidifiers, evaporative coolers Hot water tank
Asbestos	Pipe and furnace insulation Ceiling and floor tiles	Decorative sprays Shingles and siding
Radon	Soil and rock Some building materials	Water

SOURCE: *Introduction to Indoor Air Quality: A Self-Paced Learning Module,* EPA/400/3-91/002.

ranging from headaches and respiratory tract irritation to death. This section provides an overview of health effects that have been related to contaminants from combustion sources.

Sources of combustion contaminants

Residential buildings. An important concern associated with the use of vented and unvented combustion sources is safety hazards including fires, burns from contact with hot metal surfaces, and poisonings from the accidental ingestion of fuel. Fires are also a concern with the use of tobacco products, hobby, and craft activities. A second concern is the release of indoor air contaminants from all fuel-burning unvented appliances and from vented appliances which are improperly installed, poorly maintained, or improperly operated. Safety hazards will not be discussed further in this section, but potential health effects from specific combustion contaminants are summarized below.

The primary fuel sources for vented and unvented household appliances include natural gas, fuel oil, wood, coal, kerosene, and liquid propane gas. Charcoal, newsprint, and other potentially hazardous fuels should not be burned indoors.

Large combustion appliances such as gas, wood, or oil-filled central heating systems are used mainly in those areas where winter temperatures fall below 68°F. Smaller appliances such as gas water heaters, ranges, and clothes dryers are used all year. Under normal conditions the by-products of these appliances are exhausted outside of the dwelling through a flue or chimney. Contaminants can be released indoors if there is a blockage in the flue or chimney or if the appliance is not vented properly.

When a combustible fuel burns, heat and light are given off along with a broad range of contaminants including asphyxiants, irritants, carcinogens, teratogens, and mutagens. Carbon monoxide, carbon dioxide, water vapor, and the nitrogen oxides are the primary contaminants from the combustion of natural gas. The combustion of kerosene adds sulfuric dioxide and inhalable particulates, including polycyclic aromatic hydrocarbons, to the inventory. Tobacco combustion and improperly vented wood and coal combustion sources increase the list of potential contaminants, and they can release aldehydes, a variety of polycyclic aromatic compounds, and other contaminants to the indoor air.

Tobacco smoke, combustion-related hobby and craft activities, and unvented kerosene and gas space heaters pose special problems because they release contaminants directly into the living space. Tobacco smoke is of particular concern because of the many carcinogenic, teratogenic, and mutagenic chemicals in the smoke.

Another potential problem is the release of moisture from the combustion of fuel by unvented sources. It is possible for water vapor from combustion to condense onto window frames and sills and to wet surfaces such as wood and insulation which are not directly visible. In addition to structural damage which can be caused by excessive moisture, these wetted materials can provide an excellent substrate for microbial growth which can produce a variety of effects in sensitive individuals.

Commercial buildings.   In commercial buildings, important sources and pathways of combustion contaminants include tobacco smoking, garages which are attached to working spaces, and improperly located air intake vents. Air intake vents which are located at ground level or adjacent to vehicles or other combustion sources can significantly elevate indoor contaminant levels by transporting contaminants to all areas served by the air-handling system.

Health effects of combustion contaminants.   Symptoms of exposure to combustion contaminants can include headaches, decreased alertness, flu-like symptoms, nausea, fatigue, rapid breathing, chest pain, confusion, and impaired judgment. Concentrations at which these symptoms will occur depend on health status and individual variations in sensitivity, so specific responses at a given concentration of a contaminant will vary among individuals.

Each year there are unnecessary deaths due to carbon monoxide poisoning from faulty furnaces and other combustion sources. When an investigator receives a call, and the client reports headaches, drowsiness, and nausea, especially during the heating season, the inspector should be aware of potential problems with furnaces or unvented combustion appliances.

Carbon monoxide.   Carbon monoxide (CO) is a colorless, odorless, and tasteless gas which is produced from the incomplete combustion of any carbon-containing fuel. It is a chemical asphyxiant that prevents oxygen from reaching the body's tissues. Normally, oxygen is carried to the body's tissues by hemoglobin in the form of oxyhemoglobin (OHb). When CO is present, it also combines with hemoglobin to form carboxyhemoglobin (COHb). In fact, CO is about 200 times as effective as oxygen (O_2) in combining with hemoglobin. This means that when both O_2 and CO are present, hemoglobin will not be available to carry O_2 to the tissues. Once inside the body, CO has a half-life of about 5 h.

The health effects of CO exposure are generally discussed in terms of the percentage of COHb in the blood (Fig. 2.3 and Table 2.8). The level of COHb is directly related to the CO concentration in the air, the duration of the exposure, and the activity level of the individual. For a given CO dose, the COHb level will reach an equilibrium over some period of time. As the CO concentration increases or decreases from this point, the COHb level will follow.

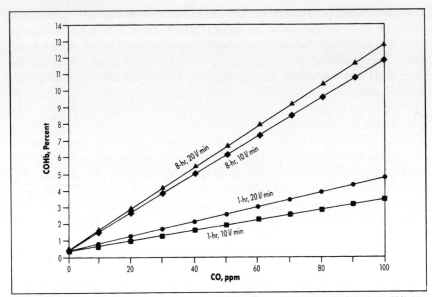

Predicted COHb levels resulting from 1- and 8-h exposures to carbon monoxide at rest (10 l/min) and with light exercise (20 l/min) are based on the Coburn-Forster-Kane equation using the following assumed parameters for nonsmoking adults: altitude = 0 ft; intial COHb level = 0.5%; Haldane constant = 218; blood volume = 5.5 l; hemoglobin level = 15 g/100 ml; lung diffusivity = 30 ml/torr/min; endogenous rate = 0.007 ml/min.

Figure 2.3 Relationship between carbon monoxide (CO) concentrations and carboxyhemoglobin (COHb) levels in blood. (*From* Introduction to Indoor Air Quality: A Reference Manual, *EPA/400/3-91/003.*)

Normally, metabolic processes in the body will result in a COHb level of 0.5 to 1.0 percent. Average COHb levels among nonsmokers are 1.2 to 1.5 percent. In cigarette smokers this level is about 3 to 4 percent on average, but it may be as high as 10 percent in heavy smokers.[43]

Continuous exposure to 30-ppm CO leads to an equilibrium COHb level of 5 percent; about 80 percent of this value occurs in 4 h and the remaining 20 percent, over the next 8 h. Continuous exposure to 20-ppm CO leads to COHb levels of 3.7 percent and exposure to 10 ppm leads to COHb levels of 2 percent. The time for equilibrium to be established is usually 8 h, but this time can be shorter if a person is physically active.[47]

Carbon monoxide can have detrimental effects on the heart, lungs, and nervous system. At COHb levels of 10 percent or less, the major effects are cardiovascular and neurobehavioral. Levels of 2.5 percent have been shown to aggravate symptoms in angina pectoris patients. No adverse health effects have been reported below 2.0 percent COHb; and findings in the range of 2.0 to 2.9 percent are inconclusive.[43] A level of 2.5 percent COHb can result from exposure to air with 50-ppm CO for 90 min or 15 ppm for 10 h.[48]

TABLE 2.8   Carboxyhemoglobin Levels and Related Health Effects

% COHb in blood	Effects associated with this COHb level
80	Death*
60	Loss of consciousness; death if exposure continues*
40	Confusion; collapse on exercise*
30	Headache; fatigue; impaired judgment*
7–20	Statistically significant decreased maximal oxygen consumption during strenuous exercise in healthy young men[†]
5–17	Statistically significant diminution of visual perception, manual dexterity, ability to learn, or performance in complex sensorimotor tasks (such as driving)[†]
5–5.5	Statistically significant decreased maximal oxygen consumption and exercise time during strenuous exercise in young healthy men[†]
Below 5	No statistically significant vigilance decrements after exposure to CO[†]
2.9–4.5	Statistically significant decreased exercise capacity (i.e., shortened duration of exercise before onset of pain) in patients with angina pectoris and increased duration of angina attacks[†]
2.3–4.3	Statistically significant decreased (about 3–7%) work time to exhaustion in exercising healthy men[†]

*From U.S. EPA (1979).
[†]From U.S. EPA (1985).
SOURCE: *Introduction to Indoor Air Quality: A Reference Manual,* EPA/400/3-91/003.

Nitrogen oxides.   There are many chemical species of the oxides of nitrogen (NO_x), but nitrogen dioxide (NO_2) and nitric oxide (NO) are of greatest concern as indoor air contaminants. Nitrogen oxides are produced when fossil fuels are burned, and most of the emissions occur as NO, which can be converted to NO_2.

Nitric oxide is a colorless, odorless, and tasteless gas that is only slightly soluble in water. The toxicological and health effects database for NO is somewhat limited. There is some evidence of inflammatory changes at the cellular level at 2 ppm.[49] The formation of the methemoglobin (met-Hb), which interferes with the transport of oxygen, has been attributed to the action of nitrite ion generated by either NO or NO_2 in solution. Background levels of met-Hb in the blood are in the range of 0.2 and 0.7 percent in the absence of high NO_x levels. Case et al.[50] provide evidence to show that met-Hb in whole blood can result from the direct uptake of NO by hemoglobin in the blood. They suggest that exposure to NO at 3 ppm may be physiologically comparable to exposure to CO concentrations of 10 ppm to 15 ppm.[50]

Nitrogen dioxide is a corrosive and highly oxidizing gas with a characteristic pungent odor which has been described as stinging, suffocating, and irritating.[43] The odor threshold has been placed between 0.11 and 0.22 ppm by different investigators.[43]

NO_2 is a deep lung irritant which has been shown to result in biochemical alterations and histologically demonstrable lung damage in laboratory animals as a result of both acute and chronic exposures. In laboratory animals, biochemical changes occur at concentrations as low as 0.2 ppm for 30 min.[43] Long-term animal studies have resulted in emphysema-like structural changes and increased susceptibility to bacterial lung infections.[43] Changes at the cellular level occur at the time of exposure, but biological effects are delayed, which complicates the understanding of long-term effects.

In humans, 80 to 90 percent of NO_2 can be absorbed upon inhalation. Controlled clinical studies have been conducted on susceptible subjects at concentrations in the range of 0.1 to 5.0 ppm. Most studies show that substantial changes in pulmonary function can be demonstrated in normal, healthy adults at or above concentration of 2 ppm.[43] The evidence at lower concentrations is not as clear. Asthmatics appear to be responsive at about 0.5 ppm, and subjective complaints have been reported at that level.[43] Below 0.5 ppm, small but statistically significant decrements in pulmonary function have been reported in asthmatics.[43] Kagawa and Tsuru[51] reported decrements in the lung function of asthmatics at concentrations as low as 0.15 ppm, but others have not substantiated these findings. Table 2.9 summarizes some of the human exposure studies that have been conducted.[51]

Epidemiologic studies suggest that children who are exposed to combustion contaminants from gas stoves have higher rates of respiratory symptoms and illness than other children. Nitrogen dioxide concentrations in these studies ranged from a low of 0.005 ppm to about 0.3 ppm.[43,49] In general, these results have not been supported in studies of adults. Table 2.10 summarizes some of the studies which have been conducted.

Carbon dioxide.   Carbon dioxide is a colorless, odorless gas. It is a simple asphyxiant, but it can also act as a respiratory stimulant. At concentrations above 1.5 percent, respiration is affected, and breathing becomes faster and more difficult. Concentrations above 3 percent can cause headaches, dizziness, and nausea. Above concentrations of 6 to 8 percent, stupor and death can result.[52]

The lowest level at which effects have been observed in both human and animal studies is about 1 percent.[53] Structural changes in the lungs of guinea pigs have been observed along with calcification of the kidneys. In humans, effects include increases in respiration, changes in blood pH and pCO_2, and decreases in the ability to perform strenuous

TABLE 2.9 Controlled Studies of the Effects of Human Exposure to Nitrogen Dioxide*

Pollutant concentration $\mu g/m^3$	ppm	Duration of exposure and activity	Number and type of subjects	Pulmonary effects	Symptoms	Reference
9400	5	14 h	8, normal	Increase of Raw during the first 30 min of exposure, with decrease during the following 4 h. Increase of Raw after 6.8 and 14 h of exposure. Reactivity to acetylcholine increased.	Not described.	Beil & Ulmer (1976)
9400	5	2 h + intermittent light exercise	11, normal	Increase of Raw and decrease in $AaDO_2$; no further increase when combined with 200 μg O_3/m^3 and 13.0 mg SO_2/m^3.	Not described.	Von Nieding et al. (1977)
7520	4	75 min including light and heavy exercise	25, normal 23, asthamatic	No effect on $SRaw$, heart rate or skin conductance.	Systolic blood pressure different; no symptoms.	Linn et al. (1985)
4700	2.5	2 h	8, normal	Increase of Raw, no change in PaO_2 or $PaCO_2$.	Not described.	Beil & Ulmer (1976)
1880	1	2 h	16, normal	Small changes in FVC.	5 subjects complained of chest tightness.	Hackney et al. (1978)
1880	1	2 h	8, normal	No increase in Raw.	Not described.	Beil & Ulmer (1976)

TABLE 2.9 Controlled Studies of the Effects of Human Exposure to Nitrogen Dioxide* (Continued)

Pollutant concentration $\mu g/m^3$	ppm	Duration of exposure and activity	Number and type of subjects	Pulmonary effects	Symptoms	Reference
940–9400	0.5–5	3–60 min	63, chronic bronchitic 25, chronic bronchitic	Increase of Raw at 3.0 mg/m³ Decrease of PaO_2 at 7.5 mg/m³; no change at 3.8 mg/m³.	Not described. Not described.	Von Nieding et al. (1971) Von Nieding et al. (1973)
940	0.5	2 h	10, normal 7, chronic bronchitic 13, asthmatic	None.	7 out of 13 asthmatic subjects suffered from symptoms such as chest tightness.	Kerr et al. (1979)
560	0.3	20 min at rest, followed by 10 min of moderate exercise (oral exposure, mouthpiece)	10, asthmatic	NO_2 plus exercise decrease in FEV_1 and partial expiratory flow rates at 60% TLC. After exposure at rest, no significant change in function.	None.	Bauer et al. (1984)
560	0.3	20 min at rest, followed by three 10-min cycles of moderate exercise (chamber exposure)	13, asthmatic	11% decrease in FEV_1, statistically significant.		Roger et al. (1990)

Concentration (µg/m³)	Concentration (ppm)	Exposure	Subjects	Effects	Reference
560 2000	0.3 1.06	1 h	8, normal	Small increase in *SRaw* at 560 µg/m³; no change at 2000 µg/m³.	Rehn et al. (1982)
380	0.2	2 h intermittent light exercise	31, asthmatic	No effect on forced expiratory function or total respiratory resistance observed with NO_2 alone. Small exacerbation by NO_2 of metacholine-induced broncho-constriction in 17 of 21 subjects tested. Fewer symptoms during NO_2 exposure compared to air.	Kleinman et al. (1983)
280 290	0.15 NO_2 0.15 O_3 0.15 NO_2+O_3	2 h intermittent light exercise	6, normal	Decrease in *SGaw/Vtg* with O_3 for 5 of 6 subjects, and all 6 for combined O_3+NO_2; very small (<5%) decrease in *SGaw/Vtg* with NO_2 alone in 3 of 6 subjects. Cough with O_3 and O_3+NO_2, but not NO_2 alone.	Kagawa & Tsuru (1979)
230 460 910	0.12 0.24 0.48	20 min at rest	8, normal 8, asthmatic	Normal: small increase in *SRaw* at 460 µg/m³; decrease in *SRaw* at 910 µg/m³; no change in reactivity to histamine. Asthmatic: no effects in *SRaw*; increase in reactivity to histamine at 910 µg/m³.	Bylin et al. (1985)
190	0.1	1 h at rest	20, asthmatic 20, normal	No effect on baseline *SGaw*, FEV_1 or V_{isov}; increased reactivity to carbachol in normal subjects and in asthmatics. None.	Ahmed et al. (1982)
190	0.1	1 h at rest	9, asthmatic hypersensitive to ragweed	No effect on baseline *SGaw*, FEV_1 and V_{isov} or reactivity to ragweed. None.	Ahmed et al. (1983)

TABLE 2.9 Controlled Studies of the Effects of Human Exposure to Nitrogen Dioxide* (Continued)

Pollutant concentration		Duration of exposure and activity	Number and type of subjects	Pulmonary effects	Symptoms	Reference
$\mu g/m^3$	ppm					
190	0.1	1 h at rest	15, normal 15, asthmatic (atopics)	No change in *SRaw* for either group; no change in sensitivity to methacholine.	None.	Hazucha et al. (1983)
190	0.1	1 h at rest	7, asthmatic	No change in response to grass pollen after exposure to NO_2.		Orehek et al. (1981)
190	0.1	1 h at rest	20, asthmatic	No effect on *SRaw*; increased sensitivity to carbachol in some subjects.		Orehek et al. (1976)

*Indication of change only described if statistically significant. Abbreviations are as follow: *SRaw*, specific airway resistance; *Raw*, airway resistance; *SGaw*, specific airway conductance, the reciprocal of *SRaw*; *FEV₁*, forced expiratory volume at 1 second; *TLC*, total lung capacity; *Vtg*, total gas volume; *Vᵢₛₒᵥ*, flow volume; *PaO₂* and *PaCO₂*, arterial partial pressure of oxygen and carbon dioxide; *AaDO₂*, difference in partial pressure of oxygen in the alveoli as against the arterial blood; *FVC*, forced vital capacity.

SOURCE: *Introduction to Indoor Air Quality: A Reference Manual*, EPA/400/3-91/003.

TABLE 2.10 Effects of Exposure to Nitrogen Dioxide Plus Other Gas-Stove Combustion Products in the Home on the Incidence of Acute Respiratory Disease in Epidemiology Studies Involving Gas Stoves

NO_2 concentration $\mu g/m^3$ (ppm)	Study population	Effects	Reference
		Studies of Children	
NO_2 concentration not measured at time of study.	2554 children from homes using gas to cook compared to 3204 children from homes using electricity; ages 6–11.	Bronchitis, day or night cough, morning cough, cold going to chest, wheeze, and asthma increased in children in homes with gas stoves.	Melia et al. (1977).
NO_2 concentration not measured in same homes studied.	4827 children, ages 5–10.	Higher incidence of respiratory symptoms and disease associated with gas stoves after controlling for confounding factors.	Melia et al. (1979).
Kitchens: 9–596 (gas) (0.005–0.317) 11–353 (electric) (0.006–0.188) Bedrooms: 7.5–318 (gas) (0.004–0.169) 6–70 (electric) (0.003–0.037) (by triethanolamine diffusion samplers)	808 6- and 7-year-olds.	Higher incidence of respiratory illness in gas-stove homes. No apparent statistical relationship between lung function tests and exposure to NO_2 levels in kitchen or bedroom.	Florey et al. (1979), companion paper to Melia et al. (1979); Goldstein et al. (1979).

TABLE 2.10 Effects of Exposure to Nitrogen Dioxide Plus Other Gas-Stove Combustion Products in the Home on the Incidence of Acute Respiratory Disease in Epidemiology Studies Involving Gas Stoves (Continued)

NO_2 concentration $\mu g/m^3$ (ppm)	Study population	Effects	Reference
		Studies of Children	
Sample of households 24-h average: gas (0.005–0.11); electric (0–0.06); outdoors (0.015–0.05); monitoring location not reported; 24-h averages by modified sodium arsenite; peaks by chemiluminescence.	128 children, ages 0–5. 346 children, ages 6–10. 421 children, ages 11–15.	No significant difference in reported respiratory illness between homes with gas and electric stoves in children from birth to 12 years.	Mitchell et al. (1974); see also Keller et al. (1979 a,b).
Sample of same households as reported above but no new monitoring reporting.	174 children under 12.	No evidence that cooking mode is associated with the incidence of acute respiratory illness.	Keller et al. (1979b).
95 percentile of 24-h indoor average; 39–116 $\mu g/m^3$ (0.02–0.06) (gas) vs 17.6–95.2 $\mu g/m^3$ (0.01–0.05) (electric); frequent peaks (gas)>1100 $\mu g/m^3$ (0.6 ppm); 24 h by modified sodium arsenite; peaks by chemiluminescence.	8120 children ages 6–10 in 6 different communities; data collected on lung function and on history of illness before the age of 2.	Significant association between history of serious respiratory illness before age 2 and use of gas stoves. Small but statistically significant decrements in lung function tests between lower FVC_1, FVC levels from gas stove homes compared with children from homes with electric stoves.	Speizer et al. (1980); Spengler, et al. (1979).
		Studies of Adults	
Preliminary measurements peak hourly 470–940 $\mu g/m^3$; max 1880 $\mu g/m^3$ (1 ppm).	Adults cooking with gas stoves, compared to those cooking with electric stoves.	No consistent statistically significant increases in respiratory illness associated with gas-stove usage.	U.S. EPA (1976).

See Mitchell et al. (1974) for monitoring.	Adults cooking with gas stoves, compared to those cooking with electric stoves, 146 households.	No evidence that cooking with gas is associated with an increase in respiratory disease.	Keller et al. (1979a, b).
See Mitchell et al. (1974) for monitoring.	Members of 441 households.	No significant difference in reported respiratory illness among adults in gas vs electric cooking homes.	Mitchell et al. (1974); see also Keller et al. (1979a, b).
See Mitchell et al. (1974) for monitoring.	Members of 120 households (subsample of 441 households above).	No significant difference among adults in acute respiratory disease incidence in gas vs electric cooking homes.	Keller et al. (1979a, b).

SOURCE: *Introduction to Indoor Air Quality: A Reference Manual*, EPA/400/3-91/003.

exercise. The significance of these effects is not clear, but a potential increase in respiratory and gastrointestinal illness has been postulated because these effects were observed in submarine crews at concentrations of 0.5 to 1 percent.[52] Table 2.11 summarizes the results of some studies which have been conducted.

Sulfur dioxide.   Sulfur dioxide (SO_2) is a colorless gas with a strong, pungent odor. The odor can be detected at about 0.5 ppm.[52] SO_2 is very soluble in water and exerts its irritant effects primarily on the upper respiratory tract, but its site of action depends on the presence of particulates and the rate, depth, and type of breathing.

There is considerable variability in the response to SO_2 among both normal, healthy subjects and asthmatics, and this makes it difficult to define a no-adverse-effect level. It has been estimated that about 5 percent of the population may be sensitive to SO_2.[43]

There is good agreement that healthy adults experience adverse effects at concentration of 0.75 to 1.0 ppm and that asthmatics experience increased airway resistance at exposures of about 0.4 ppm for 10 min, both during exercise and at rest.[43] Discernible effects have been reported below that level, but WHO concludes that the consequences of those effects are not clear.

Increased airway resistance has been reported at concentrations of 0.1 ppm among mild asthmatics who were exercising.[54] There is also some evidence that sulfur dioxide at levels of 0.15 ppm appears to act synergistically with ozone at levels of 0.15 ppm.[51] Table 2.12 summarizes some of the human exposure studies which have been conducted on asthmatic subjects.

Particulates.   In addition to the compounds listed above, other gases and particulates can be released from indoor combustion sources. In homes where wood is burned, respirable particulates which include polynuclear (polycyclic) aromatic hydrocarbons (PAH) compounds, trace metals, nitrates, and sulfates have been measured. PAH compounds and chromium[55] have also been measured from kerosene heaters.

PAHs are of particular concern because of their carcinogenic potential. PAH compounds include a large number of organic compounds which contain two or more benzene rings in their structure. These compounds are produced as the result of incomplete combustion. They are only very slightly soluble in water, but they are very soluble in fat. Although fat soluble, these compounds are metabolized rapidly in the body and do not tend to bioaccumulate in the fatty tissues. It is thought that the metabolites of PAH compounds in the body (diol-epoxides) are ultimately the carcinogens.[43]

Once PAH compounds enter the air, they can be adsorbed onto respirable-sized particles and inhaled into the lungs. PAH compounds are

TABLE 2.11 Selected Studies of Human Exposure to Carbon Dioxide

Exposure concentration and duration	Exposure method	Effects	Reference
4%, 2-wk exposure bracketed by two 2-wk control periods	Chamber, 24 subjects	No psychomotor impairment; no decrement in complex task performance by healthy young subjects.	Storm and Giannetta (1974)
4.2%, 5 days and 11 days; 3%, 30 days; exposures bracketed by two 3–5-day control periods	Chamber, 12 subjects total; 4 in each of 3 groups	Increased arterial and cerebrospinal fluid bicarbonate; decreased pH; occasional mild headaches and awareness of increased ventilation during first 24 h of exposure; some ectopic foci noted during exercise but small sample size hampered interpretation; decreased tolerance to exercise noted.	Sinclair et al. (1969)
3%, 5 days bracketed by two 5-day control periods	Space Cabin Simulator, 7 subjects	No changes in ammonia or titratable acidity; no changes in serum electrolytes, blood sugar, serum creatinine, or liver function; no significant changes in exercise or psychomotor studies.	Glatte et al. (1967)
1.5%, 42 days; 0.7–5%, 50–60 days	Chamber*; submarines (13 Polaris patrols)	Increases in respiratory minute volume, tidal volume, physiological dead space; decrease in vital capacity; respiratory acidosis, increase in pCO_2, decrease in pH; decrease of plasma chloride, red cell sodium increase, potassium decrease; decrease in plasma calcium metabolism, urine calcium, urine magnesium, increase in red cell calcium. In the submarine study a decrease in respiratory and gastrointestinal disease was noted with decreasing CO_2 (and other pollutants).	Schaefer (1979)
1% and 2%, 30 days	Chamber, 2 subjects in each of 2 exposures	At 2% significant increases in pCO_2 in blood and alveolar air, decrease in ability to perform strenuous exercise; decrease in blood pH, increase in pulmonary ventilation; changes at 1% were not considered to be significant; authors conclude that prolonged CO_2 exposure causes acidosis, hypodynamia, and fatigue but effects are reversible.	Zharov et al. (1963)

*Similar effects were noted in subjects in both the chamber exposure and submarine exposure.

SOURCE: *Introduction to Indoor Air Quality: A Reference Manual*, EPA/400/3-91/003.

TABLE 2.12 Selected Studies of Asthmatic Subjects Exposed to Sulfur Dioxide

Sulfur dioxide concentration* (ppm)	Duration of exposure (min)	Number and type of subject	Type of exposure	Type of activity	Effects†	Reference
1, 3, 5	10	7, normal 7, atopic 7, asthmatic	Mouthpiece	Rest	$SRaw$ increased significantly at all concentrations for asthmatic subjects, only at 5 ppm for normal and atopic subjects. Some asthmatics exhibited marked dyspnea requiring bronchodilation therapy.	Sheppard et al. (1981a)
1.0 0.1, 0.25, 0.5	5 10	6, asthmatic 7, asthmatic	Mouthpiece	Exercise	$SRaw$ significantly increased in the asthmatic group at 0.5 and 0.25 ppm of sulfur dioxide and at 0.1 ppm in the two most responsive subjects. At 0.5 ppm three asthmatic subjects developed wheezing and shortness of breath.	Sheppard et al. (1980, 1981b)
0.50	180	40, asthmatic	Oral chamber; nose clips	Rest	$MMFR$ significantly decreased 2.7%; recovery within 30 min.	Jaeger et al. (1979)
0.5	10	5, asthmatic	Mouthpiece	Exercise	$SRaw$ increases were observed over exercise baseline rates for 80% of the subjects.	Linn et al. (1982)
0.25, 0.5	60	24, asthmatic	Chamber	Exercise	No statistically significant changes in FVC or $SRaw$.	Linn et al. (1982)
0.30	120	19, asthmatic	Chamber	Exercise	No pulmonary effects seen with 0.3 ppm of sulfur dioxide and 0.5 ppm of nitrogen dioxide exposure compared to exercise baseline.	Linn et al. (1980)

*0.1 ppm of sulfur dioxide≈262 µg/m³; 0.05 ppm=1310 µg/m³; 1.0 ppm=2620 µg/m³; 5.0 ppm=13,100 µg/m³; 10 ppm=26,200 µg/m³; 50 ppm=131,000 µg/m³.

†Significant increase or decrease noted here refers to "statistically significant" effects, independent of whether the observed effects are "medically significant" or not. Abbreviations are as follows: $SRaw$, specific air way resistance; $MMFR$, maximum mid-expiratory flow rate; FVC, forced vital capacity.

SOURCE: *Introduction to Indoor Air Quality: A Reference Manual*, EPA/400/3-91/003.

also present in foods (smoked, broiled, refined) and water; in fact, the oral intake of PAH compounds may be much higher than the inhaled amount in the general population.[43]

PAH compounds have been shown to be carcinogenic in animal tests and mutagenic in short-term laboratory tests. Evidence for carcinogenicity is supported by epidemiological studies of coke-oven workers, coal-gas workers, and workers in aluminum production plants.[43]

Environmental tobacco smoke. *Environmental tobacco smoke* (ETS) is a term which describes the contamination released into the air when tobacco products burn or when smokers exhale. The hazards of inhaling mainstream smoke (inhaled by the smoker) and sidestream smoke (produced at the burning end of the tobacco product) are well documented. The inhalation of ETS is known as *involuntary smoking* or *passive smoking.*

Studies have shown that cigarette smoke contains over 3800 chemical compounds;[52] some of these compounds are shown in Table 2.13. Many of these gaseous and particulate contaminants are irritants, and others are carcinogens (43 identified compounds), mutagens, and teratogens. Particles in tobacco smoke are especially hazardous because they are inhalable (0.1 to 1.0 μm), remain airborne for hours after smoking stops, and attract radon decay products. Table 2.13 shows that concentration of contaminants in sidestream smoke can be several times higher than those in mainstream smoke.

In 1986 two major reports reached similar conclusions about the hazards of passive smoking; these were *Environmental Tobacco Smoke. Measuring Exposures and Assessing Health Effects,* which was prepared by the National Academy of Sciences (NAS)[56] for the EPA and the Department of Health and Human Services, and *The Health Consequences of Involuntary Smoking,* which was prepared for the Office of the Surgeon General.[57]

Both reports concluded that passive smoking significantly increases the risk of lung cancer in adults. The NAS report[56] estimates that the risk of lung cancer is about 30 percent higher for nonsmoking spouses of smokers than for nonsmoking spouses of nonsmokers and that as many as 20 percent of lung cancers in nonsmokers may stem from exposure to tobacco smoke. The Surgeon General's report[57] concludes that simply separating nonsmokers from smokers in the work environments is not sufficient to protect nonsmokers. Although the available studies did not specifically include workplace environments, tobacco smoke poses similar risks, regardless of the environment.

There was also agreement that passive smoking substantially increases respiratory illness in children. Children who live in house-

TABLE 2.13 Composition of Mainstream and Sidestream Smoke

Characteristic or compound	Concentration, mg/cigarette*		
	Mainstream smoke	Sidestream smoke	Ratio, 2:1
General characteristics:			
Duration of smoke production, s	20	550	27.5
Tobacco burned	347	411	1.2
Particles, no. per cigarette	1.05×10^{12}	3.5×10^{12}	3.3
Particles:			
Tar (chloroform extract)	20.8	44.1	2.1
	$10.2^{\dagger}$	$34.5^{\dagger}$	3.4
Nicotine	0.92	1.69	1.8
	$0.46^{\dagger}$	$1.27^{\dagger}$	2.8
Benzo [a] pyrene	3.5×10^{-5}	1.35×10^{-4}	3.9
	4.4×10^{-5}	1.99×10^{-4}	.45
Pyrene	1.3×10^{-4}	3.9×10^{-4}	3.0
	2.70×10^{-4}	1.011×10^{-3}	.37
Fluoranthene	2.72×10^{-4}	1.255×10^{-3}	4.6
Benzo [a] fluorene	1.84×10^{-4}	7.51×10^{-4}	4.1
Benzo [b/c] fluorene	6.9×10^{-5}	2.51×10^{-4}	3.6
Chrysene, benz [a] anthracene	1.91×10^{-4}	1.224×10^{-3}	6.4
Benzo [b/k/j] fluoranthrene	4.9×10^{-5}	2.60×10^{-4}	5.3
Benzo [e] pyrene	2.5×10^{-5}	1.35×10^{-4}	5.4
Perylene	9.0×10^{-6}	3.9×10^{-5}	4.3
Dibenz [a, j] anthracene	1.1×10^{-5}	4.1×10^{-5}	3.7
Dibenz [a, h] anthracene, ideno-(2,3-ed] pyrene	3.1×10^{-5}	1.04×10^{-4}	3.4
Benzo [ghi] perylene	3.9×10^{-5}	9.8×10^{-5}	2.5
Anthanthrene	2.2×10^{-5}	3.9×10^{-5}	1.8
Phenols (total)	0.228	0.603	2.6
Cadmium	1.25×10^{-4}	4.5×10^{-4}	3.6
Gases and vapors:			
Water	$7.5^{\ddagger}$	298§	39.7
Carbon monoxide	18.3	86.3	4.7
	—	72.6	—
Ammonia	0.16	7.4	46.3
Carbon dioxide	63.5	79.5	1.3
NO_x	0.014	0.051	3.6
Hydrogen cyanide	0.24	0.16	0.67
Acrolein	0.084	—	—
	—	0.825	—
Formaldehyde	—	1.44	—
Toluene	0.108	0.60	5.6
Acetone	0.578	1.45	2.5
Polonium-210, pCi	0.04–0.10	0.10–0.16	1–4

*Unless otherwise noted.

†Filtered cigarettes.

‡3.5 mg in particulate phase; rest in vapor phase.

§5.5 mg in particulate phase; rest in vapor phase.

SOURCE: *Introduction to Indoor Air Quality: A Reference Manual*, EPA/400/3-91/003.

holds where there are smokers are more likely to have respiratory infections (including bronchitis and pneumonia) than children in non-smoking households. Additional effects in children include increases in coughing, wheezing, sputum production, slower lung function growth, and low birthweight babies in mothers who are nonsmokers but are exposed to ETS. The prevalence of these effects has been found to increase with the number of smokers in the home.

The evidence for these effects was so strong that the National Research Council's Committee on Passive Smoking voted to recommend eliminating tobacco smoke from any area where there are small children or infants.

Pesticides. Pesticides are chemicals which are used to kill or control pests. A pest is any organism that is not wanted in a particular location (for example, in the home or garden). Termites, cockroaches, fleas, rodents, ants, moths, caterpillars, dandelions and other weeds, fungi, bacteria, and molds in buildings are examples of pests. Pesticides can be categorized into insecticides, herbicides, fungicides, rodenticides, disinfectants or antimicrobial agents, and plant growth regulators.

Because most pesticides are inherently toxic, proper use and storage are needed to minimize the potential adverse effects from exposure. Unfortunately, consumers tend to be casual about pesticides, perhaps assuming they are innocuous since they can be purchased in grocery, drug, and hardware stores and because these products can be used without a license or special protective clothing. As a result, each year there are cases of poisonings by these products which could have been prevented through proper use of the products or through the application of alternative methods of pest control.

The use of pesticides is widespread. In 1985 U.S. agricultural uses accounted for 77 percent of the total usage (over 1 billion pounds), and farmers spent about $4.6 billion on pesticides.[58] Nonagricultural uses of pesticides are also significant. During 1984, almost 230 million pounds of herbicides, insecticides, fungicides, and rodenticides were used for nonagricultural purposes.[59] Of this total, about 28.7 percent was used in homes and gardens, and the remainder was used by industry, government, and commerce.

Measured concentrations in homes. A nationwide survey conducted by EPA during 1976 and 1977 of household pesticide use found that about 91 percent of households use pesticides.[58] In the home, pesticides are used to kill pests on lawns, trees, shrubs, flowers, and vegetables. Pesticides are almost universally used to control termite infestations either before or after construction. Pesticides are applied to living spaces to rid them of unwanted pests. And, people use these products on themselves or their pets to prevent the bites of mosquitos, chiggers, flies, ticks, fleas, and other pests.

In 1985, EPA extended its earlier work by developing a methodology for determining pesticide exposures in the general U.S. population.[60] The methodology used in this study, which is known as the "Non-occupational Pesticides Exposure Study (NOPES)," was designed as a means of developing estimates of exposure to some of the most commonly used household insecticides via air, drinking water, food, and dermal contact. In the two cities which were studied (Jacksonville, Florida, and Springfield/Chicopee, Massachusetts), the average number of pesticides in the home was 4.2 for Jacksonville and 5.3 in Springfield/Chicopee.

For the majority of the 33 target compounds which were studied, indoor air concentrations were substantially higher than outdoor air concentrations, and personal air concentrations were usually similar to indoor air concentrations. Another finding of this study was that seasonal variations existed for many of the compounds. This effect appears to be compound specific and complex, and it probably reflects the interaction of many variables, including temperature, patterns of pesticide usage, use of heating and cooling systems, and occupant activities.

The study also attempted to assess the relative contributions of air, food, water, and dermal exposure in the two tested cities. Based on limited data, it appears that exposure from water ingestion was negligible. Food appeared to be a dominant contributor for some compounds, while air dominated for others. Limited data were collected for dermal exposures, and the importance of this pathway needs further study.

Table 2.14 summarizes some additional measurements of pesticides in buildings under different conditions. These and other data suggest some pesticides which are sprayed will persist for long periods at varying concentrations. It is also possible for these chemicals, particularly termiticides, to migrate up and down through cracks and crevices in the building and by air currents.

Health effects of pesticides

Poisonings.   During 1987, 57,430 cases of pesticide exposure were reported to poison control centers, and 98 percent of these were due to accidental exposures. Insecticides accounted for about 66 percent of the total cases, followed by rodenticides (17 percent), moth repellents (7.7 percent), herbicides (7.2 percent), and fungicides (2.3 percent). About 60 percent of the cases involved children less than 6 years of age.[61]

During the period 1980 to 1985, at least 46.5 percent of the accidental pesticide-related deaths in the United States occurred in the home

TABLE 2.14   Measurements of Pesticides in Buildings

Pesticide	Concentration range, μg/m³	Comments	References
		Dormitory	Leidy et al. (1982)
Diazinon (emulsion)	38.4	Treatment room, day of treatment	
	9.7	Treatment room, 7 days later	
	7.1	Treatment room, 21 days later	
	0.9	Adjacent room, day of treatment	
	1.0	Adjacent room, 21 days later	
	0.4, 0.5	Rooms above and below treatment Room; day of treatment	
	0.6, 0.4	Rooms above and below; 21 days later	
		Dormitory	Wright et al. (1981)
Bendiocarb (0.5% wettable powder)	7.7	Day of treatment	
	ND*	3 days later	
Carbaryl (5% dust)	1.3	Day of treatment	
	0.2	1 day later	
	0.01	3 days later	
Acephate (1% suspension)	1.3	Day of treatment	
	2.9	1 day later	
	0.3	3 days later	
Diazinon (1% suspension)	1.6	Day of treatment	
	0.6	1 day later	
	0.4	3 days later	
Chlorpyrifos (0.5% suspension)	1.1	Day of treatment	
	1.1	1 day later	
	0.3	3 days later	
Fenitrothion (1.0% suspension)	3.3	Day of treatment	
	1.1	1 day later	
	0.5	3 days later	
Propoxur	15.4	Day of treatment	
	2.7	1 day later	
	0.7	3 days later	
		6 Single-family Homes	Wright & Leidy (1982)
Chlordane (1% emulsion)	2.75 ± 1.33	3 houses, day of treatment	
	3.32 ± 1.38	6 months later	
	5.01 ± 0.97	12 months later	
Termide® (0.5% chlordane)	4.48 ± 1.70	3 houses, day of treatment	
	5.81 ± 5.01	6 months later	
+	2.77 ± 2.69	12 months later	
0.25% heptachlor)	1.41 ± 0.64	3 houses, day of treatment	
	1.80 ± 1.47	6 months later	
	1.00 ± 0.70	12 months later	
		Carpet swatches were contaminated with pesticide after application	

TABLE 2.14   **Measurements of Pesticides in Buildings (Continued)**

Pesticide	Concentration range, $\mu g/m^3$	Comments	References
		17 Houses	Dobbs & Williams (1983)
gamma-HCH (17 houses)	0.01–2.9; 0.56 (mean)	Concentrations in interior areas other than roof voids, from 1 to 10 years after treatment	
Dieldrin (16 houses)	0.01–0.5; 0.11 (mean)		
		4368 Houses	Olds (1987)
		Results for initial sampling; considerable variability on resampling; time between application and sampling not given	
Chlordane/Heptachlor	3.00–87.7	0.89%>NAS guideline	
Aldrin	1.40–1.55	0>NAS guideline	
Chlorpyrifos	0.51–34.62	0.02%>NAS guideline	
Diazinon	0.51–34.62	No NAS guideline	
		5038 Houses	Lillie & Barnes (1987)
Chlordane		% of houses with identical level (time between treatment and sampling not given)	

		Time of treatment	
		Preconstr., %	Postconstr., %
NDL[†]			
	Slab (ducts in slab)	77	28
	Crawl space	84	5
	Slab (ducts in attic)	47	96
NDL to ≤2			
	Slab (ducts in slab)	17	49
	Crawl space	11	48
	Slab (ducts in attic)	53	4
>2 to ≤5			
	Slab (ducts in slab)	5	18
	Crawl space	4	28
	Slab (ducts in attic)	0	0
≥5			
	Slab (ducts in slab)	1	5
	Crawl space	1	19
	Slab (ducts in attic)	0	0

*ND—not detected.
[†]NDL—nondetectable level.
SOURCE: *Introduction to Indoor Air Quality: A Reference Manual*, EPA/400/3-91/003.

(40.9 percent of the locations were not specified). Organophosphate insecticides were responsible for about 32 percent of the deaths. Seventeen percent of the victims were under the age of 5; 29.6 percent were between 25 and 44 years of age; 23.9 percent were between 45 and 64 years of age; and 22 percent were over the age of 65.[61]

Pesticide poisonings are the second most common source of childhood poisonings. A new trend to develop products with less offensive odors makes poisonings more likely. Consumers should know that the availability of these products is increasing in the marketplace, and the absence of this warning signal may lull users into a false sense of security.

Prevention of poisoning through proper selection, storage, and use of pesticides is the key to reducing adverse health effects. Although medical treatments can counteract the pesticide poisoning, they apply to acute exposures and many treatments pose risks to the health of patients.

Symptoms of acute and chronic exposures.   Many pesticides (for example, organophosphates and organochlorines) affect more than one organ system and produce a variety of symptoms which can progress rapidly from mild to fatal. Some pesticides produce reactions almost immediately, while others result in delayed reactions. The specific symptoms that will result from a given exposure situation depend on the pesticide and its site of action, the dose received, and the sensitivity of the exposed individual. It should be noted that some individuals may be more sensitive to pesticides and other chemicals than the general population.

Irritation of the skin, eyes, and respiratory tract are common effects of pesticides. Skin exposure can result in itching, redness, swelling, blistering, or an acne-like condition. The mucous membranes and the lining of the respiratory tract are especially sensitive, and inhaled pesticides can produce stinging, swelling, difficulty breathing, and increased mucous production. Flu-like symptoms are common.

Gastrointestinal tract symptoms include salivation, nausea, vomiting, abdominal cramps, and diarrhea. Nervous system effects include fatigue, headache, dizziness, weakness, behavioral and mood disturbances, decreased or blurred vision, tingling and numbness of the extremities, tremors, pinpoint and nonreactive pupils, paralysis, coma, and death. Shock, hypertension, and arrhythmias of the heart can result when the cardiovascular system is affected. The kidneys and blood can also be damaged.

Some pesticides are sensitizers, and they result in more severe and potentially life-threatening reactions with subsequent exposures to small amounts.

Chronic exposure to some pesticides can result in damage to the liver, kidneys, and nervous system. Typical clinical findings include muscular weakness and numbness and tingling of the extremities (peripheral neuropathy).

A history of recent pesticide use and the presence of these types of symptoms should suggest the possibility of pesticide poisoning.

Health effects data.   There are significant gaps and uncertainties in the health effects database. For example, the lowest dose that results in acute effects is not known with certainty for most pesticides. In addition, the effects of chronic exposures and the doses at which these effects occur are not well documented. Deficiencies in the database for long-term health effects are also important because of the potential exposure to pesticides in schools, parks, retail stores, mass transit vehicles, or other public areas; and nonoccupational exposures, in general, are poorly characterized.

Of particular concern are the carcinogenic, mutagenic, and teratogenic potential of pesticides. The database for assessing these effects is inadequate to support definitive conclusions, but some animal and short-term tests suggest that many pesticides may be carcinogenic or genotoxic.[59]

In addition to the animal and cell studies, there are epidemiologic studies of occupationally exposed workers which suggest that subacute poisoning does occur as a result of continuous low-level exposure.[65–67] Also, a study by Lowengart et al.[68] underscores the concern for health effects in children resulting from home pesticide use. Although this study was not designed to evaluate the relationship between household chemicals and cancer, the data in the study showed an association between pesticide exposure in children and infants and childhood leukemia. However, other studies confirming this work are needed.

Regulatory framework

Federal.   EPA regulates pesticide formulations under the Federal Insecticide, Fungicide and Rodenticide Act (FIFRA) of 1947 and its amendments. All pesticides must be registered with EPA before the products can be sold or distributed. Each product must have a label which identifies the EPA registration number, ingredients, proper use, health effects, warnings, and cautions.

Registration is based on an overall risk/benefit standard which requires the EPA to consider the economic, environmental, and social costs and benefits of pesticide use. Pesticides can be registered if the pesticide performs its stated function when used according to label instructions, without posing an *unreasonable risk* of adverse effects on human health or the environment. EPA has a Science Advisory Panel of outside experts which reviews major pesticide decisions or regulations.

The toxicological data that are required for registering pesticides used in and around the home depend on the nature, magnitude, and duration of expected exposures if the pesticide labels are reasonably followed. Some basic data such as acute toxicity studies for labeling the pesticide formulation are required routinely. Longer-term studies such as reproduction carried over two generations of breeding and cancer studies in rats and mice are required only for nonfood uses, which could result in high exposures over a significant period of a person's lifetime. Pesticides used on food crops have been tested in all types of studies including long-term chronic and cancer testing.

An important provision of FIFRA requires EPA to review "old" pesticides (previously registered) to ensure that these products meet current scientific and regulatory standards. Pesticides which were considered to be "reasonably safe" were to be reregistered, and the registrations of those which were considered to be "unreasonably unsafe" were to be canceled. Prior to 1988, EPA was able to evaluate 185 active ingredients of about 600 previously registered pesticide active ingredients. The 1988 amendments accelerate and expedite the reregistration process, which should enable EPA to evaluate the remaining chemicals more quickly.

EPA can also place a pesticide into "Special Review" if it believes the chemical poses a serious potential health or environmental risk. Special Review is an intensive investigation of the pesticide's risks and benefits.

EPA can limit the use of a chemical in some applications but may decide its use is safe in others. For example, diazinon is one of the most widely used ingredients in consumer pesticide products. In 1988 EPA banned the use of diazinon on sod farms and golf courses because of its toxicity to certain birds and other nontarget species. Diazinon can still be applied to lawns because lawns are not the usual habitat for the waterfowl that are at risk.

If a pesticide is considered to be a significant health hazard, EPA or another appropriate agency can take one of the following actions: (1) cancel the registration, (2) cancel the registration and withdraw the product, (3) place restrictions on use or application of the compound, (4) suspend the registration pending resolution of the hazard or receipt of data, (5) set tolerance limits for pesticide residues on foodstuffs, or (6) establish maximum permissible limits for the pesticide in drinking water.

As EPA evaluates pesticides, it publishes fact sheets which identify the manufacturer, date of registration, uses, toxicity, and regulatory action. These fact sheets and registration information for individual pesticides are a useful source of information.

Warning labels.   EPA requires pesticides to be labeled according to one of four toxicity categories based on a series of tests which relate to acute effects such as eye or skin irritation and other harmful effects that result shortly after the pesticide exposure occurs.

Depending on the health effects evaluation, products may be labeled *DANGER* (highly poisonous), *WARNING* (moderately poisonous), or *CAUTION* (least hazardous). Unfortunately, based on EPA's 1987 survey, it seems highly likely that many consumers do not discriminate among these different labels.

Registration and labeling, however, have limitations. In 1986 the General Accounting Office (GAO) noted, "The public is not told about the uncertainties surrounding chronic health risks."[59] In 1988 the California Senate Office of Research echoed the GAO's concerns when it concluded that "labeled precautions for consumers may often provide only a minimal, and in certain instances inadequate, basis for avoiding hazards, especially infants and children."[69]

EPA does require some pesticide products to contain warnings about potential chronic effects, but the labeling regulations do not require disclosure of chronic health hazards or the lack of full assessments of chemicals.

Local authority. Regulation of lawn chemicals is one area in which state and local jurisdictions have attempted to inform the public about pesticide use. Some states such as Rhode Island, Massachusetts, Maryland, Minnesota, and Iowa have enacted laws which require the posting of warnings for the application of lawn chemicals. These regulations require notifications of pesticide applications, listing of the pesticides to be applied, and the disclosure of health and environmental effects.

Formaldehyde and other volatile organic compounds

Sources of formaldehyde

Residential buildings. Formaldehyde (HCHO) is a flammable, colorless gas with a characteristic odor. The odor threshold for HCHO is about 1 ppm, but it can be detected at levels as low as 0.05 ppm by some people.[52] It is one of the most widely used chemicals in the United States. About half of the HCHO produced annually (6 billion pounds in 1983) is used to make urea and phenol-HCHO) resins which, in turn, are used to produce adhesives, bonding and laminating agents, foam insulation, fabrics, coatings, and paper.[70] Phenol-HCHO resins are used only on interior-grade products because they are susceptible to moisture deterioration.

HCHO can be released from a variety of products (Table 2.15), but the primary residential sources are hardwood plywood, particleboard, medium-density fiberboard (MDF), and other pressed wood products. All of these pressed wood products are produced by combining wood pieces or chips with an adhesive and other chemicals (including urea-HCHO resins) and pressing them together in hot hydraulic presses.

TABLE 2.15   Potential Sources of Formaldehyde Indoors

Pressed-wood products	Hardwood plywood, particle board, medium-density fiberboard (MDF), decorative paneling
Insulation	Urea-formaldehyde foam insulation (UFFI), fiberglass made with HCHO binders
Combustion sources	Natural gas, kerosene, tobacco, automobile exhaust
Paper products	Grocery bags, waxed paper, facial tissues, paper towels, disposable sanitary products
Stiffeners, wrinkle resisters, and water repellents	Floor coverings (rugs, linoleum, varnishes, plastics), carpet backings, adhesive binders, fire retardants, permanent press textiles
Other sources	Plastics, cosmetics, deodorants, shampoos, disinfectants, starch-based glues, adhesives, laminates, paints, fabric dyes, inks, fertilizers, fungicides

SOURCE: *Introduction to Indoor Air Quality: A Reference Manual*, EPA/400/3-91/003.

The potential for HCHO emissions is the greatest for MDF, followed by particleboard and hardwood plywood.

Measured concentrations of HCHO. Formaldehyde is perhaps one of the most widely characterized indoor air contaminants. Table 2.16 summarizes some of the measurements which have been made in mobile homes, conventional homes, offices, and a variety of public buildings. These and other studies have shown that manufactured housing could be expected to have higher average concentrations of HCHO than conventional housing, probably because of the greater number of sources and higher surface-to-volume ratio. It should be noted that construction techniques have changed for manufactured housing and average concentrations in these homes may be lower than in the past.

HCHO concentrations in conventional houses insulated with urea-formaldehyde foam insulation (UFFI) are generally higher than in houses with other types of insulation. Measurements of HCHO concentrations in nonresidential buildings have generally demonstrated lower concentrations than in conventional or mobile homes.

Although general trends have been noted, the reported data also show that a wide range of concentrations can exist in any type of construction, depending on the age of the structure, season, time of day, climatic factors, and presence of sources.

Health effects of formaldehyde. Concerns about exposure to HCHO have resulted in thousands of complaints to agencies such as the U.S. Consumer Product Safety Commission (CPSC) and in numerous lawsuits. These complaints have related primarily to effects resulting

TABLE 2.16   Measurements of Formaldehyde Concentrations in Different Types of Buildings

Type of building	Concentration (ppm)			Reference
	Minimum	Maximum	Mean	
Conventional homes with chipboard (n = 23)	0.07	1.82	0.51	Andersen et al. (1975)
Conventional homes (n = 80)	0.4*	8.1*	—	Sardinas et al. (1979)
All homes (n = 100)	<0.1	3.68	0.35 (median)	Dally et al. (1981)
U-F foamed conventional homes (n = 14)	0.1	1.09	0.47 (median)	
U-F wood products conventional homes (n = 13)	0.1	0.92	0.1 (median)	
Mobile homes (n = 65)	<0.1	3.68	0.1 (median)	
Mobile home day care centers (n = 7)	0.2	0.45	0.35	Olsen & Dossing (1982)
Permanent day care centers (n = 2)	0.04	0.09	0.07	
Mobile homes (n = 39)	0.02	3.69	0.42	Ritchie & Lehnen (1985)
Conventional homes (n = 489)	0.01	5.52	0.15	
Mobile homes (n = 137)	0.1	2.84	0.46	Hanrahan et al. (1985)
Conventional homes (n = 36)	<0.008	<0.14	0.04	Stock & Mendez (1985)
Energy-efficient homes (n = 7)	0.04	0.11	0.07	
Apartments (n = 19)	0.02	0.27	0.08	
Condominiums (n = 10)	<0.008	0.29	0.06	
Energy-efficient condominiums (n = 3)	0.15	0.2	0.18	
Nonmanufactured homes (n = 48)			0.41	Sexton et al. (1986)
Mobile homes—all (n = 633)	<0.010	0.464	0.072	
Pre-1981 mobile homes (n = 266)	<0.010	0.386	0.061	
Post-1981 mobile homes (n = 391)	0.012	0.464	0.080	

TABLE 2.16   Measurements of Formaldehyde Concentrations in Different Types of Buildings   (Continued)

Type of building	Concentration (ppm)			Reference
	Minimum	Maximum	Mean	
New buildings[*] (n = 3)	ND	0.192	—	Shelden et al. (1987)
Old buildings[‡] (n = 3)	ND	0.103		
Office buildings (n = 3)	0.025	0.039	0.031	Bayer & Black (1988)

*Draeger tubes.

[†]Office, nursing home, hospital.

[‡]Office, office/school, nursing home.

SOURCE: *Introduction to Indoor Air Quality: A Reference Manual,* EPA/400/3-91/003.

from acute exposures, but increasingly consumers are concerned about health effects resulting from chronic exposures and the potential carcinogenicity of HCHO.

HCHO is a known irritant and sensitizer. The frequency and severity of irritant effects from HCHO has been shown to increase with concentration and length of exposure. Symptoms of upper airway irritation include a tingling sensation in the nose, dry throat, and sore throat. These symptoms usually coexist with tearing, burning, stinging, and pain in the eyes.[52] These effects can occur within a few minutes after exposure to HCHO depending on the exposure concentration and the sensitivity of the individual. At higher levels, inhalation of HCHO produces lower airway irritation and pulmonary effects which are characterized by coughing, chest tightness, and wheezing.

Skin contact with HCHO has been reported to result in irritation, allergic contact dermatitis, and urticaria. These effects may be caused by direct contact with HCHO or formalin (HCHO in solution with methanol) or by HCHO-releasing agents (cosmetics, germicides, incompletely cured resins) and the decomposition of HCHO-containing resins (textiles). Repeated contact with low concentrations of HCHO can result in sensitization reactions.

Additional reported effects of HCHO exposure include nosebleeds and runny noses, persistent swell of nasal turbinates, headaches, fatigue, memory and concentration problems, nausea, dizziness, and breathlessness.[71]

Irritant effects have been associated with concentrations in the range of 0.1 to 3 ppm, and concentrations as low as 0.03 ppm have been reported to cause effects in sensitive individuals. It has been estimated that 10 to 12 percent of the U.S. population may have hyperactive airways which may make them more susceptible to the irritant effects of HCHO; this estimate includes asthmatics.[52]

According to the NRC, the Committee on Toxicology of the National Academy of Sciences evaluated data available in 1980, and it concluded that there is no population threshold effect level for the irritant effects of HCHO in humans.[52] Based on its review, the Committee concluded that less than 20 percent of the population would experience slight to mild irritation and discomfort when exposed to less than 0.25 ppm HCHO. More recently, CPSC also concluded that there may not be a threshold limit concentration for HCHO.[72] In 1983, the WHO Working Group on Assessment and Monitoring of Exposure to Indoor Air Pollutants concluded that indoor HCHO concentrations of less than 0.05 ppm were of limited or no concern and concentrations greater than 0.10 ppm were of sufficient concern to call for corrective action.

The most controversial health effect from exposure to HCHO is its carcinogenic potential in humans. The debate surrounding the role of HCHO as a carcinogen began with a study sponsored by the Chemical Industry Institute of Toxicology (CIIT) in 1980 in which it was reported that nasal cancer developed in 103 of 240 laboratory rats exposed to 14.3 ppm HCHO and in two rats exposed to 5.6 ppm HCHO. Nasal cancer also developed in 2 of 240 mice exposed to 14.3 ppm HCHO.[73]

Since the results of the CIIT study were made available, there have been other animal and human epidemiologic studies which suggest that HCHO should be presumed to pose a carcinogenic risk to humans. The Federal Panel on Formaldehyde,[74] the International Agency for Research on Cancer,[75] the CPSC,[72] and the U.S. EPA[71] have concluded that HCHO poses a carcinogenic risk to humans.

In 1987, the U.S. EPA classified HCHO as a "Probable Human Carcinogen" (Group B1) based on sufficient animal and limited human evidence and other supporting data.[71] In 1989, EPA, in consultation with EPA's Science Advisory Board, undertook efforts to update the 1987 assessment in light of new hazard data and recent advances in risk assessment methodology. The new methodology incorporates pharmacokinetic data which provides a closer approximation to a delivered dose and uses monkey DNA binding data as the basis for human dosimetry. This update effort is likely to significantly reduce the 1987 cancer risk estimates.

Sources of other volatile organic compounds

Sources.   Organic compounds can be divided into three categories based on volatility. Volatile organic compounds (VOCs) exist entirely in the vapor phase at ambient temperature and have vapor pressures greater than about 1 mm Hg. Semivolatile organic compounds (SVOCs) have vapor pressures in the range of 10^{-7} to 1 mm Hg and are present both in the vapor and particle-bound state. Nonvolatile organic compounds are those that are present only as particulates and have vapor pressures less than 10^{-7} mm Hg.[76]

Over 250 different organic compounds have been measured in indoor air at levels greater than 1 ppb,[77] and over 900 VOCs have been identified in indoor air.[78] These compounds are incorporated into almost all materials and products that are used in construction materials, consumer products, furnishings, pesticides, and fuels. Drinking water (typically well water) that is contaminated with VOCs can also be an indoor air source when contaminated water is used for showering, bathing, cooking, and other uses that potentially result in the release of VOCs. Some examples of VOCs and the products which contain them are given in Table 2.17. Table 2.18 contains examples of some emission rates for selected VOC-containing products.

A national survey conducted by EPA[79] on the usage of household solvents has provided insight into the sources of six solvents contained in consumer products and the usage of those products by consumers. The solvents which were studied include methylene chloride and five potential substitute chemicals: 1,1,1-trichloroethane, trichlorethylene, tetrachloroethylene, carbon tetrachloride, and 1,1,2-trichlorotrifluoroethane. EPA examined a total of 1026 brands of household products, which were grouped into 67 product categories, and the use patterns of 5000 adults. These studies demonstrated that exposure to VOCs is widespread through the use of consumer products, but the significance of these exposures is not known.

Almost half of the brands surveyed contained at least one of the six target chlorocarbons. Methylene chloride and 1,1,1-trichloroethane were the predominant chemicals—34 percent of the brands tested positive for methylene chloride and 14 percent for 1,1,1-trichloroethane. Methylene chloride was found in 78 percent of the paint removers/strippers and 60 percent of the aerosol spray paints tested, and 1,1,1-trichloroethane was found in most of the typewriter correction fluids, suede protectors, and brake quieters/cleaners tested.

Less than 4 percent of the brands tested were positive for any of the four remaining chlorocarbons. Trichloroethylene was found in 78 percent of the typewriter correction fluids tested. Tetrachloroethylene was found in 58 percent of the brake quieters/cleaners tested. Carbon tetrachloride was not found at the 1 percent level in any of the products tested.

In addition to the findings of specified concentrations of chemicals in household solvent products, the study found that concentrations of chlorocarbons varied considerably between brands of the same product type, and in a few brands, concentrations differed by geographic

TABLE 2.17   Health Effects and Sources of Selected Volatile Organic Compounds

Compound	Health effects*	Sources and uses
Formaldehyde	Probable human carcinogen; eye and respiratory tract irritant; a variety of low-level symptoms	Listed in Table 2.15
Benzene	Carcinogen; respiratory tract irritant	Plastic and rubber solvents; cigarette smoking; paints, stains, varnishes, filler, other finishes; inhalation of gasoline vapor
Xylenes	Narcotic; irritant; affects heart, liver, kidney and nervous system	Adhesives, joint compound, wallpaper, caulking compounds, floor covering, floor lacquer, grease cleaners, shoe dye, tobacco smoke, kerosene heaters, varnish, solvent for resins, enamels; used in non-lead automobile fuels, pesticides, dyes, pharmaceuticals
Toluene	Narcotic; may cause anemia	Solvents, solvent-based adhesives, water-based adhesives, edge-sealing, moulding tape, wallpaper, joint compound, calcium silicate sheet, vinyl floor covering, vinyl coated wall paper, caulking compounds, paint, chipboard, kerosene heaters, tobacco smoke
Styrene	Narcotic; affects central nervous system; possible human carcinogen	Plastics, paints, synthetic rubber, and resins
Toluene diisocyanate (TDI)	Sensitizer; probable human carcinogen	Polyurethane foam aerosols
Trichloroethylene	Animal carcinogen; affects central nervous system	Solvent for paints, varnishes, oil and wax, cleaning compounds, degreasing products, drycleaning

TABLE 2.17   Health Effects and Sources of Selected Volatile Organic Compounds (Continued)

Compound	Health effects*	Sources and uses
Ethyl benzene	Severe irritation to eyes and respiratory tract; affects central nervous system	Solvents, in styrene-related products
Methylene chloride (Dichloromethane)	Narcotic; affects central nervous system; probable human carcinogen	Paint removers, aerosol finishers; acoustical office partitions
Para-dichlorobenzene	Narcotic; eye and respiratory tract irritant; affects liver, kidney, and central nervous system	Moth crystals, room deodorizers
Benzyl chloride, Benzal chloride	Central nervous system irritants and depressants; affects liver and kidney; eye and respiratory tract irritant	Vinyl tiles plasticized with butyl benzyl phthalate
2-Butanone (MEK)	Irritant; central nervous system depressant	Floor/wall covering, calcium silicate sheet, fiberboard, caulking compounds, particleboard, tobacco smoke
Petroleum distillates	Central nervous system depressant; affects liver and kidney	Cleaning products, solvents, paint thinners
4-Phenylcyclohexene	Eye and respiratory tract irritant; central nervous system effects	By-product of styrene butadiene latex, an adhesive used in most synthetic fibers carpets

*For many indoor pollutants, there is insufficient data to determine the levels at which the specific effects listed would actually occur and the extent to which these levels are experienced in non-industrial indoor environments.

SOURCE: *Introduction to Indoor Air Quality: A Reference Manual,* EPA/400/3-91/003.

TABLE 2.18   Examples of Volatile Organic Compound Measurements in Indoor Air

Contaminant	Concentration ($\mu g/m^3$) Minimum	Maximum	Mean	Reference
Benzene				
Kitchens (n = 15)	6	7	15	Seifert &
Other rooms (n = 15)	6	14	18	Abraham
Outdoors, next to dwellings (n = 5)	4	33	29	(1982)
Toluene				
Kitchens (n = 15)	34	3800[a]	60	
Other rooms (n = 15)	17	173[a]	62	
Outdoors, next to dwellings (n = 5)	16	60	35	
m- and p-Xylene				
Kitchens (n = 15)	18	77[a]	29	
Other rooms (n = 15)	10	47	21	
Outdoors, next to dwellings (n = 5)	4	32	28	
Ethylbenzene				
Kitchens (n = 15)	6	33	15	
Other rooms (n = 15)	1	22	11	
Outdoors, next to dwellings (n = 5)	4	20	13	

Various Types of Buildings[b]			Wallace et al. (1983)
Benzene	0.4	120	20
Carbon tetrachloride	0.5	14	2.5
Trichloroethylene	0.3	47	3.6
Chloroform	0.2	200	8
Dichlorobenzenes	0.2	1200	41
Ethylbenzene	0.3	320	13
o-Xylene	0.4	49	7.8
m- and p-Xylene	0.4	120	21
Styrene	0.1	54	3.1
1,1,1-Trichloroethane	0.7	880	50
Tetrachloroethylene	0.2	250	10

Two Schools, Two Homes, and One Office		van der Wal et al. (1987)
n- and i-Pentanal	10	12
n-Hexanal	2	7
n-Octanal	1	21
N-Nonanal	7	50
m-Decanal	2.5	17
Benzaldehyde	4	5
Toluene	13	69
Higher Aromatic Hydrocarbons	14	600
n-Alkanes	8	1700
Chlorinated Hydrocarbons	4	42

New Buildings, (Office, Nursing Home, Hospital)	Sheldon et al. (1988)
Total VOCs[c]	21–1100
Aromatic Hydrocarbons[d]	11–270
Aliphatic Hydrocarbons[e]	4.7–810
Chlorinated Hydrocarbons[f]	3.9–56
Oxygenated Hydrocarbons[g]	ND–9.6

TABLE 2.18   Examples of Volatile Organic Compound Measurements in Indoor Air (Continued)

Contaminant	Concentration ($\mu g/m^3$)			Reference
	Minimum	Maximum	Mean	
Older Buildings, (Office, Office/School, Nursing Home)				Sheldon, et al. (1988)
Total VOCs[c]			18–130	
Aromatic Hydrocarbons[d]			12–74	
Aliphatic Hydrocarbons[e]			1.9–18	
Chlorinated Hydrocarbons[f]			4.7–46	
Oxygenated Hydrocarbons[g]			ND–4.3	
Three Nonresidential Buildings[h]				Bayer and Black (1988)
Total VOCs			237–1090	
1,1,1-Trichloroethane			14.8–214	
Benzene			12.9–43.2	
Ethylbenzene			1.16–17.2	
o-Xylene			3.66–16.8	
Toluene			7.84–98.7	
3-Methylpentane			1.42–37.6	
Hexane			4.7–68.7	
1,2,3-Trimethylbenzene			<0.02–0.522	
Heptane			1.24–38.9	
1, 4-Dioxane			<0.02–20.1	
Acetone			11.1–62.7	
4-Methyl-1-pentanone			0.343–27.9	
Butylacetate			10.6–48.3	
Homes in 2 Cities over the Course of 3 Sampling Periods in 3 Years				Wallace (1987)
Total VOCs			200–338	
1,1,1-Trichloroethane			45–94	
m, p-Dichlorobenzene			45–71	
m, p-Xylene			36–52	
Tetrachloroethylene			11–45	
Benzene			NC[i]–28	
Ethylbenzene			9.2–19	
o-Xylene			12–16	
Trichloroethylene			4.6–13	
Chloroform			4.0–8.0	
Styrene			2.1–8.9	
Carbon Tetrachloride			ND[i]–9.3	

TABLE 2.18   Examples of Volatile Organic Compound Measurements in Indoor Air (Continued)

Contaminant	Concentration ($\mu g/m^3$)			Reference
	Minimum	Maximum	Mean	
	Homes in 1 City over the Course of 3 Samplings Periods in 1 Year			Wallace (1987)
n-Octane			2.3–5.8	
n-Decane			2.0–5.8	
n-Undecane			2.7–5.2	
n-Dodecane			2.1–2.5	
α-Pinene			2.1–6.5	
o-Dichlorobenzene			0.3–0.6	
1,1,1-Trichloroethane			16–96	
m- and p-Xylene			11–28	
m- and p-Dichlorobenzene			5.5–18	
Tetrachloroethylene			5.6–16	
o-Xylene			4.4–13	
Ethylbenzene			3.7–11	
Trichloroethylene			3.8–7.8	
Styrene			1–3.6	
Chloroform			0.6–1.9	
Carbon tetrachloride			0.8–1.3	
1, 2-Dichlorobenzene			0.1–0.5	
p-Dioxane			0.2–1.8	

[a]Not included in the calculation of the mean.

[b]Overnight air samples, Elizabeth-Bayonne, NJ; additional measurements are given in Wallace (1987) and TEAM publications.

[c]Specific levels of individual contaminants are given in Shelden et al. (1988).

[d]Benzene; o- and m-xylene; styrene; ethylbenzene; isopropylbenzene; n-propylbenzene; o- and m-toluene; 1,2,3-trimethylbenzene; 1,2,4-trimethylbenzene; 1,3,5-trimethylbenzene.

[e]α-pinene, n-decane, n-undecane, n-dodecane.

[f]1,2-dichloroethane; 1,1,1-trichloroethane; trichloroethylene; p-dichlorobenzene.

[g]n-butylacetate; 2-ethoxyethylacetate.

[h]Atlanta, GA; spring season; additional VOCs are given in Bayer and Black (1988).

[i]Not calculated-high background contamination.

[j]Not detected in most samples.

SOURCE: *Introduction to Indoor Air Quality: A Reference Manual,* EPA/400/3-91/003.

regions of the country. One of the most important findings of this study was that product labels are often inadequate; only 56 percent of the brands with chlorocarbons were labeled as containing these chemicals.

Measured concentrations.   The database for VOCs and other organic compounds includes studies of healthy and sick buildings. Some examples of VOCs measurements in residential and nonresidential

TABLE 2.19   Examples of Selected Volatile Organic Compound Emission Rates for Materials and Typical Household Products Found Indoors

Compound name	Emission rates of selected materials (μg/g)							
	Adhesives	Coating	Fabric	Foam	Lubricant	Paint	Rubber	Tape
1,2-Dichloroethane	0.80	—	—	0.75	—	—	—	3.25
Benzene	0.9	0.6	—	0.7	0.20	0.90	0.10	0.69
Carbon tetrachloride	1.00	—	—	0.18	—	—	4.20	0.75
Chloroform	0.15	—	0.10	0.04	0.20	—	0.90	0.05
Ethylbenzene	—	—	—	—	—	527.8	—	0.20
Limonene	—	—	—	—	—	—	—	—
Methyl chloroform	0.40	0.20	0.07	1.00	0.50	—	0.10	0.10
Styrene	0.17	5.20	—	0.02	12.54	33.50	0.15	0.10
Tetrachloroethylene	0.60	—	0.30	65.00	0.60	—	0.20	0.08
Trichloroethylene	0.30	0.09	0.03	0.10	0.10	—	0.07	0.09
Sample size (n)	98	22	30	68	23	4	90	66

Compound name	Emission rate of selected household products (μg/g)								
	Cos-metics	Deodo-rants	Health and beauty aids	Elect. equip.	Misc. house-wares	Ink and pen	Paper	Photo equip.	Photo film
1,2,-Dichloroethane	—	—	—	0.06	—	—	—	—	—
Benzene	—	—	1.85	0.02	1.10	0.40	0.03	1.51	0.04
Carbon tetrachloride	—	—	—	0.00	0.04	0.20	—	2.50	—
Chloroform	—	—	—	0.23	4.85	10.00	0.10	2.50	0.10
Ethylbenzene	—	—	—	0.80	—	—	—	10.50	0.13
Limonene	—	0.40	1.00	—	1.80	—	—	—	—
Methyl chloroform	0.20	—	0.01	0.03	0.19	0.10	0.26	0.08	1.90
Styrene	1.10	0.15	0.17	0.05	0.02	0.30	—	0.04	0.10
Tetrachloroethylene	0.70	—	—	0.05	—	2.00	0.42	—	—
Trichloroethylene	1.90	—	0.11	0.01	0.06	0.07	0.10	0.03	0.13
Sample size (n)	5	9	23	71	23	25	12	35	26

SOURCE: *Introduction to Indoor Air Quality: A Reference Manual*, EPA/400/3-91/003.

buildings are given in Tables 2.19 and 2.20. These data, along with the consumer use surveys conducted by EPA, show that exposure to VOCs is widespread and highly variable. In general, VOCs can be expected to be higher in buildings immediately after construction or renovation compared to older buildings. The use of consumer products can be expected to predominate VOC emissions after building-related VOCs decrease in concentration.

The Team Studies conducted by Wallace and others[80] have provided important information about actual exposures to VOCs. These studies showed that:

- Indoor personal exposures were greater than mean outdoor concentrations for each of 11 target VOCs.

- Breath levels correlated significantly with personal air exposures but not with outdoor air levels for nearly all the chemicals.

- Inhalation accounted for more than 99 percent of the exposure for all contaminants studied, except for the trihalomethanes.

- Specific sources of exposure were identified and included smoking (aromatics such as benzene, styrene, ethylbenzene, and m,p-xylene in breath), passive smoking (same chemicals in indoor air), visiting dry cleaners (tetrachloroethylene in breath), pumping gas or being exposed to auto exhaust (benzene in breath), various occupations such as chemicals, plastics, wood processing, scientific laboratories, garage or repair work, metal work, printing (aromatic chemicals in daytime personal air).

- Other sources which were hypothesized included room air fresheners, toilet bowl deodorizers, or moth crystals (p-dichlorobenzene in indoor air) and use of hot water in the home (chloroform in indoor air).

Health effects of other VOCs.   Exposure to VOCs can result in both acute and chronic health effects. Table 2.17 summarizes some health effects for selected contaminants. Most of the available health effects data have been developed from animal or occupational studies. In general, the health effects database for VOCs, especially low-level or intermittent exposures, is not complete.

Many of the VOCs are potent narcotics and result in the depression of the central nervous system. VOCs can also result in irritation of the eyes and respiratory tract and sensitization reactions which involve the eyes, skin, respiratory tract, and heart. At higher concentrations, many of these chemicals have been shown to result in liver and kidney damage.

Symptoms of VOC exposure (depending on the dose) could include fatigue, headache, drowsiness, dizziness, weakness, joint pains, peripheral numbness or tingling, euphoria, tightness in the chest, unsteadiness, blurred vision, skin irritation, irritation of the eyes and respiratory tract, and cardiac arrhythmias.[81]

The term *solvent encephalopathy* is used to describe a group of symptoms (major symptoms—headache, irritability, difficulty concentrating, and fine-motor deficits) attributed to VOC exposures. A dose-effect relationship has not been described, but effects occur at levels well below the threshold limit values for individual solvents, and there appears to be a relationship between duration of exposure and the time required to resolve symptoms after exposure stops. VOCs are present in office environments at concentrations that have been associated with solvent encephalopathy.[82]

TABLE 2.20   Additional Examples of Volatile Organic Compound Emission Rates for Selected Materials Found Indoors

Material*	Emission rate ($\mu g/m^2/hr$)			
	Aliphatic oxygenated aliphatic hydrocarbons	Aromatic hydrocarbons	Halogenated compound	All target hydrocarbons
Latex caulk	252	380	5.2	637
Latex paint (Glidden)	111	52	86	249
Carpet adhesive	136	98	—†	234
Vinyl cove molding	31	26	1.4	60
Linoleum tile	6.0	14	0.62	46
Large diameter telephone cable	14	35	4.0	45
Black rubber molding	24	78	0.88	103
Small diameter telephone cable	33	26	1.4	60
Carpet	27	9.4	—	36
Vinyl edge molding	18	12	0.41	30
Particle board	27	1.1	0.14	28
Polystyrene foam insulation	0.19	20	1.4	22
Tar paper	3.2	3.1	—	6.3
Primer/adhesive	3.6	2.5	—	6.1
Latex paint (Bruning)	—	3.2	—	3.2
Water repellent mineral board	1.1	0.43	—	1.5
Cement block	—	0.39	0.15	0.54
PVC pipe	—	0.53	—	0.53
Duct insulation	0.13	0.15	—	0.28
Treated metal roofing	—	0.19	0.06	0.25
Urethane sealant	—	0.13	—	0.13
Fiberglass insulation	—	0.08	—	0.80
Exterior mineral board	—	0.03	—	0.03
Interior mineral board	—	—	—	—
Ceiling tile	—	—	—	—
Red clay brick	—	—	—	—
Plastic laminate	—	—	—	—
Plastic outlet cover	—	—	—	—
Joint compound	—	—	—	—
Linoleum tile cement	—	—	—	—

*Emission rates for cove adhesive are not reported; sample was overloaded. It is estimated that cove adhesive is one of the emitters of VOCs with emissions of target compounds >4700 $\mu g/m^2$.

†No detectable emissions.

SOURCE: *Introduction to Indoor Air Quality: A Reference Manual,* EPA/400/3-91/003.

Many of the VOCs which have been measured indoors are known human carcinogens (benzene) or animal carcinogens (carbon tetrachloride, chloroform, trichloroethylene, tetrachloroethylene, and p-dichlorobenzene). VOCs such as 1,1,1-trichloroethane, styrene, and α-pinene are mutagens and possible carcinogens. Other VOCs such as octane, decane, and undecane are possible cocarcinogens.

Cancer risk estimates. Cancer risk estimates have been developed by EPA for exposure to some VOCs. Other investigators have also estimated the cancer risk from VOCs. Wallace[83] estimated that six VOCs (benzene and the other five animal carcinogens listed above) contribute 1000 to 5000 excess cancer cases per year nationwide. Tancrede et al.[84] estimated the cancer risk of 9 VOCs which had previously been measured in New Jersey (Bayonne and Elizabeth), 19 VOCs in California (Los Angeles), and 44 VOCs in Dutch houses. The estimated mean individual risk (the sum of the mean individual risks for each of the VOCs) was 0.019 to 0.03 for the residents of New Jersey and 0.002 for the residents of California. The estimated mean risk for the contaminants based on the Dutch data was 0.001 to 0.002. The unit risk estimates were computed using human and animal data, by analogy with other chemicals, and other methods.

When the risks were computed based only on those chemicals for which there was either animal bioassay data or human epidemiological data, the estimated risk was 0.003 for New Jersey, 0.001 for California, and 0.0002 to 0.001 for The Netherlands. Estimated risks for radon (0.0520), passive smoking (0.002 to 0.008), and formaldehyde (0.034) were also shown for comparison. Tancrede et al. concluded that even though their estimates were conservative, the calculations suggested exposure to VOCs through indoor air were important. Although there are few risk assessments available for VOCs in indoor air, VOCs appear likely to pose a significant cancer risk.[78]

Sick building syndrome and multiple chemical sensitivity. There is some evidence that VOCs can provoke some of the symptoms typical of SBS. Molhave observed increased mucous irritation and impaired memory in healthy subjects (who previously demonstrated symptoms of SBS) who were exposed to 22 VOCs at total VOC concentrations of 5 mg/m^3 and 25 mg/m^3.[85]

Kjaergaard et al.[86] also demonstrated a dose-dependent response in 63 randomly selected healthy subjects who were exposed to n-decane in the range of 0 to 100 ppm. Exposed subjects experienced mucous membrane irritation, decreased tear film stability, and sensation of increased odor intensity and reduced air quality. The authors concluded that these results support the hypothesis that VOCs can provide some of the symptoms of SBS.

Individuals who appear to demonstrate multiple chemical sensitivity report severe reactions to a variety of VOCs and other organic compounds which are released by building materials and various consumer products including cosmetics, soaps, perfumes, tobacco, plastics, dyes, and other products. Many of the chemicals contained in these products are potent sensitizers.

These reactions can occur after exposure to a single sensitizing dose or sequence of doses, after which time a far lower dose can provoke symptoms. Reactions can also be provoked as a result of chronic exposure to low doses. Ashford and Miller[87] summarize some of the studies that have been conducted that attempt to link multiple chemical sensitivity to exposure to VOCs and other organic compounds.

Biological contaminants. The home and workplace can harbor a variety of airborne allergens and pathogens. About 50 to 60 percent of all community-acquired illness is due to respiratory infections and most of these are caused by viruses;[88] but, bacterial diseases and allergic reactions caused by biological sources can pose significant problems in homes and public facilities such as day care centers, hospitals, hotels, nursing homes, schools, and office buildings.[88]

Pathogens and illness. Biogenic agents (those produced by living organisms) in the indoor environment generally have limited direct toxicity and, more often, result in infection or allergic responses. The term *bioaerosol* refers to biogenic agents that are airborne.

Most viral and bacterial diseases are spread by direct person-to-person contact (kissing, hugging, touching) or indirectly as a result of droplets in air which are produced by talking, sneezing, and coughing.

In addition to these modes of transmission, some evidence suggests that these diseases can be transmitted through building-related airborne pathways (such as the heating, ventilating, and air-conditioning system). For example, an epidemic of measles (28 cases after an incubation period of about 10 days) in an elementary school near Rochester, New York, was traced to a student in the second grade and ventilation system that served 14 classrooms. The ventilation system recirculated air from room to room before being exhausted outside. The investigators concluded that the ventilation system was responsible for the outbreak since the student did not occupy the same room as the other children who became infected.[89]

In a more recent study, Brundage et al.[90] demonstrated that army trainees who were housed in new energy-efficient barracks with mechanical ventilation had acute febrile respiratory disease rates that were 51 percent higher, on average, than trainees who were housed in older barracks. These results support the hypothesis that

risks of respiratory infection are increased among susceptible populations in buildings that have tightly sealed envelopes and closed ventilation systems.

Infectious agents can also enter the indoor environment from the
outside air. Once inside, they can be incubated, amplified, and disseminated by humidifiers, air conditioners, and other building components.

Legionella.   *Legionella* is a major cause of respiratory illness world
wide and accounts for 1 to 13 percent of all pneumonia seen in hospitals in the United States, Canada, England, and Germany.[88] The bacteria are ubiquitous and can survive in water for long periods of
time—up to a year under certain conditions.[91]

Epidemics caused by *Legionella* occur most commonly during the
summer and early fall, while sporadic cases of disease occur throughout most of the year. The characteristics and causes of some of these
epidemics are discussed in Imperator and Band et al.[92,93]

Sources of *Legionella* in residences and office buildings include contaminated forced-air heating systems, humidifiers, water flooding,
hot water systems, hot tubs, vaporizers, nebulizers and external
sources, primarily cooling towers and evaporative condensers but also
dusts from construction and landscaping activities. *Legionella* has
also been isolated from potable drinking water.

Two important bacterial diseases which are both caused by
Legionella pneumophila are Legionnaires' disease and Pontiac fever.
These two diseases, which are referred to as legionellosis, are not
spread via person-to-person contact. Rather, they can be spread both
indoors and outdoors through the soil/air or water/air link.

Legionnaires' disease.   One of the most dramatic and frightening cases
of indoor airborne bacterial infections is the mysterious illness that
affected veterans attending the American Legion Convention in
Philadelphia in 1976. A pneumonia-like illness was contracted by 182
persons who were either in or near the Bellevue Stratford Hotel.
Twenty-nine people died.[94] The organism that caused the disease, a
gram negative bacillus named *Legionella pneumophila,* was first isolated in 1977 at the Centers for Disease Control. The illness, named
after the group that was most affected in 1976, has come to be known
as Legionnaires' disease.

Legionnaires' disease is a form of legionellosis that is a very severe
multisystemic illness that can affect the lungs, gastrointestinal tract,
central nervous system, and kidneys. It is characterized by a low
attack rate (2 to 3%), long incubation period (4 to 10 days), and severe
pneumonia. Hospitalization is required, and about 2 to 3 percent of
cases are fatal even with proper treatment. It has been estimated
that in the United States *Legionella* species account for 8 to 10 percent, or 50,000 to 60,000 cases, of community-acquired pneumonia.[95]

Pontiac fever. Pontiac fever was first recognized in 1968 when, during a 1-week period, 95 of 100 employees at the Oakland County Health Department in Pontiac, Michigan, became sick with a flu-like illness.[96] Although a causative agent was not conclusively demonstrated, *L. pneumophila* was implicated 10 years later based on indirect fluorescent antibody tests on sera from patients who came down with the illness. The air-conditioning system was identified as the source and mode of transmission of the agent.

Pontiac fever is a milder clinical form of legionellosis. It is characterized by a high attack rate (90 percent) and a short incubation period (2 to 3 days). It is not fatal, and it can be resolved without hospitalization. Characteristic symptoms include fever, chills, headache, and muscle ache; additional symptoms may include sore throat, coughing, nausea, diarrhea, and chest pain.

Allergens. The terms *allergic reaction* and *sensitization reaction* refer to a condition in which an immune response results in exaggerated or inappropriate reactions that are harmful to the host. An individual typically experiences an allergic reaction after the second contact with a specific allergen. In order for a substance to produce an allergic reaction, the substance or metabolic product of the substance has to act as a hapten and combine with endogenous protein to form an antigen. The antigen is capable of eliciting the formation of antibodies. The initial exposure results in an antigen-antibody interaction which results in the manifestation of allergy.

Allergies are commonly acquired health problems which are mediated by a variety of immunologic processes. The substances that cause allergies are called allergens or antigens. The term *airborne allergen* refers to allergens that are carried by the air.

Allergens do not affect most people; rather, they provoke an allergic response in a small subset of the population. Allergens that cause reactions include both viable and nonviable agents. Viable agents include bacteria, fungi, amoebae, and algae. Common nonviable agents include house dust, insect and arachnid body parts and hulks, animal danders, mite fecal pellets, cockroach feces, remains of molds and their spores, pollens, and dried animal excretions.

Chemicals found in the home or workplace (plastics, metals, pharmaceuticals, detergents, hair dyes, bleaches) are not biogenic agents, but they have been known to produce allergic reactions in sensitive individuals.

Illness caused by allergens. Several patterns of illness can arise from exposure to allergens including allergic reactions on the skin, in the nose, in the airways, or in the alveoli. It is not known why some people are allergic to otherwise harmless pollen grains or other airborne particles, but it is presumably due to differences in their immune systems. These differences may be partly genetic since allergy-based diseases (allergic rhinitis, asthma, contact dermatitis) often run in families. It has been estimated that about 20 percent of the U.S. population may have a genetic predisposition toward allergies.[97]

In the respiratory tract, allergic reactions begin with a localized inflammatory reaction that may eventually be accompanied by secondary effects such as bacterial colonization.[52] The airborne allergens that have the most potential to affect the lower lung are those with small aerodynamic diameters and include molds and organic dusts. Most pollens have diameters greater than 12 μm and affect the upper respiratory tract, but some may reach the lower portions of the lung.

Several important conditions are caused by airborne allergens including allergic rhinitis, allergic asthma, allergic bronchopulmonary aspergillosis, hypersensitivity pneumonitis, and humidifier fever; they are discussed below:

1. *Allergic rhinitis.*   Allergic rhinitis is an acute condition that resolves readily when the source is removed. It is commonly called *hay fever* when it is related to pollens produced by the change of seasons, and it affects about 15 percent of the population.

It is characterized by dilation and edema of the nasal mucosa and mucus secretion; typical symptoms include sneezing, itching, excessive mucus secretion, and obstruction of nasal passages. Conjunctivitis (irritation, itching, and reddening of the eyes) may also be associated with allergic rhinitis. Secondary bacterial infections may result from blocked sinuses and eustachian tubes.

2. *Allergic asthma.*   Allergic asthma affects about 3 to 5 percent of the U.S. population.[98] It is characterized by bronchospasm, edema of the bronchial mucosa, accumulation of bronchial mucus, or any combination of these conditions. The narrowing of the airways and production of mucus can block the airways. Typical symptoms include wheezing, shortness of breath, sneezing, itching of the nose, and rhinorrhea. Repeated attacks can lead to a narrowing of the airways, which is reversible over short periods of time (spontaneously or with treatment).

Allergic asthma can be caused by a variety of viable and nonviable biological agents. Factors related to IAQ such as cigarette smoke, sulfur dioxide, and other particles and gases can precipitate attacks. Emotional stress and exposure to cold have also been known to result in asthmatic attacks.

3. *Allergic bronchopulmonary aspergillus (ABPA).*   ABPA is an uncommon, progressive disease that is caused by an allergic reaction to the inhalation of a widely distributed soil fungus, *Aspergillus fumigatus.* Spores are about 3 μm in diameter and grow at body tempera-

tures. Episodes of ABPA most frequently occur during the winter when the counts of *Aspergillus fumigatus* are highest. Other species of *Aspergillus* can also result in a variety of syndromes. ABPA is characterized by recurrent episodes of pulmonary eosinophilia, usually associated with asthmatic attacks. As the disease progresses, bronchiectasis (dilation of the bronchial tubes associated with significant mucus production), irreversible airway narrowing, and pulmonary fibrosis may occur in the upper lobes of the lung. Typical symptoms include coughing, wheezing, difficulty breathing, and low-grade fever.

   4. *Hypersensitivity pneumonitis.* Hypersensitivity pneumonitis (also called extrinsic allergic alveolitis) is primarily an occupational disease of agricultural and industrial workers who are exposed to sensitizing agents in organic (especially fungal spores) and inorganic dusts. However, it can and does occur as a result of exposures to sensitizing agents in residential and office environments. Some examples of hypersensitivity pneumonitis include pigeon-breeder's or bird fancier's lung, which is caused by the inhalation of serum proteins in the droppings of pigeons and parakeets. The attack rate has been estimated to be between 0.1 and 21 percent in pigeon breeders.[99] The inhalation of thermophilic actinomycetes (a group of filamentous bacteria that superficially resemble fungi) growing in moldy hay can produce farmer's lung. Exposure to inorganic compounds such toluene diisocyante (isocyanate lung) and copper sulfate (vineyard sprayer's lung) can also produce pneumonitis. Exposure to thermophilic actinomycetes in residential or office ventilation systems can result in ventilation pneumonitis. Fungi which have been implicated in ventilation pneumonitis include *Aspergillus, Penicillum, Alternaria, Rhizopus, Paecilomyces,* and *Aureobasidium.* Regardless of the agent, estimated rates of pneumonitis in office workers range from 1.2[100] to 4 percent.[101]

   Hypersensitivity pneumonitis can result from intermittent exposure to high concentrations of allergens. The symptoms and progression of the disease are the same, regardless of the agent causing the disease.[52] Continuous exposure to low concentrations of allergens often does not result in the appearance of overt symptoms, but at a later time, less reversible stages of the disease can develop.

   Sensitization causes an inflammatory reaction in the alveolar walls and peripheral bronchioles due to an allergic reaction between the agent and circulating antibodies and sensitized lymphocytes. The diagnosis of hypersensitivity pneumonitis is made by the physician based on the patient's history and results of some tests. These include restrictive pulmonary function tests, decreased exercise tolerance, granulomas and interstitial fibrosis on lung biopsy, reproduction of symptoms upon bronchial challenge with the suspected agent, and response to corticosteroid medications.[102]

An acute attack causes symptoms which are similar to the flu: chills, fever, dry cough, shortness of breath, tightness in the chest, and fatigue. Symptoms typically occur within 4 to 6 h after exposure, and may persist for 12 h to 10 days. Changes in lung function can return to normal over a period of about a month after the condition develops. Between attacks, the individual may be symptom free and feel fine. Over a period of time, the lung gradually develops fibrous scar tissue. Irreversible pulmonary fibrosis, followed by pulmonary failure, and death can occur in severe cases.

5. *Humidifier fever.*   This is a type of pneumonitis that is probably due to allergic reactions of the alveolar wall. It has been related to amoebae, bacteria, and fungi. *Bacillus subtilis,*[103] amoebae including *A. polyphaga* and *N. gruberi,*[104] and bacterial endotoxin[105] are specific agents which have been implicated in this condition. Sources of these agents include humidifier reservoirs, air coolers, air conditioners, spas, and aquaria.

The disease is characterized by episodes of flu-like symptoms (chills, muscle aches, malaise) and fever without prominent pulmonary symptoms and signs. Symptoms develop 4 to 8 h after exposure and resolve spontaneously, usually within 24 h, without long-term effects. Lung function changes may include a restrictive ventilatory defect with a decrease in gas transfer that improves over a period of days. Pulmonary fibrosis does not occur and chest x-rays do not show abnormalities.[52]

Chronic humidifier fever has been reported from residential humidifiers,[106] but the prevalence of the disease (acute and chronic forms) in the home environment has not been evaluated. In Great Britain, an attack rate of 2 to 3 percent has been estimated in office buildings with mechanical ventilation based on reports of symptoms.[107] Epidemics in the workplace are rare, but when they do occur, attack rates are high (30 to 75 percent).

An additional potential problem associated with the use of some types of humidifiers is the formation of fine particles during the operation of the humidifier. Highsmith et al.[108] measured fine particle concentrations greater than 590 μg/m^3 when an ultrasonic humidifier was operated in a kitchen using tap water containing 303 mg/l total dissolved solids. Using distilled water does reduce, but not eliminate, the formation of fine particulates. Even when the ultrasonic humidifier was operated using purchased distilled water, whole house fine particular concentrations greater than 40 μg/m^3 were measured. Fine particulate concentrations greater than 6300 μg/m^3 were measured when the ultrasonic humidifier was operated in a closed room situation.

Even when distilled water was used by the manufacturer, fine particles were generated. Impeller units generated less than one-third of the aerosol mass compared to the ultrasonic units, and steam units generated no measurable increase in fine particles. The health consequences of these particulates have not been evaluated.

Allergenic agents.   The following are allergenic agents:

1. *House dust mite.*   One important agent that has been implicated in allergenic conditions such as allergic rhinitis and allergic asthma is the house dust mite. It is not the actual house dust mite that causes disease, but allergens which are probably present in the excreta of the mite, some of which is of inhalable size.[109] The highest levels of allergens from house dust mites that occur indoors have been shown to be associated with respirable particles in the size range 0.8 to 1.4 μm.[110]

The house dust mite, which is arachnid, is about 300 μm long, and it can be found in almost every home. Mites are translucent and cannot be seen with the naked eye. The most commonly found mites include *Dermatophagoides pteronyssinus* (in Europe) and D. *Farinae* (in North America).[52]

Mite populations vary depending on atmospheric moisture and food sources. Growth is favored by a temperature of 25°C and a relative humidity (RH) greater than 45 percent. Below 45 percent RH at 20°C to 22°C, almost no house dust mites are able to survive.[111]

House dust mites are important causes of allergic rhinitis and asthma in climates with humid, mild conditions.[52] In North America, the mite population is at a maximum during the summer when windows are open and ventilation is good; levels drop in winter when the heating season begins and the relative humidity drops to 10 to 20 percent.[112]

Dust mites feed on the skin scales of humans and other animals. The mites, however, cannot feed on new skin; rather, they require skin scales that have been defatted. This explains why these mites are found in mattresses, bedclothes, and heavily used upholstered furniture. High concentrations of other specialized mites that cause allergic conditions can also be found in interior spaces that are used to store or process agricultural products.

2. *Fungi.*   Fungi are a major group (over 100,000 species) of chlorophyll-less eukaryotic organisms which are formed by hyphae with chitinous or cellulosic rigid cell walls. Most fungi are saprophytic (live off dead organic matter for food), and some fungi require specific substrates for growth and reproduction (dung and wood-rotting fungi, for example). Many can use any nonliving organic matter, providing temperature and moisture conditions are met.

Fungi reproduce either by specialized cells (spores) that are produced on fruiting branches or by fragmentation of the fungus body (mycelium). Fungi have both sexual and asexual stages which can result in allergenic effects, and there may be more than one spore type for each stage. The identification of fungi and spores can be difficult. Many fungi cannot be identified without fruiting structures. Another complicating factor is that fungal names have undergone changes, and the names for the various life cycle stages may be different because they were described at different times.[113]

Major fungi classes of interest include Zygomycetes, Ascomycetes (powdery mildews), Basidiomycetes (rusts, smuts, mushrooms), and a fourth class, Deuteromycetes or Fungi Imperfecti, which is an artificial grouping of asexual fungus stages.[113] The imperfect fungi are perhaps the most important class from an IAQ perspective because this class includes *Aspergillus, Cladosporium, Alternaria, Penicillium,* and other saprophytes which are commonly found indoors.

Any organic material that is wet can support the growth of fungi. In the outdoor environment fungi can utilize soil, animal and bird droppings, dead leaves, grass, tree bark, dead wood, and fallen fruits. Indoors, any damp, nonliving organic surface can be colonized by fungi; these surfaces include carpet, upholstery fabric and fillers, wood, concrete, painted surfaces, wall coverings, soap scum on tiles and porcelain surfaces. Humidifiers and air conditioners can also serve as reservoirs for fungi. Some fungi have even become adapted to growth in dry house dust environments[114] and carpeting that is not water damaged.[115]

(a) *Measured concentrations.*   The most abundant spore types are produced continuously outdoors during the growing season at concentrations ranging from 10^3 to $10^5/m^3$; these fungi can reach levels of 10^0 to $10^4/m^3$ indoors. In the outdoor environment, airborne spore concentrations are reduced in areas with snow cover (dispersion of spores is prevented) and where temperatures fall below freezing (spore production is decreased). Spore counts are usually highest in late summer and autumn, although *Aspergillus fumigatus* is more common in autumn and winter.[52]

Spores may be introduced into the home from the outside or result from unrestrained growth inside if conditions are favorable.

In the ambient air, concentrations of *Aspergillus fumigatus* rarely exceed 150 spores/m^3. The concentration in clean interiors is also low, ranging from 0 to 200 spores/m^3.[52] Recoveries of thermophilic actinomycetes (filamentous bacteria) in domestic air are generally less than 3000 counts/m^3 while occupational exposures can be 10 times higher.[116]

Factors such as shading of homes and organic debris outdoors have been found to be significantly associated with higher spore concentrations indoors.[117] Indoors, there is a direct relationship between mold growth and airborne spore levels and humidity levels between 25 and 70 percent.[113] Mold growth is suppressed below 25 percent RH, and humidities above 70 percent are optimal for growth.

Kozak et al.[117] reported on sources of fungi problems in 186 homes that were surveyed using rotorod and Anderson samplers over a period of 4 years in southern California. Of the 80 homes sampled with both types of sampling devices, 63 had a history of water damage and were suspected of having an endogenous mold problem. Forty-nine percent of these homes had more than one problem area.

The most likely areas with mold problems were the bathroom (31 percent of cases), living room (18.4 percent), family room/den (16.5 percent), and a bedroom (11.7 percent). The most likely materials were jute-backed carpeting and baseboards (53.5 percent of problems), wicker straw baskets (17.5 percent) and walls, ceilings, and window frames (13.6 percent). The most frequent causes were chronic water spills (35 percent of problems), followed by recurrent water leaks from plumbing (20.4 percent) and one-time disasters such as roof leaks and structural defects (10 percent).

(a) *Disease-producing fungi.* *Alternaria, Cladosporium, Aspergillus* and *Merulius lachrymans* have been identified as important causes of allergic asthma and rhinitis. Other spores which may colonize the airways include *Candida, Scedosporium, Scopulariopsis, Geotrichium,* and *Paecilomyces.*[52] Contact with the respiratory tract may be brief, followed by clearance out of the airways, or it may be prolonged and followed by colonization of the airways.

Elimination of fungal growth is necessary for spore-sensitive individuals, but there is no consensus on dose-response relationships. Holmberg[118] found that airborne levels greater than 50 CFU/m^3 of thermotolerant *Aspergillus ssp.* were a significant risk factor for irritation of the eyes and respiratory symptoms.

Some clinicians caution allergic patients against keeping living plants or processed plant materials in their homes because they have been implicated as substrates for saprophytic fungi, which are allergens. However, Burge et al.,[119] in a study of 10 homes and 3 greenhouses in Michigan, concluded that healthy undisturbed houses are not a major exposure source for airborne fungus spores. Samples were collected before and after watering and also while plant foliage was disturbed by a small fan. This study, however, was done in a colder climate, and the limited results may not apply to continuously warm and/or humid environments.

3. *Other allergenic agents.*   Insect excretions are strong sensitizers that can result in allergic responses. Roach fecal pellets are impor-

tant sensitizers, but carpet beetles, houseflies, and bedbugs may also be implicated.

Domestic animals, particularly cats, but also dogs, rabbits, guinea pigs, birds, and horses, can be important causes of allergic rhinitis and asthmatic attacks. It is generally accepted that the source of the allergen is animal dander, small scales of feathers or hair, or saliva (cat). Animal danders are very strong sensitizers, and highly sensitive people may develop allergic eczema or urticaria (hives) as a result of direct contact with the allergen. The feces of birds (parakeets and pigeons) can also result in allergic rhinitis, asthma, and hypersensitivity pneumonitis; the original source of the allergen is serum proteins which are secreted in the gut.[98]

Some individuals may also be allergic to components in tobacco smoke, chemical cleaners, dyes in carpeting, hair sprays, evergreen Christmas trees, and other chemical agents.

2.4   The Application of Industrial Hygiene Methodology to IAQ

The American Industrial Hygiene Association (AIHA) has published a guide to IAQ investigations for industrial hygienists.[120] The guide addresses the recognition and evaluation tenets of industrial hygiene (see Sec. 2.2) as applied to diagnosing an IAQ problem. A phased approach is recommended.

Design and construction of buildings since the 1950s have moved toward creating indoor environments that are tightly contained and which are controlled by increasingly sophisticated systems. Synthetic construction materials, windows that do not open, and complicated HVAC systems which require competent maintenance are all factors which make air quality in buildings today different from that in pre-World War II facilities.[121]

Synthetic chemicals enter the indoor environment in building materials (paints, pressboard, carpets, caulkings, etc.), pesticides, cleaning agents, deodorizers, personal products (perfumes, colognes, hair spray, etc.), and hosts of other materials and products. The 1970s brought an awareness that energy supplies are exhaustible and a concomitant effort to reduce building energy consumption. Building design, construction, and operation moved to seal buildings more tightly and to reduce the introduction of outside air for dilution ventilation. Considering these facts, deductive reasoning leads to the conclusion that air in buildings today contains chemicals not present in indoor air several decades ago and not prevalent in outside air today. The U.S. EPA has concluded that indoor air concentrations of VOCs are substantial-

TABLE 2.21   Some Factors Which May Influence IAQ

Environmental tobacco smoke (ETS)
Combustion sources, both indoor and outdoor
VOCs from building materials, furnishings, or maintenance products
Ozone from outdoor air, laser printers, or office machines
Fiberglass insulation
Poor maintenance of HVAC systems
Microbiological contamination of ventilation systems or interiors
Insufficient amounts of outside air to occupants

SOURCE: *The Industrial Hygienist's Guide to Indoor Air Quality Investigations,* Patrick Rafferty, ed., p. 5. Used with permission of American Industrial Hygiene Association, Fairfax, Va.

ly greater than outdoor levels. The agency's data also indicate that the indoor air concentrations of VOCs are highly variable building to building by several orders of magnitude. This suggests that these concentrations are significantly influenced by the unique sources and ventilation characteristics of any building.[122]

Studies and experience of practitioners have shown that many IAQ problems relate directly or indirectly to HVAC systems. Poor operation and/or maintenance practices, inadequate design, and improper installation, singularly or in combination, can result in chemical, biological, and physical problems. Investigations have also determined that discomfort due to temperature and/or humidity, work-related stress, ergonomic stress, noise discomfort, and lighting discomfort can be mistaken for IAQ problems.[123]

In the past 50 years, the U.S. working population has become predominantly white-collar, rather than blue-collar. Office workers expect a cleaner and more comfortable work environment than do industrial workers.[123] Industrial and construction workers generally are acclimatized to more severe conditions than office personnel, so the perception of poor air quality by an office worker is expected to differ greatly from the perception of an industrial or construction worker. Table 2.21 lists various factors which may influence IAQ.[124]

IAQ studies of existing facilities are usually driven by one of two events, excluding research:

1. Complaints are received by building management from building occupants about symptoms. These symptoms may be perceived by those affected as being IAQ related, or building managers may

review the complaints and conclude that poor IAQ is a possible cause.

2. The lease of space or purchase of property may be contingent upon an IAQ assessment. A report of poor IAQ may negate the transaction or result in negotiations to correct the problems identified.

The design of a new facility or of a renovation to an existing facility may also include an IAQ design study. This represents an acknowledgment by the building owners that good IAQ is a priority and that architectural and engineering designs must meet the objective of good IAQ in the constructed facility. Renovations of existing facilities have the additional consideration of IAQ control during the construction process if the facility is to remain occupied during the renovation.

Most texts and guidance documents about IAQ have grouped or classified the most common IAQ problems in various ways. These attempts at categorization have merit and logic, but most suffer from being too simple to adequately consider the major issues or too complex to be useful in practical application. The following strives to reach a middle ground that is both sufficiently inclusive and of practical value:

1. *VOCs.* If the sources are new building materials, the emissions will usually decay to an acceptable level with time, assuming adequate ventilation. Dealing with the time period of high emission rates is the pertinent issue. If office chemicals, such as cleaning agents or office machine products, are the sources, usage patterns may need to change or localized ventilation may be needed.

2. *Insufficient outside air, ventilation, and air distribution.* These conditions may require a change in HVAC operation or HVAC modifications.

3. *Particulates.* Correction probably lies with changes in maintenance and custodial practices. HVAC filtration systems may also be useful.

4. *Microbes.* HVAC maintenance and operational changes may be in order. Custodial practices can be important. Sources of moisture inside the building and HVAC systems may need to be eliminated or controlled. High humidity can also be a cause. In certain cases, HVAC filtration systems are warranted.

5. *Pesticides.* A change in chemicals and/or application may be sufficient. Design and construction techniques in new facilities can reduce the ability of pests to enter buildings and sustain themselves, thus reducing the required amount of chemicals. Good housekeeping practices are also important.

6. *Other chemicals.*   Depending on the chemicals and their uses, substitution of different chemicals or increased ventilation may be successful.

7. *"Classic" hazardous materials.*   These are not considered by some texts as IAQ problems because they do not produce standard IAQ symptoms; however, they do contaminate the air if they are present as an airborne particulate or gas. Asbestos-containing building materials, if improperly maintained or disturbed, can produce elevated airborne asbestos concentrations. A proper operations and maintenance program is recommended by EPA.[125] Poly-chlorinated biphenyls (PCBs) have been used in the past in the oils contained in electrical ballasts and transformers. Radon is a gas which comes from the earth and certain stone used in construction. Its presence cannot be sensed by humans, but it is, according to EPA, responsible for significant increases in lung cancer. EPA recommends that it be identified and controlled.[126] Lead is contained in many paints, and inhalation or ingestion of dust generated from lead-based paint can be toxic (see Sec. 4.3.4. on hazardous materials).

Some IAQ problems can be solved quickly and with little effort by a knowledgeable person. Others require lengthy investigations and exhaustive measurements to identify sources and effectuate adequate controls. It is sensible, therefore, to use a diagnostic methodology that progresses in stages. The ideas and terminology presented in the remainder of this chapter have evolved from experience in practice and from discussions with many colleagues. Many of the ideas and terminology are drawn from the AIHA's guidance document,[127] combined with practical experience.

The staged investigation begins, from an industrial hygiene perspective, with *recognition* and preliminary *evaluation* of the problem. These two steps complete stage 1. Stage 2 is a more extensive *evaluation* and stage 3 is the design, specification, and installation of *control* devices and/or the initiation of *control* actions.

2.4.1   Stage 1

Stage 1 is gaining a thorough understanding of the problem statement and all information pertinent to that statement. This review process should include historical as well as current information. The objective is to develop some working hypotheses, which will serve as a guide for a walk-through survey and for a review of the HVAC system.

Stage 1, step 1. Problem statement. A clear understanding of the problem, as articulated by the entity requesting the investigation, is the proper beginning point for any diagnostic study, be it medicine, science, engineering, or industrial hygiene. As a business matter for those investigators in private practice, the problem statement should also be a matter of contract and should be related to the contractual scope of professional services. It is usually desirable to have a specific, rather than general, problem statement. For example, "possible IAQ problems" is less helpful than "headache complaints by fifth floor staff."

Stage 1, step 2. Information collection and review. This process may begin prior to arrival at the site. Record drawings and specifications should be examined along with documentation of complaints, concerns, and relevant observations. This information should be supplied by the people who manage the building and by those who manage the people who have identified the IAQ problems and have accordingly made complaints, stated concerns, or offered observations. Medical information is helpful, if it is available, and prior building studies (e.g., energy efficiency reports, environmental site assessments, asbestos inspections and management plans, HVAC studies, and other IAQ studies) should be reviewed. The checklist in App. A is a guide to the information which might be collected and reviewed.

Stage 1, step 3. Interviews. Having reviewed the available information, it is important to interview building and personnel managers to ask questions generated by the problem review process and to attempt to complete gaps in the information. It is important to interview those who know the history of the building's design, construction, and renovations; the operation and maintenance of the facility's systems; the occupancy patterns currently and historically; past uses of the building which might be different from current uses; and planned renovation and/or maintenance projects. It is also important to interview the occupants, or at least an adequate representation, who have registered the complaints. (It may be appropriate and adequate to interview someone thoroughly familiar with the complaints, rather than interviewing the individual occupants.) Appendix B is a questionnaire to assist in discussions with occupants about health and comfort concerns.

Correlation of complaints to recent changes in the building is helpful diagnostically. Introduction of new building materials and/or furnishings can bring air quality changes. The specifics of these items are discussed in Sec. 4.2.

The use of certain chemicals in the facility must be ascertained.

Details of where, when, how much, and application technique are useful for any chemicals which seem to correlate with the symptoms. Material safety data sheets (MSDSs) should be reviewed for suspect chemicals (Fig. 2.4). Table 2.22 lists types of products commonly used in facilities related to cleaning, maintenance, and office equipment.[128]

MATERIAL SAFETY DATA SHEETS	Under OSHA regulations, responsible parties are required to document information on potentially hazardous products. These Material Safety Data Sheets (MSDS's) may be of limited help in identifying some products that may pose IAQ concerns. However, professional judgment and collection of additional information may be necessary in order to make full use of the MSDS. The following table summarizes some of the issues to keep in mind when deciding whether information from MSDS's is applicable to emission sources and exposures of concern in a building.	
Item	**Possible Uses**	**Comments**
Substances Covered	• MSDS's may identify significant airborne contaminants	• MSDS's may not be available onsite for many products • some components are listed as proprietary and are not disclosed • MSDS's do not always highlight products most likely to be airborne • contaminant byproducts inadvertently formed during manufacture won't always be listed
Personal Protection/ First Aid	• may suggest precautions for conducting source inspection	• usually relates only to high-level, worst-case exposures in general industry
Health Effects	• generally presents types of health effects that may be expected primarily at high level (e.g., industrial) exposures	• Symptoms listed may not occur at low-level concentrations found in indoor air • MSDS's may not include more subtle IAQ aspects such as nuisance factors and sensitivity to mixtures
Physical Data	• odor description may help identify sources • volatility may suggest which products are likely to be airborne • contaminants to expect in event of a fire or decomposition may be listed • reactivity data may suggest potential problems with storage or use	• reference material on how to use physical data information to predict IAQ impacts may be scarce
Control Measures	• identifies proper storage and packaging procedures • identifies steps for cleanup of gross spills	• many office chemicals are kept in much smaller amounts than found in industrial settings • spill cleanup may not eliminate airborne contamination • does not specify routine emission controls

A reasonable effort should be made to collect available MSDS's during IAQ profile development. Care should be taken to consider information that is relevant to IAQ concerns. Other important indicators of how a particular product may affect IAQ are available from direct odor and dust observations, a review of work practices, and interviews with operators and occupants. The manufacturer is a good source of follow-up information on a given product (phone number should be included on each MSDS).

Figure 2.4   Material safety data sheet. (*From* Building Air Quality: A Guide for Building Owners and Facility Managers, *EPA/400/1-91/033, p. 39.*)

TABLE 2.22   Chemicals Which Can Affect IAQ

Cleaners, disinfectants, deodorizers, waxes, and static-reducers used by cleaning crews

Pesticides and herbicides used for extermination, lawn and garden care, and maintenance of indoor plants

Disinfectants, growth inhibitors, and scale inhibitors used in maintaining the HVAC system

Materials used in photocopiers, printers, and blueprint copiers

Specialty chemicals used in darkrooms, graphic arts, building maintenance, mailing, and distribution

The information review and interviews should result in knowledge about the following:

1. The specific health and comfort complaints reported and the proportion of occupants reporting each complaint

2. Time patterns (hour, day, season) of the onset of adverse health and comfort conditions and of the diminishing of the conditions

3. Location patterns (i.e., normal work station, other work areas, degree of mobility) of the affected occupants

4. Relationship between predominant health and comfort complaints and potential source materials

5. Time and location patterns of the introduction of potential source materials into the indoor environment

6. Potential deficiencies in the distribution of adequately conditioned air, including the amount of outside air distributed to occupied areas

7. Understanding of the design, installation, operation, and maintenance of the HVAC system concerning potential contaminant pathways

8. Available medical opinions about the cause of any adverse health conditions attributed to IAQ[129]

Smoking policies and practices should be reviewed. Combustion sources and their respective fuel types should be identified, along with their schedules of operation and the way in which combustion gases are handled.

Water or water vapor penetration through the building skin (roof, walls, etc.) and leaks of internal systems (plumbing, mechanical, etc.)

can result in wet or damp areas conducive to microbial growth. Any cause of high humidity should be considered a potential microbial problem.

From this knowledge, hypotheses should be developed about sources and pathways. These are used to guide the initial walk-through, which may result in conclusions upon which action can be taken or the decision that more study is warranted.

Stage 1, step 4. Initial walk-through.   This function is usually accomplished by unaided visual, olfactory, and auditory means (i.e., the investigator walks through the building and uses his or her eyes, nose, ears, and professional inquisitiveness to test hypotheses, alter them, or develop new ones). The investigation should include the building's external environment, internal problem areas, and internal areas perceived by occupants as free of IAQ problems (these are to be the investigator's controls, for comparison to problem areas). The purpose of the walk-through is to identify potential contributors to the IAQ problem and the probable pathways that allow contributing pollutants to reach occupants. Synergistic contributors should be considered. For example, a source that emits VOCs is certainly a contributor, but an HVAC system that does not adequately ventilate the space containing the VOC source also contributes by allowing a stagnant air pathway to the occupants in the space.

This initial walk-through should be conducted in a manner specific to the given building and the attendant circumstances. It should be influenced by the information gathered and the resulting hypotheses. However, the investigator should be open to learning new and highly relevant facts during this initial survey that could redirect the investigation. Professional attentiveness to any clues and persistent pursuit of suggestive evidence are encouraged.

There are certain sources that are common to the majority of office buildings: large photocopiers, which emit significant amounts of heat, and blueprint copiers, which can be sources of ammonia and acetic acid.[130] It is important to note poor lighting conditions (e.g., insufficient light, too much light, glare, or reflection). Noise sources can be stressors also (e.g., HVAC units, copiers, electrical capacitors and transformers, and printers). Any discomfort to the investigator, such as an uncomfortable temperature or humidity, should be noted. As a rule of thumb, discomfort due to lighting, noise, temperature, and humidity could be pertinent to the study because occupants may confuse symptoms caused by these stressors with IAQ-related symptoms.

It is appropriate to remember that certain stressors cannot be sensed directly by the occupants or investigator. Radon and electromagnetic radiation are two examples. While some practitioners do not consider these as classic IAQ problems, this text treats them as items to consider during an IAQ investigation. Asbestos-containing building materials are also considered as potential contributors to air quality concerns. The U.S. EPA considers both asbestos and radon to be significant health hazards.[126,131] The health effects of certain electromagnetic fields (EMFs), which are associated with electrical power transmission, are being studied currently.[132] Whether or not these hazards are to be addressed in an IAQ investigation should be a matter of contract. Building managers may consider these as more appropriately dealt with in an environmental site assessment. Asbestos and radon are discussed in Sec. 4.3.

The initial walk-through is completed by gaining any additional information needed to understand thoroughly how the HVAC system works and how the building managers operate and maintain it. This topic is covered extensively in Sec. 3.2.

Stage 1, step 5. Second walk-through.   Stage 1, step 5, begins the evaluation process and is based on the information gained during the recognition process in the various investigative components of stage 1. Step 5 should begin after the observations, facts, and hypotheses from steps 1 through 4 are considered, consolidated, and correlated. The objectives of stage 1, step 5 are to refine hypotheses and to collect initial data. Often, the investigation can reach convincing conclusions after step 4, and step 5 may not be necessary. If this is the case, control actions can be initiated without further study.

A second walk-through is useful to take certain semiquantitative measurements, depending on what stressors are suspect at this point in the investigation. Table 2.23 summarizes several parameters that should be considered for this walk-through.[133] Instruments are suggested, with the measurement range in which the instruments should be valid and a general "acceptable range." This acceptable range means only that additional investigation is indicated if the measurement is outside this range.

It is best to make measurements throughout the day to determine if changes occur during the work day. Data should be sufficient to compare conditions before workers arrive to those at other times during the work day, including after work hours. In deciding when to take measurements, it is appropriate to consider the HVAC system operation, especially if the system is controlled differently after hours and on weekends from working hours. The measurements suggested in Table 2.23 should be taken in problem areas, in control areas, inside air-handling components of the HVAC system, and outdoors.[134] The following should be considered:[135]

TABLE 2.23   Common IAQ Measurement Techniques

Parameter	Instrument	Range of measurement	Acceptable range
Temperature	Thermometer; thermocouple	30° to 120°F	69° to 79°F
Relative humidity	Capacitive detector; sling psychrometer	0 to 100% RH	30 to 60% RH
Carbon monoxide	Electro-chemical detector; colorimetric tube	1 to 50 ppm	0 to 2 ppm above ambient, <9 ppm avg.
Carbon dioxide	Infrared detector; colorimetric tube	200 to 4000 ppm	<850 ppm
Airflow rate	Smoke tube; thermal anemometer; flow hood	Qualitative only 10 to 2000 fpm 10 to 2000 cfm	20 cfm outside air/person

SOURCE: *The Industrial Hygienist's Guide to Indoor Air Quality Investigations,* Patrick Rafferty, ed., p. 16. Used with permission of American Industrial Hygiene Association, Fairfax, Va.

CO_2

1. Indoor source is usually human respiration.
2. It has been used as a marker for inadequate outside air in a given area or inadequate air distribution.
3. The usefulness of CO_2 as a predictor of ventilation and air distribution efficiency depends on the occupant load in the building (i.e., a few people in a large space won't generate enough CO_2 to use as a predictor—generally, less than 7 people per 1000 ft^2 is too few).
4. Indoor levels should be below 1000 ppm.

Airflows.   The American Society for Heating, Refrigerating, and Air-Conditioning Engineers (ASHRAE) recommends 20 cfm per person of fresh air for most office environments.

Temperature and humidity

1. ASHRAE recommends 69 to 79°F.
2. ASHRAE recommends 30 to 60 percent RH.
3. High or low temperatures are uncomfortable.
4. Low humidity results in dry skin, lips, and nasal mucosa, sore throats, and nose bleeds.

5. High humidity can provide surface conditions suitable to growth of molds, yeasts, and dust mites.

CO

1. If measurably above outside levels, this may indicate improperly controlled and exhausted combustion sources and/or improper fresh air intakes for the building.
2. Smoking may cause elevated levels, depending on ventilation conditions.

This second inspection allows collection of useful data which may provide answers to the problem without the necessity of expensive searches for specific airborne chemicals. This should be done in conjunction with an initial evaluation of the HVAC. In stage 1 the investigator, via documents review and interviews, gains an understanding of the HVAC system type, how it is operated, and how it is maintained. Now an inspection of the system is in order. This should be done by an investigator thoroughly knowledgeable of HVAC systems, such as a licensed mechanical engineer. Sections 3.2 and 3.4 of this book are dedicated to HVAC systems and their investigation. Building materials are in the domain of architecture, and reliance on this discipline is suggested for industrial hygienists unfamiliar with building materials and systems. Architecture, related to IAQ, and chemicals emitted from various building materials are discussed in Sec. 4.2.

2.4.2   Stage 2

If completion of stage 1 does not render a problem characterization sufficient to recommend control measures, stage 2 is warranted. Stage 2 is a more detailed evaluation, usually involving measurements for classes of pollutants (e.g., volatile organic compounds) or for specific pollutants (e.g., formaldehyde). The sampling and analysis strategies and methodologies should be determined based on everything learned in stage 1 and on the best hypotheses developed to this point.

Measurements for most of the important IAQ culprits are discussed in Sec. 2.5. However, probably the most fundamental decision is how to interpret the data collected during stage 2. What are the appropriate standards and guidance? Much of the answer, of course, depends on the health consequences and medical characteristics involved in each specific diagnostic project. Headaches experienced by some occupants and related to noisy office machinery may merit a less stringent approach than headaches related to high carbon monoxide levels.

The AIHA guide makes the following statement:

> Several air quality standards and guidelines have been used in interpreting IAQ studies. None of these is sufficiently comprehensive to accommodate the variety of chemicals found in commercial environments, nor have any of the standards or guidelines been developed to provide an indication of "acceptability" for the office environment. Available guidelines do not adequately take into account exposure to multiple contaminants at low levels, which is recognized as a common problem in interpreting IAQ data.
>
> Some investigators have suggested applying a safety factor to occupational guidelines to account for multiple exposures and the possibility that the exposed population might not be as healthy as the population for which occupational limits were developed. The industrial hygienist should critically examine any IAQ literature to determine the extent to which earlier studies might have developed reliable guideline concentrations.[136]

See Table 2.24 for a summary of standards that have been found useful in interpreting IAQ information.[137] Some guidance does exist in the literature for acceptable levels of individual contaminants. In addition to data interpretation by comparison to standards, valid conclusions may be drawn by comparison to measurements taken in control areas where occupants do not exhibit symptoms. If all other relevant factors are equal, or have been properly compensated if different between control and problem areas, these comparisons may be the most valid and most helpful. Exceptions are, of course, situations where regulatory standards are exceeded or conditions exist which are

TABLE 2.24   Air Quality Standards and Guidelines

Canada Environmental Health Directorate: Exposure Guidelines for Residential Indoor Air Quality

American Industrial Hygiene Association (AIHA): Workplace Environmental Exposure Levels (WEELs)

Occupational Safety and Health Agency (OSHA): Permissible Exposure Limits (PELs)

American Conference of Governmental Industrial Hygienists (ACGIH): Threshold Limit Values (TLVs®)

National Institute for Occupational Safety and Health (NIOSH): Recommended Exposure Levels (RELs)

U.S. Environmental Protection Agency (EPA): National Ambient Air Quality Standards (NAAQS)

World Health Organization (WHO): Air Quality Guidelines for Europe

American Society of Heating, Refrigerating and Air-Conditioning Engineers: Standard 62-1989

immediately dangerous to health. Some data and guidelines for certain pollutants were discussed in Sec. 2.3.

Stage 2 evaluation may also include medical examinations and diagnoses, comprehensive HVAC studies, and epidemiological studies.[138] Table 2.25 summarizes some common IAQ complaints, possible symptoms, and possible causes.[139]

2.4.3 Stage 3

Stage 3 brings the investigator to the final, hoped for result—the problem solution. Control strategies can generally be categorized into one of the following:

Source removal.   The source of the air pollutant is removed. If the source is a building material, such as carpet adhesive, a replacement material must be installed and must be one that will not cause the same or a different IAQ problem. If removal means cleaning up a contaminant source, such as mildew on a damp wall, the cleaning process must be done with controls sufficient to prevent spread of the contaminant to other parts of the building. The underlying cause of the problem must also be corrected, or source removal brings only a short-term benefit (i.e., if the moisture that is dampening the mildewed wall is not eliminated, the mildew will eventually return). It is advisable to consult with an architect knowledgeable in IAQ resolution, or an engineer if engineering systems are involved, when designing such control solutions. Source removal may be the selection of a different pesticide or pesticide application methodology or the selection of different janitorial chemicals.

HVAC modification.   This may involve increasing fresh air to the occupants, redistributing air flow, exhaust ventilation of airborne pollutants, and temperature and humidity control. Design and specifications of such modification should be done by a licensed mechanical engineer (see Sec. 3.4).

Containment.   This strategy separates the occupants from the source by means of a suitable barrier. Large copy machines might be relocated to a dedicated room, which is ventilated and adequately cooled.

Administrative controls.   Building operations or personnel management changes are types of administrative controls. A smoking policy may be instituted to restrict smoking to a properly contained area. Building maintenance activities which have IAQ implications, such as painting, may be restricted to weekends.

TABLE 2.25 Common Problems and Solutions

Complaint	Symptoms might include	Possible causes	Predisposing factors	Prevalence
Sick building syndrome	Headaches, irritation, congestion, fatigue	Not related to sources of emission or contamination	Worst when and where ventilation is inadequate	Common (a small number of cases may occur in well-maintained buildings)
Allergic reactions	Swelling, itching, congestion, asthma	Unsanitary conditions (excessive dust or mold growth)	Individuals usually have history of allergies (about 10–20% of population)	Common
Hypersensitivity illness	Cough, shortness of breath, fever, chills, fatigue	Repeated exposure to microbial aerosols	Initially sensitized to high level of microbial contamination	Rare
Irritation	Watering, burning or dryness of eyes, nose or throat, may be accompanied by other nonspecific symptoms such as headache, nausea, or fatigue	Excessive concentrations of volatile chemicals such as solvents or formaldehyde; might also be because of very dry air	Some people more sensitive; tends to be worse during peak emissions or driest air	Moderate
Carbon monoxide poisoning	Headache, dizziness, discoloration, positive blood test, nausea, coma	Uncontrolled combustion	Cardiac conditions in more sensitive individuals	Rare
Neurological	Headaches, tremors, loss of memory	Insecticide misuse	Some people more sensitive	Rare
Infections	Diagnosed infection such as Legionnaire's or Aspergillus	Should be related to specific contaminant in building	Previously weakened immune system	Rare

TABLE 2.25 Common Problems and Solutions   (Continued)

Complaint	Symptoms might include	Possible causes	Predisposing factors	Prevalence
Comfort (thermal)	Too hot, too cold, too stuffy, too drafty	HVAC	"You can't please all of the people all of the time"	Common
Comfort (nuisance)	No symptoms, just concern for unusual odor or other conditions	Inadequate control of source emissions or contamination	Psychosocial	Moderate
Psychosocial stressors	Headaches, fatigue, muscle aches	Poor labor relations, overcrowding, unrelated concerns	Poor communication	Common
Mass hysteria	Hyperventilation, fainting, scratching	Symptoms spread by power of suggestion	Direct contact between affected individuals	Rare
Ergonomic problems	Muscle aches, fatigue, eyestrain	Uncomfortable seating, repetitive motion		Moderate
Lighting	Eyestrain, headaches	Insufficient light, glare, flicker		Moderate
Noise	Headaches, hypertension	Annoying noise interferes with concentration		Moderate
Cluster of adverse health effects	Any disease or health event that occurs in a building	Might be contagious, hereditary, etc., might not be related to IAQ	Occupants read about IAQ in media	Rare

SOURCE: *The Industrial Hygienist's Guide to Indoor Air Quality Investigations,* Patrick Rafferty, ed., App. D. Used with permission of American Industrial Hygiene Association, Fairfax, Va.

Time and scheduling.   Introduction of new building materials may result in off-gassing at a high initial rate, but this may decay to an acceptable level after a given time. If temporary ventilation can be provided through the high emission rate period, the products' impact on IAQ can be controlled.

Many of these control strategies may be involved in *commissioning.* This term refers to actions which should be taken prior to occupying a new or renovated facility to reduce the probability of IAQ problems. Commissioning procedures for IAQ relate primarily to allowing sufficient time before occupancy for the emission rates from new building materials to decay to lower levels. Increased ventilation may be provided during this time (see Secs. 3.5 and 4.7 for a comprehensive discussion).

Proper selection, design, and specification of problem solutions will probably involve other disciplines. The interdisciplinary issues were discussed in the Introduction.

2.5   Sampling, Analysis, and Interpretation

Characterizing IAQ by sampling and analysis can be done in a variety of ways, depending on the suspected contaminant or contaminants. These data are useful for solving IAQ problems, but proper test methods must be used, and valid interpretation of the data is crucial. For a given contaminant, a method ordinarily used in an industrial setting may not be sufficiently sensitive to test for the low concentrations expected in an office environment. Testing may be done using an integrated air sampling method, followed by laboratory analysis of the samples, or by direct-reading instruments, with or without real-time recording capabilities. Existing methods are being improved and new methods are being developed by various organizations. This section reviews techniques that have been used successfully for some of the major indoor air contaminants and is organized according to major groups of pollutants.

The major categories of concern are organic chemicals, inorganic chemicals and elements, particles and fibers, microbials, and radioactive elements. Sources of specific contaminants are discussed in Secs. 4.2 and 4.3. Symptoms caused by some IAQ problems are listed in Secs. 2.3 and 2.4. "It is prudent to begin a program of chemical sampling only if symptoms or observations strongly suggest that a specific pollutant or a specific source may be the cause of the complaint and if sampling results are important in determining an appropriate corrective action."[140]

Airborne concentrations are expressed in units of measure which depend on the contaminant being sampled. Units will be explained in the discussions of the major contaminant categories. Emission rates are measures of the quantity of a chemical released into the air from a given quantity of a source during a given amount of time. For example, Bayer and Black reported that an adhesive, under certain laboratory conditions, emitted 62 mg/h of benzene from a square meter (m^2) of the product. This emission rate is expressed as 62 mg/m^2-h.[141] As products age, the emission rate declines, or decays. This decay rate can be an important predictor of the time required for a new building product to cease emitting a contaminant at a rate sufficient to cause an IAQ problem. Decay rates are expressed in units of h^{-1}.

An organic compound was originally defined as a substance formed by living matter. The definition is expanded today to include any compound which contains the element carbon.[142] (Certain applications of chemistry have exceptions to this definition, but this general explanation will suffice here.) The classifications and nomenclature of organic compounds are indeed complex and beyond the scope of this discussion; however, a few terms important in IAQ must be generally understood. A *hydrocarbon* is an organic compound comprised exclusively of carbon and hydrogen.[143] If the carbon atoms are attached to each other in a straight chain or in a branched chain, the compound is an *aliphatic*.[144] *Aromatic* compounds are characterized by carbon atoms linked together into rings, rather than straight chains. These are typified by benzene, which is a ring containing six carbon atoms.[145] An organic compound with four or more ring structures is called *polycyclic* or *polynuclear*.[146] These compounds are often referred to in IAQ studies as *polycyclic aromatic hydrocarbons* (PAHs) or *polynuclear aromatic hydrocarbons* (PNAs). Cigarette smoke is a source of PNAs.[147] *Chlorofluorocarbons* (CFCs) are compounds made of chlorine, fluorine, carbon, and hydrogen.[148] A *halogenated hydrocarbon* has had one or more hydrogen atoms replaced by fluorine, chlorine, bromine, or iodine. (CFCs are a subgroup of the halogenated hydrocarbons.) Many of these compounds are highly toxic, and some of the chlorinated types are used as insecticides.[143] PCBs are compounds containing two benzene rings and at least two chlorine atoms. They are highly toxic.[149]

Volatility is an expression of the tendency of a solid or liquid to produce a vapor.[150] The volatility of a substance depends on the pressure and temperature. For IAQ purposes, volatile compounds are loosely defined as those which produce detectable vapors at normal room temperature and pressure. VOCs are defined in Sec. 2.3. This grouping is used to designate an important class of indoor air pollutants. Specific VOCs may be sampled, or *total volatile organic compounds* (TVOCs) may be measured.

The sampling method chosen for VOCs should be one that has been validated for the low levels typically found in nonindustrial environments. EPA has developed the following methods to measure VOCs at the parts-per-billion level:[151]

1. *Method TO-1.* Determination of VOCs in ambient air using Tenax® adsorption and gas chromatography/mass spectroscopy (GC/MS)

2. *Method TO-2.* Determination of VOCs in ambient air by carbon molecular sieve adsorption by GC/MS

3. *Method TO-14.* Determination of VOCs in ambient air using SUMMA® polished canister sampling and GC with appropriate detector [e.g., flame ionization detector (FID), electron capture detector (ECD), or nitrogen-phosphorus detector (NPD)]

Formaldehyde (HCHO) is a specific organic compound which contains oxygen in addition to carbon and hydrogen. It is an off-gassing product of many building materials (e.g., plywood and particle board). It can be measured using colorimetric indicator tubes, passive diffusion badges, OSHA Method 52(XAD-2 media), and NIOSH methods 3500 and 3501 (impinger).[152] Sampling sites should include control and complaint areas, and data should be correlated with the severity of the complaints in the sampling areas.

Formaldehyde and VOC measurement techniques are summarized in Table 2.26.[153] Measurement of specific organic compounds in indoor

TABLE 2.26 VOC Measurement Techniques

Parameter	Instrument	Range of Measurement	Acceptable Range
Total VOCs	Photoionization detector (PID); flame ionization detector (FID)	0.1–10 ppm	0–1.0 ppm
Formaldehyde	Passive diffusion badge impinger; specialty sorbent tube	0.01–1.0 ppm	0–0.1 ppm
Specific VOCs	Specialty sorbent tube; passive diffusion badge	0.001–10 ppm contaminant	Depends on SUMMA canister

SOURCE: *The Industrial Hygienist's Guide to Indoor Air Quality Investigations,* Patrick Rafferty, ed., p. 29. Used with permission of American Industrial Hygiene Association, Fairfax, Va.

air requires methods of sampling and analysis which have been validated for the expected levels of contaminant. The following organizations provide useful information for selecting specific measurement
techniques:

Air Pollution Control Association (APCA)
  Box 2861
  Pittsburgh, PA 15230
  (412-232-3444)

American Conference of Governmental Industrial Hygienists (ACGIH)
  6500 Glenway Avenue, Building D-7
  Cincinnati, OH 45211
  (513-661-7881)

American Industrial Hygiene Association (AIHA)
  2700 Prosperity Avenue, Suite 250
  Fairfax, VA 22031
  (703-849-8888)

American National Standards Institute, Inc. (ANSI)
  1430 Broadway
  New York, NY 10018
  (212-354-3300)

American Public Health Association (APHA)
  1015 15th Street, NW
  Washington, DC 20005
  (202-789-5600)

American Society for Testing and Materials (ASTM)
  Committee D-22 on Sampling and Analysis of Atmospheres
  1916 Race Street
  Philadelphia, PA 19103
  (215-299-5400)

National Institute for Occupational Safety and Health (NIOSH)
  Centers for Disease Control
  Robert A. Taft Laboratories, MS-R2
  4676 Columbia Parkway
  Cincinnati, OH 45226
  (513-533-8236)

U.S. Environmental Protection Agency (EPA)
  Environmental Monitoring Systems Laboratory
  Methods Standardization Branch
  Quality Assurance Division (MD-77)
  Research Triangle Park, NC 27711
  (919-541-2622)

Consultation with a competent analytical laboratory is advised.

The EPA's *Introduction to Indoor Air Quality: A Self-Paced Learning Module* and *Introduction to Indoor Air Quality: A Reference Manual* both contain valuable information about IAQ measurement methods. The remainder of this chapter is reproduced in part from Unit 2: Lesson 6 of the *Learning Module*.[154] Note that the cost information contained herein is in 1990 dollars, and costs will vary with time and geographic region.

2.5.1 Types of measurement methods

The term *measurement* is a broad term that encompasses the measurement of air contaminants; physical parameters such as temperature, humidity, atmospheric pressure, ventilation rates, and air exchange rates; characteristics of the buildings being investigated; and the health and activity patterns of occupants.

Before indoor air contaminants can be characterized, they must be collected and analyzed. *Measurement method* describes the overall procedure that is used (sampling plus analytical method). *Sampling method* is a term that describes the collection of the air contaminant; these methods and the equipment used for collection (samplers) do not analyze the data. Sampling methods can be active (pumps move air) or passive (air movement by diffusion). *Analytical method* refers to the chemical method that is used to identify and quantify the contaminant. *Monitoring method* refers to measurement methods in which electronically based equipment is used to both collect and analyze the air contaminant. Active or passive methods can be used to deliver air to the detector, but a power source is typically required for analysis. The terms *sampling equipment* and *samplers* are also used to refer to monitoring equipment and monitors.

Measurement methods can be direct or indirect reading. Direct-reading methods are those in which sample collection and analysis are accomplished in one stop; the results are determined as the sample is collected. Many of these methods are electronically based in which a sensor detects an input signal that is converted by mechanical and electrical components into a concentration or other measurement that can easily be interpreted. Other direct-reading methods rely on colorimetric indicators to react chemically with a contaminant to produce a color change which can be interpreted according to a calibrated scale. Although most direct-reading methods require moderate to large capital expenditures, they can be economical if many analyses are required (for example, in routine sampling for carbon monoxide, carbon dioxide, radon, particulates, and other contaminants.)

TABLE 2.27   Factors to Consider in the Selection of Measurement Methods and Equipment*

Measurement objectives	Screening or in-depth
Operating specifications	Size; weight; power source requirements; range; flow rates; heat output; temperature requirements; exhaust requirements; noise
Performance specifications	Accuracy; precision; range; minimum detectable limits; zero and span drift; interferences; linearity; recording capability; lag, rise and fall times
Labor requirements	Operation; calibration; maintenance; analysis; personnel (number and expertise)
Costs	Purchase of equipment and supplies; operation; calibration; maintenance; training

*References that provide useful descriptions of equipment include Lioy (1983); Nagda and Rector (1983); Nagda, Rector and Koontz (1987); and Wallace and Ott (1982).

SOURCE: *Introduction to Indoor Air Quality: A Self-Paced Learning Module,* EPA/400/3-91/002.

Indirect-reading methods are those in which sampling and analysis are accomplished in two steps. The sample is collected onto or into a substrate which undergoes a separate analysis, typically in a laboratory. Particulates can be collected onto a filter and gases can be collected into a liquid or onto solid chemicals or chemically treated papers. Some indirect-reading analytical methods such as the gravimetric analysis of particulates are relatively moderate in cost (about $25 for each gravimetric analysis), but other methods such as gas chromatography and/or mass spectroscopy for gases can be very expensive ($200 to $300 per sample analyzed). If the costs for sampling and analysis are combined, these methods can be characterized as moderate to expensive.

Measurement methods can also be grouped according to required sampling times, portability, presence of an air mover system, and collection and analytical methods. Section 6 of the EPA *Reference Manual* contains a summary of indoor air sampling equipment with information on these and other parameters including lower detectable limits, sampling rates, estimated prices, weight, and dimensions. The final selection of equipment will depend on operating and performance specifications, labor requirements, and costs which are outlined in Table 2.27.

Sampling time. Based on the length of time a contaminant is measured, sampling equipment (and monitoring equipment) can be classified as continuous, integrated, or grab:

Continuous samplers provide a real-time record of contaminant concentrations. The equipment can provide very reliable data, but it is generally expensive and time intensive and requires extensive training to use.

Integrated samplers provide an average concentration over a period of time ranging from minutes to weeks to months. Some samplers can provide data sequentially in an automatic mode without needing a technician to change parameters. One disadvantage of integrated methods is that concentration highs and lows are lost. Equipment for integrated methods is low to moderate in cost and some training is required for use, but the required training is not as extensive as for continuous methods.

Grab samplers provide a concentration measurement at a single point in time. The equipment is inexpensive to moderately expensive, depending on the number of samples to be taken. Minimal training is required, but the data are not very reliable.

Portability.   After the required time frame for sampling has been identified, sampling equipment can be selected based on the need for mobility or spatial variation. Based on this criterion, equipment can be classified as stationary, portable, or personal:

Stationary samplers operate from a fixed location. The equipment is generally bulky and heavy and requires a power source. Continuous samplers are usually stationary.

Portable samplers are small enough to be conveniently carried from place to place. Most equipment uses batteries for power, but some also has the option of using direct current. Integrated and grab samplers are typically portable, but some continuous equipment can also be portable.

Personal samplers are lightweight and quiet and can easily be carried or worn by a person. Although personal samplers may be preferred for many sampling problems, they are not available for all contaminants. If personal samplers are not available, portable methods are usually favored over stationary methods because they are generally less expensive and easier to use.

Air mover systems.   Air mover systems, which are classified as either active or passive, transport contaminated air into the air sampling measurement device. Particles and gases can be sampled using either system.

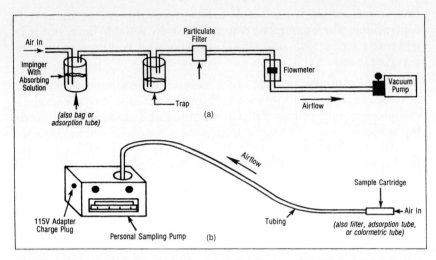

Figure 2.5 Examples of active samplers. (*a*) Portable sampler for gases; (*b*) personal sampler. (*From* Introduction to Indoor Air Quality: A Self-Paced Learning Module, *EPA/400/3-91/002.*)

Active samplers. Active samplers (Fig. 2.5) use an air mover system powered by a pump to draw the contaminated air through a collector or sensor. Continuous, integrated, or grab samples of gases or particles can be collected; these samples can be analyzed on site or taken to a laboratory for further processing. The volume of air moving through an active sampler and the resulting concentrations can be determined more accurately than with passive samplers. On the other hand, these samplers require more training than passive samplers, and they are also noisier and bulkier.

Active samplers range in complexity from simple bellows and piston pumps, which are used with colorimetric tubes or dosimeter badges, to mass flow-controlled direct-reading instruments.

The personal sampling pump is an active air mover system that is widely used in indoor air measurements. These compact battery-operated units can handle flow rates from 1 ml/min to 4500 ml/min. They are easy to operate, require minimal training, and can sample a broad range of contaminants using adsorption tubes, filters, bubblers, colorimetric tubes, and air bags to collect the contaminant for further analysis.

Passive samplers. Passive samplers (Fig. 2.6) do not have pumps to move the air through the sampling device; rather, contaminants diffuse or permeate through the collecting medium. Contaminant concentrations can be read directly, or further analysis may be required. These samplers have the advantages of being lightweight, compact,

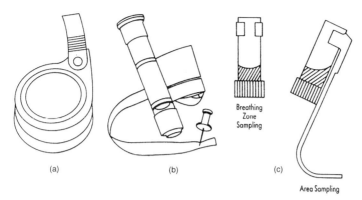

Breathing
Zone
Sampling

(a)   (b)   (c)

Area Sampling

Figure 2.6 Examples of passive samplers. (a) HCHO diffusion monitor; (b) NO_2 diffusion monitor; (c) SO_2 passive bubbler. (*From* Introduction to Indoor Air Quality: A Self-Paced Learning Module, *EPA/400/3-91/002.*)

and inexpensive for single samples. They are easy to use and require little or no training. They are good for initial screenings and are commonly worn by an individual to estimate personal exposures. Disadvantages include decreased sensitivity and limited accuracy (usually ±25 percent or more). Passive samplers provide integrated data rather than real-time data. If the sampler is not direct reading, the additional time required for analysis may be a drawback to its use. Section 6 of the EPA *Reference Manual* provides a summary of some passive sampling methods.

Collection methods

Particles and aerosols. Particles and aerosols can be sampled using filtration, inertial, gravity, electrostatic, or thermal collectors. Section 6 of the EPA *Reference Manual* summarizes some commonly used collection methods for asbestos, other fibers, inhalable particulates, and metals. Filtration and inertial collectors have been the most widely used methods because of ease of use, low cost, and broad applications.

Filtration is a technique in which filters are used to collect particles which are subsequently analyzed for metals, organic compounds, fibers, microorganisms, and radon progeny. The choice of filter type in a given situation depends on the general characteristics of the filter, background filter impurities, flow resistance over time, collection efficiency, ease of analysis, cost, and availability. A wide variety of filters is available including cellulose, glass fiber, membrane, and nucleopore. Interest in collecting respirable particles (those that are 10 μm or less in diameter) has resulted in the increased use of inertial collectors. These collectors can separate particles in the gas stream according to particle size using impaction, impingement, or centrifugal force.

Gases and vapors. Gases and vapors can be collected using both active and passive systems with two basic collection techniques: (1) collection into a suitable container such as a bag, bottle, or canister and (2) removal from the air and concentration by adsorbing or absorbing the gas onto a solid or into a liquid solution.

Plastic sampling bags can be used for collecting integrated samples for periods ranging from instantaneous samples to 8-h samples. Samples can remain stable for hours to several days. Some common bag materials include Mylar®, Teflon®, and polyethylene.

Absorption is a process in which gases are transferred into a liquid or solid medium in which they dissolve. The concentration of the gas that is dissolved in the liquid or solid increases until an equilibrium is established with the concentration of the gas in the air. Continued sampling past this point will not increase the concentration of the gas in the solution.

Adsorption is a method of collecting gases in which the gas is attracted to, concentrated in, and retained on a substrate. After the gas has been collected, it can be removed from the adsorbent for analysis by treatment with chemicals, heat, or inert gases. Solid sorbents have been used to determine volatile organic compounds in indoor air; activated charcoal has been a commonly used sorbent in passive and active samplers. Other adsorbing agents include activated alumina, silica gel, and porous polymers (Tenax-GC, Chromosorb, Porapak Series, Amerlite XAD-2).

Solid sorbents can provide an integrated sample of varying time (typically 8 to 12 h), and because of the small size of sampling tubes and pumps, they are easy to use in a variety of indoor situations.

Analytical methods. The number of analytical methods available for identifying and quantifying contaminants and physical stressors can be overwhelming. Most IAQ investigations will be handled by relatively few methods, but it is useful to have an awareness of other methods that could be used in special circumstances.

Physical stressor detectors
Temperature. Room air temperature can be measured by liquid-in-glass thermometers (alcohol or mercury), resistance thermometers (platinum, thermistors), thermocouples, and bimetallic thermometers. Analog thermometers can be purchased for less than $10; the cost of digital thermometers is about $35 to $100.

Humidity. Humidity is commonly measured as the relative humidity which is the ratio of the amount of water vapor in the air at a specific temperature to the maximum amount of water vapor that the air could hold at that temperature. Relative humidity can be measured using hygrometers or psychrometers.

Analog hygrometers can be purchased for as little as $35; digital units that can also measure temperature and are traceable to the National Institute of Standards and Technology (NIST), formerly the National Bureau of Standards (NBS), can be purchased for about $200. (See discussion below under "Standard Materials.")

The sling psychrometer has a thermometer holder that telescopes into a swivel handle which has a slide rule that contains scales for relative humidity and wet- and dry-bulb temperatures. The psychrometer is whirled by hand to produce the air velocity required to determine the wet-bulb temperature which is needed along with the dry-bulb temperature to read the relative humidity. Sling psychrometers can be purchased for about $75. A powered psychrometer can be purchased for about $350.

Light.   The intensity of visible light can be measured using light meters. These meters measure the quantity of light per unit area in foot-candles (fc). Light meters can measure light intensities over a broad range (from 0 to 99,900 fc). Analog meters can be purchased for about $100; digital meters can range from about $150 to $300, depending on the range of light to be measured and whether the meters are traceable to NIST.

Air motion.   In most situations air movement can be measured using analog or digital meters and smoke tubes. When using meters to measure air motion, it is important to use devices that are nondirectional or to monitor the orientation of the meter carefully to ensure that the true air speed is being measured.

Air velocity can be measured in rooms or inside heating and ventilating ducts, grilles, and diffusers. The unit of measurement for air velocity is feet per minute (fpm) or meters per second (mps). Some meters also contain scales for measuring static pressures in ducts. A mechanical air velocity meter kit that can measure velocities and differential pressures at a variety of locations costs about $1000. Mini-sized air velocity meters, which can measure the same air velocity range but not static pressures, can be purchased for about $250 to $500. These mechanical systems do not require power sources or batteries.

Direct readings of airflow [in cubic feet per minute (f^3/min) or cubic meters per second (m^3/s)] can be obtained with air volume meters. Standard-sized units cost about $1700 and mini-sized meters cost about $1000. Both units have hoods of different sizes which fit directly over supply and exhaust openings that channel the air through a manifold to a specially designed base that senses airflow and averages the results. A wide range of flows can be measured (0 to about 2000 ft^3/min).

Smoke tubes or smoke candles release visible smoke which blends readily with air to aid in observing airflow. These devices should be used cautiously because they can trigger fire alarms and the smoke can be irritating. Smoke tubes or candles can be purchased in different sizes depending on the amount of smoke to be generated. Costs are about $2 to $7 per tube or candle.

Noise.   There is a variety of equipment available for measuring noise. For most evaluations, the sound level meter (A-weighted scale) will provide sufficient information. In some instances an octave band analyzer may be needed. Meters with the A-weighted scale only can be purchased for about $300; an acoustical calibrator (about $200) must also be purchased. Meters that have more capability are slightly more expensive.

Particle and aerosol detectors.   Particles and aerosols are most commonly collected onto a filter medium and then analyzed gravimetrically or by other methods, but instruments are available which can provide a direct reading of particles without an intermediate step. These instruments are relatively complex and expensive (from $500 to over $10,000). They operate by sensing some property of the particulate such as size, electrical charge, or mass.

Instruments for measuring particulates can be grouped into four categories: optical, piezoelectric, beta attenuation, and electrical detectors. Optical detectors can be useful in routine IAQ investigations. The other techniques are probably more appropriate in outside air quality, occupational, or research investigations.

Optical detectors are based on the interaction of particles with light. These instruments can determine particle size and number. Particles in the size range from 0.5 to 10 μm can be detected with single particle detectors. Instruments which can analyze fibrous aerosols, including asbestos, are also available but are generally less reliable than collection onto a filter, followed by laboratory analysis.

Gas and vapor detectors.   There are many instruments that can detect contaminants in the gaseous phase at the same time they are being sampled. Although they are more expensive than indirect-reading methods (typically, several thousand dollars to over $10,000) and require skilled operators, they may be cost effective for contaminants which are routinely measured.

Some situations such as the investigation of faulty furnaces or gas leaks require direct-reading instruments. In other situations, the convenience of a direct reading is attractive because it eliminates potentially lengthy turnaround times in a laboratory.

In general, there are seven analytical methods that can be applied to the analysis of gases and vapors.[155] These methods are electrical, electromagnetic, chemielectromagnetic, thermal, gas chromatography, magnetic, and radioactive. They can be incorporated into direct-reading field instruments or laboratory-based instruments and techniques. They are described in Sec. 6 of the EPA *Reference Manual.*

Direct-reading colorimetric indicator devices. One of the most commonly used techniques for gases (and some particulates such as lead) is the colorimetric indicator device. These devices, which can be active or passive, are widely used in industrial hygiene and emergency response applications to sample contaminants at relatively high concentrations (in the range of the OSHA standards). This technique is generally inadequate for indoor air monitoring because of the lack of specificity of some tubes and accuracy. Nevertheless, there may be some instances when these devices can be usefully employed.

These devices rely on the chemical reaction between a contaminant and a reagent to produce a color which can be interpreted visually or optically. They may consist of liquid reagents, chemically treated papers, and glass indicating tubes containing solid chemicals. The color changes can be observed as a length of stain on a calibrated tube or a color change in a tube or badge which is compared to a standard color chart.

If these methods are used, cautions should be observed. Devices should be refrigerated, stain fronts or color changes should be read immediately after sampling, and pumps should be checked for leaks and calibrated regularly. And, most important, the accuracy and lower detectable limits should always be foremost in the mind of the investigator when selecting these devices and interpreting results.

2.5.2   Minimizing errors

Sampling protocol.   One important way of minimizing errors is to develop a sampling protocol or written plan before sampling begins. The protocol is a valuable tool which can ensure that the measurement problem has been thought out and that time, money, and resources will be optimized to provide quality data. The protocol should include basic information such as what will be sampled and how, where, when, and by whom the sampling will be accomplished. A key component of the protocol is the evaluation of data reliability through the use of a quality assurance plan.

The selection of appropriate equipment and the proper operation, routine maintenance, and calibration of equipment are critical to the success of any sampling program. Calibration is a check on the sample collection system and the analytical method to verify that accurate measurements are made. It is the cornerstone of any sampling protocol and can make or break the validity and usefulness of the collected data.

It is the investigator's responsibility to know each piece of equipment or method that will be used and to identify maintenance and calibration requirements before sampling begins. Maintenance and calibration schedules should be delineated in the protocol and followed strictly.

Instructions should also be included on sample handling, storage, and transport. Directions for calculations and criteria for accepting data should also be included in the protocol along with other quality assurance procedures. In developing the protocol, it is a good idea to seek advice from a chemist, an industrial hygienist, or another person who has expertise with the proposed analytical methods and from a statistician, if the project involves multiple locations or measurements. If the sample is to be collected and then analyzed at a later time in the laboratory, the investigator must also be sure that the laboratory personnel follow a quality assurance (QA) program.

A major objective in designing a sampling program is to collect a representative sample, one that reflects the exposure that is being experienced. This requires careful attention to sample size and selection of methods (Sec. 6 of the EPA *Reference Manual*). Failure to collect a representative sample can be an important source of error in any investigation.

Quality assurance.   Quality assurance describes the activities needed to provide assurance that high-quality data are being collected. The objectives of a QA program are to ensure that the data are accurate, precise, complete, representative, and comparable. Factors in a quality assurance program include:

1. Adequately trained and experienced personnel
2. Proper equipment and facilities in good working order
3. Written sampling, calibration, and maintenance procedures and schedules
4. Data validation programs
5. Chain-of-custody procedures
6. A supportive management team

Quality control refers to that part of the QA plan that directly measures data reliability through calibrations and other checks such as blanks and duplicates.

Ideally, a good IAQ sampling program will have a written plan that incorporates as many of the components of an ideal QA program as possible. Although such a plan may not be required, it is sound practice to develop and use as many of the components as feasible. Additional information on the elements of quality assurance programs for quality measurements are discussed in EPA ambient air QA documents[156–158] and in the compendium of methods for indoor air.[151] An example QA plan for indoor environments is given in GEOMET Technologies, Inc.[159]

Accuracy and precision.   All measurement methods are subject to error. Accuracy and precision are two measures of data quality that help evaluate errors in the measurement process (Sec. 6 of the EPA *Reference Manual* discusses each in greater detail). Accuracy is a measure of how close data points are to the true result, and precision describes the variation or scatter among the results (Fig. 2.7). Precision is a measure of the uncertainty of the average concentration—it is not related to the true concentrations.

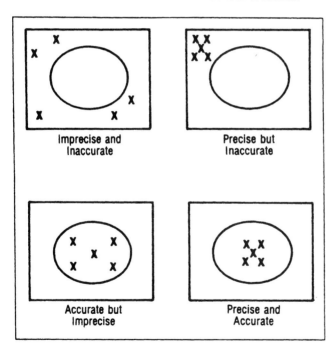

SOURCE: Adapted from *The Industrial Environment - Its Evaluation and Control.* C.H. Powell and A.D. Hosey. (eds). 1965. Health Services Publication No. 614. U.S. Dept. Health, Educ., and Welfare: Cinncinati, OH.

Figure 2.7 Accuracy and precision. (*From* Introduction to Indoor Air Quality: A Self-Paced Learning Module, *EPA/400/3-91/002.*)

Accuracy is affected by sources of error that can be identified and controlled. These errors are known as systematic errors because they result in measured values that are consistently above or below the true value. Systematic errors can arise from many sources including errors in calculation, incorrect calibrations, contaminated reagents, interferences, improper operation of equipment, and improper handling and storage of samples. Systematic errors cannot be treated by statistical methods.

Precision is affected by sources of error that are random and cannot be controlled. Sources of random error include variations in equipment such as airflow fluctuations, variations in the contaminants being tested, and variation in the analytical methods, including instrument responses. Random errors can vary in magnitude and direction, and they are never completely eliminated. Random errors can be accounted for and minimized by statistical techniques. For example, random errors can be minimized by increasing the size of the sample.

Ideally, the sampling or analytical method that is employed will be both accurate and precise. However, it is possible for a method to have high precision but low accuracy because of improperly calibrated equipment or inaccurate measurement techniques. Alternatively, a method can be accurate but imprecise because of low instrument sensitivity or factors beyond the investigator's control.

Interferences.   Interferences are chemicals or factors other than the contaminant of interest which react during sampling or analysis to give concentrations that are higher or lower than the true value. Interferences can result in significant sampling errors and must be considered before a sampling method is selected. Most standard methods and equipment specifications identify major interferences.

When standard methods are not used, it is important to review the literature to obtain information on potential interferences. The potential impact of interferences on the data can be estimated, and then a decision can be made to try another method, ignore the interference, or correct for the interference. Ignoring interferences and correcting results are common practices, but they should be approached cautiously.

Reporting only corrected results obscures information that affects the validity of the data. For example, data that have a 5 percent correction factor for interferences will likely be viewed differently than those that have a 25 or 50 percent correction factor. If correction factors are applied, they should always be reported along with the data.

Limit of detection and limit of quantification.   The limit of detection (LOD) is the smallest quantity or concentration of a contaminant for which an analytical method will show a response. The limit of quantification

(LOQ) is the smallest quantity or concentration that can be quantified in an environmental sample.

Blanks, duplicates, and standard materials

Blanks. The term *sample blank* refers to the concentration of a contaminant that is present in the medium (chemical, filter) that is used to collect the sample. For example, if radon is sampled using track-etch detectors and all samplers are deployed, it will not be possible to know if there is any contamination of the sampler. However, if a number of samplers are held back and remain sealed and unexposed, they can be sent back to the laboratory and analyzed, allowing any contamination to be detected. The value of the sample blank should always be subtracted from the measured concentration. If the blank concentration is greater than the measured concentration, the collected data should be regarded as invalid.

About 10 percent of the total number of samples collected should be blanks, and at least one blank should be included in each measurement batch.

Duplicates. Duplicate samples are those which are collected and handled in exactly the same way as the regular samples. Duplicate samples should be collected for indirect-reading methods and some direct-reading methods. The use of duplicate instruments for direct-reading methods is usually reserved only for research applications when the method is being investigated.

Duplicate samples provide an additional check on the quality of the data, and they should agree very closely with one another. A useful guideline is to have duplicates for about 10 percent of the total number of samples collected.

Standard materials. Standard materials are those for which purity and concentration have been verified by an outside agency. NIST, EPA, and NIOSH all provide standard materials that can be used in the calibration of equipment and laboratory analytical methods. Section 6 of the EPA *Reference Manual* contains a list of materials which can be obtained from NIST; a list of the EPA's regional Quality Assurance Offices which can be contacted to obtain more information about standard materials is also included. EPA does provide, at *no charge,* cylinders of standard gases, including hazardous organic compounds, that may be used to audit the performance of indoor air measurement systems.

Calibration. Calibration is the establishment of a relationship between various standard materials and the measurements of them obtained by all or part of a measurement system. The levels of standard materials which are used should bracket the range of levels for which measurements will be made.

In the case of direct-reading instruments, calibration standard materials (calibration standards) are used to quantify the relationship between the output of a sensor and contaminant concentrations. This relationship allows the user to know that the instrument is responding accurately (or inaccurately) to contaminants in the air.

Without proper calibration of equipment and methods, the sampling results cannot be assumed to be accurate and reliable. Considerable money and time can be wasted in the long run when investigators skimp on calibration.

Sampling pumps, flowmeters, analyzers, calibration gases, and laboratory analytical procedures must all be calibrated. It is essential for any chemical reagents or gases that are used in the calibration to be of the highest reliability. This means they must be certified in some manner; materials that can be traced back to NIST will provide the highest reliability.

The frequency of calibration varies depending on the requirements of data acceptability, performance between scheduled calibration, and manufacturer's recommendations. The conditions under which the instruments are used and the number of people using the instruments and their skill levels should also be considered. A general rule is to calibrate before and after each sampling period if equipment is turned off or transported between measurements.

Methods of calibration for equipment and laboratory methods are specified in EPA methods and several references;[151,157,160–162] these should be used whenever possible. Section 6 of the EPA *Reference Manual* contains more information on the calibration of equipment.

Proficiency testing. Proficiency testing is an external quality control check that involves the analysis of reference samples once or twice a year. Certified samples are sent to laboratories for analysis. The laboratory's performance is judged by the accuracy of the analysis. Proficiency testing is a commonly used technique in industrial hygiene and environmental analysis. It provides additional assurance about the quality of the data produced by laboratories.

Proficiency testing is not routinely available in IAQ work; however, programs do exist for the measurement of radon and asbestos. These programs are administered by EPA, and EPA publishes a list of companies that pass the performance tests. Selecting a company that passes the proficiency test provides additional assurance that quality data will result. EPA also provides comparison standards (audit materials) for the compendium methods through the Atmospheric Research and Exposure Assessment Laboratory, Quality Assurance Division, MD-77B, Research Triangle Park, NC 27711.

Validation of collected data. The validation of data is a final critical point in the measurement process, and the investigator should have a set of criteria by which to judge the validity of collected data. These criteria should include the following:

1. Instruments should operate properly during sampling periods (if an instrument or pump is not operating at the end of a designated sampling period, the data collected during that time period should not be used).

2. Analysis of blanks and duplicate samples and calibrations must be performed properly and be within predetermined limits during the times the data were collected.

3. Extreme values must be checked to determine causes.

4. Calculations and data transfers must be performed properly.

5. Results should be evaluated to determine if they are consistent with other measurements.

In general, it is best to flag data which are outside the designated data validation criteria. Data which do not meet the designated acceptable criteria, with few exceptions, should not be included in statistical summaries. There is a real temptation to rationalize the inclusion of data that are outside the designated data validation bounds because of the effort that goes into data collection, but this should be resisted. Report only those data in which there is confidence.

There are instances when data will be useful in qualitative evaluation even though they may not pass all of the validation criteria. If data that have not met the inclusion criteria are included in a report, be sure to flag them for the reader, clearly pointing out the problems and deficiencies.

Always keep in mind how data will be used. Will a decision about a health risk be made? Will a policy decision be made? If the data are to be used for critical decisions, it is far better to repeat measurements and incur the extra expense rather than including lesser-quality data that may have far-reaching consequences. The investigator must exercise careful judgment in deciding the validity of data.

Data that are within predesignated acceptable criteria but are either much higher or lower than other measurements should be included in the data summary. Statistical tests can be applied to determine if a value is an outlier, but even when outliers are verified statistically, they should be included in the report of the data. Under no circumstances should data arbitrarily be excluded from a report simply because they do not fit the mold. If, after careful evaluation of the entire sampling process, no reason can be found to exclude the data, they should be reported as valid. However, outliers may be treated differently in the analysis and interpretation of data.

2.5.3 Standard methods

Standard methods or procedures do not currently exist for the measurement of all indoor air pollutants, but EPA has developed 21 methods for 9 categories of contaminants plus two methods for determining air exchange rates.[151] In addition, there are some ambient air quality and industrial hygiene procedures which are suitable for IAQ investigations.

EPA's compendium of methods for indoor air. In response to the need for specific guidance on the determination of indoor air contaminants, EPA has developed methods for the determination of selected contaminants in indoor air. However, EPA cautions that these methods at this time are not certified and are not officially recommended or endorsed by EPA. The following methods have been developed:

1. Volatile organic compounds using SUMMA® stainless steel canister sampling or solid adsorbents

2. Nicotine using XAD-4 solid adsorbent, active filter cassettes, or passive filter cassettes

3. Carbon monoxide and carbon dioxide using nondispersive infrared spectroscopy or gas filter correlation

4. Nitrogen dioxide using continuous luminox LMA-3, Palmes diffusion tube, passive sampler badge, or a transducer technology electrochemical technique

5. Formaldehyde using solid adsorbent Sep-Pak 2,4-DNPH cartridge, passive sampler badge or a continuous CEA monitor

6. Benzo(a)pyrene and other polynuclear aromatic hydrocarbons in air using a combination quartz filter/adsorbent cartridge with subsequent analysis by gas chromatography with flame ionization and mass spectrometry detection or high-performance liquid chromatography

7. Selective pesticides using low-volume polyurethane foam sampling with gas chromatography/electron capture detector

8. Acid, bases, aerosols, and particulate matter using an annular denuder coupled with filter pack assembly or transition flow reactor

9. Particulate matter using an impactor with filter pack assembly or a continuous particulate monitor

10. Air exchange rate using perfluorocarbon tracer or tracer gas

Whether or not a specific method will be appropriate for a given application will depend on economic resources, available expertise, and the application itself. Not all methods will be appropriate or possible for routine sampling applications.

Information on the EPA methods can be obtained from the EPA Atmospheric Research and Exposure Assessment Laboratory, Research Triangle Park, NC.

Canadian indoor air test kit. The Building Performance Division of Technology, Architectural and Engineering Services within Public Works Canada has developed an IAQ test kit (Public Works Canada, 1988) which is intended to be simple and easy to use and to require little technical training. This kit includes an investigation strategy that begins with a preliminary assessment followed by measurements with simple instruments and complex instruments, if needed.

Step-by-step instructions are contained in the test kit, which includes equipment for measuring carbon dioxide, carbon monoxide, formaldehyde, radon, volatile organic compounds, relative humidity, temperature, and air movement.

More information about this kit can be obtained by contacting the Architectural and Engineering Services Division, Public Works Canada, Sir Charles Tupper Building, Riverside Drive, Ottawa, Ontario, K1A OM2.

NIOSH analytical methods. NIOSH publishes a manual of analytical methods that includes 350 methods for over 600 substances.[151] However, these methods were developed for the industrial environment, and many of the substances are not relevant for other IAQ problems. Nevertheless, some of the methods, particularly those for formaldehyde and VOCs, are used successfully by NIOSH in investigating nonindustrial workplaces. The manual is available from the U.S. Government Printing Office.

References

1. *The Random House Dictionary of the English Language,* 2d ed., Unabridged, Random House, New York, 1987, p. 1544.
2. Plog, Barbara A., Benjamin, George S., Kerwin, Maureen A., *Fundamentals of Industrial Hygiene,* National Safety Council, Chicago, Ill., 1988, p. 3.

3. *The Third Wave of Asbestos Disease: Asbestos in Place,* Proceedings of the Collegium Ramazzini, William Hines (ed.), The Workplace Health Fund, Washington, D.C., 1990.
4. *Bulletin of the American Board of Industrial Hygiene,* American Board of Industrial Hygiene, Lansing, Mich., October 1, 1993, p. 7.
5. Plog, Benjamin, and Kerwin, p. 5.
6. *Ibid.*, p. 6.
7. *Ibid.*, p. 335.
8. *Ibid.*, pp. 850, 862, 867, 876, 887, 893.
9. Millette, J. R., and Hays, S. M., *Settled Asbestos Dust Sampling and Analysis,* Lewis Publishers, Chelsea, Mich., 1994, Chap. 2.
10. *Ibid.*, Glossary.
11. U.S. Environmental Protection Agency (EPA), *Respiratory Health Effects of Passive Smoking: Lung Cancer and Other Disorders,* EPA/600/6-90/006F, December 1992, p. 2-1.
12. *The Random House Dictionary of the English Language,* p. 1611.
13. Plog, Benjamin, and Kerwin, pp. 21–22.
14. *Ibid.*, p. 21.
15. *Ibid.*, p. 429.
16. *Threshold Limit Values for Chemical Substances and Physical Agents and Biological Exposure Indices,* American Conference of Governmental Industrial Hygienists, Cincinnati, Ohio, 1993, p. ii.
17. *Ibid.*, p. 2.
18. *Ibid.*, p. 3.
19. *Ibid.*, p. 50.
20. Plog, Benjamin, and Kerwin, p. 394.
21. *Threshold Limit Values for Chemical Substances and Physical Agents and Biological Exposure Indices,* p. 2.
22. Ibid, p. 3.
23. *Documentation of the Threshold Limit Values and Biological Exposure Indices,* 5th ed., American Conference of Governmental Industrial Hygienists, Cincinnati, Ohio, 1990.
24. Hansen, Shirley J., *Managing Indoor Air Quality,* Fairmont Press, Lilburn, Ga., 1991, p. 1.
25. *Ibid.*, p. 2.
26. *Building Air Quality: A Guide for Building Owners and Facility Managers,* United States Environmental Protection Agency, EPA/400/1-91/033, December 1991, p. 154.
27. Fiedler, Nancy, Maccia, Clement, and Kipen, Howard, "Evaluation of Chemically Sensitive Patients," *J. of Occupational Medicine,* 34(5) 529, May 1992.
28. *Building Air Quality: A Guide for Building Owners and Facility Managers,* pp. 153–156.
29. *The Random House Dictionary of the English Language,* p. 1215.
30. Plog, Benjamin, Kerwin, p. 878.
31. *The Random House Dictionary of the English Language,* p. 210.
32. *Ibid.*, p. 1213.
33. *Ibid.*, p. 1214.
34. Nester, Eugene W., et al., *Microbiology: Molecules, Microbes, and Man,* Holt, Rinehart and Winston, New York, 1973, p. 53.
35. *Ibid.*, p. 59.
36. *The Random House Dictionary of the English Language,* p. 1219.
37. Nester et al., p. 62.
38. *The Random House Dictionary of the English Language,* p. 209.
39. Plog, Benjamin, and Kerwin, p. 850.
40. Millette, J. R., and Hays, S. M., Chap. 2.
41. *The Random House Dictionary of the English Language,* p. 560.
42. Plog, Benjamin, and Kerwin, p. 124.

43. World Health Organization, *Air Quality Guidelines for Europe,* Series no. 23, WHO: Copenhagen, Denmark, 1987.
44. Calabrese, E. J., *Pollutants and High-Risk Groups, The Biological Basis of Increased Human Susceptibility to Environmental and Occupational Pollutants,* John Wiley, New York, 1978.
45. Rudolph, L., and Forest, C. S., "Female Reproductive Toxicology," Chap. 23, *Occupational Medicine,* J. LaDou (ed.), Appleton & Lange, Norwalk, Conn., 1990.
46. Pushen, J. S., and Nelson, C. B., "EPA's Perspective on Risks from Residential Radon Exposure." *J. Air Poll. Control Assoc.,* 39(7), 915–920, 1989.
47. Doull, J., Klaassen, C. D., and Amdur, M. O. (eds.), *Toxicology,* 2d ed., Macmillan, New York, 1980.
48. Turiel, I., *Indoor Air Quality and Human Health,* Stanford University Press, Stanford, Calif., 1985.
49. U.S. Environmental Protection Agency, *Air Quality Criteria for Oxides of Nitrogen,* EPA-600/8-82-026F, U.S. EPA, Research Triangle Park, N.C., 1982.
50. Case, G. D., Dixon, J. S., and Schooley, J. C., "Interactions of Blood Metalloproteins with Nitrogen Oxides and Oxidant Air Pollution," *Environ. Res.,* 20, 43–65, 1979.
51. Kagawa, J., and Tsuru, K., "Effect of 2-Hour Exposure to O_3 and SO_2 with Intermittent Exercise on Human Pulmonary Function," *Nippon Eiseigaku Zasshi,* 34, 690–696, 1979. As translated by Literature Research Company, Annandale, Va.
52. National Research Council, *Indoor Pollutants,* National Academy Press, Washington, D.C., 1981.
53. U.S. Consumer Product Safety Commission, "Hazard Assessment for Pollutants Emitted During Use of Kerosene Heaters," *Kerosene Heater Briefing Package,* U.S. CPSC, Washington, DC., 1983.
54. Sheppard, D., et al., "Exercise Increases Sulfur Dioxide-Induced Broncho-Constriction in Asthmatic Subjects, *Am. Rev. Resp. Dis.,* 124, 257–259, 1981.
55. Tu, K. W., and Hinchliffe, L. E., "A Study of Particulate Emissions from Portable Space Heaters," *Am. Ind. Hyg. Assoc. J.,* 44(11), 857–862.
56. National Research Council, *Environmental Tobacco Smoke. Measuring Exposures and Assessing Health Effects,* National Academy Press, Washington, D.C., 1986.
57. U.S. Department of Health and Human Services, *The Health Consequences of Involuntary Smoking,* U.S. DHHS, Office on Smoking and Health, Rockville, Md., 1986.
58. U.S. Environmental Protection Agency, *A Consumer's Guide to Safer Pesticide Use,* OPA 87-013, U.S. EPA, Office of Public Affairs, Washington, D.C., 1987.
59. U.S. General Accounting Office, *Nonagricultural Pesticides. Risks and Regulations,* GAO/RCED-86-97, U.S. GAO, Washington, D.C., 1986.
60. U.S. Environmental Protection Agency, *Nonoccupational Pesticide Exposure Study (NOPES),* EPA/600/3-90/003, U.S. EPA, Atmospheric Research and Exposure Assessment Laboratory, Research Triangle Park, N.C., 1990.
61. Blondell, J., Personal Communication, U.S. Environmental Protection Agency, Health Effects Division, Washington, D.C., 1989.
62. Börzsönyi, M., Török, Pintér, and Surján, A., "Agriculturally-Related Carcinogenic Risk," IARC (International Agency for Research on Cancer) Scientific Publication Series, vol. 56, M. Börzsönyi, N. E. Day, K. Lapis, and H. Yamasaki (eds.), World Health Organization, Geneva, Switzerland, 1984.
63. U.S. General Accounting Office, *Lawn Care Pesticides. Risks Remain Uncertain While Prohibited Safety Claims Continue,* GAO/RCED-90-134, U.S. GAO, Washington, D.C., 1990.
64. AMA Council on Scientific Affairs, "Cancer Risk of Pesticides in Agricultural Workers," *JAMA,* 260(7), 959–966, 1988.
65. Sharp, D. S., et al., Delayed Health Hazards of Pesticide Exposure," *Am. Rev. Public Health,* 7, 441–471, 1986.
66. Xue, S., "Health Effects of Pesticides: A Review of Epidemiologic Research from the Perspective of Developing Nations," *Am. J. Indust. Med.,* 12, 269–279, 1987.

67. Stokes, C. S., and Brace, K. D., "Agricultural Chemical Use and Cancer Mortality in Selected Rural Counties in the U.S.A.," *J. Rural Studies,* 4(3), 239–247, 1988.
68. Lowengart, R. A., et al., "Childhood Leukemia and Parents Occupational and Home Exposures," *J.N.C.I.,* 79(1), 39–46, 1987.
69. Jennings, B. H., "Issue Brief. Pesticides at Home: Uncertain Risks and Inadequate Regulations," California Senate Office of Research, Sacramento, Calif., 27 pp., 1988.
70. U.S. Department of Housing and Urban Development, "Manufactured Home Construction and Safety Standards; Final Rule," *Federal Register,* 49(155), 31995–32013, 1984.
71. U.S. Environmental Protection Agency, *Assessment of Health Risks to Garment Workers and Certain Home Residents from Exposure to Formaldehyde,* U.S. EPA, Office of Pesticides and Toxic Substances, Washington, D.C., 1987.
72. U.S. Consumer Product Safety Commission, *Briefing Package on Formaldehyde Emissions from Urea-Formaldehyde Pressed Wood Products,* U.S. CPSC, Washington, D.C., 1986.
73. Kerns, W. D., et al., "Carcinogenicity of Formaldehyde in Rats and Mice After Long-Term Inhalation Exposure," *Cancer Research,* 43, 4382–4392, 1983.
74. "Federal Panel on Formaldehyde Report," *Environ. H. Persp.,* 43, 139–168, 1982.
75. International Agency for Research on Cancer, "Formaldehyde," *IARC Monographs on the Evaluation of the Carcinogenic Risk of Chemicals to Humans,* vol. 29, *Some Industrial Chemicals and Dyestuffs,* Lyons, France, World Health Organization, Geneva, Switzerland, pp. 345–389, 1982.
76. Riggin, R. M., and Petersen, B. A., "Sampling and Analysis Methodology for Semivolatile and Nonvolatile Organic Compounds in Air," *Indoor Air and Human Health,* R. B. Gammage, S. B. Kaye, and V. A. Jacobs (eds.), Lewis Publishers, Chelsea, Mich., pp. 351–358, 1985.
77. Sterling, D. A., "Volatile Organic Compounds in Indoor Air: An Overview of Sources, Concentrations, and Health Effects," *Indoor Air and Human Health,* R. B. Gammage, S. B. Kaye, and V. A. Jacobs (eds.), Lewis Publishers, Chelsea, Mich., pp. 387–402, 1985.
78. U.S. Environmental Protection Agency, *Report to Congress on Indoor Air Quality. Vol. II. Assessment and Control of Indoor Air Pollution,* EPA 400/1-89-001C, U.S. EPA, Washington, D.C., 1989.
79. U.S. Environmental Protection Agency, *Household Solvent Products: A National Usage Survey, Final Report,* U.S. EPA, Office of Pesticides and Toxic Substances, Washington, D.C., 1987.
80. Wallace, L. A., *The Total Exposure Assessment Methodology (TEAM) Study: Summary and Analysis: Vol. 1,* EPA/600/6-87-002a, U.S. EPA, Office of Research and Development, Washington, D.C., 1987.
81. Rosenberg, J., "Solvents," Chap. 27, *Occupational Medicine,* J. LaDou (ed.), Appleton & Lange, Norwalk, Conn., 1990.
82. Hodgson, M. A., "Health Risks of Indoor Pollutants," *IAQ 88, Engineering Solutions to Indoor Air Problems,* ASHRAE, Atlanta, Ga., pp. 284–293, 1988.
83. Wallace, L. A., "Cancer Risks from Organic Chemicals in the Home," *Environmental Risk Management: Is Analysis Useful? Proceedings,* Air Pollution Control Association, Chicago, Ill., pub. no. 50-55, 1986.
84. Tancrede, M., et al., "The Carcinogenic Risk of Some Organic Vapors: A Theoretical Survey," *Atm. Environ.,* 21(10), 2187–2205, 1987.
85. Mølhave, L., Bach, B., and Pedersen, O. F., "Human Reactions to Low Concentrations of Volatile Organic Compounds," *Env. Intl.,* 8, 117–127, 1987.
86. Kjaergaard, S., Mølhave, L., and Pedersen, O. F., "Human Reactions to Indoor Air Pollution: n-Decane," *Indoor Air '87, Vol. 1, Volatile Organic Compounds, Combustion Gases, Particles and Fibres, Microbiological Agents,* Oraniendruck GmbH, Berlin, Germany, pp. 97–101, 1987.
87. Ashford, N. A., and Miller, C. S., *Chemical Sensitivity. A Report to the New Jersey State Department of Health,* December 1989.
88. Feeley, J. C., "Impact of Indoor Air Pathogens on Human Health," Chap. 12, *Indoor Air and Human Health,* R. B. Gammage and S. V. Kaye (eds.), Lewis Publishers, Chelsea, Mich., 1985.

89. Riley, E. C., Murphy, G., and Riley, R. L., "Airborne Spread of Measles in a Suburban Elementary School," *Am. J. Epidemiol.*, 107, 421–432, 1978.
90. Brundage, J. F., et al., "Building-Associated Risk of Febrile Acute Respiratory Diseases in Army Trainees," *JAMA*, 259(14), 2108–2112, 1988.
91. Skaliy, P., and McEachern, H. V., "Survival of Legionnaires' Disease Bacterium in Water," *Ann. Intern. Med.*, 90, 662–663, 1979.
92. Imperato, P. J., "Legionellosis and the Indoor Environment," *Bull. N.Y. Acad. Med.*, 57(10), 922–935, 1981.
93. Band, J. D., et al., "Epidemic Legionnaires' Disease," *JAMA*, 245(23), 2404–2407, 1981.
94. Fraser, D. W., et al., "Legionnaires' Disease. Description of an Epidemic of Pneumonia," *N. Engl. J. Med.*, 297, 1189–1203, 1977.
95. Fang, G. D., et al., (abstract) "A Prospective Multi-Center Study of 359 Cases of Community-Acquired Pneumonia," *American Society of Infectious Diseases*, 1988.
96. Glick, T. H., et al., "Pontiac Fever: An Epidemic of Unknown Etiology in a Health Department. I. Clinical and Epidemiologic Aspects," *Am. J. Epidemiol.*, 107, 149–160, 1978.
97. Burge, H. A., "Environmental Allergy: Definition, Causes, Control," *IAQ 88. Engineering Solutions to Indoor Air Problems*, ASHRAE, Washington, D.C., 1988.
98. Reed, C. F., "Allergic Agents," *Bull. N.Y. Acad. Med.*, 57(10), 897–906, 1981.
99. Parkes, W. R., *Occupational Lung Disorders*, 2d ed., Butterworths, London, England, 1982.
100. Arnow, P. M. et al., "Early Detection of Hypersensitivity Pneumonitis in Office Workers," *Am. J. Med.*, 64, 236–242, 1974.
101. Gamble, J., et al., "Building-Related Respiratory Symptoms: Problems in Identification," *IAQ 86. Managing Indoor Air for Health and Energy Conservation*, ASHRAE, Atlanta, Ga., pp. 16–30, 1986.
102. Kreiss, K., "The Epidemiology of Building-Related Complaints and Illness," *Occupational Medicine: State of the Art Reviews*, 4(4), 575–592, 1989.
103. Parrott, W. F., and Blyth, W., "Another Causal Factor in the Production of Humidifier Fever," *J. Soc. Occup. Med.*, 30, 63–68, 1980.
104. Edwards, J. H., "Microbial and Immunological Investigations and Remedial Action After an Outbreak of Humidifier Fever," *Br. J. Ind. Med.*, 37, 55–62, 1980.
105. Rylander, R., et al., "Humidifier Fever and Endotoxin Exposure," *Clin. Allergy*, 8, 511–516, 1978, and "Airborne Endotoxins and Humidifier Disease," *Clin. Allergy*, 14, 109–112, 1984.
106. Kreiss, K., and Hodgson, M. J., "Building Associated Epidemics," Chap. 6, *Indoor Air Quality*, P. J. Walsh, C. S. Dudney, and E. D. Copenhaver (eds.), CRC Press, Boca Raton, FL, 1984.
107. Finnegan, M. J. et al., "The Sick Building Syndrome: Prevalence Studies," *Br. Med. J.*, 289, 1573–1575, 1984.
108. Highsmith, V. R., et al., "Indoor Particle Concentrations Associated with the Use of Tap Water in Portable Humidifiers," *Environ. Sci. Technol.*, 22(9), 1109–1112, 1988.
109. Tovey, E. R., et al., "Mite Faeces are a Major Source of House Dust Allergens," *Nature*, 289, 592–593, 1981.
110. Reed, C. E., and Swanson, M. C., "Indoor Allergens: Identification and Quantification," *Indoor Air. Vol. 1. Recent Advances in the Health Sciences and Technology*, Swedish Council for Building Research: Stockholm, Sweden, pp. 99–108, 1984.
111. Korsgaard, J., "Preventive Measures in House-Dust Allergy," *Am. Rev. Resp. Dis.*, 125, 80–84, 1982.
112. Arlian, L. G., et al., "The Prevalence of House Dust Mites, *Dermatophadoides spp*, and Associated Environmental Conditions in Homes in Ohio," *J. Allergy Clin. Immunol.*, 69, 527, 1982.
113. Burge, H. A., "Fungus Allergens," *Clin. Rev. Allergy*, 3, 319, 329, 1985.
114. Rijckaert, G., "Exposure to Fungi in Modern Homes," *Allergy*, 36, 277–279, 1981.
115. Gravesen, S., et al., "Demonstration of Microorganisms and Dust in Schools and Offices," *Allergy*, 41, 520–525, 1986.

116. Burge, H. A., et al., "Microbial Prevalence in Domestic Humidifiers," *Appl. Environ. Microbiol.,* 39(4), 840–844, 1980.
117. Kozak, P. P. et al., "Endogenous Mold Exposure: Environmental Risk to Atopic and Nonatopic Patients," *Indoor Air and Human Health,* R. B. Gammage and S. V. Kaye (eds.), Lewis Publishers, Chelsea, Mich., 1985.
118. Holmberg, K., "Indoor Mould Exposure and Health Effects," *Indoor Air '87. Vol. 1. Volatile Organic Compounds, Combustion Gases, Particles and Fibers, Microbiological Agents,* Oraniendruck GmbH, Berlin, W. Germany, pp. 637–645, 1987.
119. Burge, H. A., et al., "Evaluation of Indoor Plantings as Allergen Exposure Sources," *J. Allergy Clin. Immunol.,* 70(2), 101–108, 1980.
120. Rafferty, Patrick J. (ed.), *The Industrial Hygienist's Guide to Indoor Air Quality Investigations,* The American Industrial Hygiene Association, Technical Committee on Indoor Environmental Quality, Fairfax, Va., 1993.
121. *Ibid.,* p. 3.
122. *Ibid.,* pp. 3–4.
123. *Ibid.,* p. 4.
124. *Ibid.,* p. 5.
125. *Managing Asbestos in Place: A Building Owner's Guide to Operations and Maintenance Programs for Asbestos-Containing Materials* (Green Book), U.S. EPA, Office of Pesticides and Toxic Substances, Washington, D.C., 20T-2003, July 1990.
126. Clarkin, M., and Brennan, T., *Radon-Resistant Construction Techniques for New Residential Construction,* U.S. EPA, Office of Research and Development, Washington, D.C., EPA/625/2-91/032, February 1991.
127. Rafferty, Patrick J. (ed.), pp. 1–67.
128. *Ibid.,* p. 10.
129. *Ibid.,* pp. 7–8.
130. *Ibid.,* p. 11.
131. *Guidance for Controlling Asbestos-Containing Materials in Buildings* (Purple Book), U.S. EPA, Office of Pesticides and Toxic Substances, Washington, D.C., EPA 560/5-85-024, June 1985.
132. "More EMF-Health Risk Research Needed; Experts Provide Some Simple Tips to Avoid Exposure," *Indoor Air Review,* April 1993, p. 20.
133. Rafferty, p. 16.
134. *Ibid.,* p. 15.
135. *Ibid.,* pp. 16–18.
136. *Ibid.,* pp. 25–26.
137. *Ibid.,* p. 26.
138. *Ibid.,* p. 25.
139. *Ibid.,* pp. 66–67.
140. EPA/NIOSH, *Building Air Quality: A Guide for Building Owners and Facility Managers,* p. 76.
141. *Design and Protocol for Monitoring Indoor Air Quality,* N. L. Nagda and J. P. Harper (eds.), American Society for Testing and Materials, Philadelphia, 1989, p. 243.
142. Roberts, J. D., and Caserio, M. C., *Modern Organic Chemistry,* W. A. Benjamin, New York, 1967, p. 3.
143. *The Condensed Chemical Dictionary,* 9th ed., rev. by Gessner G. Hawley, Van Nostrand Reinhold, New York, 1977, p. 449.
144. *Ibid.,* p. 25.
145. *Ibid.,* p. 74.
146. *Ibid.,* p. 697.
147. *Design and Protocol for Monitoring Indoor Air Quality,* p. 139.
148. *The Condensed Chemical Dictionary,* p. 196.
149. *Ibid.,* p. 696.
150. *Ibid.,* p. 921.
151. U.S. Environmental Protection Agency, 1989 *Compendium of Methods for the Determination of Air Pollutants in Indoor Air.* Draft. U.S. EPA, Atmospheric

Research and Exposure Assessment Laboratory, Office of Research and Development: Research Triangle Park, N.C., 1989.

152. Rafferty, Patrick S. (ed.), p. 28.

153. *Ibid.,* p. 29.

154. U.S. Environmental Protection Agency, U.S. Public Health Service, National Environmental Health Association, *Introduction to Indoor Air Quality: A Self-Paced Learning Module,* EPA/400/3-91/002, July 1991, pp. 64–76.

155. Nader, J. S., Lauderdale, J. F., and McCammon, C. S., "Direct Reading Instruments for Analyzing Airborne Gases and Vapors," Chap. V, *Air Sampling Instruments,* 6th ed. American Conference of Governmental Industrial Hygienists. Cincinnati, Ohio, 1983.

156. U.S. Environmental Protection Agency, *Quality Assurance Handbook for Air Pollution Measurement Systems. Volume I—Principles.* U.S. EPA, Quality Assurance and Environmental Monitoring Laboratory, Office of Research and Development: Research Triangle Park, N.C., 1975.

157. U.S. Environmental Protection Agency, *Quality Assurance Handbook for Air Pollution Measurement Systems. Volume II—Ambient Air Specific Methods.* (Rev. July 1984 and September 1985) EPA-600/477-027a. U.S. EPA, Environmental Monitoring Systems Laboratory, Office of Research and Development: Research Triangle Park, N.C., 1977.

158. U.S. Environmental Protection Agency, *Interim Guidelines and Specifications for Preparing Quality Assurance Project Plans.* EPA QAMS-005/80. U.S. EPA, Office of Monitoring Systems and Quality Assurance, Office of Research and Development: Washington, D.C., 1980.

159. GEOMET Technologies, Inc., "Quality Assurance Plan for Indoor Environment Program," GEOMET Report No. ES-1528, GEOMET Technologies, Inc., Germantown, Md., 1985.

160. Taylor, J. K. (ed.), *Sampling and Calibration for Atmospheric Measurements,* ASTM STP 957, American Society for Testing and Materials, Baltimore, Md., 1987.

161. Katz, M. (ed.), *Methods of Air Sampling and Analysis,* 2d. ed., American Public Health Association, Washington, D.C., 1977.

162. U.S. National Institute for Occupational Safety and Health, *NIOSH Manual of Analytical Methods,* 3d ed., P. M. Eller (ed.), NIOSH, Cincinnati, Ohio, 1984.

3

Mechanical Engineering and IAQ

3.1 Introduction

In 1987, NIOSH conducted a study of 529 facilities whose occupants had complaints regarding IAQ. The results of this survey were documented in the much-quoted ranking of the major causes of IAQ ,as follows:[1]

Inadequate ventilation (53 percent)

Inside contamination (15 percent)

Outside contamination (10 percent)

Microbiological contamination (5 percent)

Building materials contamination (4 percent)

Unknown (13 percent)

Clearly the data indicated that a majority of IAQ problems in the tested facilities was caused by inadequate ventilation. The ASHRAE 62-1989 Standard: Ventilation for Acceptable Indoor Air Quality, published in 1989, supported the NIOSH results. It was the publication of this standard in 1989 that revised the recommended minimum ventilation requirements for commercial office buildings from a value of 5 cfm per person, the ASHRAE 62-1973 Standard, to 15 cfm per person.[2] As could be expected from such a drastic revision in design practice (a three-fold increase in a minimum recommended design value), facilities designed and constructed between 1973 and 1989 suddenly were considered to be inadequately ventilated. The minimum ventilation requirements used by HVAC design engineers as an acceptable design recommendation for nearly two decades were suddenly viewed as a deficient design practice and, as NIOSH so substantiated, a major cause of IAQ problems.

Experience and research have contributed new thinking to the 1987 NIOSH study, which attributed inadequate ventilation as a cause of poor IAQ. NIOSH is due to publish new findings as a result of their further investigations of IAQ problems in public facilities. Increasing the amount of ventilation air is a solution for diluting airborne contaminants—the real causes of IAQ problems—prior to building occupants' exposure to the contaminants. Inadequate ventilation is not the problem. Contaminants are the problem. Ventilation is a solution.

Driven by energy conservation concerns, there were advances in building materials and construction technology during the 1970s. Thermal resistivity values of insulation materials improved. At the same time, the demand for energy conservation dictated that buildings be designed with tighter envelopes—with the use of inoperable windows, weatherstripping, and sealants—in an effort to reduce outdoor air infiltration.

ASHRAE and the construction building materials industry were in agreement: Design buildings to save energy; bring in a minimum amount of outside air (just enough to dilute body odors); and create the "tight" building with energy expenditure at a minimum. The IAQ issues faced today are found primarily in buildings that were constructed during the use of ASHRAE 62-1973 and ASHRAE 62-1981 (roughly from the early 1970s to the late 1980s) and in older buildings that were renovated during this time. Energy conservation measures are important and necessary, but good IAQ should not be compromised to achieve their benefits.

This chapter will discuss how the HVAC system can affect IAQ in two ways. First, the HVAC system can be the *source* of indoor air contamination due to dirt and moisture buildup caused by improper maintenance or equipment age. Second, the HVAC system can act as the *pathway* through which other contaminants enter the airstream and are circulated throughout the building.

The three basic variables that are controlled by the commercial HVAC system are ventilation, temperature, and humidity. These three variables are interrelated and must be balanced to maintain a comfort level for the occupants. If one of these factors is controlled improperly, occupant comfort and IAQ can be in jeopardy.

3.1.1   Ventilation

ASHRAE 62-1989 is the widely accepted standard that most U.S. HVAC design firms utilize for minimum outside air design requirements for commercial buildings. Many building codes, such as the Standard Building Code, have officially incorporated ASHRAE 62-

1989 by reference, thereby making minimum ventilation standards an enforceable regulation.

Ventilation, or outdoor, air is important to the HVAC design engineer for two reasons: (1) Ventilation air is a means of controlling indoor air contamination through dilution with fresh, "uncontaminated" (or "clean") outdoor air, and (2) additional ventilation air has an impact on the energy consumption of the building's heating and cooling equipment.

There are several terms that describe the amount of ventilation air in a building. Bearg lists five evaluation "yardsticks." The term *cfm of outdoor air* refers to the absolute quantity of outside air. *Percentage of outdoor air in the supply air* is a calculation of the mixture of outdoor air and air recirculated from the building, both of which combine to achieve total air volume. Buildings are generally operated with a minimum setting of outdoor air at 15 to 20 percent of the total supply air. *CFM of outdoor air per person* is a calculation where the absolute quantity of outdoor air being delivered is divided by the number of people present or potentially present. ASHRAE 62-1989 lists minimum recommended ventilation rates expressed in these units. *CFM of outdoor air per square foot* expresses the ventilation rate in terms of outdoor air per area or space. This recognizes that people are not the only source of contaminants in a building. *Air changes per hour of ventilation* is an expression of the quantity of outdoor air divided by the building volume. These units express the rate at which the ventilation system actually dilutes and removes the air contaminants present in the space.[3]

The emphasis beginning in 1973 was on the *minimum* introduction of outdoor air in an effort to minimize the impact on the energy required to heat or cool the outdoor air used for ventilation. The recommended amount of ventilation air was based on such criteria as the amount of air required to expel exhaled air, to remove moisture from indoor air, and to maintain CO_2 levels below established limits. It is important to note that while CO_2 itself is not considered a contaminant at these established levels, it is considered to be a surrogate, or indicator, for adequate ventilation within a space. Research was also conducted investigating acceptable minimum ventilation rates required to reduce body-generated odors while maintaining comfortable levels of temperature and humidity (see Fig. 3.1). The basic parameter used by ASHRAE to determine minimum outside air requirements is the concentration of CO_2 generated by occupants in the space. The concentration of CO_2 in a steady-state condition is given by

$$C_i = \frac{C_o + S}{Q}$$

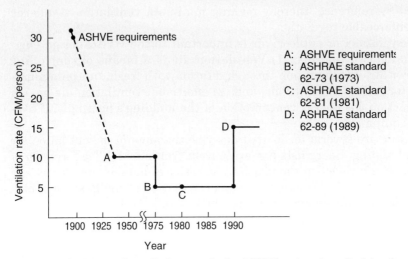

Figure 3.1 Evolution of ventilation standards. ASHVE = American Society of Heating and Ventilating Engineers. (*Based on* IAQ and HVAC Workbook *by D. Jeff Burton, IVE, Inc., 1993, p. 1. Used with permission of IVE, Inc., Bountiful, Utah.*)

where C_i = concentration of CO_2 inside the space

C_o = concentration of CO_2 outdoors

S = generation rate of CO_2

Q = ventilation rate (outside air only).[4]

ASHRAE 62-1989 establishes two procedures for determining an acceptable ventilation rate. The Ventilation Rate Procedure specifies a minimum ventilation rate based upon the space functions within given building types. The Ventilation Rate Procedure tables are derived from respiration rates, which are based on occupants' activities. This procedure that established the 15 cfm per person minimum in 1989 is the same as used by ASHRAE in 1973 that established a 5 cfm per person minimum, except that the acceptable concentration of CO_2 allowed inside the space was reduced from 0.25 percent in 1973 to 0.1 percent in the 1989 Standard (0.1 percent corresponds to maintaining indoor CO_2 levels below 1000 ppm; 0.25 percent corresponds to maintaining levels below 2500 ppm). The ASHRAE requirements for minimum ventilation rates, summarized in Table 3.1, indicate that the more active the building occupants are, the more outside air should be introduced due to their increased metabolism and subsequent increased generation rate of CO_2.

The second procedure described by ASHRAE 62-1989 is the Indoor Air Quality Procedure. This procedure requires maintaining certain indoor air contaminants below specified values. The "certain" contam-

TABLE 3.1 Outdoor Air Requirements for Ventilation*

Commercial Facilities (Offices, Stores, Shops, Hotels, Sports Facilities)

Application	Estimated maximum† occupancy P/1000 ft² or 100 m²	Outdoor air requirements						Comments
		cfm/ person	L/s‡ person	cfm/ft²	L/s · m²	cfm/room	L/s · room	
Dry cleaners, laundries								Dry-cleaning processes may require more air.
Commercial laundry	10	25	13					
Commercial dry cleaner	30	30	15					
Food and beverage service								
Dining rooms	70	20	10					
Cafeteria, fast food	100	20	10					
Bars, cocktail lounges	100	30	15					Supplementary smoke-removal equipment may be required.
Kitchens (cooking)	20	15	8					Makeup air for hood exhaust may require more ventilating air. The sum of the outdoor air and transfer air of acceptable quality from adjacent spaces shall be sufficient to provide an exhaust rate of not less than 1.5 cfm/ft² (7.5 L/s · m²).
Hotels, motels, resorts, dormitories								Independent of room size.
Bedrooms						30	15	
Living rooms						30	15	
Baths						35	18	Installed-capacity for intermittent use.
Lobbies	30	15	8					
Conference rooms	50	20	10					
Assembly rooms	120	15	8					See also food and beverage services, merchandising, barber and beauty shops, garages.
Dormitory sleeping areas	20	15	8					

TABLE 3.1 Outdoor Air Requirements for Ventilation* (Continued)

Commercial Facilities (Offices, Stores, Shops, Hotels, Sports Facilities)

Application	Estimated maximum† occupancy P/1000 ft² or 100 m²	Outdoor air requirements cfm/person	L/s‡ person	cfm/room (cfm/ft²)	L/s·room (L/s·m²)	Comments
Offices						
Office space	7	20	10			Some office equipment may require local exhaust.
Reception areas	60	15	8			
Telecommunication centers and data entry areas	60	20	10			
Conference rooms	50	20	10			Supplementary smoke-removal equipment may be required.
Public spaces						
Corridors and utilities				0.05	0.25	
Public restrooms, cfm/wc or cfm/urinal		50	25			
Locker and dressing rooms	70			0.5	2.5	Normally supplied by transfer air. Local mechanical exhaust with no recirculation recommended.
Smoking lounge		60	30			
Elevators				1.00	5.0	Normally supplied by transfer air.
Retail stores, sales floors, and show room floors						
Basement and street	30			0.30	1.50	
Upper floors	20			0.20	1.00	
Storage rooms	15			0.15	0.75	
Dressing rooms				0.20	1.00	
Malls and arcades	20			0.20	1.00	
Shipping and receiving	10			0.15	0.75	
Warehouses	5			0.05	0.25	Normally supplied by transfer air, local mechanical exhaust; exhaust with no recirculation recommended.
Smoking lounge	70	60	30			

Application	Estimated Maximum Occupancy P/1000 ft²	cfm/person	L/s·person	cfm/ft²	L/s·m²	Comments
Specialty shops						
Barber	25	15	8			
Beauty	25	25	13			
Reducing salons	20	15	8			
Florists	8	15	8			Ventilation to optimize plant growth may dictate requirements.
Clothiers, furniture				0.30	1.50	
Hardware, drugs, fabric	8	15	8			
Supermarkets	8	15	8			
Pet shops				1.00	5.00	
Sports and amusement						
Spectator areas	150	15	8			When internal combustion engines are operated for maintenance of playing surfaces, increased ventilation rates may be required.
Game rooms	70	25	13			
Swimming pools (pool and deck area)				0.50	2.50	Higher values may be required for humidity control.
Playing floors (gymnasium)	30	20	10			
Ballrooms and discos	100	25	13			
Bowling alleys (seating areas)	70	25	13			
Theaters						
Ticket booths	60	20	10			
Lobbies	150	20	10			
Auditorium	150	15	8			
Stages, studios	70	15	8			Special ventilation will be needed to eliminate special stage effects (e.g., dry ice vapors, mists, etc.)
Transportation						
Waiting rooms	100	15	8			
Platforms	100	15	8			
Vehicles	150	15	8			Ventilation within vehicles may require special considerations.

TABLE 3.1 Outdoor Air Requirements for Ventilation* (Continued)

		Commercial Facilities (Offices, Stores, Shops, Hotels, Sports Facilities)				
	Estimated maximum† occupancy P/1000 ft² or 100 m²	Outdoor air requirements				Comments
Application		cfm/ person	L/s‡ person	cfm/ft²	L/s · m²	
		Institutional Facilities				
Education						
Classroom	50	15	8			
Laboratories	30	20	10			Special contaminant control systems may be required for processes or functions including laboratory animal occupancy.
Training shop	30	20	10			
Music rooms	50	15	8			
Libraries	20	15	8			
Locker rooms				0.50	2.50	
Corridors				0.10	0.50	
Auditoriums	150	15	8			
Smoking lounges	70	60	30			Normally supplied by transfer air. Local mechanical exhaust with no recirculation recommended.
Hospitals, nursing and convalescent homes						
Patient rooms	10	25	13			Special requirements or codes and pressure relationships may determine minimum ventilation rates and filter efficiency. Procedures generating contaminants may require higher rates.
Medical procedure	20	15	8			
Operating rooms	20	30	15			
Recovery and ICU	20	15	8			
Autopsy rooms				0.50	2.50	Air shall not be recirculated into other spaces.
Physical therapy	20	15	8			

Correctional facilities			
Cells	20	20	10
Dining halls	100	15	8
Guard stations	40	15	8

*Prescribes supply rates of acceptable outdoor air required for acceptable IAQ. These values have been chosen to control CO_2 and other contaminants with an adequate margin of safety and to account for health variations among people, varied activity levels, and a moderate amount of smoking. Rationale of CO_2 control is presented in App. D of ASHRAE Standard 62-1989.

†Net occupiable space.

‡L/s = liters per second.

SOURCE: Based on ASHRAE Standard 62-1989, Table 2. ©1989 American Society of Heating, Refrigerating and Air-Conditioning Engineers, Inc., Atlanta, GA. Used by permission from *ANSI/ASHRAE 62-1989.*

inants and their levels are based upon concentrations determined by research of the U.S. EPA and the ACGIH and by such subjective evaluation as odor. The maintenance of the contaminant levels below specified values may be achieved through source control, the use of air cleaning, or local exhaust ventilation. In some instances, the minimum ventilation rate of 15 cfm per person required in the Ventilation Rate Procedure may be reduced by utilizing the Indoor Air Quality Procedure. ASHRAE 62-1989 includes a list of contaminants and their acceptable levels of concentration.

The increase of ventilation air is often recommended as a solution to IAQ problems in existing buildings in order to dilute indoor air contaminants. But, as will be further discussed in Sec. 3.3, the ramifications of "opening up" the HVAC system or building to additional outside air are many. The presence or absence of contaminants in the outdoor air must first be established. The U.S. EPA has set acceptable levels of certain contaminants in outside air as shown in Table 3.2. Other contaminants may be present at the building site where, by the act of increasing the outside air for ventilation, the HVAC system becomes a pathway through which these contaminants can travel into the indoor environment. An example is the case of an air-handling unit intake louver located in the ground floor of a building. Increasing the outdoor air from a 10 percent minimum position to a 20 percent minimum position could

TABLE 3.2 National Primary Ambient-Air Quality Standards for Outdoor Air as Set by the U.S. EPA

Contaminant	Long term			Short term		
	Concentration			Concentration		
	$\mu g/m^3$	ppm	Averaging	$\mu g/m^3$	ppm	Averaging
Sulfur dioxide	80	0.03	1 year	365*	0.14*	24 h
Particles (PM 10)	50[†]		1 year	150*		24 h
Carbon monoxide				40,000*	35*	1 h
Carbon monoxide				10,000*	9*	8 h
Oxidants (ozone)				235[‡]	0.12[‡]	1 h
Nitrogen dioxide	100	0.055	1 year			
Lead	1.5		3 months[§]			

*Not to be exceeded more than once per year.

[†]Arithmetic mean

[‡]Standard is attained when expected number of days per calendar year with maximal hourly average concentrations above 0.12 ppm (235 $\mu g/m^3$) is equal to or less than 1, as determined by App. H to subchapter C, 40 CFR 50.

[§]Three-month period is a calendar quarter.

SOURCE: ©1989 American Society of Heating, Refrigerating and Air-Conditioning Engineers, Inc., Atlanta, GA. Used with permission from *ANSI/ASHRAE 62-1989*.

allow a greater volume of contaminants such as pesticides, pollutants from traffic, or contaminants from nearby facilities to enter the indoor environment.

Another effect of increasing ventilation air into existing HVAC systems is the increased demand for heating and cooling because of the increased volume of outside air. A limiting factor may be the capacity of existing heating and cooling systems. Also as important as the energy required to heat and/or cool the outside air to acceptable supply air temperature is the energy required to dehumidify (in summer conditions) or humidify (in winter conditions) the outside air.

The implementation of air-to-air energy recovery systems will continue to increase as the additional ventilation requirements go into effect for new building design. The air-to-air system typically takes the form of a heat wheel which exchanges heat between the conditioned building exhaust air and the incoming outside air. Figure 3.2 is a heat wheel energy selection example. Tables 3.3 and 3.4 show energy operating costs for selected buildings in various U.S. cities, summarized from a 1990 study.

3.1.2   Temperature

The HVAC system is designed to provide and control ventilation, temperature, and humidity to the building occupants' environment. In addition to the ASHRAE Standard 62-1989: Ventilation for Acceptable Indoor Air Quality, ASHRAE has published the Standard 55-1992: Thermal Environmental Conditions for Human Occupancy, which recommends indoor air comfort levels for occupants, based upon occupant activity levels and clothing. ASHRAE states that the purpose of this standard is "to specify the combinations of indoor space environment and personal factors that will produce thermal environmental conditions acceptable to 80 percent or more of the occupants within a space."[5]

Temperature and humidity are often overlooked with regard to IAQ; however, their impact on occupant comfort and on occupant illnesses related to their fluctuations is not disputed. As will be discussed later in this chapter, a good HVAC investigation of buildings with known IAQ problems should begin with measurements and questions related to occupant temperature and humidity conditions.

ASHRAE publishes ranges of indoor temperature and humidity based upon specific building occupant clothing and activity levels. These temperature and humidity ranges are reproduced from the ASHRAE 55-1992 Standard in Fig. 3.3.

ASHRAE defines the operative temperature as the uniform temperature of an imaginary black enclosure in which an occupant would exchange the same amount of heat by radiation plus convection as in

Heat Wheel Energy Selection Example

Design Parameters:

Supply Air Flow:	12,000 CFM
Return Air Flow:	14,400 CFM
Outside Air:	95°F db / 78°F wb (0.0168 lb/lb)
Return Air:	75°F db / 61°F wb (0.0083 lb/lb)
O.A. Side Static Pressure:	3.50 in. W.G.
R.A. Side Static Pressure:	1.00 in.W.G.

Model HWL-96 is desired.

Step 1

Determine Energy Recovery Effectiveness

Effectiveness is the ratio of actual energy transfer to the maximum theoretical energy transfer. Effectiveness may be defined in regard to total, sensible or latent energy. Effectiveness can be quantified by the following equation:

Supply Air E	$= Vs (X1-X2) / Vmin (X1-X3)$	eq. #1
Exhaust Air E	$= Ve (X4-X3) / Vmin (X1-X3)$	eq. #2

Therefore

Supply Air Condition X2
$$= X1 - (E)(Vmin/Vs)(X1-X3) \qquad eq.\ \#3$$
Exhaust Air Condition X4
$$= X3 + (E)(Vmin/Ve)(X1-X3) \qquad eq.\ \#4$$

Air Flow Ratio $K = Vmax / Vmin$ Ratio   eq. #5

E	=	Effectiveness
Vs	=	Supply Air Flow (CFM)
Ve	=	Exhaust Air Flow (CFM)
$Vmax$	=	The larger of Vs or Ve
$Vmin$	=	The smaller of Vs or Ve
Xn	=	Dry bulb (T), humidity ratio (W), or enthalpy (h)

Typical Air Flow Arrangements

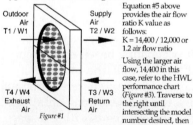

Outdoor Air T1 / W1 — Supply Air T2 / W2 — T4 / W4 Exhaust Air — T3 / W3 Return Air

Figure #1

Equation #5 above provides the air flow ratio K value as follows:
K = 14,400 / 12,000 or 1.2 air flow ratio

Using the larger air flow, 14,400 in this case, refer to the HWL performance chart (*Figure #3*). Traverse to the right until intersecting the model number desired, then read up until reaching the proper K ratio. Finally, traverse to the left until intersecting the resulting unit effectiveness. In this case, the unit effectiveness is 84.6% for the HWL-96.

Step 2

Determine Air Pressure Drop & Face Velocity

Traverse down on the chart to read the face velocity and air pressure drop. For this example, the face velocity is 600 FPM with an air pressure drop of 0.59 in W.G.

Step 3

Calculate Exit Air Conditions

Using equations #3 and #4, the supply and exhaust air conditions can now be calculated as follows:

Supply Air Condition:
$T2_{db} = 95°$ F - 0.846 x (14,400 / 14,400) x (95° F - 75° F)
$T2_{db} = 78.1°$ F
W2 = 0.0168 - 0.846 x (14,400 / 14,400) x (0.0168 - 0.0083)
W2 = 0.0096 lb/lb
Exhaust Air Condition:
$T4_{db} = 75°$ F + 0.846 x (12,000 / 14,400) x (95° F - 75° F)
$T4_{db} = 89.1°$ F
W4 = 0.0083 + 0.846 x (12,000 / 14,400) x (0.0168 - 0.0083)
W4 = 0.0143 lb/lb

Step 4

Determine the Purge Angle & Air Flow

An adjustable purge section is provided to avoid exhaust air cross-contamination into the supply air. An added small portion of outside air will be required for the purge operation. This air flow will have to be added to either the supply or exhaust air fan capacity, depending on the fan arrangements. For the purge to operate properly, the outside air side of the energy wheel must be positive pressure in respect to the return air side. *Figure #2* demonstrates three fan locations that provide effective purge operation. The fourth fan arrangement must not be used if cross-contamination is a concern.

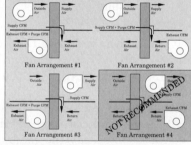

Figure #2

To determine the purge angle and air flow, the pressure differential between the outside and the return air sides of the wheel must be calculated with the following equation:

$$Pressure\ Differential = P_{oa} - P_{na} \qquad eq.\ \#6$$

Referring to *Figure #4*, locate the intersection of the pressure differential and the model number. Traversing to the top determines the required purge angle and traversing to the left determines the required purge air flow.

For this example,
Pressure Differential   =   3.50 - 1.00 = 2.50 in. W.G.
Wheel Model Number   =   HWL-96

Referring to *Figure #4*, the required purge angle is 2.5° and the purge air flow is 1,300 CFM.

Figure 3.2 Heat wheel energy selection example. (*From Governair Air-Conditioning product literature. Used with permission of Governair Air-Conditioning, Inc., Oklahoma City, Okla.*)

TABLE 3.3 Summary of Building Characteristics

	Medium office	Small office
Size	4,524 m² (48,680 ft²)	209 m² (2,250 ft²)
Shape	3 floors, rectangular	1 floor, square
Construction	Steel frame superstructure, 4-in precast concrete walls	Wood frame, brick veneer
Glazing	36% of wall area, equally distributed	50% north and south, 10% west, 3% east
Operation	8 a.m. to 6 p.m. weekdays, with some evening work, 30% occupancy on Saturday; closed Sundays and holidays	Identical to medium office
Thermostat settings	24.4°C (76°F) cooling 22.2°C (72°F) heating (night and week-end setback) 16.7°C (62°F)	Identical to medium office
Internal loads	25.8 W/m² (2.4 W/ft²) lighting 5.4 W/m² (0.5 W/ft²) equipment	Identical to medium office
Occupancy	13.7 m²/person (148 ft²/person)	11.0 m²/person (118 ft²/person)
HVAC air-side	Dual-duct system with variable speed fan; dry bulb economizer set at 18.9°C (66°F)	Variable air volume, direct expansion, rooftop unit; dry bulb economizer set at 18.9°C (66°F)
Heating plant	Gas-fired hot water boiler (eff. = 75%)	Baseboard electric
Cooling plant	Air-cooled, hermetic reciprocating chiller (coefficient of performance = 2.4)	Direct-expansion (coefficient of performance = 2.8)

SOURCE: "The HVAC Costs of Increased Fresh Air Ventilation Rates in Office Buildings, Part 2," *Proceedings of the 5th International Conference on Indoor Air Quality and Climate, Indoor Air '90*, Toronto, Canada, July, 1990. Used with permission of J. Eto.

TABLE 3.4 Annual Energy Operating Cost Impacts

	5 L/s person = 10 cfm/person (1987$/m²)	Percentage increase from 5 L/s person = 10 cfm/person				
		7.5 L/s person = 15 cfm/person	10 L/s person = 20 cfm/person	12.5 L/s person = 25 cfm/person	15 L/s person = 30 cfm/person	17.5 L/s person = 35 cfm/person
Small office						
Atlanta	0.16	2.0	4.0	6.4	8.7	11.3
Boston	0.35	3.8	8.5	14.0	19.0	25.3
Chicago	0.41	1.3	2.8	5.4	8.0	10.9
Dallas	0.13	1.9	3.7	5.8	8.3	11.3
Miami	0.21	1.9	3.5	5.4	7.1	9.0
Minneapolis	0.14	3.6	7.4	11.9	16.0	20.6
New York	0.27	2.7	5.8	9.5	13.1	17.4
San Diego	0.17	1.3	2.5	3.8	5.0	6.5
Seattle	0.06	2.9	6.2	10.2	14.3	19.1
Washington	0.25	1.2	2.3	3.7	5.0	6.5
Medium office						
Atlanta	0.13	2.1	4.1	6.2	8.2	10.4
Boston	0.13	1.6	3.2	4.9	6.8	9.2
Chicago	0.13	1.6	3.1	4.8	6.8	9.1
Dallas	0.14	2.1	4.2	6.4	8.6	10.8
Miami	0.14	2.8	5.7	8.7	11.8	14.9
Minneapolis	0.14	1.2	2.9	5.0	7.5	10.2
New York	0.13	1.8	3.5	5.2	7.3	9.6
San Diego	0.12	0.9	1.7	2.5	3.3	4.2
Seattle	0.12	0.6	1.1	2.0	2.8	3.8
Washington	0.13	2.3	4.6	7.0	9.5	12.0

SOURCE: "The HVAC Costs of Increased Fresh Air Ventilation Rates in Office Buildings, Part 2," *Proceedings of the 5th International Conference on Indoor Air Quality and Climate, Indoor Air '90,* Toronto, Canada, July, 1990. Used with permission of J. Eto.

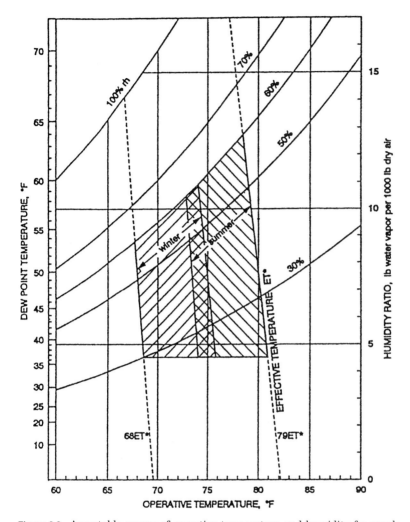

Figure 3.3 Acceptable ranges of operative temperature and humidity for people in typicl summer and winter clothing during light, primarily sedentary activity (≤1.2 met). The ranges are based on a 10 percent dissatisfaction criterion. (©1992 American Society of Heating, Refrigerating and Air-Conditioning Engineers, Inc., Atlanta, Ga. Used by permission from ANSI/ASHRAE 55-1992.)

the actual nonuniform environment. The difference in optimum operative temperatures for the indoor environment in summer and winter is due to the type and amount and, thus, the thermal insulation value, of clothing. The ranges of temperature and humidity are based upon a 10 percent dissatisfaction criterion.

Occupant activity is an important variable in adequately controlling temperature and humidity. The greater the activity level, the greater the increase in the metabolic level of the occupant. The control of temperature and humidity in the occupied space is very much dependent upon occupant activities and equipment which may reject heat into the indoor environment. The IAQ investigation should note any changes in use or equipment that have occurred in the occupied environment. The designer should understand occupant activity levels anticipated in spaces prior to calculating heating, cooling, and humidity loads for the HVAC unit.

Also affecting indoor comfort are such parameters as air distribution, temperature gradients, and radiant surface temperatures. Poor air distribution can cause local cooling of portions of the body; this condition is known as draft. Draft can many times be avoided or reduced by decreasing air velocity or increasing air temperature at the point of discomfort (usually where the occupant's skin is exposed). Temperature gradients occur more frequently in spaces with high ceilings. The layout of air-distribution grilles and diffusers can play an important role in proper air mixing and temperature control within a space. A radiant heat source acting as the sole source of heat within a space will create the most dramatic temperature gradient. The occupants closest to the radiant source may experience a much higher ambient temperature than those occupants only 10 ft away. For this reason, radiant heaters such as steam and electric baseboard types should not be used as the sole means of comfort space heating.

The classic example of occupant discomfort caused by temperature gradients is the case of a ducted heating system designed to supply warm air through diffusers from a ceiling height of 15 ft above occupant floor level. Due to the difference between the warm, heated supply air and the cool, ambient indoor air conditions on a cold day, the warm supply air has no chance of reaching the occupied level unless supplied with a greater-than-normal velocity. The tendency of warm supply air to cling to the ceiling is increased if system return grilles are ceiling mounted. This situation would at least be predicted to cause discomfort at the floor levels of the occupied space.

To improve the severe temperature gradient caused by high ceilings, return air grilles should be at the floor levels and in locations sufficient to pull the supply air from the ceiling area, through the occupied zones, and down to the floor level grille(s). Ceiling fans have also proven to be effective in pushing the warmer air down to occupant zone levels.

3.1.3 Humidity

There has been much research on the effects of humidity on occupant comfort. Relative humidity is the percentage of moisture in the air relative to the amount it could hold if saturated at the same tempera-ture. Not only can humidity affect how the occupant subjectively feels, but studies are indicating that occupants become more susceptible to adverse health conditions, such as allergies, based upon the humidity levels to which they are exposed. ASHRAE 55-1992 recommends that relative humidity in occupied spaces be maintained between 30 and 60 percent.[5] Such humidity control is often ignored by those who recom-mend additional outside air to flush indoor air contaminants. Increasing the amount of more humid outside air, as occurs in the summer months, can increase indoor humidity levels. This can cause moisture damage to interior finishes and can lead to an increased growth of microbiologicals. Likewise, increasing outside air in the low-humidity winter months can cause dehydrated mucous membranes, sinus irritation, headaches, and other adverse health effects. See Fig. 3.4 for optimum relative humidity ranges for health.

The effects of increased ventilation on humidity control is of special concern in hot, humid climates. Schools are particularly susceptible to the adverse effects of humidity in hot, humid climates. The minimum requirement in classrooms of 15 cfm per person may cause HVAC sys-tems serving the classrooms to provide minimum outside air capaci-

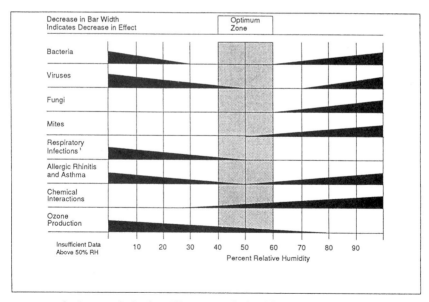

Figure 3.4 Optimum relative humidity ranges for health. (*Used with permission ©1985 American Society of Heating, Refrigerating and Air-Conditioning Engineers, Atlanta, Ga., from ASHRAE Transactions, Part 1B, 1985.*)

ties greater than 50 percent of their total supply air delivery.[6] Along with increased heating and cooling loads, humidity control becomes an important consideration.

3.2   Classifications of HVAC Systems

The HVAC system is at the heart of most IAQ issues. As discussed earlier, the lack of adequate ventilation has been documented by NIOSH to be a "cause" of IAQ problems in approximately 53 percent of buildings in a 1987 study. However, ventilation is now considered a means of solving IAQ problems, rather than the root cause. The professional investigating IAQ problems must, therefore, be familiar with the components and operations of HVAC systems in order to make an accurate diagnosis of IAQ problems and offer strategies for remediation. The HVAC system can affect IAQ by being a source of contamination or by serving as a pathway for other contaminants to be transported through a building. A variety of HVAC systems can be found in commercial buildings. Systems differ according to building size, the diversity of occupant activities, climate (and, subsequently, geographic location), and even building age, which can place restrictions on the amount of space available above the ceiling and can critically affect the requirements for certain types of HVAC systems. The following systems are discussed in terms of their installation and operation in commercial buildings. These systems have been included for discussion because they are those most commonly found in commercial buildings.

ASHRAE categorizes air-handling unit systems as either all-air, air-and-water, all-water systems, or as packaged unitary equipment systems. *All-air systems* provide cooling and heating in the air supplied by the system. Examples of all-air systems include:

Single zone (see Sec. 3.2.2)

Single zone with reheat (see Sec. 3.2.3)

Variable volume with reheat (see Sec. 3.2.4)

Dual duct (see Sec. 3.2.5)

Multizone (see Sec. 3.2.6)

Air-and-water systems utilize air and water which are distributed into the space where room or space terminals provide the control of supply air (referred to as *primary air*) and supply water (referred to as *secondary water*) to meet room conditions. An example is induction unit systems. The primary air supply in induction unit systems is typically designed for providing ventilation air to the space, and it is, therefore, critical for the IAQ investigator to verify the proper operation of the primary air handling unit.

All-water systems provide space conditioning by circulating chilled or hot water through fan coil units. Electric or steam heating coils can also be utilized in lieu of hot water. Failure to provide adequate ventilation air to spaces conditioned by fan coil units is common. Too often fan coil units are placed in locations where they only recirculate the air in the space. There must be a source of outside air provided for these systems or to the spaces conditioned by these systems so that ventilation air is supplied to the occupied zone. Examples of all-water systems include:

Two-pipe fan coil units (see Sec. 3.2.7)

Four-pipe fan coil units (see Sec. 3.2.8)

An IAQ problem that is inherent with all-water systems is that cooling coils are an integral part of the fan coil units, which are typically installed one per space. The increased number of cooling coils increases the opportunity for problems associated with condensation moisture, compared to the all-air systems. A common practice is to install an auxiliary drain pan below the fan coil unit to prevent excess condensation or cooling coil water leaks from damaging the building finishes. The presence of these auxiliary drain pans should be noted as an area of concern by the IAQ investigator, especially if these pans are located in an air pathway. The potential for standing water to accumulate within an air plenum significantly increases the possibility of microbiological contamination to be spread throughout the HVAC system. The potential for condensation and moisture problems located in the proximity of occupied spaces is an IAQ problem associated with all-water systems.

The IAQ investigator will also find that many designs utilizing all-water systems disregarded minimum ventilation requirements. All-air systems satisfy minimum ventilation requirements through the use of outside air intakes at the mixing plenum of a central air-handling unit. Because water system fan coil units are commonly scattered throughout buildings, sometimes in each occupied space, designers are faced with a much more challenging job of introducing fresh air to each of these units in a manner such that the ventilation air can be supplied into the occupied zone. Experience shows that the issue of providing ventilation air to occupied spaces was largely ignored in the design of all-water systems.

Packaged unitary systems are characterized as having factory-assembled components that include a refrigeration cycle (compressor, evaporator and condenser coils, and refrigerant piping). Components are matched to meet specific project and performance specifications. Examples of packaged unitary systems include:

Split systems (see Sec. 3.2.9)

Packaged rooftop units (see Sec. 3.2.10)

Heat pumps (air-to-air and water source)

Window units

Indoor unitary equipment

In commercial buildings, the IAQ investigator will encounter air systems more often than water or packaged unitary systems. However, all systems can be sources of IAQ problems and can act as pathways for IAQ contamination.

3.2.1 Central plant

The central plant provides the heating and cooling heat transfer medium (air/water) and energy source (electricity/gas) for the HVAC system(s). An understanding of the HVAC system begins in the central plant because the plant is the source of the mechanical equipment that provides heat via hot water or steam and cooling via chilled water or refrigerant to be distributed to the air-handling units, which may or may not be located in the central plant. It is, therefore, important for the IAQ investigator to determine how significantly the central plant figures into the IAQ equation. Is it a source of contamination, and, if so, how are the contaminants transported to occupied areas of the building? Is it a pathway through which contaminants are transmitted to other building areas? Or is a deficiency in central plant equipment affecting air quality conditions in other occupied areas? The IAQ investigator should consider these questions before plunging headlong into an exhaustive central plant investigation.

Descriptions of typical equipment most commonly found in the central plants of commercial buildings follow.

Boilers. Most commercial buildings have a boiler to provide heating. In fact, many central plants are commonly referred to as "the boiler room." Boilers generate either hot water or steam for heating applications. Hot water is transported from the boiler to the air-handling or terminal units by pumps and associated hydronic equipment. Steam boilers can generate steam at varying pressures [typically between 15 and 80 pounds per square inch (psi) for commercial applications] and transport the steam to heating coils through the pressurized piping system. Components of both hot water and steam boiler systems are listed below:

Hot water boilers

  Pumps

  Water strainers

  Expansion tanks

  Chemical feed systems

  Hot water supply and return piping (insulated)

  Boiler flue

Steam boilers

  Condensate return pumps

  Boiler feed units

  Heat exchangers or convertors (and associated pumps, piping, etc.)

  Chemical feed systems

  Steam supply and condensate return piping (note the presence of steam traps in condensate pipe)

  Boiler flue

Boilers can be equipped with burners that are gas fired, oil fired, coal, electric, or a combination burner (gas and oil fired, for example). Boilers equipped with stacks, or flues, typically need permits from local or state agencies that may require special exhaust/flue cleaning treatment and filtration. The IAQ professional should note the exhaust point of any boiler in relation to adjacent openings, especially outside air-intake openings for building air-handling systems.

Chillers. The refrigeration machines in the central plant are commonly referred to as chillers. Chillers are typically classified as centrifugal, reciprocating, or absorption machines, depending upon their compressor type. The chiller condensing units are classified as water cooled or air cooled based upon their method of heat rejection. A cooling tower which is often found in commercial applications is a heat-rejection device used as a component of a water-cooled condenser, which in turn may be a component of a centrifugal chiller system.

Refrigeration applications up to 60 tons (t) generally utilize reciprocating chillers. From 60 to 200 t, either reciprocating or centrifugal chillers are typically utilized. Above 200 t of capacity, centrifugal or absorption machines are utilized.[7] The term *chiller* in this text implies the refrigeration process of chilling water by circulation through the heat exchangers of a refrigeration machine. Typical components of the chiller system found in the central plant are listed below:

Refrigeration machine (condenser and evaporator)

Pumps

Water strainers

Expansion tanks

Chemical feed systems

Chilled water supply and return piping (insulated)

Cooling towers (or closed circuit coolers)

Pressure relief (purge) devices

Packaged equipment also may be referred to as refrigeration equipment because internal compressors and condensers do produce a refrigeration effect. However, these systems place the supply airstream in direct contact with the refrigeration process through the cooling coil, which acts as an evaporator in the refrigeration process. Therefore, equipment utilizing this type of direct expansion (DX) refrigeration process is rarely found in the central plant but is more commonly found in packaged equipment (see Secs. 3.2.9 and 3.2.10) that would be located closer to the area being conditioned.

Pumps and piping systems.   Any of a variety of pumps might be found in the central plant, if water is used as the heat transfer medium for heating and cooling. In general, IAQ contaminants are rarely traced to the actual design of water systems but are more related to the malfunctioning of these systems. The potential for leaks in piping systems or for condensate from exposed piping is of obvious importance to the IAQ investigator, especially when water has collected in areas in contact with the recirculated airstream. Components of piping systems that can be found in the central plant are listed below:

Chilled water pumps

Hot water pumps

Condenser water pumps

Domestic hot water pumps [many times found as a package system with the hot water storage tank(s)]

Domestic water pumps

Fire pump

Fuel oil pump

Expansion tanks

Hot water converters (or heat exchangers)

Condensate return pumps (found in steam boiler systems)

Strainers, valves, gauges

Piping

Piping systems for circulated water should be chemically treated to reduce the potential for algae buildup and corrosion within pipes which can impair water flow.

Miscellaneous central plant equipment.   Walking into a central plant can be intimidating to an IAQ investigator who has little experience. The array of piping, equipment, conduit, noise, odor, heat, and vibration can in itself be an environmental stressor that could cause worker discomfort. Other miscellaneous equipment and/or systems that can be found in the central plant are listed below. Their effects on IAQ are minimal unless they are operating improperly.

Control air compressor

Domestic hot water storage tanks

Chemical feed storage tanks and containers

Water softeners

Electrical switch gears and motor control panels

Emergency generator

Ventilation and exhaust fans and louvers

Air-handling units (see the following system descriptions)

3.2.2   Single-zone air-handling system

Figure 3.5 is a diagram of a single-zone air-handling system. The basic components of this unit are:

Air-handling unit

Air-distribution system

Central plant and controls

Air-handling unit.   Air enters the air-handling unit at the mixing plenum, where outside air and building return air mix to create the heat-transfer coil's entering air temperature (EAT). The IAQ investi-

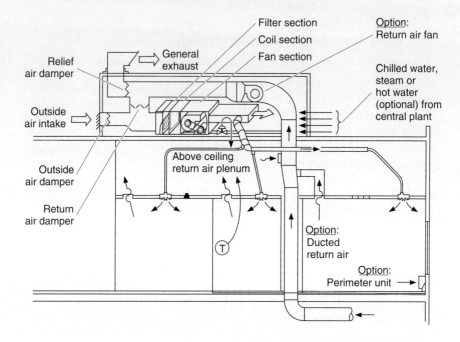

Figure 3.5 Single-zone air-handling system. (*Used with permission of Gobbell Hays Partners, Inc., Nashville, Tenn.*)

Characteristics:
1. One thermostat per air handler.
2. No reheat coil.
3. Draw-thru air handler is shown.
4. Relief air dampers are installed when air economizer is utilized.

gator typically is able to locate the outside air intake dampers and the return air dampers within the mixing plenum. Obviously, the relationship of these two dampers is critical to the investigation for determining the percentage of outside air entering the unit and, subsequently, being delivered to the occupied spaces.

The mixed air then enters the air-handling unit's filter section, where the mixed air passes through a filter prior to entering the coil section of the unit. Filter sections should be reasonably accessible to the investigator, and it is important to note the condition and type of filters. If this section is not accessible, this should alert the investigator that filter maintenance is difficult to perform and may not be occurring regularly. Filter replacement is usually recommended, depending upon the type of filter, at least three times a year.

The coil section of a single-zone air-handling unit has, as a minimum, a cooling coil, and, in most instances, a heating coil. If the heating coil is downstream of the air-handling unit and installed in the ductwork, this system is known as a reheat system (see Sec. 3.2.3). In colder climates or on systems requiring a large minimum outside air capacity, a heating coil might be in a preheat position. The preheat coil is designed to increase the entering air temperature from the mixing plenum temperature (for example, 30°F) to a temperature at the entering side of the air-handling unit's coil section that would prevent coil freezing (for example, 50°F). A heating coil in the air-handling unit or in the reheat position then warms the supply air to an acceptable temperature for space heating (for example, 90°F). Heating coils can be hot water, steam, or electric.

The fan section of the air-handling unit typically follows the coil section. The type of arrangement depicted in Fig. 3.5 (the fan section downstream of the coil section) is called a *draw-thru* configuration. If the fan section precedes the coil section, the configuration of the unit is called *blow-thru.*

Air-distribution system.   Ductwork leaves the fan section of the single-zone air-handling unit and is routed to the spaces to be conditioned. Diffusers and grilles are connected to the ductwork branch lines (typically above ceiling) and located in the space (typically in the ceiling) to provide adequate air movement at a supply air temperature to satisfy occupant comfort needs. Other air distribution components that might be found in the ductwork system of single-zone systems are fire, smoke, or combination fire and smoke dampers; manual or automatic volume dampers; and humidifiers. Dampers, when not properly functioning, can affect the thermal comfort of the occupants. Improperly functioning humidifiers can affect the thermal comfort of occupants and can introduce contaminants into the airstream.

Central plant and controls.   Heating and cooling for single-zone air-handling systems is typically provided by hot water or steam for heating and chilled water for cooling. If the heat transfer medium is a refrigerant, the system is referred to as a *split system* because the refrigeration system is contained within its own package (the condensing unit) and is separated, or split, from the air-handling unit (see Sec. 3.2.9).

The control of a single-zone air-handling system is activated from a room thermostat or sensor which regulates the operation of hot water and chilled water valves at the air-handling unit coil section. For single-zone systems, there is one thermostat for each air-handling unit. The operation of an economizer cycle (where 100 percent outside air is introduced through the system for "free cooling") can also be sequenced with the operation of the heating and cooling valves. The single-zone air-handling system is a constant air volume, variable temperature control system (i.e., the airflow capacity remains constant while the supply air temperature varies).

3.2.3 Single-zone air-handling system with reheat

Figure 3.6 is a diagram of a single-zone air-handling system with reheat. The basic components of this system are the same as the single-zone air-handling system:

Air-handling unit

Air-distribution system

Central plant and controls

Air-handling unit. The mixing plenum, filter sections, and fan sections of the single-zone unit with reheat are no different from the single-zone unit (see Sec. 3.2.2). The air-handling unit may have only a cooling coil. If a hot water or steam coil is located in the coil section of a reheat type system, it most commonly will be operated as a preheat coil. The reheat coil is located downstream of the cooling coil in the supply ductwork. One advantage of reheat systems is their ability to provide more individual space control. A single-zone air-handling system with reheat has independent "zones" of heating control rather than a single heating coil in the unit providing control for all spaces. Another aspect of the reheat system is the dehumidification that can be achieved by cooling the supply air prior to heating. These two aspects, individual zone control and dehumidification, make the reheat-type systems attractive to designers and building owners and popular for use in commercial buildings.

Air-distribution system. The air-distribution system on single-zone air-handling systems with reheat is similar to the single-zone system components with the addition of the reheat coils. Most single-zone systems are low-pressure supply systems, which means that the static pressure in the supply ductwork ranges from 0.1 in to a maximum of 2.5 in of water. Reheat coils in low-pressure supply ductwork systems are installed by transitioning from the supply ductwork to the reheat coil flange connection. Reheat coils are most commonly hot water but can also be electric or steam.

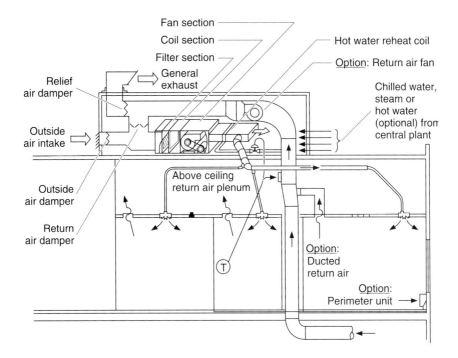

Characteristics:
    1. One thermostat per reheat coil.
    2. Reheat coils are normally used for the perimeter zones.
    3. Reheat could be by hot water or gas-fired duct furnace.
    4. Draw-thru air handler is shown.

Figure 3.6 Single-zone with reheat. (*Used with permission of Gobbell Hays Partners, Inc., Nashville, Tenn.*)

Central plant and controls. The central plant provides hot water, steam, and chilled water for the single-zone system with reheat in a similar manner as in the single-zone air-handling system. The heating piping systems that supplied the heating coil for the single-zone system at the air-handling unit will now supply reheat coils that are distributed at different locations in the supply ductwork.

The control of the single-zone air-handling systems with reheat is generally regulated by a discharge air sensor. This sensor is set so that it controls the cooling coil valve and the operation of outside air and mixed air dampers to maintain a constant temperature leaving the cooling coil section (typically 55°F). A room thermostat will then regulate the reheat coil control valve, which controls the capacity of the reheat coil to heat the entering air (typically 55°F) up to the designed leaving air temperature (typically 90 to 100°F) to maintain occupant thermal comfort levels. Economizer cycles are commonly found on these units.

3.2.4   Variable air volume systems (with hot water reheat)

Figure 3.7 is a diagram of a variable air volume (VAV) system with hot water reheat, which is perhaps the most prevalent system in commercial buildings. The components of the VAV system are similar to the other all-air systems:

Air-handling unit

Air-distribution system

Central plant and controls

Air-handling unit.   The basic configuration of the air-handling unit for the VAV system is no different from other all-air systems (see Sec. 3.2.2). However, a fan controller compensates for reduced cooling demand in the occupied spaces by reducing the air volume in the system. Airflow is typically regulated through a variable speed controller or inlet vanes. Critical in VAV system air-handling units from an IAQ perspective is the control and maintenance of minimum outside air as the total supply air volume is reduced.

Air-distribution system.   Supply air is controlled into the individual occupied space through volume dampers located in duct-mounted terminal units. The volume dampers are either pneumatically or electronically powered. Variable volume reheat systems have a heating coil (hot water or electric coil) in series with the volume damper and contained as a single manufactured terminal unit. Access doors should be installed in the ductwork on the coil side of the terminal box for maintenance of the coil. Duct pressures and velocities in VAV systems are substantially greater than other all-air system types.

Central plant and controls.   The central plant provides hot water, steam, and chilled water for the VAV system with reheat in a similar manner as in the single-zone air-handling system. The hot water heating piping system supplies reheat coils that are distributed at dif-

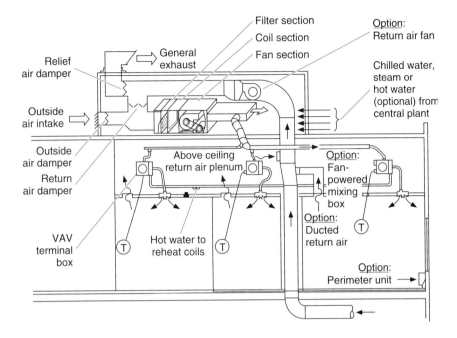

Figure 3.7 Variable air volume air-handling system. (*Used with permission of Gobbell Hays Partners, Inc., Nashville, Tenn.*)

Characteristics:

1. Simultaneous heating and cooling is possible.
2. VAV box zone control is achieved pneumatically or electrically.
3. Exterior zones are reheat zones, and interior zones are cooling only.
4. All VAV boxes have a minimum position setting for the outside air requirements.
5. Electric reheat is sometimes used in lieu of hot water reheat.
6. Static pressure sensors monitor building pressurization.

ferent locations (zones) in the supply ductwork. Systems located in colder climates or systems with a large minimum outside air capacity may have preheat coils installed in the central air-handling unit.

The control of the VAV air-handling system with reheat cooling coil is generally regulated by the room thermostat. A discharge air sensor is set to control the cooling coil valve and the operation of outside air and mixed air dampers to maintain a constant supply air temperature leaving the cooling coil section (typically 55°F.). A room thermostat will then regulate the sequencing of the reheat coil control valve and the position of the volume damper to satisfy the room load conditions. Economizer cycles are often found on these units. The supply fan speed is controlled by a system static pressure sensor located at a designated point in the supply ductwork (typically two-thirds the distance from the supply fan to the end of the main supply duct). As the pressure at the static pressure sensor increases due to volume dampers closing, the pressure controller signals the fan speed controller (inlet vanes or variable speed controller) to a reduced airflow setting, thus maintaining a constant pressure. The prevalent use of VAV systems is due to their ability to track building loads through the space thermostats, reducing the volume of air required to be supplied to the spaces with no loads and thus reducing the fan motor horsepower and electrical requirements for the air-handling unit fan.

3.2.5 Dual duct system

Figure 3.8 is a diagram of a dual-duct system. Although not commonly used in designs today, dual-duct systems may be found in many older buildings. The components of a dual-duct system are similar to those of other all-air systems:

Air-handling unit

Air-distribution system

Central plant and controls

Air-handling unit. The difference between a dual-duct air-handling unit and the air-handling units previously described in all-air systems is that heating and cooling coils are aligned in parallel position rather than in series position. This stacked alignment creates separate hot and cold decks within a single air-handling unit. From the air-handling unit fan section the air is distributed to the conditioned spaces through two ducts to a terminal mixing box. One duct supplies cold air and one supplies warm air, providing the capability for both heating and cooling at all times. A dual-duct reheat system will have the heating coil downstream of the fan rather than stacked on top of and parallel to the cooling coil. This allows the total supply air volume to pass through the cooling coil prior to the separation of ductwork into cold and warm air decks. The reheat coil is positioned in the hot air deck on the leaving air side of the fan.

Air-distribution system. The predominant aspect of dual-duct systems is the two supply air ducts that run from the fan section to the mixing box. The mixing boxes are equipped with volume dampers on both the cold and warm air supply duct inlets that blend the two airstreams until the room thermostat conditions are satisfied. Complications from this type of system exist in that leakage occurs at the mixing

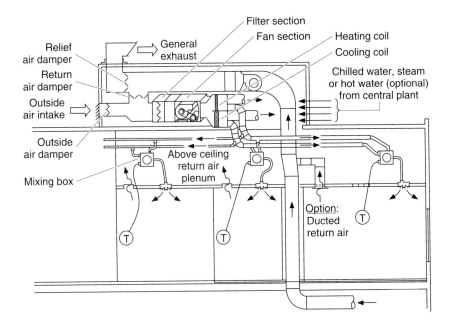

Relief air damper
Return air damper
Outside air intake
Outside air damper
Mixing box

General exhaust
Filter section
Fan section
Above ceiling return air plenum

Heating coil
Cooling coil
Chilled water, steam or hot water (optional) from central plant

Option: Ducted return air

Characteristics:
1. Simultaneous heating and cooling is possible.
2. VAV box control is achieved pneumatically or electrically.
3. All VAV boxes have a minimum position setting for the outside air requirements.

Figure 3.8 Dual duct air-handling system. (*Used with permission of Gobbell Hays Partners, Inc., Nashville, Tenn.*)

box dampers, and this leakage may cause supply air temperature to be unachievable. Mixing boxes can be provided as either variable volume or as constant volume, which is most common.

Central plant and controls.   The central plant provides hot water, steam, and chilled water or gas for the dual-duct system in a similar manner as other all-air air-handling systems. The heating and cooling piping systems will supply the air-handling unit at its central location rather than distributing hot water throughout the occupied spaces serving zone terminal boxes, unless it is a reheat system.

The control of the dual-duct air-handling system is generally maintained through the zone thermostat's control of the cold and warm air volume dampers at the mixing box terminal. The leaving air temperatures of the hot and cold decks are generally set according to outside and return air temperatures. For variable volume systems, the same control strategies apply as in standard VAV design (see Sec. 3.2.4).

3.2.6 Multizone air-handling system

Figure 3.9 is a diagram of a multizone air-handling system, which is another all-air system that is no longer commonly installed and is more likely to be found by the IAQ investigator in older buildings. The unique aspect of a multizone system is that all of the zone dampers are located at the air-handling unit rather than at a terminal position. The system components are similar to other all-air systems:

Air-handling unit

Air-distribution system

Central plant and controls

Air-handling unit. In multizone systems, the heating and cooling coil sections of the air-handling unit are configured similar to that of the dual-duct unit (i.e., the coils are stacked in parallel position). However, instead of having the mixing box of the dual-duct system, the multizone unit has a damper section containing zone dampers, one section for the cold deck and one for the warm deck, downstream of the coils section. The multizone unit is commonly configured in the blow-thru fan position. Multizone cooling coils can be either chilled water or DX packaged, commonly found on rooftop units. Heating can be provided by hot water or steam coils or by a gas furnace.

Air-distribution system. The dampers for each zone are contained in a damper section at the unit. Each zone is supplied by a dedicated duct-work system. Typical ductwork components for each zone of a multi-zone system are similar to those of single-zone systems (see Sec. 3.2.2). The multizone unit is generally limited to smaller projects requiring few individual zones of control due to the physical limitations of aligning and accurately constructing a zone damper section for numerous zones.

Central plant and controls. The central plant provides hot water, steam, and chilled water or gas for the multizone system in a similar manner as other all-air air-handling systems. The heating and cooling piping systems supply the air-handling unit at its central location rather than distributing water throughout the occupied spaces to terminal boxes.

The control of the multizone air-handling system is generally maintained through the zone thermostat's control of the cold and warm air

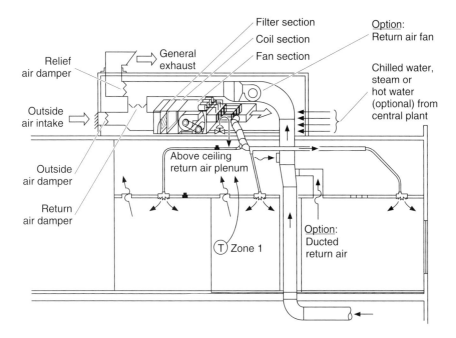

Characteristics:
1. Parallel heating and cooling air sections.
2. Simultaneous heating and cooling is possible.
3. The zone dampers mix hot and cold air until the zone demand is satisfied.
4. Direct expansion cooling with gas-fired heating systems have same characteristics.
5. Blow-thru air handler is shown.
6. A third deck is sometimes added (bypass deck) for economizer cooling.

Figure 3.9 Multizone air-handling system. (*Used with permission of Gobbell Hays Partners, Inc., Nashville, Tenn.*)

volume dampers at the air-handling unit zone damper section. The temperatures of the hot and cold decks are generally set according to outside and return air temperatures. The space thermostat controls a hot deck and cold deck damper at the air-handling unit to provide the air temperature to satisfy the space load.

3.2.7 Two-pipe fan coil system

Figure 3.10 is a diagram of a two-pipe fan coil system, which is the most basic of an all-water system. With the two-pipe system, the conditioned building is either on all heating or all cooling with no ability to switch easily between the two. The advantages of the two-pipe system are the low installation cost and the system's ability to physically

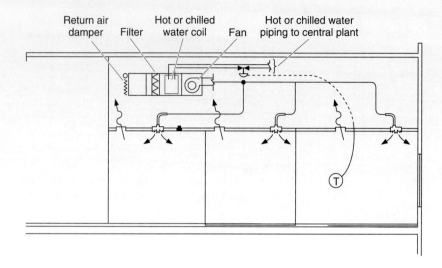

Return air damper   Filter   Hot or chilled water coil   Fan   Hot or chilled water piping to central plant

Characteristics:
  1. No simultaneous heating and cooling is possible.
  2. Typically used for extreme weather conditions, hotels.
  3. Lower initial installation cost.
  4. Ventilation air is often provided by a separate, independent fan system.

Figure 3.10 Two-pipe fan coil system. (*Used with permission of Gobbell Hays Partners, Inc., Nashville, Tenn.*)

fit into tight architectural spaces. The reason their use has diminished recently is the lack of individual occupant zone control. The building occupants are at the mercy of the entire building's demand for either heating or cooling. The components of a two-pipe system are:

Fan coil unit

Distribution piping

Central plant and controls

Fan coil unit. The fan coil units are typically located at perimeter locations, either above ceiling with a minimal amount of ductwork or, more commonly, as cabinet units along exterior walls and under windows. Outside air can be introduced directly into the fan coil unit by either the construction of a mixing plenum or, for perimeter installations, direct individual intake openings for each fan coil unit. Many designs utilize a separate air-handling system to introduce outside air to interior zones.

Distribution piping. A common configuration of fan coil units in high-rise buildings is to be aligned vertically from floor to floor, with each terminal unit in a vertical run connected by a common water piping riser. These vertical piping risers can easily be concealed in chases or walls. The potential exists for condensation from uninsulated chilled water piping. The extensive use of water pipes throughout the facility adds to the probability of water leaks and condensate damage.

Central plant and controls. Either chilled water or hot water is supplied through the same piping for two-pipe systems. The system works well in hot weather when all spaces have a requirement for cooling and in cold weather when all spaces require heating. However, spring and fall temperatures may cause some spaces to need cooling while others need heating. Both demands cannot be simultaneously satisfied in the simple two-pipe system. To compensate for this, some two-pipe systems are installed with electric resistance heat so that simultaneous cooling and heating can occur in the system. System changeover from cooling to heating is typically controlled by outside air temperature or manually operated valves.

3.2.8   Four-pipe fan coil system

Figure 3.11 is a diagram of a four-pipe fan coil system, which is similar to the two-pipe system except that in the four-pipe system, there are independent hot water and chilled water coils in the fan coil terminal units. These systems are prevalent in certain applications because they give individual space control to occupants. They are primarily used in hotels. The components of the four-pipe fan coil unit are:

Fan coil unit

Distribution piping

Central plant and controls

Fan coil unit. Four-pipe fan coil units are typically located at perimeter locations, either above ceiling with a minimal amount of ductwork or, more commonly, as cabinet units along exterior walls and under windows. The same outside air considerations that apply to two-pipe systems apply to the four-pipe systems.

Distribution piping. The four-pipe fan coil system utilizes four pipes—hot water supply and return and chilled water supply and return—that are independently piped and connected to their respective central plant equipment. As with the two-pipe system, the four-pipe units are commonly found vertically arranged in high-rise applica-

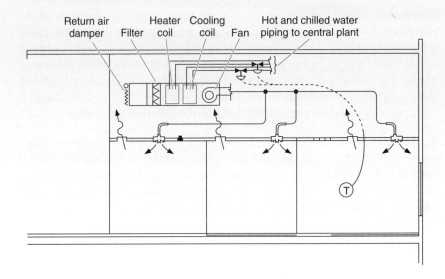

Characteristics:
1. Simultaneous heating and cooling is possible.
2. One thermostat per fan coil.
3. Typical hotel room system.
4. Ventilation air is often provided by a separate, independent fan system.

Figure 3.11 Four-pipe fan coil system. (*Used with permission of Gobbell Hays Partners, Inc., Nashville, Tenn.*)

tions and, unlike the two-pipe system, can simultaneously provide heating and cooling to different spaces in the building. The potential exists for condensation from uninsulated chilled water piping.

Central plant and controls.   Chilled and hot water are independently controlled in four-pipe systems and are piped to their respective coils and control valves within the fan coil cabinets. In intermediate weather conditions, the occupant is able to maintain control via a space thermostat, which operates the hot and chilled water control valves in individual fan coil units.

3.2.9   Split system

This is a very popular and inexpensive HVAC system found in low-rise commercial buildings. Split system units are characterized by having their air-handling unit located inside of the building (usually in a closet or above ceiling) and their condensing units located outside. Split system condensing units can be either water or air cooled.

Another type of split system is the water source heat pump. The basic components are a cooling tower, hot water boiler, and circulating pumps. Water is used as the heat-transfer medium in these systems. In this system, the loop water is circulated to all of the heat pump units and is maintained at between 60 and 90°F. Each individual unit utilizes the loop water with the refrigeration system within the unit to supply the required heating or cooling to the zone. The attraction of these systems is that they are relatively inexpensive. Disadvantages from an IAQ perspective are the same as with fan coil units in that the many separate coils can produce moisture problems. Also, on the water source heat pump units, there is the addition of the cooling tower component. The potential for biocontaminant growth and amplification associated with cooling towers can be a disadvantage if they are not properly designed or maintained. Cooling tower water must be chemically treated to prevent biological growth.

Figure 3.12 is a system description of a water source heat pump.

3.2.10   Packaged air-handling unit

Figure 3.13 is a diagram of a packaged air-handling unit, which is another prominent type of HVAC system. Their lower equipment and installation cost make them desirable for many small commercial applications, especially rooftop mounted. The components of the packaged systems are similar to those of the single-zone system:

Packaged air-handling unit and condensing unit

Air-distribution system

The notable difference between the single-zone and packaged systems is the lack of the central plant for the packaged systems. The function of the central plant is provided by the condensing unit and heating module, which are located in the "package."

Packaged air-handling unit and condensing unit.   The basic components of the packaged air-handling unit are similar to the single-zone air-handling unit. Many packaged units are manufactured with their outside air dampers at a preset opening size. The diversity of filter selection may be more limited in the packaged units due to the physical constraints of the filter section sizes available from the manufacturer. If, for example, a special or unique filter is required for a particular application, a packaged unit may not be the best equipment selection.

The cooling coil on a packaged unit is a DX refrigerant coil. The refrigerant system is prepiped inside of the unit so there is basically no other piping (and associated pumps, valves, fittings, etc.) to be

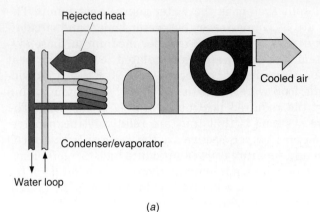

Rejected heat

Cooled air

Condenser/evaporator

Water loop

(a)

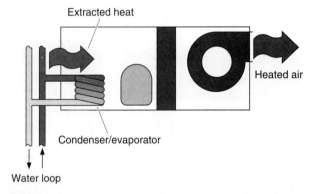

Extracted heat

Heated air

Condenser/evaporator

Water loop

(b)

Figure 3.12   Water source heat pump.
The water source heat pump is essentially a heat recovery system. The heat recovery function is made possible by piping all of the condenser/evaporator heat exchangers to a common water loop. (*a*) When in the cooling mode, the condenser/evaporator, water-side heat exchanger functions as a condenser, rejecting heat extracted from the space to the water loop. (*b*) Conversely, when in the heating mode, the condenser/evaporator, water-side heat exchanger functions as an evaporator, extracting heat from the same water loop to be rejected to the space. Therefore, during times of the year when heating needs occur, an energy saving potential exists when the interior units are cooling, rejecting heat to the loop, and the perimeter units are heating, taking heat from the loop. In other words, unneeded heat is transferred from the interior to heat the perimeter of the building. (*From* Water Source Heat Pump Design, *Trane Air Conditioning Applications Engineering Manual, 1981, p. 2. Reprinted with permission of the Trane Company, LaCrosse, Wisc.*)

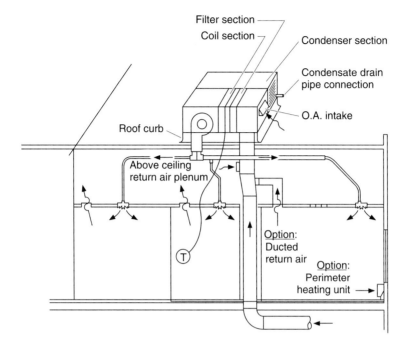

Filter section
Coil section
Condenser section
Condensate drain
pipe connection
O.A. intake
Roof curb
Above ceiling
return air plenum
Option:
Ducted
return air
Option:
Perimeter
heating unit

Characteristics:
1. Found most commonly in roof-mounted installations.
2. Condenser section can be replaced by a chilled water coil system.
3. Heating can be in the form of:
   a. Heat pump system (with electric auxiliary)
   b. Gas-fired furnace as a part of the unit
   c. Gas-fired or hot water duct heater
   d. Hot water or electric coil inside the unit

Figure 3.13 Packaged air-handling units. (*Used with permission of Gobbell Hays Partners, Inc., Nashville, Tenn.*)

added for cooling when installing these systems. Heating can be provided in a variety of forms but is most commonly found as a gas-fired furnace or electric heater. A heating section can be specified internal to the unit or can be specified in the reheat position, such as in a duct-mounted gas furnace.

The condensing unit section of the packaged units contains the condenser and the compressor. Rooftop units are an air-cooled type of condenser. Water-cooled package systems are also available but are not as common as air-cooled ones and can be distinguished by an evaporative cooler loop water supply. The most attractive feature of these packaged units is their ease of installation and economical cost.

Air distribution. The ductwork and associated air distribution for a packaged system is similar to the single-zone unit. Although most commonly seen as constant volume systems like the single-zone unit, packaged units may be designed as VAV. The VAV packaged system uses variable volume dampers or boxes as a part of the air distribution. For rooftop units, there may be internal ductwork insulation at duct locations around the penetration of the roof at the curb. This is a common practice to prevent noise from rooftop units being transmitted to occupied spaces below.

3.3   IAQ Issues for HVAC

The HVAC system can affect IAQ in two ways: by the HVAC system's ability to transport contaminants generated from sources within the building and by the HVAC system's ability to act as a source of contaminant generation. The system can be a pathway through which indoor contaminants are entrained and distributed via air recirculation to the occupied spaces. These contaminants can be generated either from sources external to the HVAC system or from the system itself. The HVAC system can be the cause of thermal comfort problems by being of deficient design or by being improperly maintained, and, as discussed earlier, occupant discomfort is often attributed to poor IAQ.

Increasing outside air for ventilation is not the panacea for solving IAQ problems. Additional outside air, which was intended to dilute indoor contaminants, could introduce contaminated outside air into the building or could cause a reduction in building occupant comfort (temperature and humidity) due to lack of adequate heating or cooling capacity. HVAC issues related to IAQ are important for the design of new buildings as well as in remediation of existing IAQ problems.

3.3.1   HVAC as source of contamination

Because the HVAC system is responsible for providing comfort by controlling temperature, humidity, and ventilation to building occupants, it is an integral part of investigating IAQ. We have categorized HVAC systems into air and water systems and have briefly described some systems commonly found in commercial buildings. To investigate the HVAC system as a source of contamination, an understanding of the materials and equipment used in the installation is necessary.

Materials and equipment. This discussion of the materials used in HVAC systems will begin with the equipment itself, either the air-handling unit for air systems or fan coil units for water systems. Manufacturers typically provide the components of the air-handling equipment as a single prefabricated package, consisting of a fan and a coil section contained in a sheet metal housing. The entering air side of the air-handling unit consists of a mixing plenum for mixing of return air and outside air and a filter system which provides a specified level of air filtration prior to the air entering the coil section of the unit. Typically, the air-handling unit is constructed of materials resistant to corrosion or degradation, and material problems are not usually associated with the units themselves. However, it is not uncommon in smaller packaged systems to find a factory-insulated fiberglass or neoprene lining inside of the air-handling unit. Fiberglass, or any porous insulating material when wet, can act as a breeding ground for fungal and bacterial growth, and the condensation from cooling coils could potentially provide such a wet environment. Figure 3.14 shows internal lining in ductwork.

Sheet metal ductwork typically circulates air from the central air-handling unit or fan coil into the occupied zone. Insulation is generally installed on supply ductwork to prevent condensation and heat loss. Supply ductwork insulation is typically a fiberglass blanket insulation from ½ to 1 in thick and is generally adhered to the outside of the ductwork. The fiberglass blanket insulation is normally provided with a foil or cloth cover which enhances the insulation's vapor-retardant characteristics. Some designs call for internal insulation of supply ductwork and, more prevalent, internal insulation of return ductwork at or near the return air connections to the air-handling

Figure 3.14 Internal lining in ductwork. (*Used with permission of Gobbell Hays Partners, Inc., Nashville, Tenn.*)

unit. Internal insulation at these areas is usually a fiberglass board or blanket applied with adhesive to the inside of the ductwork and may be installed for noise reduction purposes as much as for thermal insulation.

Internal insulation, especially composed of fibrous materials, can present IAQ problems. First and foremost is the release of fibers into the airstream, where they can be transported through the system and into the occupied space. On the supply side of the ductwork, it is recommended to avoid internal insulation due to the potential for insulation degradation and resultant fiber release. The same potential for degradation exists in return ductwork, but the filter should be able to prevent most fiber recirculation through the unit into the occupied space. Also, internal insulation, when it is wet, can be a source of microbial growth and amplification. For most commercial buildings, dirt and debris will accumulate in the pores of internal insulation due to a lack of high-efficiency filtration. This insulation is likely to become moist during the normal operation of the HVAC unit, especially downstream of cooling coils or humidifiers. Morey has presented a case study in which *Cladosporium* fungi were increased from 500 colony forming units per square inch (CFU/in^2) on insulation from a mixing plenum to 1,500,000 CFU/in^2 on insulation immediately downstream of steam humidifiers in the supply ductwork. For this case, as with most cases where porous materials have collected moisture and caused amplification of microbials, removal of the material, under controlled conditions, was recommended.[8]

Within the last 10 years, fiberglass board ductwork has been promoted for use in small commercial and residential construction. The attractiveness of these systems is their low cost compared to traditional sheet metal ductwork. Careful consideration of the IAQ issues discussed above for internal lining should be made prior to the use of this material for supply air systems.

Fan coil and heat pump units are often specified to be provided with internal lining. These linings are installed for noise reduction and thermal insulation purposes. Fan coil units are generally installed very near the occupied space (in cabinets, above ceilings, etc.) or exposed in the occupied space, as in hotels, where noise reduction is important to occupant comfort. The internal insulation in these units can be subject, over the years, to disintegration and the erosion of fibers into the airstream and into the occupied zones. There is also the tendency with these units for condensation and moisture buildup at the cooling coil, which could cause the internal lining to become damp and support biocontaminant growth.

VAV terminal units are often specified with internal insulation when they are located above or near sensitive areas to reduce noise.

Although not commonplace, mastics are sometimes applied to the inside of ductwork and have the potential of emitting VOCs. The presence of VOCs is stronger at the first application of these mastics and would certainly be most suspect in new ductwork at building start-up or after building renovations. As will be discussed later, a good commissioning program is beneficial in reducing VOC emissions before occupancy.

Gas-fired heating equipment can also produce indoor air contaminants if the equipment is not installed correctly or not properly operated and maintained. The most prevalent and potentially dangerous contaminant resulting from incomplete combustion is CO. Gas and building codes set very specific requirements for gas-fired equipment that include flue stack and makeup air specifications. If adequate outside air is not provided for proper combustion, levels of CO and nitrogen dioxide may be generated at levels that exceed OSHA PELs. Inadequate makeup air can cause back-drafts through the flue into occupied spaces. Makeup and combustion air should be provided through louvers directly communicating to the outside. Louver intake dimensions are dependent upon gas-fired equipment rated input British thermal unit per hour (Btu/h) capacity. If gas-fired equipment cannot be located in rooms where direct communication with the outside is possible, provisions are allowed in most codes for confined space installation where makeup and combustion air can be provided from adjacent unconfined areas. The IAQ investigator should understand what building and gas codes require for makeup and combustion air. Obviously, any louvers communicating with the outside that provide makeup and combustion air for gas-fired equipment should be unobstructed (see Fig. 3.15).

Moisture collection in humidifiers, cooling coils, and other areas of the HVAC system. Part of the cooling process is dehumidification of air, which creates condensation at the cooling coil. Both air and water systems have condensate drain pans that are designed into the air-handling or fan coil equipment to collect moisture from the cooling coil. From this pan, condensate is then drained to the sanitary sewer or stormwater system. The potential for moisture collection of the cooling coil condensate pan is greater with systems in high-humidity areas and with older systems that are more likely to have fouled condensate drain piping. When performing an IAQ investigation, inspect the condensate drain pans and note any evidence of algae or biocontaminant buildup. It is important to include cleaning of these condensate pans as routine practice in the IAQ preventative maintenance program. See Fig. 3.16 for an example of a condensate pan.

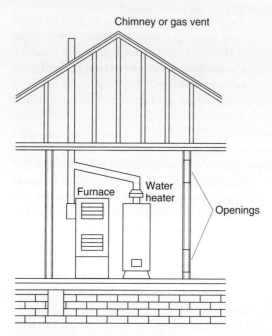

Note: Each opening shall have a free area of not less than 1 in^2 per 1000 Btu/hr of the input rating of all appliances in the enclosure but not less than 100 in^2.

Figure 3.15 Appliances in confined spaces. All air from inside the building. (*Used with permission from* Standard Gas Code, *Southern Building Code Congress International, Inc., Birmingham, Ala., 1985, p. 39.*)

Figure 3.16 Condensate pan. (*Used with permission of Gobbell Hays Partners, Inc., Nashville, Tenn.*)

Commonly, condensate from the cooling coil sections of air-handling equipment is piped into the sanitary sewer system. A p-trap at the drain connection must be installed prior to the connection of the drain pipe into the sanitary piping system. The p-trap is used to prevent sewer gases from migrating up into the sanitary piping and entering the occupied space, either directly or through the airstream of the air-handling unit. For air-handling units located above ceilings or in other areas where water damage to building finishes would be critical, a secondary drain pan is often installed below the unit's condensate pan to collect overflow. If the drain from this secondary pan is piped into the sanitary system, a p-trap should be installed. Many times these secondary pans are piped to a location that would be noticeable to maintenance personnel so that the problem of overspill from the unit's condensate pan can be quickly detected.

Proper collection and removal of moisture from the cooling coil of the air-handling system is important in controlling IAQ and is an area that is often neglected in design, construction, and maintenance. The moisture on the surface of cooling coils can be a source of microbiological buildup. If the air filtration has low efficiency or is improperly maintained, small particles will tend to collect on the coil surface. These particles and moisture, if allowed to remain on the coil, can produce microbiological growth.

The humidification process is intended to add moisture to the airstream in the air-handling unit or, most commonly, in the supply ductwork. Humidifier types fall into two general categories: adiabatic process humidifiers and isothermal process humidifiers.[9] In the adiabatic humidification process, no heat is added to or taken from the supply air. The sensible heat of the air is exchanged for the latent heat of the water. Examples of adiabatic-type humidifiers are air washers, evaporative coolers, water atomizers, and wetted media. The isothermal humidification process adds moisture already converted to water vapor directly into the airstream. These types are categorized into steam humidifiers and vapor generators. Humidifiers that inject water vapor directly into the airstream should not be located in ductwork that has internal insulation. Nor should these humidifiers be installed immediately upstream of ductwork turns, transitions, or internal obstructions such as dampers. As discussed above, moisture collecting in the ductwork at these areas could create conditions of biocontaminant growth in the ductwork, as well as accelerate disintegration of any internal lining.

The steam injected into the airstream enters as 100 percent saturated vapor, mixes with the cooler supply airstream, causing it to become "supersaturated," and condenses, creating a fog of microscopic drops of water. This fog will be carried downstream of the humidifier until further mixing with unsaturated air causes the fog to evaporate and disappear. The fog distance inside of the ductwork is dependent upon steam pressure at the humidifier, air velocity inside of the ductwork, configuration of the ductwork, and airstream temperature. The condensation and collection of this vapor inside of the ductwork can also be contaminated from anticorrosion chemicals injected into the steam boiler that migrate through the steam supply system. See Fig. 3.17 for an illustration of the behavior of steam in a duct.

Bioaerosols. Bioaerosols are airborne microbiological particulate matter containing viruses, bacteria, fungi, protozoa, mites, pollen, and their components.[10] Their sizes generally range from a minimum of 0.01 μm to an upper limit in the 50- to 100-μm range. Filters rated at dust spot efficiencies of 70 percent should prove capable of controlling bioaerosols.[11] Although their presence occurs naturally in both indoor and outdoor environments, the abundance of standing water in cold, dark locations amplifies their growth. Areas within ductwork or air-handling units around condensate pans, humidifiers, and other sources of water (such as porous pockets of internal duct lining) can be sites of microbial growth and amplification. Turbulence caused by air movement within the air-handling system and vibration caused by the intermittent operation of supply fans can dislodge these contaminants and result in their transport into the indoor environment.

Cooling towers can be a source of biocontaminant growth. Cooling towers are generally used in association with centrifugal chiller systems which are used to chill water in large buildings (generally greater than 100 t of cooling capacity). Cooling towers are designed to circulate warm water from the heat-rejection loop of the chiller and

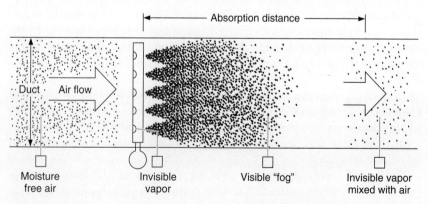

Figure 3.17 Steam humidifier in a duct. (*From* Humidification Handbook, *1982, p. 63. Used with permission, Dri-Steem Humidifier Co., Eden Prairie, MN.*)

disperse it over a series of plates and/or fins exposed to the atmosphere. Cooling towers are located outdoors and usually in the vicinity of the central plant where the chiller is located. The water is thus evaporatively cooled to the saturation temperature of the outside air. The sump of the cooling tower is typically an open basin containing standing water that provides temperature, water, and nutrient conditions suitable for microorganisms such as *Legionella*. Legionnaires' disease and Pontiac fever are two illnesses traceable to microorganisms that thrive in environments such as cooling towers and evaporative condensers. These microorganisms become airborne through their exposure to the wind during the evaporative cooling process. Occupants can be exposed to the microorganisms either by direct contact or by the entrainment of the microorganisms into the HVAC system via the outside air intake. It is important to chemically treat the water that circulates through the cooling tower to prevent microorganism growth as part of IAQ maintenance programs.

Dirt. Another source of contamination related to the HVAC system is dirt. At the start-up of the HVAC system, dirt and debris present inside of the equipment or ductwork may become dislodged by the vibration caused when the supply fan starts and then may be dispersed throughout the occupied zones by the air velocity within the duct system. This dirt and debris can be from internal sources, such as internal lining or sheet metal filings, or it may have accumulated during the construction of the building when sheet metal was erected and left open. It is not uncommon for fast-track construction projects to have much of the ductwork installed prior to or during some of the dirtiest phases of general construction work. The most common example would be erected ductwork left open and unprotected while fireproofing is being sprayed. For the IAQ investigator, if the outside of the sheet metal and hangers are covered with dirt, debris, or fireproofing, this is an indicator that fireproofing and other dirt and debris may also be inside the ductwork. Assurance that the ductwork was completely sealed and protected during the phase of construction in which it was erected will be difficult to find. A good commissioning program would prevent this problem by enforcing the closure of any open ends of erected ductwork during other phases of general construction. Figure 3.18 shows dust inside sheet metal ductwork.

Dust is defined by ASHRAE as particles less than 100 μm.[12] However, airborne particles occur naturally in the environment down to the 0.01-μm range. Particles above the 10-μm size settle rapidly unless disturbed by strong air movement. As a reference, tobacco smoke consists of particles in the 0.01- to 1.0-μm range. The amount and size of airborne particles in the air affect the selection of air fil-

Figure 3.18   Dust inside sheet metal ductwork. (*Used with permission of Gobbell Hays Partners, Inc., Nashville, Tenn.*)

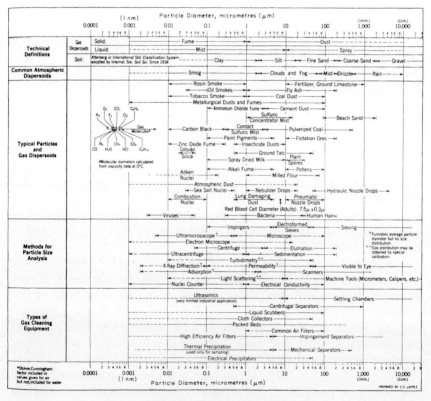

Characteristics of Particles and Particle Dispersoids
(Courtesy of Stanford Research Institute)

Figure 3.19   Characteristics of particles and particle dispersoids. (*From* 1993 ASHRAE Handbook: Fundamentals, *I-P Ed., ASHRAE, Atlanta, Ga. Used with permission of ASHRAE.*)

ters for the HVAC unit. Air filters are typically located in draw-thru systems at the entering side of the cooling coil after the return air and outside air are mixed. Dirt and airborne particles generated from the supply side of the system are distributed into the occupied zone without passing through the air filter. Therefore, as good as the unit's air filter efficiency may be, its effectiveness is dependent upon where the dirt is generated in the HVAC system. See Fig. 3.19 for characteristics of particles and particle dispersoids.

3.3.2 Pathway: HVAC as contaminant transport

Figure 3.20 shows the HVAC as a pathway for contaminant transport. All new HVAC systems should provide, at a minimum, adequate outside air for ventilation according to ASHRAE Standard 62-1989. HVAC systems installed prior to 1989 should at least provide some means for introducing outside air into the occupied space, even though perhaps not at the 62-1989 recommendations. The location of the outside air intakes on the exterior of the building is very important to the

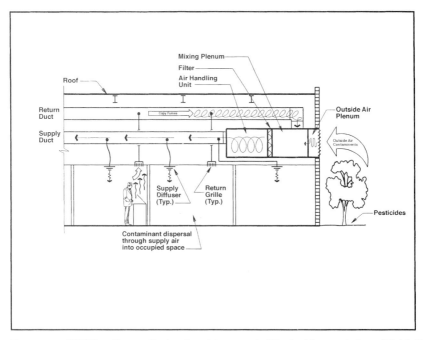

Figure 3.20 HVAC pathway: Contaminant transport. (*Used with permission of Gobbell Hays Partners, Inc., Nashville, Tenn.*)

HVAC designer and IAQ investigator. The intent of ASHRAE 62-1989 was to increase ventilation for the removal of human-generated CO_2 and for the dilution of other possible indoor pollutants, not to inadvertently increase outside air which could act as a pathway through which exterior pollutants could travel. ASHRAE 62-1989 does not ignore the possibility, especially in urban areas, of introducing contaminated outside air. The standard is based on the National Ambient Air Quality Standards (NAAQS) ambient air levels for allowable outside air contamination. The levels associated with a particular city or site should be investigated prior to design, and levels higher than the NAAQS may indicate potential IAQ problems.

A common condition found in sick buildings is the location of outside air intakes near parking lots, loading docks, or garages. The exhaust from idling cars and traffic contains many hazardous contaminants, most notoriously CO, which can be introduced into the building's HVAC system. When outside air intakes are located near the ground, the use of pesticides or other chemicals that emit noxious odors or VOCs suddenly affects IAQ. Since many of these activities occur outside the building, occupants easily remain unaware of the potential hazards caused by these unseen sources. See Fig. 3.21 for an example of drums stored beneath an outside air intake.

Fortunately, the location of outside air intakes has long been recognized as a potential for creating IAQ problems, and most building codes have adopted stringent regulations for the minimum distances

Figure 3.21 Drums stored beneath outside air intake. (*Used with permission of Gobbell Hays Partners, Inc., Nashville, Tenn.*)

that intakes can be located from possible sources of contaminants. Typically, codes specify a minimum distance for outside air intakes of 25 ft from plumbing vent openings and building exhaust fans discharge. Hospital and laboratory codes may specify even greater minimum distances from particularly hazardous exhausts. Infiltration of outside air can occur at points other than this HVAC intake. Pockets of positive pressure can be created at building exteriors as the result of wind pressure and velocity. The stack effect in high-rise buildings creates a negative pressure at lower openings (doors, windows, etc.) that can at times be stronger than exhausts from fan-powered systems. To compensate for this, exhaust velocities should be designed in the 1200- to 1500-fpm range.

Another way that HVAC systems can transport contaminants is through improper zoning of the HVAC system. In general, the air from each occupied space within an HVAC system is returned and mixed with the return air from other spaces within that zone. Improper zoning becomes a greater problem as a building evolves over the years and space functions change. The addition of materials or equipment that emit VOCs or other contaminants to a space originally designed for general office use, with its return air mixed with other office use spaces, could cause contamination of all offices served by the HVAC system.

Certainly the most common example of zoning problems occurs with tobacco smoke. It is a good indicator of zoning problems because its odor is easy to trace. Unfortunately, most occupants agree that being an indicator is the only thing that makes it good. Smoking areas should not share the same return air pathway with other areas where people are smoke-sensitive. This is why it is so common in indoor air investigations to hear occupants complain that they know when Mr. Smith is smoking even though his office might not necessarily be near the occupants who have complained. The solutions to these zoning problems are usually not very complicated, but they can be expensive. For tobacco smoke, solution options would include:

1. Installing improved air filtration either at Mr. Smith's return grille or at the HVAC unit serving the office area zone

2. Providing a localized exhaust in Mr. Smith's office area (and noting the effect of additional outside air on the HVAC unit and pressure relationships around adjacent offices)

3. Creating a smoke-free office environment.

Return air plenums are commonly found in commercial office buildings. Their prevalence is in part due to their economic benefits: Eliminating return air ductwork from the occupied space to the air-handling unit saves the building owner the cost of material and labor for the ductwork installation. Although typically not a huge cost savings in comparison to the entire mechanical systems cost, return air plenums are often promoted to building owners as a cost reduction that will have little or no adverse effect on system operation and occupant thermal comfort. In fact, return air plenums can have a significant impact on IAQ by acting as an open pathway through which contaminants can travel. In return air plenums, the return air is in direct contact with the above ceiling environment. The above ceiling area of a building is not a well-maintained, clean area. The potential for the airstream to become contaminated with suspended airborne particles, dust, and moisture-related biocontaminants is much greater above ceiling than below. If return plenums are used, the following practices should be maintained:

1. Avoid PVC piping or coated wiring in plenums due to their fire and smoke hazards (many codes outlaw their use in plenum spaces).

2. Keep the plenum clean and dry.

3. Keep ceiling tile in place to maintain proper airflow mixing in occupied spaces.

4. Be aware that fire walls (that extend to the deck structure) will interrupt airflow above ceilings; install openings with rated fire dampers when needed.

Figure 3.22 is a view of an above ceiling plenum.

The types of contaminants that can be transported by the HVAC airstream are particulate and gaseous. As will be discussed later, air

Figure 3.22 View of above ceiling plenum. (*Used with permission of Gobbell Hays Partners, Inc., Nashville, Tenn.*)

filtration can be an effective means to clean some of these contaminants from the airstream, but a thorough knowledge of the type and behavior of the contaminant must be known. Many of the contaminants can be controlled by installing localized exhaust systems and by controlling pressure relationships between the source generator and surrounding areas. For example, radon is a gas which is emitted naturally from the soil in some areas of the country and typically infiltrates into buildings through cracks and holes in the foundation or at subgrade levels. Once radon enters the lower level of a building, it can be transported throughout the building via the HVAC system, depending on the zoning. However, by providing localized ventilation and exhaust at the building's lower level and by keeping the lower floors level at a relatively lower pressure level than the upper floors, the risks of radon migration throughout the building can be significantly reduced.

3.3.3 HVAC deficiency factors

It is not uncommon in IAQ investigations to find the HVAC system affecting the indoor air environment due to some malfunction or maintenance problem. Even the best IAQ design will eventually be reduced to the level of IAQ expertise of the HVAC maintenance personnel. Although all components of the HVAC system must be working properly to ensure comfort and good air quality, the following facets of HVAC systems are most significant in maintaining good air quality.

Ventilation. Ventilation has already been discussed regarding its importance in providing an air exchange rate in occupied areas to dilute contaminants and to dispel CO_2 buildup from occupants breathing. According to ASHRAE's Ventilation Rate Procedure, the amount of outside air required to be introduced is mostly dependent upon the occupants' activity levels and metabolic rates, as well as such factors as clothing and diet. Lack of adequate ventilation is often mistakenly referred to as the most prevalent cause of IAQ problems. ASHRAE revised the recommended minimum requirements for ventilation in 1973 to 5 cfm per person as an energy conservation measure. At the same time, architects were designing building envelopes that were more resistant to air infiltration through windows and doors, and the construction industry was introducing new synthetic building materials and adhesives which off-gassed as part of their natural aging process. These factors created a synergistic effect of more pollutants in the indoor air environment combined with less means for dilution of these pollutants to occur.

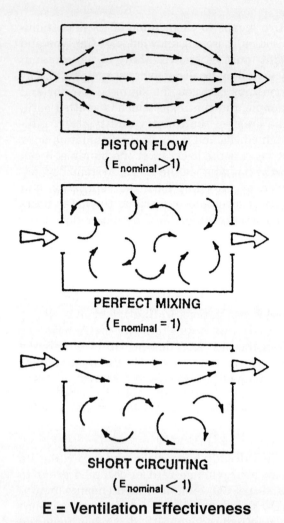

PISTON FLOW
$(E_{nominal} > 1)$

PERFECT MIXING
$(E_{nominal} = 1)$

SHORT CIRCUITING
$(E_{nominal} < 1)$

E = Ventilation Effectiveness

Figure 3.23 Representative examples of ventilation air movement. (*Used with permission from* Managing Indoor Air Quality, *Shirley Hansen, The Fairmont Press, Lilburn, Ga., 1991, p. 177.*)

Ventilation effectiveness is defined as the ratio of outside air delivered to the occupied zone to the outside air delivered to the space. The values of minimum outside air published in Table 3.1 assume perfect mixing within the space and assume that all outside air is reaching the occupied zone. Supply diffusers are often located in ceilings immediately adjacent to return or exhaust grilles. In these cases, it would not be uncommon for the ventilation air provided for that space through the supply air to completely bypass the occupied zone. The ventilation effectiveness would be significantly less than 1 (a value of 1.0 would be obtained under perfect mixing conditions), and minimum ventilation rates established in Table 3.1 would need to be increased to compensate for a poor air-distribution system. Ventilation effectiveness is difficult to measure in the field. Several procedures have proven successful for determining the outside air levels at the occupied zone.[13] The transitional steady-state (TSS) method is somewhat typical of these procedures, whereby a tracer gas, usually sulfur hexafluoride (SF_6), is injected into the outside air intake at a constant rate until equilibrium has been reached in the building. The tracer gas concentration is then measured at the occupied breathing zone level and at the air supply at the ceiling diffuser. At steady-state conditions,

$$\text{Ventilation effectiveness} = \frac{\text{concentration of } SF_6 \text{ at occupied zone}}{\text{concentration of } SF_6 \text{ at supply air}}$$

Deficient ventilation may not be detected at the air-handling unit where the investigator finds that adequate amounts of outside air are being introduced through the outside air intake but may be detected in the occupied space due to the layout and airflow patterns of the air-distribution system. In this type of situation, complaints of thermal discomfort would probably be prevalent, indicating that the conditioned supply air is bypassing the occupied zone. See Fig. 3.23.

In cases where ventilation in a given space is below the recommended levels of 62-1989, an alternate method of complying with the ASHRAE standard is to filter the recirculated air. Another situation where this method would be used is when the outside air is contaminated beyond acceptable NAAQS guidelines. If recirculated air is cleaned and introduced into the occupied spaces in amounts less than the minimum criteria described by the Ventilation Rate Procedure, the Air Quality Procedure must be used. The requirement for minimum outside air may be reduced depending upon the filter location, the efficiency of the filter with regard to the contaminant in question, the contaminant generation rate, the supply air rate (and the fraction of the air recirculated), and the ventilation effectiveness.

Sample calculation illustrating the cleaning of recirculated air (from ASHRAE 62-1989, App. E)

The amount of outdoor air specified when using the Ventilation Rate Procedures may be reduced by recirculating air from which offending contaminants have been removed or converted to less objectionable forms. The amount of outdoor air required depends on the contaminant generation in the space, the contaminant concentrations in the indoor and the outdoor air, the filter location, the filter efficiency for the contaminants in question, the ventilation effectiveness, the supply air circulation rate, and the fraction recirculated.

Figure 3.24 shows a representative system. A filter may be located in the recirculated airstream (location A) or in the supply (mixed) airstream (location B). The ventilation effectiveness will depend on the location of the supply outlet, the return inlet, and the design and performance of the supply diffuser. Figure 3.24 is a schematic of a typical system with the supply outlet and the return inlet in the ceiling.

All of the exhaust is shown in the figure as being taken from the return airstream. Many systems will have part or all of the exhaust taken directly from the space.

VAV systems reduce the circulation rate when the thermal load is satisfied. This is accounted for by a flow reduction factor F_r. The supply air temperature is normally held constant in a VAV system. Constant-volume systems require a variable supply air temperature. VAV systems also may have a constant or proportional outdoor airflow rate.

A mass balance for the contaminant may be written to determine the space contaminant concentration for each of the system arrangements. The various permutations for the air-handling and distribution systems are described in Table 3.5. There are seven variations. The mass balance equations for computing the space contaminant concentrations for each system are presented in the table.

If the allowable space contamination is specified, the equations in Table 3.5 may be solved for the outdoor flow rate V_o. When the outdoor airflow rate is specified, the equations may be solved for the resulting contaminant concentration as shown in the table.

Filters are effective for removing particles. They are less effective in removing gases and vapors. Therefore, when designing a filtration system, consideration must be given to contaminants that are poorly filtered or not filtered at all. The ventilating rate may only be reduced until some contaminant reaches its maximum acceptable limit.

Many of the problems associated with ventilation in existing buildings are due to adjustments made to outside air dampers. Minimum outside air is typically set using dampers by one of two methods: by the installation of a separate minimum outside air damper with an independent controller and a damper motor separate from the economizer outside air damper or by the installation of a minimum set point end switch that allows a single outside air damper to close only to a minimum preset position. Because HVAC controls are probably the least understood of all mechanical maintenance items, it is not uncommon to see the outside air dampers fixed in their closed position or with their damper motor linkages disconnected. Complaints from building occupants of being too hot in the summer or too cold in the winter may have led the maintenance personnel to close or block off the outside air intake damper in an effort to ease the load on either the heating or cooling coil. Thermal comfort may have been satisfied

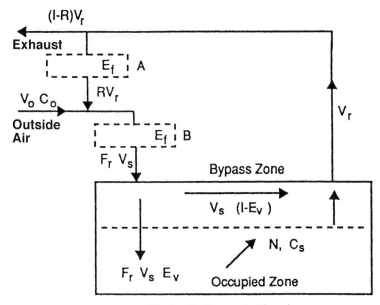

Figure 3.24 Recirculation and filtration. (*From* ASHRAE Standard 62-1989, *ANSI/ASHRAE, Atlanta, Ga., 1989, p. 23. Used with permission.*)

by this action, but the probability of increased levels of indoor contaminants would have been significantly increased.

Many office buildings constructed during the 1970s and 1980s were speculative. The owners were constructing buildings as money-making ventures, sometimes without knowing who or what type of tenant would eventually occupy the building. As with any other profit-oriented business, construction costs were held as low as possible. This abbreviated history of construction techniques during the 1970s and 1980s is mentioned because, depending upon the stringency of local building code administrations, the IAQ investigator may find office buildings with no ventilation air being introduced into the occupied spaces. The impact of such a condition on IAQ can be severe. The

TABLE 3.5 Required Outdoor Air or Space Contaminant Concentration with Recirculation and Filtration

Class	Required recirculation rate				Required outdoor air	Space contaminant concentration	Required recirculation rate
	Filter location	Flow	Tempera-ture	Outdoor air			
I	None	VAV	Constant	100%	$V_o = \dfrac{N}{E_v F_r(C_s - C_o)}$	$C_s = C_o + \dfrac{N}{E_v F V_o}$	Not applicable
II	A	Constant	Variable	Constant	$V_o = \dfrac{N - E_v \, RV_r E_f C_s}{E_v(C_s - C_o)}$	$C_s = \dfrac{N + E_v V_o C_o}{E_v(V_o + RV_r E_f)}$	$RV_r = \dfrac{N + E_v V_o(C_o - C_s)}{E_v E_f C_s}$
III	A	VAV	Constant	Constant	$V_o = \dfrac{N - E_v F_r RV_r E_f C_s}{E_v(C_s - C_o)}$	$C_s = \dfrac{N + E_v V_o C_o}{E_v(V_o + F_r RV_r E_f)}$	$RV_r = \dfrac{N + E_v V_o(C_o - C_s)}{E_v F_r E_f C_s}$
IV	A	VAV	Constant	Proportional	$V_o = \dfrac{N - E_v F_r RV_r E_f C_s}{E_v F_r(C_s - C_o)}$	$C_s = \dfrac{N + E_v F_r V_o C_o}{F_r E_v(V_o + RV_r E_f)}$	$RV_r = \dfrac{N + E_v F_r V_o(C_o - C_s)}{E_v F_r E_f C_s}$
V	B	Constant	Variable	Constant	$V_o = \dfrac{N - E_v \, RV_r E_f C_s}{E_v[C_s - (1 - E_f)C_o]}$	$C_s = \dfrac{N + E_v V_o[(1 - E_f)C_o]}{E_v(V_o + RV_r E_f)}$	$RV_r = \dfrac{N + E_v V_o[(1 - E_f)C_o - C_s]}{E_v E_f C_s}$
VI	B	VAV	Constant	Constant	$V_o = \dfrac{N - E_v F_r RV_r E_f C_s}{E_v[C_s - (1 - E_f)C_o]}$	$C_s = \dfrac{N + E_v V_o(1 - E_f)C_o}{E_v(V_o + F_r RV_r E_f)}$	$RV_r = \dfrac{N + E_v V_o[(1 - E_f)C_o - C_s]}{E_v F E_f C_s}$
VII	B	VAV	Constant	Proportional	$V_o = \dfrac{N - E_v F_r RV_r E_f C_s}{E_v F_r[C_s - (1 - E_f)(C_o)]}$	$C_s = \dfrac{N + E_v F_r V_o(1 - E_f)C_o}{E_v F_r(V_o + RV_r E_f)}$	$RV_r = \dfrac{N + E_v F_r V_o[(1 - E_f)C_o - C_s]}{E_v F_r E_f C_s}$

SOURCE: *ASHRAE Standard 62-1989*, ANSI/ASHRAE, Atlanta, GA, 1989, p. 23. Used with permission.

financial burden necessary to alter the HVAC system can be significant to the owner who purchased the building with the assumption that the mechanical systems were adequately designed.

Filtration.   Air filters in commercial buildings are primarily designed and installed to remove particulates from the airstream. Filters should be designed and installed based upon the size and characteristics of the airborne particles to be removed. High-efficiency filters can be beneficial by providing cleaner air and by providing cleaner HVAC system coils, ductwork, diffusers, etc., which reduces maintenance costs. Higher efficiencies also mean higher costs. The deficiency of air filtration in some systems is due to having the wrong filter installed when trying to achieve specific clean air criteria.

Characteristics which distinguish the performance of different filter types are efficiency, resistance, and dust-holding capacity. Efficiency measures the ability of the filter to remove particulates from the airstream. The longer a filter is used in a system, the greater the buildup of particles on the media. This buildup of filtered particles increases the efficiency of the filter, which is helpful. The buildup also increases resistance to airflow, which causes more fan energy to be expended. Average values of initial and final resistance should be used for design and filter evaluation. Resistance is the static air pressure drop across the filter at a given air speed. Dust-holding capacity defines the amount of a specific dust particle size that a filter can accept before the filter begins to drastically lose efficiency. The loading of filters increases efficiency only to a point before the media becomes overloaded and air resistance becomes a detriment to the HVAC system performance.

In general, four types of tests are used to rate efficiency, resistance, and dust-holding capacity for particulate air filters:

1. *Arrestance test.*   A known airborne concentration of a test dust of known size is fed at a constant rate and the concentration is measured at the leaving side of the filter. This test is good for determining dust removal capabilities for particles the size of the test dust and larger but gives little indication for the removal capacity of smaller particles.

2. *Dust spot efficiency test.*   This test measures the change in light transmitted through dust particles in air before and after they pass through the filter media. Because dust particles have the capacity to soil interior walls and surfaces, this measurement of efficiency determines the filter's ability to reduce soiling.

3. *Dust-holding capacity test.*   A measured amount of test dust of known size is fed into a filter until the manufacturer's maximum

operating resistance is met. The amount of dust captured by the filter is then measured and compared to the total amount fed into the filter. The reported results are an average of at least four tests.

4. *DOP penetration test.*   This test is particularly useful in measuring the performance of high efficiency filters. A known concentration of dioctyl phthalate (DOP) vapor is fed through the filter and measured by a light-scattering photometer. Penetration is usually measured in this test because high-efficiency particulate air (HEPA) filters have nearly a 100 percent capture rate at DOP smoke particle sizes (0.3 μm).

Filters used in commercial building applications are generally panel types designed for particulate control. They have the benefits of low cost and easy maintenance. They are commonly provided in premanufactured panels of up to 24- by 24-in size and can range from ½ to 4 in thick.

Panel filters, such as residential furnace filters, have a low packing density of coarse glass fibers, animal hair, vegetable fibers, or synthetic fibers. These fibers are often coated with a viscous substance, such as oil, which causes particles to adhere to the filter. Characteristics of panel filters are low pressure drop, low cost, and high efficiency for particles larger than 10 μm in diameter, such as lint. For particles smaller than 10 μm in diameter, these filters have a negligible efficiency.

Extended surface filters increase particle collection efficiency by decreasing the glass fiber size and increasing the fiber packing density, but these measures also increase airflow resistance. The air velocity through the media is reduced by extending the surface area of the filter media. This reduces the pressure drop across the filter. One way to extend the media surface area is to deploy the media in a folded or pleated form. The larger ratio of media surface area to face area allows the use of denser and hence more efficient filter media while maintaining acceptable pressure drops. These filters also offer much higher dust-holding capacities.

HEPA filters are special types of extended-surface filters which are capable of removing submicron particles. Developed for use in nuclear material processing plants to control concentrations of fine airborne radioactive particles, a HEPA filter has a minimum particle removal efficiency of no less than 99.97 percent for 0.3-μm-diameter particles and a maximum pressure drop, when clean, of 1.0 in of water (IWG) when operated at rated airflow capacity. Typically, the filter core is constructed by pleating a continuous web of filter media over corrugated separators that add strength to the core and form air passages between the pleats. HEPA filter media are composed of very fine submicron glass fibers in a matrix of larger-diameter (1 to 4 μm) fibers. Various grades of high-efficiency fibrous filters are commercially available. Minimum efficiencies range from 95 percent for hospital grade to 99.99 percent for HEPA grade.[14] Figure 3.25 shows approximate efficiency versus particle size for typical air filters.

There is much new technology being developed in the air filtration market. Many air filtration manufacturers are taking advantage of the recent publicity regarding IAQ and promoting a wide range of products as the guaranteed solution to a clean environment. Although not readily found in the commercial market, electronic air filters have received a lot of this recent attention. Electronic filters utilize electro-

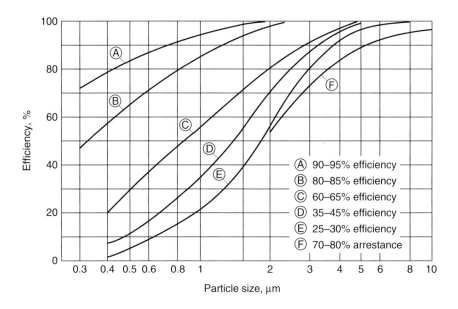

Filter	Dust spot eff., %	Outdoor air eff., %	ETS[‡] eff., %
A	90–95	99	60
B	80–85	91	42
C	60–65	72	20
E	25–30	55	0
F	70–80*	45	0

*Arrestance
‡ETS = environmental tobacco smoke

Figure 3.25 Approximate-efficiency versus particle size for typical air filters. (*From Indoor Air Quality, Vol, II* (*MGI Management Institute*)*, pp. 8-43 and 8-44. Used with permission of ASHRAE, Atlanta, Ga.*)

static precipitation to remove and collect particulate contaminants such as smoke, dust, and pollen. The dust particles become positively charged as they enter the filter section and collect on grounded plates. These filters have been proven to be up to 98 percent efficient by the dust spot test method. However, disadvantages include space requirements for the charging/collection process to occur, the failure of particles to be collected on the plate so that they enter the occupied space where they tend to cling to surfaces, and the generation of ozone. Continuous arcing and brush discharge in an electronic air filter may create ozone levels that are mildly toxic.[15]

The concern for the removal of gaseous pollutants has also produced new products. The primary target of these air filtration devices is tobacco smoke, but they also are marketed for the removal of VOCs from cleaning agents, cosmetics, pest control agents, and building materials such as carpet, particleboard, adhesives, and paints. Absorbers consist of a media, either solid or liquid, into which the gaseous contaminant dissolves. Disadvantages of liquid media absorbers is their potential for becoming an airborne contaminant through the reaction process or, if water is the medium, the potential for the addition of humidity into the airstream. Adsorbers provide a media surface to which gaseous contaminants become bound. Typical adsorption medias include activated aluminas and activated carbons. The loading of these media beds by the gaseous contaminant is not an instantaneous process, and removal efficiency is dependent upon time, gaseous contaminant concentration in the airstream, and media depth and thickness.

Efficiencies and maintainability of adsorption filters is questionable and is currently the subject of much research. Some tests have shown removal efficiencies of charcoal filters of approximately 95 percent for ozone and approximately 70 percent for selected VOCs.[16] These tests, conducted in a test duct, also revealed no noticeable degradation of filter performance over an 18-month period. The concentrations of the selected VOCs in this study were typically in ranges below 3 μg/m^3.[16] Other studies have shown that efficiencies of charcoal filters decrease drastically (within hours) after heavy exposure to gaseous contaminants. The use of carbon filters for gaseous pollutant removal should be carefully investigated prior to installation and given the following considerations before choosing a filter:

1. Type of contaminant being targeted

2. Rate of contaminant generation

3. Maintenance staff capabilities

4. Cost

5. Size constraints and limitations

Filter selection is an important facet in the control of IAQ. The knowledge of what type of contaminant is or could be present in the building environment is often not known by HVAC designers who make the filter selection. For existing buildings with existing HVAC systems, the addition of a more efficient filter may not provide a simple solution to IAQ problems. Without considering the effects of additional air resistance to the existing fan, the results could increase occupant discomfort levels by hindering supply airflow.

Air distribution.   No amount of outside air will provide dilution of contaminants if the outside air is not being delivered to the occupied zone. The efficiency with which outside air is provided into the occupied zone is called ventilation effectiveness. ASHRAE 55-1992 defines the occupied zone to be between the floor and 6 ft above the floor and more than 2 ft from walls or fixed equipment. Within the thermally acceptable ranges for occupant satisfaction (see Sec. 3.1), there is no minimum air speed that is required for comfort. There is only the necessity to avoid creating drafts. Ideally, air-distribution systems should create relatively uniform air velocity, temperature, humidity, and air quality conditions within the occupied zone.

The layout of supply diffusers and return air grilles in occupied spaces is determined by air volume, space characteristics, layout of furnishings, sources of heat gain or heat loss, and diffuser type. The movement of air within the space from supply to return/exhaust should direct supply air toward and across sources of heat generation. Localized exhaust grilles should be installed above or near the source of vapor or odor generation. In high-ceiling areas, location of return grilles near the occupied zone (the range between the floor and 6 ft above the floor) will prevent the tendency for the supply air to stratify. Ceiling-mounted fans are also useful in pushing down warm supply air to the occupied zone in high-ceiling areas.

O&M, controls and test and balance.   Maintenance of the HVAC system is perhaps the single most important concept for the control of IAQ. Maintenance for IAQ is much more than responding to occupant complaints as they occur. A preventive maintenance plan should be incorporated into the building management scheme that emphasizes procedures to identify and correct IAQ problems. Along with the routine maintenance actions normally instituted for HVAC systems, include such measures as:

1. Investigate condensate drain pans for signs of moisture buildup or algae growth.

2. Operate the HVAC system through heating and cooling cycles to ensure proper temperature control operation.

3. Resolve employee thermal comfort problems proactively.

4. Note changes in space functions, including the additions or deletions of equipment that might be contaminant sources.

Of all HVAC system components, the control systems are perhaps the least understood by maintenance personnel and designers. With the advent of direct digital controls (DDC), the temperature control industry has evolved at such a rapid pace that the manufacturers are having to become involved in the design process as the engineers find it difficult to stay abreast of equipment and technology advances. From the maintenance perspective, a lack of understanding of the control systems components can have serious effects on IAQ.

The results of an improperly functioning control system are usually manifest in occupant discomfort. Each valve and damper that has an impact on the amount of heating or cooling, the timing of heating or cooling, and the cutoff (set point) of heating or cooling is acting from the response of a control signal. Most newer control systems are DDC or electronic. Buildings constructed or renovated during the 1950s through the 1980s are more likely to have pneumatic controls. The approach to heating and cooling control is the same in both DDC and pneumatic systems. How a particular HVAC system is controlled depends upon the type of system (VAV, multizone, split systems, etc.) and the components within the system (preheat coil, reheat coil, face and bypass damper, economizer, etc.). If faulty controls are suspected of being the cause of IAQ problems, it is recommended that a controls service contractor be contacted to provide a survey and evaluation of the existing system. Such an analysis should include simulating the HVAC system response in the heating and the cooling mode, the reaction and response of outside air dampers, and the response of dampers that may be installed at the occupied zone (VAV operation, etc.).

Another useful tool available to the IAQ professional is the use of a certified test and balance contractor. There is no better way to determine if an HVAC system is performing as it was designed than by the use of these services. The test and balance report should give actual airflows for supply, return, and exhaust systems, at each diffuser/grille and at each fan and air-handling unit. This information can then be compared to either the design quantities or the current quantities as needed to provide occupant comfort. Another service that the test and balance contractor can provide is measuring air pressure relationships between occupied zones. From this information, pathways of potential indoor air contaminants can be traced within the building. The test and balance report is a quick and generally economical way to determine HVAC system deficiencies caused by inadequate airflow.

Alterations in design load. HVAC systems sometimes fail to provide acceptable air quality through no fault of their design or their performance. They fail because the function of the spaces which they serve has been altered and no modifications to the HVAC system have been made to compensate for the new space load conditions. A change in functional area of a space can affect the HVAC system in many ways:

1. Occupant activity levels may be changed, affecting the metabolic rates and thus the CO_2 generation rate of the occupants in the space.

2. Equipment, appliances, or lighting may be changed, adding to or subtracting from the internal heat generation within the space.

3. Wall partitions, especially the demountable-type partitions, may be revised in a manner to affect airflow and air-distribution patterns within the occupied space.

4. New materials that generate strong off-gassing of VOCs or other contaminants may be added to the space.

5. Process machinery or equipment that generates airborne particulates may be added to the space.

Occupant loading in commercial buildings is a variable in HVAC design that is difficult to control. Most designers approach general office settings based upon an occupant load of approximately one person per 100 ft^2 of floor area. In reality, many office areas may have a concentrated occupant load much higher than this value. In existing buildings, the higher occupant load levels may be coupled with a designed ventilation rate of 5 cfm per person which, as we have discussed, is now generally recognized as an inadequate ventilation rate by a factor of three.

In minor building renovations, the HVAC system is often neglected except to the extent that the locations of diffusers and grilles may be adjusted to track employee relocations. These minor adjustments in the HVAC system are difficult to distinguish in the field and are rarely recorded in building record drawings, which makes detection of these changes by the IAQ investigator a near impossibility. Understanding the impact on the HVAC system of functional alterations is an important measure for avoiding future IAQ problems.

3.4   Existing Buildings: Investigation and Corrective Strategies

This section is intended to assist with the HVAC-related elements of an IAQ investigation. It also offers corrective strategies. An understanding of HVAC systems in general, as described in Sec. 3.2, and familiarization with the subject building's HVAC system in particular are essential to a successful, systematic, and methodical approach. An important part of this methodology is an HVAC checklist. This checklist, as provided in App. C, complimented by the *Occupant Health and Comfort Questionnaire,* is a valuable part of the remediation process.

In the remaining portion of this section, the individual components of the HVAC checklist are analyzed, and investigative and corrective strategies are offered. Depending on the size of the building or nature of the IAQ complaint, this checklist can be utilized for an entire building or portions of it, or it can be used for each individual air-handling system serving a building.

3.4.1 Temperature and humidity readings

Depending on the size of the building or extent of the IAQ problem, it may be necessary to record temperature and relative humidity in several locations inside and outside of the building. Some of the factors contributing to changes in temperature and humidity are occupant and equipment loads and outside air ventilation rates. Temperature and relative humidity can be measured directly with digital instruments. Relative humidity can also be measured indirectly by a sling psychrometer using wet and dry bulb temperature readings.

If the above readings are outside the comfort zone, which was discussed in Sec. 3.1, the IAQ complaints may be linked to the design, performance, and capacity of the existing HVAC system. The original design parameters should be investigated and compared with the actual readings. Some of these design parameters include temperature, relative humidity, occupant load, equipment and lighting load, and ventilation rates. Humidity levels within a space may affect more than occupant comfort levels. High humidity has been shown to slow the process of curing for some adhesives, which may increase the life of VOC emissions.[17]

As part of the investigation, it must be verified that all of the components of the HVAC system are operating properly. For example, proper operation of humidifiers, fan belts, and the refrigeration cycle needs to be verified, the ductwork system should be checked for possible leaks, and the condition of filters should be determined. These are all factors that inhibit the performance of the HVAC system and adversely affect IAQ.

If design parameters do not coincide with actual conditions, new heating and cooling calculations should be performed. The internal loads (occupants, lighting, equipment, etc.) should reflect the existing conditions. If the existing HVAC equipment is not capable of satisfying the current load demands, it should be replaced, modified, or supplemented with additional equipment in order to provide temperature and relative humidity within the comfort zone.

3.4.2 Outside air intake

A potential cause of IAQ problems is contaminated outdoor air which enters the building via the outside air intake opening of the air-handling unit. This contaminated air mixes with the building return air and is distributed through the building by the supply air ductwork. Therefore, the outside air intake should be designed and located in such a manner that contaminated outdoor air cannot enter the building. Some building codes specify that any outside air intake should be located at least 25 ft from any building exhaust or combustion gas emission stack. This requirement is even more stringent and critical for hospitals and health care facilities. It is also important to note that merely satisfying the building codes may not prevent the entrance of contaminated air through the outside air intake because of prevailing wind direction. Prevailing winds can even cause the emissions from adjacent properties to enter the building.

The corrective strategy for contaminants entering through the outside air intake is to relocate the outside air intake, to remove or relocate the source of the contamination, or to provide additional filtration at the location of the outside air intake.

Wire mesh, or "bird" screens, should be installed on all outside air intake openings to protect the HVAC system from the introduction of large debris.

Outside air intake louvers adjacent to parking garages and highly congested streets can be subject to the introduction of CO gas through the outside air intake. See Fig. 3.26. One remedy is to relocate the

Figure 3.26 Outside air intake. (*Used with permission of Gobbell Hays Partners, Inc., Nashville, Tenn.*)

outside air intake away from the contamination source. This is typically accomplished by raising the outside air intake above street levels or congested traffic areas by a ductwork extension. Another option is to investigate adding a charcoal filter to the outside air intake opening to prevent CO gas from entering the system.

3.4.3 Outside air requirements

It is likely that buildings designed in accordance with the ASHRAE requirement of 5 cfm per person, before ASHRAE Standard 62-1989 revised the minimum outside air requirement to 15 cfm per person, are now providing inadequate ventilation. The minimum outside air requirement is achieved by either a minimum set point position for a single air damper or by a separate and independently controlled minimum outside air damper. The temperature controls of most HVAC systems are designed to provide up to 100 percent outside air when the outdoor temperature is in a range that additional tempering of the outside air will not be required. This is known as the economizer, or free cooling, cycle.

As explained earlier, a variable air volume HVAC system is designed in a manner that total system air quantity increases as the demand from individual zones increases. Conversely, when the total demand from these zones decreases, the system supply fan speed is automatically decreased, thereby providing energy savings from reduced fan horsepower requirements. The disadvantage of this system in relation to IAQ is that, normally, outside air is introduced to the mixing plenum of the air-handling unit from which it is delivered to individual zones through the supply airstream. When the supply air is decreased in response to demand, the outside air quantity is also decreased proportionally.

There are several instruments available in the market to measure airflow quantities. They differ depending primarily upon the desired location of the reading. The ideal instrument for use is the one that provides a direct air volume rate reading (cubic feet per minute). For example, a balancing hood with the appropriate adapter is ideal for measuring the air volume rate leaving an air diffuser in cubic feet per minute. The hot wire anemometer is best when measuring low air velocities and a vane anemometer is best for larger ventilation systems. The velocity readings from the anemometer are then converted into cubic feet per minute by multiplying the reading by the duct cross-sectional area. Manometers are sometimes used for measuring the air pressure at any location in a duct run. This air pressure can then be converted into air velocity, which can be converted to cubic feet per minute as described above.

Another method of tracking the adequacy of outside air in a building is to measure the CO_2 concentration. However, the use of CO_2 as an indicator of ventilation is not always accurate because of the variability of the CO_2 generation rate of building occupants and the uncertainty as to whether CO_2 buildup in a space or building has ever reached equilibrium. The CO_2 concentration can be measured by CO_2 gas analyzers, which are available in the market. Some analyzers are equipped with recording software capabilities. This software provides a profile of CO_2 concentrations in parts per million during an extended amount of time. These data are useful in developing corrective strategies. Chapter 2 provides guidelines on acceptable levels of CO_2. The percentage of outside air can be estimated by measuring CO_2 concentration C in the return air RA, supply air SA and outside air OA according to the equation:

$$OA\% = \frac{C_{RA} - C_{SA}}{C_{RA} - C_{OA}} \times 100$$

Sample calculation (estimating ventilation rates in existing buildings from CO_2 concentrations)

When CO_2 concentrations are allowed to reach an equilibrium state within a space, and then suddenly the source is removed (such as when people leave a building at 5:00 p.m.), the following concentration-decay method can be used to estimate the ventilation rate:

$$V_o = \frac{\ln(C_{ii} - C_o) - \ln(C_{if} - C_o)}{}$$

where V_o = air exchange rate
C_{ii} = CO_2 concentration indoors, initial (ppm)
C_{if} = CO_2 concentration indoors, final (ppm)
C_o = CO_2 concentration, outside (ppm)
t = time (h)

So for the conditions in a 64,000-ft³ space of an indoor CO_2 concentration at 5:00 p.m. of 1000 ppm, CO_2 concentrations at 8:00 p.m. of 400 ppm, and an outside C_o concentration of 330 ppm, the estimated air change rate within the space is

$$V_o = \frac{\ln(C_{ii} - C_o) - \ln(C_{if} - C_o)}{t}$$

$$V_o = \frac{\ln(1000 - 330) - \ln(400 - 330)}{3}$$

$$V_o = \frac{6.5 - 4.25}{3}$$

$V_o = 0.75$ air changes per hour

or

$$V_o = \frac{0.75 \times 64,000}{60} = 800 \text{ cfm of outside air}$$

Corrective strategies can begin with analyzing the outside air portion of the air-handling system. A new heating and cooling load calculation should be performed in order to include the ASHRAE minimum ventilation rate requirement according to the Ventilation Rate Procedure. The new calculations should also include any other changes to the original design criteria. If the HVAC system is not capable of accommodating the new criteria, it should be modified or complimented by additional equipment.

Regardless of whether additional HVAC equipment is needed or whether the introduction of additional outside air is accomplished by opening up the outside air damper, it is safe to say that the energy consumption of the building will increase. The amount of increase in energy consumption is related to both the geographic location of the building and the number of people occupying it. Air-to-air heat recovery systems can be effective in reducing the energy impact.

The increase in outside air quantity, specifically in more humid climates, can adversely affect the relative humidity levels in a building. This fact is critical in facilities which require exact control of humidity for occupant health, such as health care facilities, and manufacturing plants, where specific relative humidity levels are required for the operation of equipment and processes. Humidity control can become a significant part of the corrective action plan.

Another source of outdoor air entering the building is through the operation of a building's HVAC system under a negative pressure. This situation occurs when the intake of outside air is less than the air exhausted through exhaust fans. Ideally, buildings should operate at a slightly positive pressure to assist in overcoming infiltration. Figure 3.27 is a schematic of building pressurization scenarios.

3.4.4 Mixing plenums

The mixing plenum is the housing or sheet metal section where the building return air is mixed with the outside air before entering the building as supply air through the air handler. Dampers operate the mixing between outside air and return air. It is important to verify that the return and outside air are mixed properly before entering

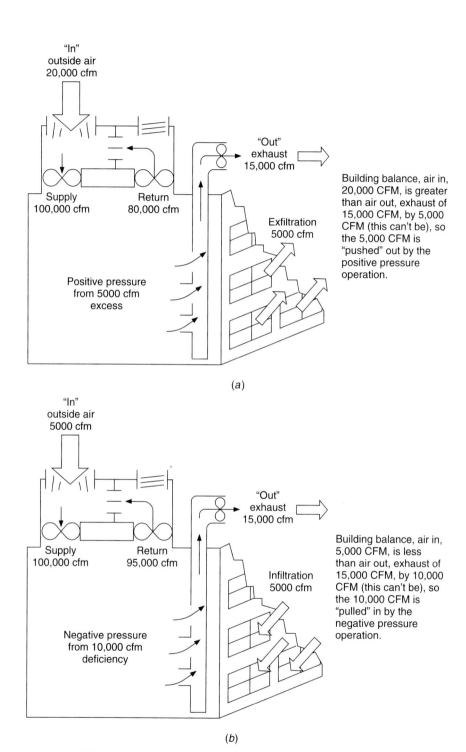

"In"
outside air
20,000 cfm

"Out"
exhaust
15,000 cfm

Supply
100,000 cfm

Return
80,000 cfm

Exfiltration
5000 cfm

Positive pressure
from 5000 cfm
excess

Building balance, air in, 20,000 CFM, is greater than air out, exhaust of 15,000 CFM, by 5,000 CFM (this can't be), so the 5,000 CFM is "pushed" out by the positive pressure operation.

(a)

"In"
outside air
5000 cfm

"Out"
exhaust
15,000 cfm

Supply
100,000 cfm

Return
95,000 cfm

Infiltration
5000 cfm

Negative pressure
from 10,000 cfm
deficiency

Building balance, air in, 5,000 CFM, is less than air out, exhaust of 15,000 CFM, by 10,000 CFM (this can't be), so the 10,000 CFM is "pulled" in by the negative pressure operation.

(b)

Figure 3.27 Schematic of building pressurization (a) Positive pressurization; (b) negative pressurization. (*From* "Ventilation System O & M: A First Step for Improving IAQ," *presented at IAQ '93, Philadelphia, Penn., Nov. 7–10, 1993. Used with permission of ASHRAE, Atlanta, Ga.*)

the filter section side of the air-handling unit and that all of the visible debris is removed by filters before reaching the cooling coil. The proper operation and sequencing of all dampers, linkages, and manual and automatic controls need to be verified. It should also be noted whether all of the mixing plenum housings are equipped with floor drains for draining carryover moisture from the outside air intake. If a drain is present, the investigator should verify that it is properly trapped.

As a part of corrective strategies, all of the deficiencies in the operation of the dampers and linkages need to be corrected. Traditionally, the insulation of any exposed ductwork, including the mixing plenums, is in the form of internal lining. This internal lining and the adhesive attaching this insulation to the interior portion of the ductwork are potential contributors to an IAQ problem, as discussed in Sec. 3.3. If it is determined that this lining is in fact contributing to the IAQ problem, it should be removed and replaced with appropriate weatherproof external insulation.

3.4.5   Air filtration

The concept of filtration was discussed in Sec. 3.3. To start the investigation of the system's filter section, a review of the HVAC system design must first be conducted in order to verify that the installed filters meet the type and efficiency of the design. As explained in the previous section, filters come in different media types and efficiencies.

The filters should also be checked for their cleanliness and proper frame seatings. Any debris that gets through the filter is a potential contributor to an IAQ problem. Moisture accumulation could contribute to biocontaminant growth, and any such evidence, like stains, should be noted. The maintenance log should be checked or interviews with the maintenance staff should be performed to determine the frequency of filter replacement. Figure 3.28 illustrates improperly maintained filters.

As part of corrective actions, any discrepancy between the design intent and the actual conditions should be corrected. A preventative maintenance plan (see Sec. 3.6) should be established or closely followed if one already exists. Appropriate static pressure gauges should also be installed at the filter banks to indicate when filters are becoming loaded and need to be replaced.

Sometimes, as part of a comprehensive investigation, it is determined that more efficient filters need to be installed. It should be noted that an increased static pressure drop across the more efficient filters will possibly require adjustments to the supply fan motor belts and sheaves and may even require a larger fan motor. More efficient

Figure 3.28 Dirty filter. (*Used with permission of Gobbell Hays Partners, Inc., Nashville, Tenn.*)

filters installed with an inadequate supply fan will not be able to deliver the required amount of air and, consequently, will create a bigger IAQ problem.

Sample calculation (effects of installing a higher-efficiency filter on an existing HVAC system)

Fan motor horsepower can be estimated by the following equation:

$$\text{HP} = \frac{\text{SP} \times Q \times K_L}{6356 \times N_{\text{eff}} \times d}$$

where SP = static pressure (in H_2O)
$\quad\ \ Q$ = airflow (cfm)
$\quad\ \ K_L$ = factor for drive loss
$\quad\ \ N_{\text{eff}}$ = fan efficiency
$\quad\ \ d$ = density correction factor

What is the effect on a supply fan of replacing a 1-in-thick pleated filter (average static pressure drop between initial and final resistance = 0.5 in H_2O) with a HEPA filter with an average resistance listed at 1.4 in H_2O?

Assumptions K_L = 1.0
$\qquad\qquad\quad d$ = 1.0
$\qquad\qquad\ \ N_{\text{eff}}$ = 0.8
$\qquad\qquad\quad Q$ = 5000 cfm
Fan system static pressure (except air filters) = 1.5 in H_2O

$$\text{Existing HP} = \frac{(1.5 + 0.5) \times 5000}{6356 \times 0.8} = 1.97 \qquad \text{with 1-in pleated filter}$$

$$\text{New HP} = \frac{(1.5 + 1.4) \times 5000}{6356 \times 0.8} = 2.85 \qquad \text{with HEPA filter}$$

3.4.6 Cooling coils and moisture

The cooling coils, whether as the primary coils at the main air handler or as a part of the individual-zone cooling systems, should be checked along with the condensate drain system for any microbial growth. If a maintenance program is already in place, all of the records should be checked to see if maintenance is taking place. Excessive water accumulation around the cooling coil should be investigated, and any water leaks or stains should be traced back to the source. Proper installation of the condensate drain system, including piping connections, should also be verified. The drainage system should be trapped, and the proper slope from the condensate pan to the approved drain locations should be achieved.

Secondary or auxiliary condensate pans, including the trap and the piping system, should be checked to ensure that they were installed as recommended by the equipment manufacturer. Excessive amounts of water accumulation in the condensate drainage system could be indicative of inadequately sized HVAC equipment or a clogged condensate drain system. This situation might arise if, for example, the outside air quantity is increased to satisfy ASHRAE's 15-cfm-per-person recommendation.

Any visible microbial growth should be cleaned. Care should be taken in specifying the proper disinfectant and cleaning schedule in order to ensure that workers are not exposed to toxic chemicals that may be present in the disinfectant or biocide. In a system where the condensate drain pan is overloaded and does not drain properly due to the lack of sufficient slope or the drain location, perhaps a condensate drain pump can remedy the problem. It should also be verified that all of the traps are wet (contain water) so that the sewer gases cannot enter the airstream.

Other areas to evaluate for the presence of moisture when performing IAQ investigations include:[18]

- Outside air intakes
- Filters
- Humidifiers, water sprays, and air washers
- Insulation

- Finishes damaged by water
- Any areas with greater than 70 percent humidity
- Ductwork (where the potential of leakage from outside sources has occurred)
- Building functions that create water vapor (cooking, showers, etc.)

3.4.7 Fan section

Any visible sign of moisture or microbial growth that has entered into the fan section needs to be investigated. Any debris not removed by the filters should be attended to. The maintenance records in relation to the fan section should be reviewed for reoccurring problems. The proper operation of fan belts, blades, pulleys and drives that affect the supply air delivery process should be verified. If the fan is capable of operating at different speeds, it should be verified that it is, in fact, operating at the right speed.

As a part of corrective strategies, all visible moisture and microbial growth should be cleaned under controlled conditions as described in the cooling coil section. If necessary, adjust and lubricate the components of the fan sections. The verification of the supply fan performance and system balance is highly technical and requires the proper instrumentation. If the in-house capability of the above work is not available, it should be contracted out to the appropriate companies.

3.4.8 Heating coil

As described earlier, heating coils are used in a variety of forms. A heating coil can be used as a primary source of heat, or it can be used as a reheat coil downstream from an air-handling unit, usually installed in the ductwork. There is also a variety of heat-exchanging mediums used in heating coils. Hot water, gas-fired, and electric coils represent the most common types of heating coils operating in buildings today.

In the case of gas-fired heating coils, the possible IAQ problems are directly related to the effect that both combusted and uncombusted gases have on the indoor environment. As part of the investigation, it should be verified that the gas furnace is properly vented, especially if the venting system is a gravity-type system for which the flue gases should be ducted straight, properly sloped, and with a minimum of horizontal runs. Also, it should be verified that a sufficient amount of makeup air is available for the combustion process. The required amount of air is usually regulated by local governing codes. Combusted or uncombusted gases must not be able to find their way through the building by way of ductwork or plenums.

Any deficiencies in the installation of the gas-fired furnace need to be corrected, including the installation and adequate sizing of flue ductwork and the provision of sufficient makeup air for combustion. In all types of heating coils, any deficiencies in controls, including the sequencing of valves and step controllers, should be corrected.

3.4.9 Humidification and moisture control

Steam humidifiers are located in the air-handling unit or, most often, in supply ductwork. Common types of humidifiers used in most commercial buildings are direct steam injectors, dry steam, and electric. Since the general principle behind all steam humidifiers is to inject steam into the supply airstream, special attention should be given to the accumulation of moisture and ultimately to the accumulation of microbial growth inside of the ductwork.

Humidifiers should be installed in straight duct runs. A general rule of thumb is to provide a minimum of 10 ft of straight duct section following the point at which steam mixes with the airstream before any sheet metal elbows or fittings are installed.

Check all drains and makeup water connections for proper installation. In the direct steam injector units, steam typically comes from a boiler located in the central plant. The chemicals used in the boiler water treatment process may migrate into the supply airstream through the steam used for humidification.

Verify that the controls associated with the humidification system are working properly. These controls include the humidistat, the steam control valve, and the airflow switch. The function of the airflow switch is to stop steam flow to the humidifier in the absence of airflow in the ductwork. The humidistat controls the operation of the steam control valve and can be wall mounted or mounted in the ductwork. Recommendations to improve humidifier performance might include relocation of the humidifier to where there is a straight duct run or where higher air velocity exists. Internal duct lining that can become wet by the humidification process may need to be removed and replaced with external insulation containing a vapor barrier.

The problems associated with moisture in building materials include microbial accumulation in insulation and other porous materials. These materials should be removed before they cause problems. Remove contaminated insulation, porous materials, and finishes (carpets, walls, ceiling tile) under controlled conditions in order to prevent the dispersal of fungi into the indoor air.

Morey[9] describes a specification for the removal of wet, contaminated drywall partitions from an office building where sampling revealed levels of *Aspergillus versicolor* at 1,500,000 cfu/in^2 of wall surface.

Apply the following controls wherever workers are removing bacterial and fungal contaminated building materials:

1. Define the limits of the work area and isolate the work area from adjacent, noncontaminated ("clean") areas. Shut off the HVAC unit serving the work area to prevent airborne particles from being distributed through the HVAC system. Seal all openings from the work area to adjacent spaces. Use polyethylene sheets or some other material that is easy to clean for seals.

2. Install HEPA-filtered fan units in the work area that exhaust outdoors at exhaust points greater than 25 ft away from other building openings or intakes. Maintain a negative pressure between the work area and adjacent spaces of 0.02 in water column.

3. Construct a decontamination system consisting of airlocks, a clean workroom, and a dirty waste load out room.

4. Remove contaminated materials within the work area. Double bag the contaminated material and pass the waste bags through the waste load out room.

5. Use HEPA vacuums to clean all surfaces of the work area after the contaminated material has been removed.

6. Worker protection during the removal, bagging, and load out procedures should consist of a half-face respirator and disposable coveralls as a minimum. The type of respirator depends on the contaminant.

7. Perform air sampling before removing isolation barriers to determine airborne spore levels. Note that air sampling should also occur prior to the material removal in order to establish background levels.

3.4.10 Ductwork system

The ductwork system is probably the most important component of the mechanical system affecting the indoor environment. It becomes the pollutant pathway from the problem's point of origin to areas throughout the building. In some cases, a problem that started elsewhere in the mechanical system becomes magnified inside the ductwork. Also, the improper design and inadequate performance of a ductwork system creates thermal discomfort, causing complaints among the building's occupants. The actual ductwork is normally constructed of galvanized sheet metal, but ductwork made of aluminum and stainless steel is also found in many buildings. An IAQ investigator should examine the ductwork and determine how it is insulated. The metal ducts are sometimes lined internally with fiberglass for the purpose of sound or thermal insulation. Moisture and contaminants that were not removed by the air filtration system or removed by the condensate drain pan at the coil section can easily become trapped by this internal lining and increase the chances for microbial growth. The sudden vibration caused by the air-handling unit being cycled on and off will tend to dislodge these contaminants and allow them to spread throughout the building. Unless there are access doors, it is difficult to visually inspect the internal lining. However, an experienced person can distinguish between an internally lined metal ductwork and an unlined duct simply by tapping on the ductwork. Taps on the lined duct generate a dull sound that is lower in pitch than taps on the unlined duct. Also review the original construction drawings to determine the location of the internal lining.

Another place to look for internal fiberglass lining is inside the terminal control boxes associated with the VAV systems (see Sec. 3.2). These boxes are sometimes lined internally for acoustical purposes. In some cases the ductwork itself is constructed of hard fiberglass boards. This type of duct system is more economical to install than metal ducts wrapped with insulation. The problems associated with the fiberglass duct system are similar to those with the duct system internally lined with fiberglass insulation.

For remediation of systems where evidence of moist fiberglass lining is found, Morey and Williams[19] suggest the following options:

- Remove the internal lining and replace it with an external lining. This solution provides the only true remedy.

- Upgrade the efficiency of the air-handling unit filters to reduce the airborne levels of microbials recirculated through the HVAC system. Prior to installation, thoroughly investigate the effects of added resistance of high-efficiency filters to the supply fan.

- Vacuum the air side of the internal insulation using a vacuum with a HEPA filter attachment. However, use this method only as a short-term solution, since the source of contamination has not been removed and contaminants may still amplify.

- Cover the insulation with a nonporous type of sealant. However, the IAQ professional must know the detriments of any material sprayed or applied to the inside surface of ductwork in direct contact with the airstream.

- Do not use biocides, since the dead microorganisms created by this disinfection provide nutrients for future growth of spores.

In recent years, preinsulated flexible ductwork has become popular in low-pressure duct systems due to its easy installation. In this type of premanufactured duct system, the fiberglass insulation is separated from the airstream by aluminum or other flexible corrugated metals and then wrapped with a vinyl cover as a vapor barrier. The problem with this type of duct system is that it can easily get damaged (tears, kinks, bends, etc.) during construction and adversely affect the airflow quantities to the building.

Another component of the duct system is the dampers. They can be in the form of manual or automatic volume dampers or fire and/or smoke dampers. If a lack of airflow seems to be the cause of the IAQ problem, there is a possibility of damper malfunction. The fire and smoke dampers should be checked to make sure they have not been inadvertently closed, thus restricting the airflow. The volume damper settings are generally related to the total air system balance and should not be changed arbitrarily. These dampers should be adjusted and set as a part of a total system air balance by a professional who has the appropriate credentials and equipment. Ask when the system was balanced and how the balance relates to building renovation and modifications.

Air grilles and diffusers are the last place that any contaminants can be trapped before entering the indoor environment. Accumulation of dirt, moisture, or grease (in a food service facility) could be an indication that the system's air filtration is not performing adequately. The location and placement of diffusers and grilles in relation to the building occupants directly affects IAQ and can result in occupant complaints. For example, if supply and return diffusers are located too close to each other, the air, which also includes fresh outdoor air, exits the area before reaching the building occupants (known as bypass or short circuiting). IAQ complaints also arise if the supply air diffuser is positioned where it creates a draft or is situated directly above a workstation. A well-designed and well-installed ductwork and air-distribution system provide a building with thorough mixing and a high ventilation effectiveness.

As a part of corrective strategies, replace any internal lining that is a cause of an IAQ problem with either an external wrapping designed for thermal insulation or sound baffles for acoustical insulation. Repair or replace any damaged flexible ductwork and open all closed fire and smoke dampers. Consider possible building renovations and alterations when balancing the air system, and evaluate grilles and diffusers for their ventilation effectiveness.

3.4.11   HVAC controls

An IAQ investigator must become familiar with the building's HVAC system and the manner in which it is controlled. HVAC controls are either pneumatic or electric. Pneumatic systems use compressed air to operate dampers and actuators. Figure 3.29 shows a pneumatic motor operating an automatic damper. Electric systems use either line or low-voltage wiring to operate the system. In the 1970s, simple energy management systems (EMSs) were introduced to the HVAC industry. These systems allowed HVAC systems to operate on sophisticated control strategies, shut down according to complex time-of-day schedules, and automatically shed electrical components based on preset electrical demand loads. With DDC, this level of sophistication has reached a point at which a building engineer or a maintenance person can diagnose and sometimes even correct control-related problems without even entering the building.

However, improperly functioning control systems can cause an increase in the HVAC system's energy consumption and IAQ problems as well. For example, malfunctioning outside air dampers that fail in a "closed" position may not provide the required outside air quantities to dilute contaminants generated within a space or HVAC zone. Outside air damper operations that fail in their "open" position can cause unwarranted heating and/or cooling to occur when the outside air temperature affects the unit's mixed air temperature. Any alteration to or maintenance of the building controls and the energy management system should be performed strictly by or with the consultation of the manufacturer of control devices.

When investigating HVAC control systems, the first step should include observing the operation of the control components at the air-handling unit mixing plenum where outside air enters the system and is blended with the return air. Operate the equipment in both the cool-

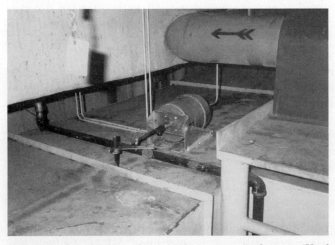

Figure 3.29 Pneumatic motor operating automatic damper. (*Used with permission of Gobbell Hays Partners, Inc., Nashville, Tenn.*)

ing and heating cycles. A visual inspection of the mixing plenum dampers during their operation from closed to open to closed will allow the investigator to make judgments regarding the amount of outside air being delivered to the unit. Obvious damper malfunction, such as no response from a control signal or damaged damper blades that impede or restrict damper activity, should be noted and corrected.

Other temperature control issues that need to be investigated are the individual thermostat set points, including setbacks (lowering zone thermostat set points at unoccupied hours) and time clock schedules that shut off HVAC systems operations at predetermined times. The building occupant schedules should correspond to the actual schedules programmed at the time clock.

Humidification or dehumidification components are a part of the control system. The operation of the humidifier control valve should be verified. For dehumidification, a reheat system is usually employed; therefore, the operation of the reheat valve or reheat controller should be verified. Attention should be given to the HVAC control in special-purpose areas such as kitchens, print rooms, laboratories, and computer rooms. These areas may have different schedules and humidity, temperature, and ventilation requirements than other building areas. For example, a computer room may be a 24-h operation area which should not be affected by time clocks. Kitchens, laboratories, and print rooms usually require separate and independent local exhaust systems. The makeup air systems and their interlocks with the exhaust fans should be investigated and verified for these special-use areas. Inadequate makeup air will cause building pressurization problems, which can lead to IAQ problems. Familiarization with the building control system and its capabilities and limitations can help the investigator recommend steps for correcting IAQ problems.

3.4.12   Alterations in design load

A common cause of IAQ problems in many buildings is that the building's current HVAC requirements differ from the original design. These alterations are usually caused by increased occupancy and subsequent altered office layouts or by a new tenant's requirements which the existing HVAC system cannot satisfy. During the investigation, determine whether or not the building's function has changed from the original design. Signs that indicate a change in the building's function include areas with a high occupant density, equipment such as copy machines and computers operating in a standard office space layout, offices partitioned without considerations to the HVAC system's air-distribution layout, and offices without at least one supply and one return diffuser.

As a corrective step, new heating and cooling load calculations incorporating new design conditions should be performed for the building. Depending upon the outcome of these calculations and the capacity and capabilities of the HVAC system, different approaches can be made to solve this problem. Examples of such approaches include moving people and equipment, increasing the ventilation rate, modifying the ductwork system and air distribution, and modifying or replacing the HVAC equipment.

3.4.13   Pathways

The HVAC system air-distribution components (ductwork, grilles, and diffusers) can be a pathway for indoor air contaminants. The most common pathway other than ductwork is the return air plenum. Generally, a return air plenum is the horizontal area between a ceiling and the floor above or between the ceiling and the roof structure, which is used to transport air from the conditioned space back to the HVAC air-handling unit. The air-handling unit is often located above the ceiling in the return air plenum. In these cases, little or no ductwork is associated with the return air, and the air-handling unit's filter section is exposed to the plenum. In other cases, a return air grille will collect the air from the plenum in a central location and then transport the return air to the air-handling unit via ductwork. Contaminants within the plenum can be transported into the air-handling unit where they may spread through the supply ducts into the indoor air environment.

Another problem associated with the return air plenum is difficulty in balancing and adjusting airflows. This can lead to pressurization problems inside the building. The balancing difficulty occurs when volume dampers are not installed for the return air grilles located in the ceiling. In these situations, the air will follow the path of least resistance, and more air will be returned from the area closer to the air-handling unit than from other parts of the zone.

The most cost-effective approach to eliminating contaminants from a return air plenum is to develop and implement a cleaning and maintenance program for the plenum area. Another approach might be to install a ducted return air system from the plenum area to the air-handling unit. The availability of space for installing return ductwork, as well as the impact on the air-handling unit's fan motor caused by additional ductwork, must be considered.

3.4.14   Mechanical equipment rooms (central plant)

The mechanical equipment rooms, or central plants, are normally unoccupied areas; therefore, they may not have an immediate and direct impact on the majority of building occupants. However, many documented cases have traced the roots of serious IAQ problems to the central plant. The central plant is where most of the major equipment and components of the HVAC system are located, including boilers, chillers, cooling towers, pumps, and air-handling units. Equipment such as the boilers and cooling towers require chemical treatment of the supplied water that is circulated through their heat exchangers. As a part of the IAQ investigation, the water treatment systems should be checked for possible interaction with the building air system. Such as where steam from the boiler is directly injected into the airstream, as is the case with some types of humidifiers. Drains and drain pans should be inspected for biocontaminant growth. The central plant is rarely air conditioned and, therefore, is not capable of being dehumidified. The nature of the equipment in the central plant, in conjunction with the lack of dehumidification control, makes this area a haven for the growth of bacteria. Regular maintenance of the central plant can prevent many of these problems.

3.4.15 Special-use areas

Within commercial buildings there are many types of special use areas that have a potential for creating poor IAQ due to the occupant activities or equipment that is associated with them. These areas include toilets, print rooms, smoking areas, garage and parking areas, and basements.

Toilets. The IAQ investigator should verify that toilet exhaust fans operate properly and that air is exhausted to the outside of the building. Also verify that the exhaust fan is equipped with a backdraft damper to prevent outside air from flowing back through the exhaust ductwork when the fan is not operating. The fan should operate continuously during the building's occupied hours, and there should be some means of providing makeup air to the toilet. The ASHRAE 62-1989 outdoor air recommendation for public restrooms is 50 cfm per water closet or urinal. Confirm that all floor drains and plumbing vents are installed properly and note any signs of leaks or moisture.

Print rooms. Verify the availability of adequate exhaust and makeup air in print rooms. The capacity of the exhaust system should be adequate to remove emissions from equipment and any stored chemicals. In some cases, the installation of a localized exhaust hood directly above printing equipment is an effective way of removing odors and emissions generated by the printing process. The IAQ investigator should inventory the chemicals used and VOC emissions involved with the printing process. If the contaminants from the printing areas are well defined, the use of air filtration units might be an effective way to clean the air. However, these units must be properly maintained, and the filters (especially adsorbent types) must be changed regularly to avoid recirculation of contaminated air.

Smoking areas.   The use of a separate exhaust system in smoking areas is highly recommended. ASHRAE 62-1989 recommends 60 cfm per person of outdoor air to be provided by the ventilation system of smoking lounges. Special filtration equipment such as electrostatic air cleaners and charcoal adsorption filters can be useful in smoking areas to eliminate the airborne contaminants found in tobacco smoke. Maintain negative pressurization of these areas in relation to adjacent areas to prevent the migration of contaminated air.

Sample calculation (estimating ventilation requirements for a proposed smoking lounge)

An existing space is proposed to be renovated into a smoking lounge. The space is 20 × 30 × 8 ft and supplied with 600 cfm of air through two ceiling diffusers. An estimated 15 percent outside air is at the air-handling unit that serves this room. Establish a dedicated ventilation system for this smoking lounge.

1.   Determine smoking lounge room volume:

$$20 \times 30 \times 8 \text{ ft} = 4800 \text{ ft}^3$$

2.   Determine the ventilation requirements using ASHRAE 62-1989 rates of 60 cfm per person. From information provided by the building owner, the lounge should be designed for 10 smokers. Required outside air ventilation is therefore

$$10 \text{ people} \times 60 \text{ cfm per person} = 600 \text{ cfm}$$

3.   Determine the estimated amount of outside air entering the space under current conditions:

$$Q_{SA} = 600 \text{ cfm}$$
$$Q_{OA} = 600 \text{ cfm} \times 0.15 = 90 \text{ cfm}$$

where Q_{SA} = volumetric airflow of supply air
Q_{OA} = volumetric airflow of outside air

As expected, the existing ventilation rate is insufficient to provide the outside air needed for the smoking lounge.

4.   Design considerations of adding a dedicated exhaust for the smoking lounge capable of removing 600 cfm are:

- How can the existing HVAC system be modified to maintain a negative pressure within the smoking lounge?
- How should a new exhaust fan be controlled? Can and should there be an "activity/no activity" control for the exhaust fan, or should it continuously operate?
- What, if anything, should be done with the room's existing return air grille? If the new fan runs continuously, is the return air grille needed? If intermittent operation of a new fan is specified, should the smoking lounge air be returned to the HVAC unit during periods of no use? Should two-speed exhaust fan operation be considered?
- What are the effects of additional exhaust on the existing HVAC unit? Is additional outside air required to compensate for the additional exhaust? Can the existing unit's capacity sufficiently handle additional outside air heating/cooling requirements?

Garage and parking areas.   The IAQ investigator should verify the amount of exhausted air for garage and parking areas (see Fig. 3.30). ASHRAE 62-1989 recommends a minimum of 1.5 cfm/ft^2 of outdoor air ventilation in parking garages. Local codes should also be consulted and may be more stringent than ASHRAE's recommendations. Sufficient makeup air via unobstructed outside air louvers, ducts, or supply fans should be provided. A CO alarm system is required by some local codes. During the investigation, verify that the exhausted air does not become reentrained into the building's HVAC system through outside air intakes located near the exhaust locations.

Figure 3.30 Underground garage. (*Used with permission of Gobbell Hays Partners, Inc., Nashville, Tenn.*)

Basement areas. Radon is a gas which naturally occurs in soils containing uranium. The EPA has recommended that all homes be tested for the presence of radon, although there are no existing recommendations or requirements for commercial buildings. Consequently, the areas most suspect to high levels of radon are subgrade or basement levels, where cracks and holes in the building's foundation walls would allow gas to enter from the soil. Basement areas are typically below grade and therefore subject to radon infiltration and accumulation.

One recommended means of radon gas mitigation is dilution through increased ventilation. As ventilation is added, provide sufficient make-up air to avoid creating a negative pressure. An alternate method of remediation to dilution ventilation is to positively pressurize subgrade or basement levels relative to the soil gas pressure in an effort to keep the radon from entering the area. (Refer to "Radon" in Sec. 4.3.4 for further discussion of this.)

3.5   New Construction

New construction projects enable the design engineer to assimilate all that he or she knows about IAQ and apply it to construction plans and specifications. Methods and procedures can be specified for good IAQ practices during the construction of the project, during the initial occupation of the building, and throughout the building's lifetime. The requirements, controls, and procedures necessary for good IAQ are not expensive and may, in fact, when combined with energy conservation design measures, prove to have an insignificant impact on the construction cost of the building. Design measures that improve IAQ need to be analyzed in terms of their economic impact in order to make building owners aware of initial costs and future anticipated costs, such as maintenance.

An important economic consideration is that employees demonstrate increased productivity and have fewer health-related absences when working in good air quality environments, as discussed in Chap. 1.

3.5.1   Design review

The initial stage of the design phase is the review and coordination of the design goals with all disciplines of the design team. The design team for a project might include architects, mechanical engineers, electrical engineers, structural engineers, civil engineers, landscape architects, specialized equipment vendors, and an industrial hygienist. IAQ can be affected by each of these disciplines. The design team members' responsibilities relevant to IAQ can be generally summarized as follows:

Architects

Specify new building materials

Lay out space designs, functions, and relationships

Specify general construction procedures

Specify moisture and thermal resistance barriers

Determine and disseminate knowledge of occupant and internal space loads

Mechanical engineers

Specify new building materials

Specify ventilation requirements

Determine recirculated air pathways

Determine space airflow patterns

Specify air filtration

Determine HVAC zoning requirements

Develop HVAC temperature and ventilation control strategies

Specify mechanical construction procedures

Industrial hygienists

Assist the mechanical engineer in determining dilution ventilation requirements

Review building materials' emissions characteristics prior to specification and installation

Electrical engineers

Specify new building materials

Specify lighting levels in occupied spaces

Specify electrical construction procedures

Structural engineers

Specify new building materials

Specify structural construction procedures

Civil engineers

Determine soil characteristics

Specify site construction procedures

Landscape architects

Specify pesticide and herbicide treatment

Specialized equipment vendors

Specify equipment that generates heat and humidity

Stress IAQ goals throughout the design process to all team members. It is a good idea to assign an IAQ team leader to coordinate among all team members and ensure that the IAQ design intentions are being met. The logical choice for this role is a mechanical engineer because of his or her understanding of ventilation, HVAC system control, and pathways created by various pressure relationships within the building. The team leader should be responsible for the development of the cost estimate that identifies additional costs of equipment, materials, or practices that will provide the owner with good IAQ.

3.5.2 Implementation

Ventilation. ASHRAE 62-1989: Ventilation for Acceptable Indoor Air Quality specifies design guidelines for determining minimum ventilation requirements based on either the Indoor Air Quality Procedure or the Ventilation Rate Procedure. ASHRAE recommends that the designer specifically note which method was used to determine minimum ventilation in the construction plans or specifications. If occupant loads or building functions change later, the designer or engineer in responsible charge can change minimum ventilation accordingly and consistently with the original design method.

ASHRAE 62-1989 also illustrates a procedure for distributing ventilation air to multiple spaces served from a single air-handling unit. When the ventilation requirements are unequal in different spaces, the amount of ventilation air being delivered in the critical spaces can be reduced. The less critical spaces become "overventilated" and the return air from these spaces which contains "unused" ventilation air is recirculated, thus reducing the total amount of outside air needed by the system.

Sample equation (multispace ventilation from ASHRAE 62-1989, App. H)

A single HVAC system may supply air to office spaces, conference rooms, print rooms, corridors, and so on, all of which require different ventilation rates based upon the Ventilation Rate Procedure. Rather than providing outside air to all of the spaces at the rates required for the most critical space, ASHRAE 62-1989 allows credit for excess outside air being returned to the HVAC vent through the following equation:

$$Y = \frac{x}{1 + x - z}$$

where Y = corrected fraction of outside air

x = sum of all outside air divided by the total supply

z = outside air fraction required in the supply to the zone having the greatest ventilation demand

The designed amount of ventilation air for a building HVAC system is based on a thorough knowledge of the anticipated use of the occupied space. Utilizing the Ventilation Rate Procedures requires knowledge of occupant schedules and activity levels. The Indoor Air Quality Procedure requires an understanding of the contaminant generation rates within the occupied space (see sample calculation below). Both procedures assume that contaminant loads in outside air used for ventilation are below contaminant levels for ambient air established by NAAQS (see Table 3.2). In urban and industrial environments, the designer should request data from local air pollution agencies that indicate levels of airborne contaminants around the site. If such data are unavailable, sampling the ambient air is an inexpensive alternative. Analysis of this data will determine the need for any special filtration requirements and could perhaps result in the specification of an outside air prefilter to clean outside air being mixed with the return air.

Sample calculation (ventilation requirements for the dilution of known contaminants)

The ventilation rate required to dilute a known volume of vapor in steady state conditions is defined by the equation

$$Q = \frac{403 \times 10^6 \times SG \times ER}{MW \times C} \times K$$

where Q = actual ventilation rate (cfm)

403 = the volume in ft^3 that 1 pt of liquid, when vaporized, will occupy at standard temperature and pressure (STP), ft^3/pt.

SG = specific gravity of volatile liquid

ER = evaporation rate of liquid (pt/min)

MW = molecular weight of liquid

C = concentration of vapor or gas (ppm)

K = a factor to allow for incomplete mixing; K = 1.0 for perfect mixing, K = 2 to 5 for fair mixing, and K = 5 to 10 for poor mixing

or for ER given in lb/min:

$$Q = \frac{387 \times 10^6 \times ER}{MW \times C} \times K$$

To determine the minimum amount of ventilation required to keep formaldehyde levels at 0.05 ppm for 100 m^2 of newly installed particleboard, assume:

Formaldehyde (HCHO) molecular weight (MW) = 30
Formaldehyde evaporation rate (ER) = 1.5 mg/m^2/h
$K = 1.0$
Formaldehyde specific gravity (SG) = 0.815

1. Convert formaldehyde evaporation rate to pounds per minute:

$$\frac{1.5 \text{ mg/m}^2\text{/h} \times 100 \text{ m}^2}{1000 \text{ mg/g} \times 454 \text{ g/lb}} = 0.00033 \text{ lb/h}$$

$$= 0.0000055 \text{ lb/min}$$

2. Find Q, ventilation rate:

$$Q = \frac{387 \times 10^6 \times \text{ER}}{\text{MW} \times C} \times K$$

$$Q = \frac{387 \times 10^6 \times 0.0000055 \text{ lb/min}}{30 \times 0.05 \text{ ppm}} \times 1.0$$

$$Q = 1419 \text{ cfm}$$

Further information on dilution air volumes for vapors is provided in Table 3.6.

For design of new construction, there is no better opportunity to combine concern for good IAQ with energy conservation. Consider using improved control technologies during this phase of building design. One method of combining adequate outside air for ventilation with energy conservation is through the use of an air-to-air energy recovery system, or a heat wheel. A heat wheel exchanges heat from building exhaust air with the outside air used for ventilation. Besides the energy benefits of preconditioning outside air through the air-to-air heat exchanger, no pollutant transfer from exhaust to supply air takes place if these systems are properly designed and applied.[20]

Temperature and humidity. Temperature and humidity parameters that establish comfort levels that strive to satisfy 80 percent of building occupants are recommended in the ASHRAE Standard 55-1992: Thermal Environmental Conditions for Human Occupancy. As with ventilation, comfort conditions in spaces depend on occupant loads and heat generated from appliances or equipment. The design engineer

TABLE 3.6   Dilution Air Volumes for Vapors

The following values are tabulated using the TLV values shown in parentheses, parts per million. TLV values are subject to revision if further research or experience indicates the need. If the TLV value has changed, the dilution air requirements must be recalculated. The values on the table must be multiplied by the evaporation rate (pts/min) to yield the effective ventilation rate (Q').

Liquid (TLV in ppm)*	Ft^3 of air (STP) required for dilution to TLV† (per pint evaporation)
Acetone (750)	7,350
n-Amyl acetate (100)	27,200
Benzene (10)	Not recommended
n-Butanol (butyl alcohol) (50)	88,000
n-Butyl acetate (150)	20,400
Butyl Cellosolve (2-butoxyethanol) (25)	Not recommended
Carbon disulfide (10)	Not recommended
Carbon tetrachloride (5)	Not recommended
Cellosolve (2-ethoxyethanol) (5)	Not recommended
Cellosolve acetate (2-ethoxyethyl acetate) (5)	Not recommended
Chloroform (10)	Not recommended
1-2 Dichloroethane (10) (ethylene dichloride)	Not recommended
1-2 Dichloroethylene (200)	26,900
Dioxane (25)	Not recommended
Ethyl acetate (400)	10,300
Ethyl alcohol (1000)	6,900
Ethyl ether (400)	9,630
Gasoline (300)	Requires special consideration
Isoamyl alcohol (100)	37,200
Isopropyl alcohol (400)	13,200
Isopropyl ether (250)	11,400
Methyl acetate (200)	25,000
Methyl alcohol (200)	49,100
Methyl n-butyl ketone (5)	Not recommended
Methyl Cellosolve (2-methoxyethanol) (5)	Not recommended
Methyl Cellosolve acetate (2-methoxyethyl acetate) (5)	Not recommended
Methyl chloroform (350)	11,390
Methyl ethyl ketone (200)	22,500
Methyl isobutyl ketone (50)	64,600
Methyl propyl ketone (200)	19,900
Naptha (coal tar)	Requires special consideration
Naptha VM & P (300)	Requires special consideration

TABLE 3.6 Dilution Air Volumes for Vapors (Continued)
The following values are tabulated using the TLV values shown in parentheses, parts per million. TLV values are subject to revision if further research or experience indicates the need. If the TLV value has changed, the dilution air requirements must be recalculated. The values on the table must be multiplied by the evaporation rate (pts/min) to yield the effective ventilation rate (Q').

Liquid (TLV in ppm)*	Ft^3 of air (STP) required for dilution to TLV[†] (per pint evaporation)
Nitrobenzene (1)	Not recommended
n-Propyl acetate (200)	17,500
Stoddard solvent (100)	30,000–35,000
1,1,2,2-Tetrachloroethane (1)	Not recommended
Tetrachloroethylene (50)	79,200
Toluene (100)	38,000
Trichloroethylene (50)	90,000
Xylene (100)	33,000

*See Threshold Limit Values 1988–89 in App. A.

[†]The tabulated dilution air quantities must be multiplied by the selected K value.

SOURCE: *Industrial Ventilation: A Manual of Recommended Practice,* 20th ed., 1988, p. 2-3. Used with permission of American Council of Governmental Industrial Hygienists, Cincinnati, Ohio.

should be aware of temperature and humidity requirements of special-use areas within a building, such as computer equipment rooms, art galleries, libraries, laboratories, and exercise rooms. In industrial settings, temperature may be allowed to vary over a greater range, but humidity can still remain a critical factor in the success or failure of a manufacturing process, such as in paper plants.

HVAC as source. Many HVAC equipment manufacturers are making technological improvements to improve IAQ. For example, some manufacturers are installing a V-shaped condensate pan below the cooling coil of their air-handling units to improve the ability of the condensate pan to drain properly, therefore reducing the potential for water to collect. The reduction of standing water inside the air-handling unit creates less potential for biocontaminant growth. This type of improved equipment technology should be specified if it makes sense for the project and if it is economically feasible.

Avoid internal duct lining in HVAC systems in areas having a potential for collecting moisture. Along with the liners, evaluate prior to specification any types of mastics used inside of the HVAC system for possible VOC emissions. The potential health effects of the vapors, or off-gasses, created by these mastics is discussed in Chap. 2. The designer should endeavor to specify sheet metal ductwork throughout the HVAC system. Sheet metal ductwork provides excellent characteristics of airflow dynamics and presents a surface that is less likely to provide a habitat for microbials and mold growth.

The designer's control over the use of any product that is a potential source of IAQ problems is through the specification and submission review process. The designer should specify the submittal of a product MSDS for his or her review and approval prior to the product's installation. Relevant information provided by the MSDS review is found in the portion of the sheet pertaining to the product's health effects. Rarely is any product available on the HVAC market used in a manner and quantity that would cause air concentrations to approach a PEL or TLV. Nevertheless, a common sense analysis of the health effects information provided on the MSDS should enable the designer to determine, for instance, if perhaps a flushout of the HVAC system is required prior to building occupancy. Designers now usually specify such flushout periods as a standard practice prior to occupancy, not necessarily because the HVAC system acts as a contaminant source but in order to dilute potential contaminants generated by building products, such as paints, particleboard, and other mastics and adhesives.

HVAC as contaminant transport. The designer should perform pressure balance analyses and provide airflow diagrams on all new designs, especially at and around those areas where there will be known sources of contaminant generation. Using the positive air pressurization in areas adjacent to contaminated areas is an effective means to isolate the source, as well as a very inexpensive way to keep the contaminant within its controlled boundaries. This solution, however, will not eliminate the source or the problem contaminant still present in the building.

Perform a pressure balance analysis after determining the building's heating and cooling load calculations and after determining a preliminary layout of the HVAC system. Air-distribution locations should also be determined. Indicate on building floor plans the pressure relationship from space to space (either + for positive pressure, − for negative pressure, or = for equal pressure areas), working toward corridors or lobbies that lead to the building exterior openings. For upper floors, work toward open shafts (mechanical, elevator, chutes, etc.) or stairwells that act as relief points for each floor. This exercise will be helpful in understanding the potential pathways for pollutants to travel in the indoor environment (from positive to negative pressure areas) as well as to ensure that the HVAC system serving the building or floor is "in balance" and not creating too great of an over- or underpressurization problem. Ultimately, this same exercise should be conducted by a test and balancing firm after construction as part of the building commissioning plan. Figure 3.31 is an example of a pressure relationship diagram.

When the engineer uses return air plenums, special considerations of air balance and air pressure relationships must be accounted for in the design through the incorporation of balancing dampers. Above ceiling plenum areas should be clearly identified on the construction documents and understood by the contractors so that they are not inadvertently obstructed or enclosed above ceiling. Some building codes require conditional use of return air plenums. For example, the National Electrical Code requires wiring located in plenum areas to be enclosed in conduit. By the time ramifications such as the additional cost of conduit, plus other above ceiling maintenance requirements are designed into return plenum projects, the net savings gained from the use of these plenums may be minimal. As a compromise to return air plenums, designers should investigate locating centralized return grilles in ceilings at locations that minimize the distances potential contaminants would travel. This option can still be more cost efficient than routing return ductwork to each individual space, and grilles may be located near areas of heat and contaminant generation that may improve IAQ and occupant comfort levels.

Transport of contaminants can also be controlled during the construction of the building by maintaining a clean work area. Ductwork and HVAC equipment that will be subjected to the recirculated airflow when operating in a new building should be protected from the dirt, dust, and debris that is prevalent at a construction job site. Specify the installation of polyethylene or plastic sheets to cover ductwork when it is stored, fabricated, and installed on the job site. For renovations, the construction zone should be isolated from any occupied adjacent spaces to prevent transmission of noise, dust, and dirt. Keeping renovated areas under localized negative pressure also helps to keep construction contaminants under control. See Fig. 3.32 for an example of fiberboard ductwork as it might appear in a renovation.

Filtration.   Understanding the types of contaminants to which occupants can be exposed is the basis for proper filter selection. But the initial and maintenance costs of special filtration systems are still disadvantages that some building owners are not willing to accept. It is therefore necessary to weigh the cost impact of special filters with their beneficial effects on air quality. It would benefit IAQ if HEPA filters were installed in every commercial building design, but the designer should make the owner aware of the higher initial costs of these filters and the higher operating costs associated with a higher-

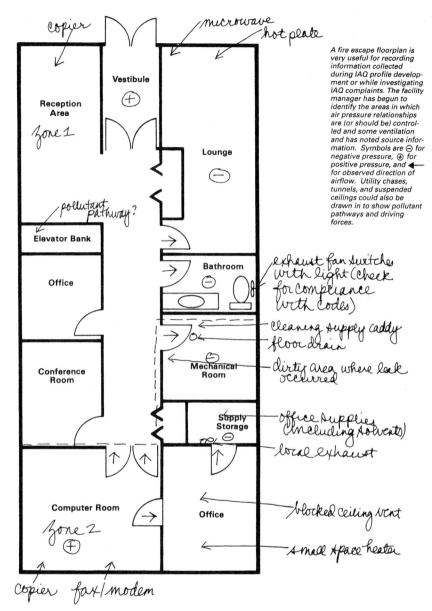

Figure 3.31 Example of pressure relationship diagram. (*From* Building Air Quality: A Guide for Building Owners and Facility Managers, *EPA/400/1-91/033, December 1991, p. 29.*)

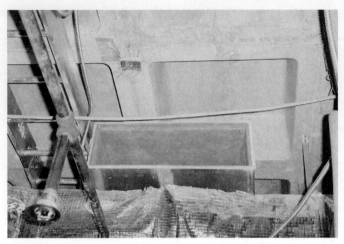

Figure 3.32 Fiberboard ductwork: In renovation areas, these openings should be sealed to prevent the collection of dust and debris. (*Used with permission of Gobbell Hays Partners, Inc., Nashville, Tenn.*)

resistance filter requiring a larger fan motor. If gaseous contaminants are suspected to be generated in building spaces, specification of carbon-activated adsorbing filters might be recommended, if not for the entire air-handling system, then for perhaps localized filtration in isolated areas where the source is localized. The use of localized filtration may have only a slight impact on the air-handling unit's total system static pressure and may not require the installation of a larger fan motor for the air-handling unit.

Air filtration can also affect the minimum ventilation air requirements for an occupied space. ASHRAE 62-1989 establishes specific procedures for the utilization of filters in recirculated air and recognizes that the reduction of recirculated contaminants is an acceptable way to reduce the minimum required amount of outside air. This method can be particularly useful in existing buildings where outside air is only available through the HVAC at a minimum fixed amount. Rather than modifying the existing air-handling unit by incorporating additional outside air ductwork, louvers, and exterior building penetrations, the addition of an air filter in the return air may reduce contaminants to an acceptable level, allowing the amount of outside air to remain unchanged.

Building codes may address minimum filtration levels based upon either building type, occupant activity, or outside air conditions. Hospitals have special filtration requirements dictated by hospital accreditation standards. Commercial building filtration should consist of media capable of providing 65, 85, or 95 percent ASHRAE dust spot efficiencies, depending upon outdoor air particulate concentrations, anticipated indoor air contaminant concentrations, and the percentage of outdoor air being used by the HVAC system. Filters below 20 percent in the dust spot test are rated according to the weight arrestance test and are not very efficient. A minimum dust spot filter efficiency of 25 percent is recommended for any HVAC equipment, including packaged units and home furnaces.

HVAC controls. DDCs are becoming more prevalent in new design due to their quick and accurate response time. DDCs have practically replaced pneumatic controls for commercial buildings on all types of HVAC systems. DDC technology is expanding rapidly, and designers have the luxury of specifying such control features as motion sensors to control HVAC system operations. HVAC controls are easily integrated with other building systems to create an automated building control system that can coordinate fire alarm and life safety functions, lighting control, and occupant comfort levels.

The designer should take advantage of rapidly developing DDC technology by making IAQ an integral part of the HVAC system control. One method used to achieve this goal is to designate contaminant levels as a control set point in critical areas where contaminants tend to accumulate. This method is commonly referred to as demand-controlled ventilation. CO_2 is used as an indicator of occupant levels. A CO_2 monitor can establish a set point (such as 800 ppm) and maintain that set point through controlling the amount of outside air entering the unit. Demand control has proven reliable in maintaining minimum outside air requirements in VAV systems at reduced airflow conditions. The CO_2 sensor is a reliable means of indicating when occupant loads are increasing (for example, in interior zones) in lieu of a temperature sensor that might be slow or fail to respond to occupant thermal load variations.

Several conditions should occur before CO_2-based demand control ventilation systems can be appropriately implemented:

1. The outside air damper must have the capability of varying the fresh air intake volume (an economizer-type setup).

2. For CO_2 control based upon occupancy, the occupancy schedules should be unpredictable. For constant or known occupancy, simpler control strategies could be put into place more effectively.

3. If economizer cycles are implemented throughout much of the heating and cooling season (thereby meeting or exceeding minimum ventilation rate requirements), demand control may not be warranted.

4. If contaminants other than people-generated CO_2 are suspected to be present, CO_2 may not be the target contaminant to control.[21]

One control strategy that is becoming more prevalent is the decentralization of the HVAC system. The decentralized HVAC system is more responsive to the needs of individual work areas. One way to decentralize is to use independent HVAC systems that are zoned and controlled for smaller areas. Modular workstations have also been designed where occupants can control temperature and airflow at their workstations by the operation of manual dampers. Each workstation is tied into an above ceiling or below floor plenum[22] that provides tempered air through the workstation. New wireless DDC thermostats have been developed to control VAV zones. The use of these thermostats can provide an effective way to adjust control set points within a zone as the load changes: simply relocate the thermostat.[23]

For VAV control, maintaining minimum outside air requirements can be the factor that determines the minimum allowable air quantity that the system can provide in the reduced flow (reduced load) mode. ASHRAE 62-1989 specifies that acceptable IAQ must be maintained throughout the occupied zone, even when the supply air is reduced by the volume box in partial load conditions. The HVAC control system strategy and air-handling unit coil design for VAV systems should account for outside air required loads at minimum supply air volume.

Architectural and occupant loads.   Understanding what is being put into a space, when designing for occupant comfort, is the essence of providing good IAQ. The HVAC system designer must ask the questions of the architect and/or building owner so that his or her understanding of the space use is as thorough and complete as it can possibly be at the design phase of the project. Usually the HVAC designer estimates occupant loads based upon information provided by ASHRAE, Carrier, or other sources. But a better method of getting this type of information might be to receive it directly from the architect. This communication at the design phase as space loads are being determined should also open up further dialogue about the scheduled use of the space, special lighting conditions, and equipment locations.

If the designer chooses to use the Indoor Air Quality Procedure to determine minimum ventilation requirements, information regarding emissions characteristics of the materials installed in the room must be ascertained. VOCs and other contaminants that may be generated within the space must be quantified and their emission rates estimated. (The emission rates for various building materials are given in Chap. 4.) The challenge for the designer using the Indoor Air Quality

Procedure is to estimate the cumulative load in a space caused by all of the different materials' emission rates.

Another characteristic of building material contaminant generation is the likelihood that the emissions will be at their highest rates when the material is initially installed or applied. Gradually the emission rates for the majority of building materials decrease or decay. Therefore, a standard practice is to flush out buildings, allowing them to remain unoccupied for a period of time in order for emission rates, and thus contaminant levels, to decrease. During this time period, operate the HVAC system in a 100 percent outside air mode.

Another preoccupancy method of contaminant reduction is to "bake out" the unoccupied building by operating the building's HVAC system in its maximum heating capacity mode to create a sustained indoor environment of 85 to 95°F. The theory behind bakeout is that the emission rates of VOCs and other gaseous indoor contaminants are increased in a warmer environment. A bakeout procedure should generally follow these steps:[24]

1. Install all furnishings and finishes prior to bakeout. Make sure that there is no standing water within the HVAC system.

2. Operate the HVAC system in the full heating mode with 100 percent electrical lighting for at least 24 h.

3. Operate the HVAC system in a normal operation for 12 to 24 h.

4. Repeat step 2 above again for 24 h.

5. Operate the HVAC system in normal operation.

One disadvantage to both flushout and bakeout is the potential for damages that could be caused to building finishes by their exposure to untempered outside air (flushout) or exposure to a warm environment (bakeout). Another disadvantage is incorporating into the construction schedule the time required to operate the systems in either of these modes. The time needed to perform these operations from the completion of building finishes to building occupancy is why it is important to discuss and coordinate with the building owner indoor air design issues (such as scheduling) at the beginning of the project.

Air distribution. Airflow patterns and currents that are created from the locations of supply diffusers and return grilles in the occupied space affect thermal comfort. ASHRAE has researched the patterns of airflows based upon location and velocity of the supplied air in terms of the coverage of the occupied zone. One innovative trend emerging in new designs is to supply conditioned air at the floor rather than the ceiling level. The conditioned air will flow from the floor level near the occupied zone and return through ceiling grilles above the occupied zone. This pattern creates a displacement air distribution method rather than the more traditional mixed air method. Figure 3.33 shows different strategies for displacement ventilation.

The importance of air distribution to IAQ and occupant comfort should be stressed to the architect and building owner at the design development phase of the project. The majority of commercial buildings with air systems have air supplied and returned from ceiling-mounted diffusers and grilles connected to above ceiling ductwork. However, a different approach to air distribution may be difficult to sell to architects and owners. Discuss and decide on the benefits of providing better indoor comfort prior to final design.

3.5.3 Building commissioning

Efforts to integrate design, construction, operation, and maintenance of a building HVAC system are often poorly coordinated and incomplete. A building HVAC commissioning plan will not only organize these efforts but will also provide IAQ guidelines for future managers and maintenance personnel. The estimated costs for performing commissioning range from 1.5 to 2 percent of the mechanical cost.[25] As outlined in ASHRAE Guideline 1-1989: Guideline for Commissioning of HVAC Systems, a building HVAC commissioning plan should include predesign, design, construction, acceptance, and postacceptance phases.

Predesign. Consultants are selected and a design team is established during this period. One of the duties of the design team is to obtain all pertinent design and building-related information. Such information might include the need for special-use facilities or systems (such as a cafeteria, kitchen, laboratory, or computer room) and coordination with representatives of facility departments to obtain each of their needs. The predesign should identify outdoor sources of potential air contaminants and verify that ambient outside air contaminant levels do not surpass the NAAQS levels. The design team should obtain the available budget from the appropriate individuals and evaluate and discuss different design options, considering the budget, with the same individuals. A commissioning plan should be developed with a designated team leader. All responsibilities should be clearly assigned by the team leader to other design team members and coordinated in a manner not to affect total design scheduling.

Design. During this period the design criteria are established and documented for the option selected in the predesign phase. Identify different HVAC system components and incorporate them into the construction documents. Specify building materials, such as carpets

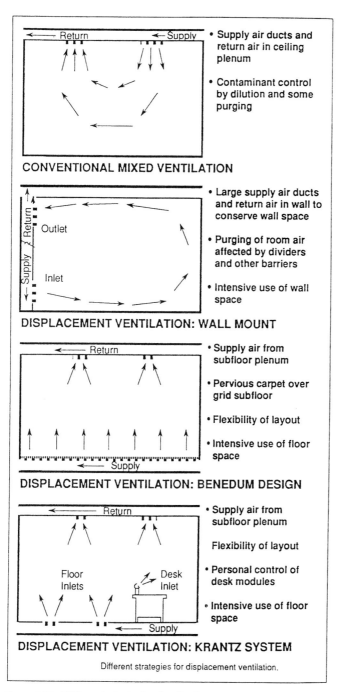

CONVENTIONAL MIXED VENTILATION

- Supply air ducts and return air in ceiling plenum
- Contaminant control by dilution and some purging

DISPLACEMENT VENTILATION: WALL MOUNT

- Large supply air ducts and return air in wall to conserve wall space
- Purging of room air affected by dividers and other barriers
- Intensive use of wall space

DISPLACEMENT VENTILATION: BENEDUM DESIGN

- Supply air from subfloor plenum
- Pervious carpet over grid subfloor
- Flexibility of layout
- Intensive use of floor space

DISPLACEMENT VENTILATION: KRANTZ SYSTEM

- Supply air from subfloor plenum

  Flexibility of layout
- Personal control of desk modules
- Intensive use of floor space

Different strategies for displacement ventilation.

Figure 3.33 Different strategies for displacement ventilation. (*From Indoor Air Quality Update, June 1991, p. 12. Used with permission, Cutter Information Corp., Arlington, Mass.*)

and adhesives, and the methods to install such materials, including engineering controls to mitigate contaminants. It is important to establish the requirement for a commissioning plan in the design document to ensure that the selected construction team is aware that it needs to follow this plan. Throughout the design phase, coordinate the HVAC system design with other design team members to ensure that occupant, material, and equipment loads within the space are taken into account, that ventilation effectiveness is maximized, and that filter selection meets the requirements for cleaning suspected indoor air contaminants. Procedures such as bakeout and flushout should be incorporated into the building design and schedule.

Construction.   Before actual construction, the selected construction firm should provide any commissioning-related submittals and shop drawings for review by the design team. During construction, the design team should make inspections of the construction site to ensure that all commissioning concerns are addressed and should provide documentation of these inspections. Address temporary ventilation to exhaust construction-related contaminants from the work site or away from partially occupied areas. The design team should participate in the HVAC equipment start-up to ensure that all HVAC components are performing properly. Testing, adjusting, and balancing of the HVAC system is the single most important aspect of the commissioning plan. Prior to the balancing procedure, it is very important to communicate with the balancing contractor that commissioning goals are to be met, proper outside air is to be delivered, and proper airflow is to be achieved. It is essential that the HVAC system is adjusted and evaluated during actual building occupancy.

Substantial completion or acceptance procedure.   Before providing the contractor with final acceptance or substantial completion documents, take the following steps:

1. Confirm and document the physical installation of all the components of the HVAC system and their compliance to the contract documents. "Record" construction drawings should be reviewed as a part of this process.

2. Review the air-balance report, including all the start-up information, calibration and testing of automatic controls, and all the airflow, temperature, and humidity readings.

3. Administer functional performance tests of the HVAC system components, including flushout or bakeout procedures for the main HVAC system and for the individual zones.

4. Review the operation and maintenance (O&M) manuals to ensure they are understood by the appropriate building management staff. O&M training should be performed by equipment manufacturers or the HVAC contractor. The maintenance staff must be trained and made aware of IAQ issues and the effect of the HVAC system on IAQ.

Postacceptance. The HVAC commissioning process does not end at substantial completion of the project. Commissioning is a process that requires continuous follow-up and attention. The following activities are necessary in order to achieve desirable IAQ:

1. Monitor and evaluate the HVAC system during a season other than the time of original HVAC start-up.
2. Perform continuous and regular O&M activities as required by equipment manufacturers; document all maintenance tasks including repair, replacement, and service of components.
3. Monitor and record all construction alterations, and evaluate the effect of the alterations on building HVAC systems and IAQ. An up-to-date record drawing will be a valuable tool for the future operator of the HVAC system.
4. Record and document all occupant complaints in order to establish a trend for a particular complaint.

See Fig. 3.34 for a Flow Diagram from ASHRAE's Guideline for Commissioning.

Construction scheduling of office space may not allow the application of all five commissioning phases defined by ASHRAE. For example, if buildings are only partially occupied after the completion of construction, the Acceptance Procedure can be only partially completed.

3.6   HVAC System Maintenance

Section 3.4 discussed the investigative techniques and corrective strategies for the identification and remediation of IAQ problems in existing buildings. Section 3.5 detailed a procedure called "HVAC Commissioning," which covered the necessary steps to attain the IAQ goals in newly constructed buildings. In order for a building to remain healthy, proper maintenance of the heating, cooling, and ventilation components is required. As discussed in earlier sections, the HVAC system has been reported by NIOSH to be the cause of over 50 percent of all IAQ problems and complaints; therefore, its maintenance is essential to the operation of a healthy building. The lack of trained

This Appendix is not part of this Guideline but is included for information purposes only.

APPENDIX A
This Flow Chart illustrates one of the many possible commissioning process arrangements.

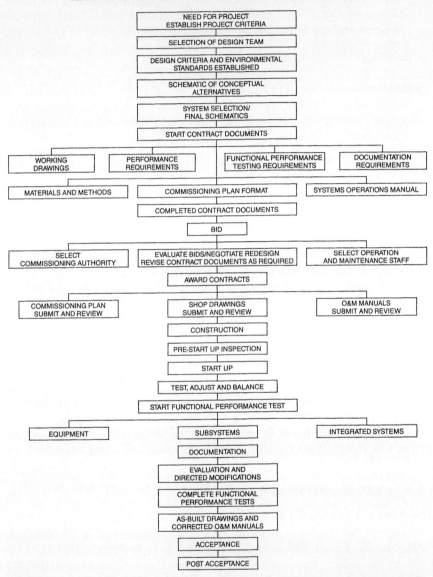

Figure 3.34 Flow diagram. (©*1989 American Society of Heating, Refrigerating and Air-Conditioning Engineers, Atlanta, Ga., from* ASHRAE *Guideline 1-1989: Guideline for Commissioning of HVAC Systems, p. 8.*)

maintenance personnel or an unsound operations and maintenance policy can be detrimental to the HVAC system's performance and can increase the risk of creating sources of contamination within the HVAC system.

3.6.1   Types of maintenance

The *ASHRAE Systems Handbook* has been used to assist in defining certain terms and aspects of HVAC maintenance programs, as follows:[26]

Preventative maintenance.   ASHRAE defines preventative maintenance as a type of maintenance in which "durability, reliability, efficiency and safety are the principal objectives, and it should be performed whether or not they are prescribed." The equipment manufacturers' guidelines should be followed as a minimum regarding the frequency of this type of maintenance.

Corrective maintenance.   ASHRAE defines corrective maintenance as strictly remedial, always to be performed before the occurrence of failure. Corrective maintenance can be performed during a shutdown caused by a failure that is not related to the corrective action.

Predictive maintenance.   Predictive maintenance is for equipment and components which are already part of the maintenance program. The basis of this type of maintenance is primarily dependent upon the experience and judgment of the maintenance staff. ASHRAE defines nondestructive testing, chemical analysis, vibration and noise analysis, and routine visual inspection as the elements of predictive maintenance.

Repair and service.   In the event of system failure, repair and service will be necessary to restore the system to a sound operating condition.

Understanding these terms and recognizing the differences between them will assist personnel in taking the appropriate maintenance action in a timely fashion and will assist in the development of an effective operations and maintenance plan.

3.6.2   Responsible parties

An effective approach to improve the IAQ profile of a building or, in the case of an already healthy building, maintaining good IAQ, is to implement a sound HVAC maintenance program.

Achieving IAQ goals is not the responsibility of one or two individuals. It requires a methodical approach by a team of individuals or departments. The team members' specific roles in relation to HVAC maintenance are listed below:

Design engineer.   A design that takes into account the minimum maintenance requirements, equipment access and serviceability, and overall equipment reliability will provide a more efficient and fine-tuned HVAC system. By specifying a sufficient amount of instrumentation devices such as control dampers, valves, and gauges and providing appropriate drawings and operation and maintenance manuals, a design engineer can play a major role in improving a building's IAQ conditions by improving the maintainability of the HVAC equipment.

Equipment manufacturer.   The equipment manufacturer provides durable and reliable equipment as well as comprehensive and accurate equipment design data, operation and maintenance manuals, and installation guides. The manufacturer should also ensure that his or her technical and sales staff are knowledgeable about the equipment and that the supply of spare parts is adequate.

Contractor.   The contractor's contributions to an HVAC system that can be effectively maintained are also essential. Proper workmanship and conformance to the plans and specifications in relation to installation and testing are the contractor's responsibility. The contractor has to make sure that the HVAC system is properly maintained prior to the start-up process and the owners' final acceptance. Appropriate operation and maintenance manuals, charts, and record drawings provided by the contractor are extremely important to the maintenance staff.

Owner or building operator.   The building owner's or operator's role in the HVAC maintenance process starts at the project's conception, in the predesign phase, and lasts throughout the useful life of the building. The owner should work closely with the design engineer to establish design requirements and criteria. The owner should also establish a sound HVAC maintenance plan related to IAQ. This plan should determine whether maintenance is to be performed by in-house personnel or by contractors. It should also require staff training appropriate for the type of HVAC system being operated and an adequate level of record keeping including inventory of equipment and parts. Finally, adequate budget and finances should be appropriated to ensure that the plan can be successfully implemented.

Building maintenance staff. Depending upon the size and complexity of the HVAC plant, a maintenance or IAQ manager might be necessary to direct and implement the HVAC maintenance plan. The manager should be able to prioritize efforts and finances in relation to different maintenance activities. The maintenance personnel should be trained accordingly prior to any maintenance work. They should follow the plan closely and be familiar with record-keeping responsibilities that need to be performed for maintenance activities.

The IAQ manager should:

- Establish a written program that documents maintenance activities and IAQ record-keeping requirements.
- Implement a smoking control policy.
- Provide IAQ training for maintenance staff and building/tenant managers.
- Develop IAQ guidelines for renovation activities.
- Establish schedules for HVAC maintenance, cleaning, and operation.
- Control and minimize the use of building materials with high contaminant emission rates.
- Develop a periodic recommissioning plan. Failure to monitor the HVAC system's performance as changes to a building occur, in conjunction with reduced operating budgets and changes in maintenance staff personnel, contributes to poor HVAC system performance.

3.6.3 Elements of an IAQ maintenance program

When organizing an IAQ maintenance program, the owner or IAQ manager should consider the following:

1. *IAQ maintenance policy.* The policy should be clear and precise and should outline the goals and directions adopted by the management staff. In order for the policy to be effective, it should contain an estimated budget and should implement the necessary controls that can be afforded.

2. *Record-keeping procedures.* The procedures should include preservation of the original construction documents, record drawings, and operation and maintenance manuals. It should also require stan-

dard procedures for updating the above documents in case of changes to the HVAC system.

3. *Procedures and schedules.*   The maintenance program should explain all of the necessary training, tools, safety measures, and reporting procedures. Appropriate forms and checklists should be created to assist maintenance personnel in their duties. A maintenance schedule and appropriate logs indicating dates, type of maintenance, and the person performing the work should be generated.

HVAC system maintenance, hand in hand with the commissioning of the HVAC system, is the major factor contributing to the health of a building. The implementation of an IAQ maintenance program is essential in eliminating IAQ complaints, which will result in higher employee productivity.

Preventative maintenance to control biocontaminants.   To control biocontaminants in a building or HVAC system, perform the following tasks as a minimum:

1. Inspect HVAC system components on a monthly basis for the presence of moisture or standing water.

2. Inspect areas of the building for moisture on a monthly basis.

3. Maintain areas below 70 percent RH.

4. Keep building areas subject to exposure to water vapor (showers and kitchens) well ventilated and well maintained. Inspect on a monthly basis.

5. Install filtration (50 to 70 percent dust spot efficiency) in areas or systems subject to moisture.

Preventative maintenance to control ventilation.   The development of a checklist to keep an adequate amount of ventilation should, as a minimum, include the following:

1. Periodically investigate the amount of building exhaust air compared to the amount of ventilation air being introduced through the air-handling unit(s). Perform this investigation during the minimum outside air mode of the air-handling unit(s). Generally, office buildings should operate under a slightly positive pressure, which means that the ventilation air supplied through the air-handling unit(s) should be greater than the building exhaust air. If exhaust air is greater than intake air, problems with infiltration of unfiltered, unconditioned, contaminated air could occur.

2. Periodically check the proper tracking of the outside air damper with the return damper. If the return damper is not closed completely in the 100 percent outside air (economizer) mode, the return air that is leaking through the damper can create overheating in the space.

3. Monitor supply fan and return fan tracking, especially on VAV systems. As the supply fan decreases output capacity on VAV systems, the return fan capacity should decrease accordingly.

4. Periodically monitor the operation of minimum outside air being introduced into VAV systems during their partial load conditions. ASHRAE minimum recommendations must be maintained.

5. Periodically investigate the proper operation of the freeze stat on cooling coils to verify that they are not completely closing minimum outside air dampers. If the freeze stat is not operating properly, it could be an indication that proper mixing of outside air and return air is not occurring.

References

1. Testimony of J. Donald Millar, M.D., Director, National Institute for Occupational Safety and Health, Center for Disease Control, Before the Subcommittee on Superfund, Ocean, and Water Protection, Committee on Environment and Public Works, U.S. Senate, Washington, D.C., May 26, 1989.
2. *Ventilation for Acceptable Indoor Air Quality,* ANSI/ASHRAE 62-1989, American Society of Heating, Refrigerating and Air-Conditioning Engineers, Inc., Atlanta, Ga., 1989.
3. Bearg, David W., *Indoor Air Quality and HVAC Systems,* Lewis Publishers, Boca Raton, Fla., 1993, pp. 61–64.
4. *1993 ASHRAE Handbook: Fundamentals,* I-P ed., American Society of Heating, Refrigerating and Air-Conditioning Engineers, Inc., Atlanta, Ga., 1993, p. 23.2.
5. *Thermal Environmental Conditions for Human Occupancy,* ANSI/ASHRAE 55-1992, American Society of Refrigerating and Air-Conditioning Engineers, Inc., Atlanta, Ga., 1992.
6. Bayer, C. W. and Downing, C. C., "Indoor Conditions in Schools with Insufficient Humidity Control," presented at IAQ '92 Environments for People, San Francisco, Calif., October 19–21, 1992, p. 197.
7. *Carrier System Design Manual, Part 7: Refrigeration Equipment,* Carrier Air Conditioning Co., Syracuse, N.Y., 1964, p. 7-2.
8. Morey, P. R., "Microbiological Contamination in Buildings: Precautions During Remediation Activities," presented at IAQ '92 Environments for People, San Francisco, Calif., October 19–21, 1992.
9. *ASHRAE Handbook: 1992 HVAC System and Equipment,* American Society of Heating, Air-Conditioning and Refrigerating Engineers, Atlanta, Ga., 1992, Chap. 20.
10. *1993 ASHRAE Handbook: Fundamental,* I-P ed., p. 37.2.
11. Burton, D. Jeff, *IAQ and HVAC Workbook,* IVE, Inc., Bountiful, Utah, 1993, p. 63.
12. *1993 ASHRAE Handbook: Fundamentals,* I-P ed., Chap. 11.
13. Farant, J. P., et al, "Impact of Office Design and Layout on the Effectiveness of Ventilation Provided to Individual Workstations in Office Buildings," presented at IAQ '91 Healthy Buildings, Washington, D.C., September 4–8, 1991.

14. Offerman, Francis, et al, "Control of Respirable Particles and Radon Progeny with Portable Air Cleaners," February 1984, in *Diagnosing and Mitigating Air Quality Problems in Buildings,* The Association of Energy Engineers, Atlanta, Ga., 1990.
15. *ASHRAE Handbook: 1992 HVAC Systems and Equipment,* Chap. 25.
16. Weschler, C. J., et al., "An Evaluation of Activated Carbon Filters for the Control of Ozone, Sulfur Dioxide, and Selected Volatile Organic Compounds," presented at IAQ '92 Environments for People, San Francisco, Calif., October 19–21, 1992.
17. Bayer, C. W. and Downing, C. C., "Indoor Conditions in School with Insufficient Humidity Control."
18. Burton, D. Jeff, *IAQ and HVAC Workbook,* pp. 64–65.
19. Morey, P. R., and Williams, C. M., "Is Porous Insulation Inside an HVAC System Compatible with a Healthy Building?" presented at IAQ '91 Healthy Buildings, Washington, D.C., September 4–8, 1991.
20. Bayer, C. W., and Downing, C. C., "Does a Total Energy Recovery System Provide a Healthier Indoor Environment?" presented at IAQ '91 Healthy Buildings, Washington, D.C., September 4–8, 1991.
21. *Indoor Air Quality Update,* June 1992, p. 8.
22. Drake, P., et al, "Strategies for Healthy Promotion through User-Based Environmental Control: A Select International Perspective," presented at IAQ '91 Healthy Buildings, Washington, D.C., September 4–8, 1991.
23. "Wireless Thermostat May Solve Several IAQ Problems, *Indoor Air Quality Update,* vol. 6, no. 9, September 1993, p. 10.
24. Meckler, Milton, "Indoor Air Quality—From Commissioning Through Building Operation," presented at IAQ '91 Healthy Buildings, Washington, D.C., September 4–8, 1991.
25. "Industry Pursues Commissioning to Prevent IAQ Problems," *Indoor Air Quality Update,* vol. 6, no. 2, February 1993, p. 9.
26. *ASHRAE Systems Handbook,* American Society of Heating, Refrigerating, and Air-Conditioning, Atlanta, Ga., 1984, Chap. 39.

Chapter

4

Architecture, Construction, and Operations

4.1 Introduction

This chapter covers a wide variety of elements that have a direct bearing on the quality of indoor air and addresses four major IAQ issues: building materials, building contamination, building functions, and other factors that affect IAQ perception. In addition, this chapter covers the diagnosis of IAQ problems and strategies for remediation in existing buildings, as well as how to optimize the IAQ of new construction. Please note that this chapter should be fully integrated with the other chapters of the book.

There are many sources of building contamination and a multitude of contaminants emitted by those sources. We have categorized the contaminant sources in the following way: Section 4.2 addresses the most common types of materials used in construction and the VOCs which they emit, generally when initially installed. Section 4.3 covers a diversity of building pollutants that affect the indoor environment. Many of these relate to construction activities or the operations of a facility. The contaminants may include other sources of VOCs, such as pesticides, and biological contaminants that are promoted by moisture. Asbestos, radon, lead, and PCBs are discussed as hazardous materials which traditionally have been addressed as separate contaminants. Asbestos, lead, and PCBs are regulated under certain conditions. As part of the discussion of building contaminants, pollutant pathways are described for contaminant transport. Section 4.4 discusses how the uses of spaces directly impact the quality of the indoor air. And finally, Sec. 4.5 includes related areas of concern which produce symptoms similar to those associated with IAQ complaints but are not really air quality problems, such as insufficient lighting and ergonomic stress.

The applications of this information are outlined in Sec. 4.6. This discussion presents practical guidelines for diagnosing and remediating contaminants and their dispersal throughout a facility. The corresponding checklist, included in App. D, is a valuable tool for the IAQ investigator when used in conjunction with the other checklists presented in this book. The final section, 4.7, explains how IAQ problems can be minimized in new facilities.

Resolution or prevention of IAQ problems requires an integrated approach, using all disciplines presented in this book. Mechanical and industrial hygiene issues have a direct bearing on the severity of the contaminants and their remediation.

4.2 Building Materials

Studies conducted by the EPA, NIOSH, the National Aeronautics and Space Administration (NASA), and the Consumer Products Safety Commission (CPSC) have shown that VOCs released from building materials and equipment constitute a major portion of indoor air contaminants.[1] The VOCs are typically a constituent of the manufacturing or installation process, and typically the emission rate of a given material will drop in relationship to the time it is exposed to the air. VOCs migrate from the material in question into the air in an effort to balance the concentrations of the compounds in the air with the vapor pressures exerted by the compounds contained in the material. As the VOCs in the material are reduced by this vaporization process, the forces driving the vaporization are concomitantly reduced; therefore, the VOCs enter the air in diminishing amounts. The reduction over time of the emission rate is called the rate of decay.

For the purpose of understanding how the majority of VOCs are released into the indoor environment, we will classify them into the following categories:

Adhesives, sealants, and *architectural coatings* are installed wet into the building and are expected to dry or cure on the premises. The release of VOCs is an inherent part of this process. The solvents used in the formulation of these materials directly relate to the VOCs emitted.

Particleboard and *plywood* are materials that are problematic because the adhesives, which are an integral part of their composition, emit the VOC urea formaldehyde (UF) after they have been manufactured. The emissions continue from these products after installation.

Carpet, resilient flooring, and *wallcovering* may bring a VOC-emitting composition into the building envelope and may use an adhesive which emits VOCs as part of their installation process. The contribution to the total VOC load is increased, and the time to reach equilibrium is extended by use of certain adhesives.

Insulation, acoustical ceiling tile, and *furnishings* can contribute VOC and particulate contaminants from a variety of sources. Depending on their composition, these materials may incorporate a variety of paints, adhesives, backing and fibrous materials, and fabrics, all of which can combine to complicate the IAQ issue.

A further complicating factor for emissions analysis is the tendency for some materials to act as sinks.[2] This term refers to the process by which VOCs released from one material may be absorbed into another and then re-released into the air.

The medical effects of VOCs are highly debatable. With formaldehyde, there is strong documentation, shown in Table 4.1, as to when a material may be uncomfortable, unhealthy, or deadly.[3] With most other VOCs, however, this kind of information has not been determined. As the significant numbers of VOCs are studied, their interaction with each other further complicates the VOC picture. Another way to assess the impact of emissions is to evaluate the TVOCs within a space.

Sections 4.2.1 through 4.2.12 examine building materials commonly used in commercial buildings. This analysis addresses the problem of VOCs emitted by these materials and discusses options that archi-

TABLE 4.1   Effect of Formaldehyde in Humans after Short-Term Respiratory Exposure

Reported ranges*	Estimated median*	Effect
0.06–1.2	0.1	Odor threshold 50% of people
0.01–1.9	0.5	Eye irritation threshold
0.1–3.1	0.6	Throat irritation threshold
2.5–3.7	3.1	Biting sensation in nose, eye
5–6.7	5.6	Tearing eyes, long-term lung effects
12–25	17.8	Tolerable for 30 min with strong flow of tears lasting 1 h
37–60	37.5	Inflammation of lung (pneumonitis), edema, respiratory distress; danger to life
60–125		Death

*Concentrations in mg/m^3; 1 mg/m^3 = 0.813 ppm.

SOURCE: National Center for Toxicological Research, 1984, Jefferson, Ark.

tects and material purchasers may follow to optimize the IAQ in a facility where new materials are installed.

4.2.1 Adhesives

An adhesive is a material or substance applied to a surface to bind one surface to another. One general characteristic of an adhesive is that it is applied in a liquid or viscous state and then reduced through curing to a solid (or more solid) state to attain proper bonding. However, the majority of adhesives on the market today release VOCs; therefore, it is typically during the application and curing processes that they pose the greatest threat to material installers and building occupants.

Adhesives have a pervasive influence on IAQ, affecting a myriad of construction materials. The adhesives may be applied with materials such as carpet, resilient flooring, and wall covering or may be a component of a material, as is the case of plywood, particleboard, movable wall panels, and office workstations. In the case of carpeting, the emissions from adhesives vary from 100 to 1000 times the emissions from the carpet fiber itself.[4]

General adhesives.   One simple method of characterizing adhesives in terms of their influence on IAQ and emissions potential is to identify the type of resin used in the base of the adhesive. A resin is a solid material with a high molecular weight which promotes better bonding of two surfaces. The resin type and percentage of solids determine the type and quantity of solvents and modifiers required. Liquid polymers and water-based emulsions have fewer emissions than solid polymers and solid rubbers because neither dry by the release of organic solvents.[1]

Resins are either natural or synthetic. Natural resin-based adhesives characteristically have low emission potential.[1] Synthetic resin-based adhesives' emissions vary dramatically, depending on specific variables.

For a general reference, Table 4.2 provides a summary of natural and synthetic resin-based adhesives in terms of specific categories, the characteristics of those categories, and the emission potential. Table 4.3 lists specific chemical names for the polymer categories found in Table 4.2.

The most effective means of determining types of solvents in adhesives is to consult the MSDS for each adhesive.

Carpet adhesives.   Within the carpet industry, the four most commonly used types of carpet adhesives are organic solvent-based styrene butadiene rubber (SBR), latex emulsion adhesives, acrylic latex adhesives

TABLE 4.2   Natural and Synthetic Resin-Based Adhesives

		Resin bases				
Natural resins based			Synthetic resin (polymer) based			
Vegetable based	Animal based	Other	Solid polymer/ solid rubber	Emulsion	Liquid polymer	Hot melt	Pressure sensitive

			Characteristics			
Vegetable resins: starches and dextrins. Animal resin: casein.		Oleoresinous: oil based. Bituminous (asphaltic): tar based.	Resins: natural rubber, synthetic rubbers and the solid synthetics polyvinyl chloride (PVC) and polyurethane (PUR).	Resins: Waterbased latexes and some polyvinyls.	Resins: Thermosetting epoxy, polyurethane, phenolics, silicone, polyvinyl alcohol, urea and melamine formaldehyde, and nitrile.	Resins: Ethylene vinyl acetate.	Resins: Natural and synthetic rubbers.

			Emissions			
Low emitting. All are water soluble, requiring small amounts of organic solvents to formulate.		Low emitting. Oleoresinous: Require small amounts of solvents since they dry by oxidation versus solvent release. Asphaltic: May be a water-based emulsion requiring no solvents or hot-pour, which sets when cool and becomes 100% solid.	Relatively high VOCs. Require large amounts of solvents to become spreadable. Dry by solvent evaporation. Fillers and additives may contain solvents.	Generally low emitting. Resins dissolve in water and dry through water evaporation. May emit low level of VOCs in the form of fillers and additives.	Generally low emitting; cure without evaporation of water or solvents. May emit VOCs through chemical reaction during curing of resins; some additives may contain solvents.	Typically low emitting. Become liquid by heating and return to solid state.	Typically low emitting. Rely on pressure for installation; adhesive remains tacky. If solvent based, may have low level of emissions.

SOURCE: Based on information from *Catalog of Materials as Potential Sources of Indoor Air Emissions*, vol. 1, prepared by Air and Energy Engineering Research Laboratory, Research Triangle Park, N.C., EPA 600/R-93-108a, June 1993.

247

TABLE 4.3   **Classification of Adhesives by Polymer Type**

I. Natural-based adhesives
    A. Natural vegetable-based adhesives
        1. Starches
        2. Dextrins
    B. Natural animal-based adhesives
        1. Casein
    C. Other natural adhesives
        1. Oleoresinous
        2. Bituminous (asphaltics)

II. Synthetic-based adhesives
    A. Solid polymer/solid rubber
        1. Styrene butadiene rubber (SBR)
        2. Neoprene rubber
        3. Nitrile rubber
        4. Butyl rubber
        5. Natural rubber*
        6. Polyvinyl chloride (PVC)
        7. Polyurethane (PUR)
    B. Liquid polymer
        1. Epoxy
        2. Polyurethane (PUR)
        3. Phenolics (resorcinol)
        4. Polyvinyl alcohol (PVOH)
        5. Amino (urea formaldehyde/melamine formaldehyde)
        6. Nitrile
        7. Silicone
    C. Emulsions
        1. Latex acrylics
        2. Polyvinyl acetate (PVAC)
        3. Styrene butadiene latex
        4. Neoprene latex
        5. Natural rubber latex*
    D. Hot melts
        1. Ethylene vinyl acetate
    E. Pressure-sensitive
        1. Natural rubber
        2. Styrene butadiene rubber
    F. Latex acrylics

*Natural rubber adhesives are included with synthetics because they are formulated in a similar way.

SOURCE: *Catalog of Materials as Potential Sources of Indoor Air Emissions,* vol. 1, prepared by Air and Energy Engineering Research Laboratory, Research Triangle Park, N.C., EPA 600/R-93-108a, June 1993.

(quick-release adhesives used to install carpet tiles), and hot-melt (ethylene vinyl acetate) adhesives.[5] Common uses of adhesives include securing carpet with a secondary backing (either fabric or latex) directly to a substrate. This process is called direct glue-down and is used primarily in high-traffic areas. A second use of adhesives is to adhere a carpet pad to a substrate and then to secure the carpet to the pad. Such a procedure is called a double glue-down and is found primarily in residential construction. Finally, carpet adhesives seal carpet seams to avoid separation, edge raveling, and delamination.

As noted in Sec. 4.2.6, much discussion and controversy exists regarding carpet systems and adhesives. Until recently little research had been done on actual emission levels of various adhesives. The adhesive industry is currently researching and developing alternatives to organic solvents, and a few products are already on the market. One manufacturer reports the development of a full line of adhesives with no emissions.[6] The adhesive and sealant industries have formed a council in cooperation with the EPA and the Carpet and Rug Institute (CRI) to study methods of reducing VOCs.

At this time, all participating manufacturers are working toward submittal of product data for their low-emission products. This information will be analyzed in association with a contracted laboratory to establish a voluntary emissions standard for indoor air quality.[6]

Due to the different degrees of emissivity, specifiers and purchasers are encouraged to ask manufacturers about their low-VOC-emitting products and to compare information from different manufacturers. The combination of emissions from resins and solvents should be kept as low as possible. Additionally, CRI recommends that systems using VOC-emitting adhesives should always be installed in areas with increased ventilation (at normal room temperature) for a period of 48 to 72 h to avoid accumulation of VOCs. When possible, 100 percent outside air and extended ventilation periods may be beneficial. The air exchange rate should also be established, based on the emission rate of adhesives being installed. Contractors should acquire and post MSDSs as required by OSHA for any hazardous material, and they should strictly comply with recommendations for installation.

4.2.2 Sealants

A sealant is a material that is applied at joints, gaps, or cavities to eliminate the penetration of liquids, air, and gases. The construction industry commonly refers to *sealants* as sealant materials suitable for exterior use and *caulks* as sealant materials generally used in interior applications.[7] In this section, we use the term *sealants* to describe materials for both exterior and interior use.

Sealants are used to seal many surface types, including glass, concrete, masonry, wood, plastic, and metals.[8] The material's flexibility factor, along with resin-base type, determines whether a sealant is suitable for exterior or interior use. Low-movement sealants (movement capability up to 5 percent) are used for window glazing, exterior siding, interior ductwork, and acoustical applications. The more versatile medium-movement sealants (movement capabilities of 5 to 25 percent) are used for glazing, pipe joints and ducts, siding, insulating glass, tub and tile caulking, and electrical applications. High-movement sealants (movement capabilities higher than 25 percent) are used in exterior construction applications, where they offer higher performance and versatility.[9] Table 4.4 categorizes base resins used in sealants by their flexibility.

The hazardous effects of sealants are prevalent during the installation and curing of the material. Most VOCs are released during the curing or drying time. Generally, however, low-movement sealants are natural-based products, creating fewer IAQ problems than higher-movement sealants, which often contain organic solvents.[10] As is the case with adhesives and architectural coatings, the emission

TABLE 4.4   Base Resins Categorized by Flexibility

Low-movement sealants: Below ±10%
Oleoresinous compounds (oil-based); includes putties, elastic glazing compounds, and architectural caulking compounds.
Butyl rubber
Asphaltic compounds (bitumens)
Some acrylic latex emulsions
Styrene butadiene rubber (SBR)
Medium-movement sealants: ±10% and above
Better-grade butyl rubber
Better-grade acrylic latex emulsions
Some solvent-based acrylic latexes
Some styrene butadiene rubber (SBR)
High-movement sealants: ±25% and above
Polysulfides
Polyurethanes
Silicones

SOURCE: Based on information from *Environmental Resource Guide Subscription,* American Institute of Architects, Washington, D.C., July 1992, I-7920, 2.

potential of various sealants is related to the percentage of solids and the base resins. The base resin is important in identifying the emission potential of a sealant since it determines the appropriate type of liquid and binders or modifiers.[1] The actual hazard presented by a sealant depends on factors such as the toxicity and volatility of its ingredients, the quantity of the sealant used, and the curing time.

One study conducted for Energy, Mines and Resources, Canada categorized sealants according to their volatile emissions. Information derived from the report is summarized in Table 4.5. Note that, although it is a low-movement sealant, SBR is not recommended for indoor use, due to toxicity of styrene and butadiene.

To minimize impact to IAQ, specifiers and purchasers should understand the toxicity of sealants and should specify the least toxic material suitable for a specific application. The location, amount, and required curing time of the sealant, as well as the construction schedule, should be considered in the development of the specifications.

During construction, installers should take precautions recommended by the manufacturer. Information on hazardous chemicals in specific products can be obtained from the manufacturer in the form of MSDSs, which OSHA requires contractors to post when hazards exist. Ventilation should be increased during installation and curing of the sealant in interior spaces. In addition, alternative water-based sealants are now available which are manufactured using nontoxic components. One such product for interior use is a vinyl adhesive sealant. Also on the market is an acrylic latex exterior sealant for building joints.[11]

Sealants are a definite IAQ concern because of their VOC emission potential. Fortunately, sealants are used inside in small quantities, and these quantities can be further reduced by judicious construction techniques and details. When the use of a high-VOC-emitting sealant is required, minimize the quantity and adjust the ventilation accordingly.

4.2.3 Architectural coatings

Architectural coatings encompass various field-applied liquids made for use on the exteriors and interiors of residences, commercial buildings, and other structures needing protection from the elements. Beyond this, there is a wide variety of architectural coatings for specific applications which need to be evaluated individually for a particular use. In this section, the term *architectural coatings* includes paints, stains, sealers, and varnishes.

Architectural coatings are a major component of the construction industry as a means of protection against corrosion, weathering, and

TABLE 4.5   The Recommended Uses of Sealants

Appropriate for Typical Indoor Use	
Asphaltic sealants	A bituminous sealant derived from tar. May be water based or hot pour which sets as it cools. Drying time: 4500 h Primary VOC emissions: Petroleum hydrocarbons
Oleoresinous sealants	Oil-based sealants which seal cracks prior to painting. This market is being overtaken by better performing latex and vinyl products. Drying time: 2000 h Primary VOC emissions: Low amounts of aliphatic hydrocarbons
Acrylic emulsion latex sealants	Water-based sealants for general interior use (popular in residential construction). Drying time: remains tacky Primary emissions: TVOCs
Polysulfide sealants	Most popular in commercial glazing applications, these very dense sealants have excellent resistance to chemicals but poor resistance to ultraviolet rays and ozone degradation. Drying time: 4900 h Primary VOC emissions: Low amounts of toluene
Polyurethane sealants	Made with synthetic resin typically used in commercial applications, with a few types marketed for residential use, these sealants adhere to most substrates, are paintable, do not shrink, are highly resistant to tearing, and may be used underwater. These products are recommended for sealing cracks in concrete foundations and slabs to prohibit radon gas exposure. Drying time: 8300 h (more than 11 months) Primary VOC emissions: Low amounts of xylene
Silicone sealants	A synthetic rubber based on silicon, carbon, oxygen, and hydrogen with high movement capabilities ($\pm 50\%$), these sealants are very resistant to extreme temperatures but less resistant to tearing and have good adhesion. Drying time: 480 h Primary VOC emissions: Low amounts of xylene

damage. In interior applications, these coatings serve as a finish to a variety of building materials and may be used as a decorative element. All coatings (paints, stains, varnishes, and sealers) have similar characteristics. They require resins and oils to form a film and aid in adhesion by promoting penetration into the substrate. All coatings also require carriers (water or organic solvents) which provide fluidity for

TABLE 4.5   The Recommended Uses of Sealants   (Continued)

Appropriate in Very Limited Quantities for Indoor Use	
Solvent-based acrylic latex sealants	Better life cycle and subject to less shrinking than acrylic emulsion latex product; precautions should be taken to avoid possible health and safety hazards. Drying time: 1000 h Primary VOC emissions: xylene
Butyl rubber sealants	Solvent-based material with strong adhesive properties, moisture resistance, and inexpensive price; material typically does not harden, has a high shrinkage rate, poor flexibility, and is difficult to install. Use in interiors should be limited and special protective measures should be taken during installation. Drying time: 430 h Primary VOC emissions: aliphatic hydrocarbons
Inappropriate for Interior Usage	
Styrene butadiene rubber (SBR)	A solvent-based synthetic rubber compound which is easier to work with than butyl rubber sealants; has poor resistance to ultraviolet rays and ozone degradation. Drying time: 100–250 h Primary VOC emissions: aliphatic hydrocarbons, xylene, toluene, & hexane

SOURCE: Based on information from a study conducted for Energy, Mines and Resources Canada, Jennings, D., Eyre, D., and Small, D., "The Development of a Knowledge Base Relating to Indoor Use of Caulks, Sealants, and Weatherstrip Products," vol. 4. "The Safety Categorization of Sealants According to Their Volatile Emissions." M91-11/1-4-1988E, October 1987; *Environmental Resource Guide Subscription,* American Institute of Architects, Washington, D.C., July 1992, Topic. 1-7920; Tucker, W. G., Environmental Protection Agency, 1988; Scott, K. and Stockton, M., "Potential Indoor Air Contaminants from Adhesives and Sealants."

application and increase adhesion through evaporation. Paints and stains require solids, including pigments, to hide the substrate and provide color variations. The presence and proportion of solids in a coating is a fundamental guide to potential VOC emission levels. A low-solid, organic solvent-based coating will have a higher percentage of solvents to solids and, therefore, a higher emission rate. Conversely, the higher the solid content, the lower the emission of VOCs. The type of carrier, either water- or organic solvent-based, further defines the potential for VOC emission. Generally water-based coatings are low-emitting, while organic solvent-based coatings are more likely to be high-emitting. The current industrial trend involves the replacement of conventional, solvent-based paints with water-based paints.[12] Presently, fewer low-emitting stains, varnishes, and sealers have been successfully adapted for low VOC emissions than have paints. In anticipation of governmental requirements, the industry is currently working to manufacture such products. The discussion in this section regarding paints also applies generally to other types of architectural coatings which contain potentially hazardous solvents.

The primary problem with paints is the VOC emission from their solvents. Short-term health effects are similar to those of intoxication: dizziness, impaired vision, nausea, and euphoria. The long-term effects may cause harm to the liver, lungs, nervous system, eyes, and genes.[13] (See Sec. 2.3 for a detailed discussion of health effects.)

Water-based paints typically have lower amounts of VOCs as part of their makeup, but this does not completely eliminate them from the arena of concern. Some water-based paints contain hazardous materials. In some cases a water-based paint mixture may not be listed as hazardous by OSHA even though it is made up of individually hazardous materials. (OSHA classifies a mixture as hazardous if it has one hazardous material which makes up 1 percent or more of the mixture.[14]) OSHA fails to classify a material as hazardous if it has individual hazardous materials, each not over 1 percent. However, in one study of 31 various building materials, the water-based latex paint was listed third highest for VOC emissions.[15]

Most water-based paint contains latex and water-soluble binders such as acrylic resins, polyvinyl acetate, and styrene butadiene. Less typical water-based paints are water-reducible coatings, such as alkyds and acrylics. Due to their chemical makeup, these require an organic solvent additive which raises the VOC emissions of that product.[16]

Unlike organic solvent-based paints, water-based paints require preservatives and fungicides such as arsenic disulfide, phenol, copper, formaldehyde and quartenary ammonium compounds.[16a] These additives are considered chemical hazards by NIOSH, 1991. Emissions from water-based paints have been shown to cause irritation of the mucous membranes and skin, leading to headaches, acute and chronic respiratory effects, and allergic eczema. Some of these emissions are suspected carcinogens.[17]

Conventional organic solvent-based paints typically have synthetic oil bases and carriers which consist of the following chemicals:[18]

1. Aliphatic hydrocarbons, which are generally considered the least hazardous (however, this category contains mineral spirits and various glycol ethers which are possibly hazardous, according to the National Paint and Coating Association, 1992[19])

2. Ketones (including acetone, methyl isobutyl ketone, methyl ethyl ketone, all listed as hazardous by NIOSH, 1991)

3. The aromatic and naphthionic hydrocarbons (including the chemicals toluene, o-xylene, and naphtha, considered to be hazardous by NIOSH, 1991)

4. Esters and acetates (including the chemicals 2-ethoxyethyl acetate and ethyl acetate, also considered hazardous by NIOSH, 1991)

Additional additives, such as styrene, vinyl toluene, methyl ethyl ketoxime, and formaldehyde, may be mixed in to attain gloss and hardness.

The sanding of organic solvent paint generates potential IAQ hazards such as the dust from talc, silica, and mica and especially from lead, which can cause permanent damage in children and adults (see Sec. 4.3). Pigments used in common paints contain potentially toxic compounds if the paint is sanded or burned.[20] Pigments that are hazardous according to NIOSH are listed in Table 4.6 as categorized by color.

VOC emissions from paint occur primarily during application and drying. As a result of increasing IAQ complaints, a few alternative paints have been recently introduced into the market in order to meet environmental demands.

Various alternative paint manufacturing processes exist in today's market: "high-solids" paint, developed as a result of Germany's Federal Emission Law of 1974; "natural" paints, which are generally free of synthetic solvents, resins, fungicides, and softeners; hypo-allergenic and low-biocide paints, developed for chemically sensitive people; and low-emission paint, containing no solvents, similar to home-made milk paint used years ago.[21]

In the German-developed high-solids paint, the amount of organic solvents is decreased and the amount of solids increased. High-solids paints must have at least 60 percent solids (versus average of 15 to 40

TABLE 4.6 Hazardous Chemicals in Pigments*

White	Antimony oxide, titanium dioxide, rutile titanium oxide
Yellow-orange-red	C.P. cadmium, cadmium lithopone, chrome yellow, molybdate orange, strontium chromate, zinc chromate
Blue	Phthalocyanine blue
Green	Chrome green, chromium oxide, hydrated chromium oxide, phthalocyanine green
Other	Copper powders, cuprous oxide

*These chemicals may be released when sanded or burned.

SOURCE: Based on Information from *Environmental Resource Guide,* American Institute of Architects, Washington, D.C., Topic. I-9900, 1992, 6; EPA, 1976; NIOSH, 1990.

percent in commercial paint). As a result, these paints have different properties from conventional paint and may be thicker and heavier with a softer film.[22]

Alternative paints do not generally perform as well as conventional paints. They are not as easily prepared or applied. They may also offer fewer colors at a higher cost.[23] Finally, they generally require more coats, which necessitates a longer drying time and could result in more total emissions of VOCs.[24]

Natural paints are composed of natural plant resins, plant and ethereal oils, mineral fillers, and pigments. Traditional synthetic solvents are usually replaced with the solvent d,l-limonene, a terpene obtained from lemon or citrus oil. There is some question as to whether d,l-limonene is a "possible carcinogen." Some reference literature classifies it as a skin irritant.[25]

Hypo-allergenic paints contain synthetic water-based emulsions. Since no preservatives are used, their shelf life is limited. They are manufactured in white and bone but may be colored on site. Low-biocide paint contains small amounts of petroleum-based chemicals but meets the limitations for VOC emissions in California. These paints do not contain fungicides.

Another low-emitting paint, made by The Old Fashioned Milk Paint Company, is in powder form, thereby avoiding any solvents. It is mixed on site, with only a water additive. The transparency of this paint is based on the proportion of water to powder.[25]

In the regulation of paints, the EPA and the CPSC are the regulatory agencies which focus on the safety of the public, and OSHA protects the worker.

Presently, the EPA is the driving force in the regulation of the paint and coating industry, but due to concern over depletion of the ozone layer, the current regulations address outside coatings rather than IAQ. Several states such as California and New Jersey have enacted emissions regulations: California: South Coast Air Quality Management District's Rule 1113 on Architectural Coatings; New Jersey: Department of Environmental Protection's Title 7, Chap. 27, Subchap. 23.

In 1990, an amendment to the Clean Air Act was enacted requiring all states to submit to the EPA plans to reduce VOC emissions by 15 percent by the year 1996. States had to comply by November 15, 1993.[26] This VOC reduction of exterior paints and coatings indirectly affected indoor paint products as alternative manufacturing techniques were developed. The movement away from solvent-based paints to water-based paints in interior applications has been driven by the paint and coatings market due to the ease of clean-up and the low odor of water-based paint. One major paint manufacturer estimates that 80 percent of their commercial-grade paint and 95 percent of their residential-grade paint sales are of water-based paint.[27] Another manufacturer has produced a paint that contains no VOCs.

Green Seal, a private organization, is considering labeling all household paints with environmental information. The proposed labeling would require paints to be certified after testing by an independent laboratory. However, the industry has concerns regarding Green Seal's proposed VOC limits, which are lower than those set by the Clean Air Act, and which current technology cannot achieve while maintaining acceptable performance.[28] Paint manufacturers maintain that these limits are redundant in light of proposed regulations by the EPA and various states. Additionally, there is concern that the labeling requirement might inhibit foreign trade since other countries have less stringent standards and since the proposed labeling standard is considered to have unrealistically low VOC limits.[29]

Paints generally cover a large surface area and are potentially high in VOC emissions for short periods of time after application. The use of low-emitting paint products is recommended. Minimal impact of VOC emissions from conventional paint requires aggressive ventilation, for at least 72 h following application.[30] Be aware that use of the HVAC system for this type of ventilation may result in transferring emissions to other parts of the building. The HVAC system may need to be modified from its normal operational mode to prevent pollutant transfer, or a temporary ventilation system may be used.

4.2.4 Particleboard

Particleboard is a composite product made from wood chips or residues, bonded together with adhesives under heat and pressure. Typically the wood chips or residues are waste from the milling or woodworking process and may vary in size from fine, powdery shavings to 1 in (2.5 cm). Particleboard is relatively inexpensive and is available in large, flat sheets, generally 4 by 8 ft. Most of the adhesives used in particleboard production (approximately 98 percent) contain urea formaldehyde (UF). Some particleboard (less than 2 percent) have adhesives which contain phenol formaldehyde (PF).[31]

Medium-density fiberboard is another pressed wood product that is used in many of the same building applications as particleboard. Again, UF adhesives are the primary bonding agents for medium-density fiberboard, and the environmental concerns and U.S. Department of Housing and Urban Development (HUD) standards are generally the same for both products.

Particleboard, used generally with wood frame construction, is rarely found as a significant part of the structural systems in concrete-

or steel-framed commercial buildings. Particleboard is used for non-structural floor underlayment, primarily in residential applications. Often a finished floor is installed over the particleboard, and this will delay the formaldehyde emissions from the material. Wall and roof sheathing is another common use of particleboard. The product is also used as the backing for interior paneling. However, by far the most common construction application of particleboard is use as a core material for doors, cabinets, and a wide variety of furnishings, such as tables and prefabricated wall systems. It may be extruded into a finished shape for items such as door frames and components of furniture systems, although this is a less common use.

Particleboard is used because it is inexpensive, flat, and, with the proper construction techniques, will not warp. It has a moderate structural integrity, which makes it an ideal backing material for other finished products. Because of its texture and appearance, particleboard is rarely used as a finished material, except in cases where utility and cost are considered more important than aesthetics.

The major IAQ concern associated with the use of particleboard is the off-gassing of formaldehyde. (The health effects of formaldehyde are discussed in Chap. 2.) While the particleboard industry is now able to manufacture the material with lower formaldehyde emissions, there is still reason for concern because of the possibility of large surface areas of this material in relationship to the volume of a given room or building (i.e., the total amount of UF or PF released to a space may be large, even from low-emission products, because so much of the product may be used in a small space).

UF, the most common adhesive ingredient used in the manufacturing of particleboard, is a resin polymer made up of urea and formaldehyde. While urea is odorless and mildly toxic by injection, the primary concern is with formaldehyde, which has a distinctive odor and is considered hazardous. It has been classified as a probable human carcinogen.[32]

PF is used in particleboard where a high-moisture environment is anticipated, specifically, exterior applications, restrooms, and kitchens. Phenol is a poisonous substance and is hazardous, even in small amounts when ingested or when it comes into skin contact. However, after the resin is cured during the particleboard manufacturing process, phenol has no significant toxicological effects. In fact, particleboard containing PF emits far lower amounts of formaldehyde than particleboard made with UF.[33]

Emissions of trace amounts of formaldehyde can continue for several months or even years. In 1986, a study was conducted to determine particleboard formaldehyde emissions rates. Formaldehyde emissions testing by the National Particleboard Association (NPA) and several particleboard manufacturers indicated that emissions levels can be expected to decrease over time, although this rate of decrease is not constant. In the sample of 16 particleboard products, emission levels decreased on average by 25 percent in 38 days. Of the 14 samples tested long enough to reach a half-life, 216 days was the average for a 50 percent decrease in emission levels. Generally, the higher the initial emission level, the greater the initial decay rate.[34] Figure 4.1 shows emissions rates diminishing over a natural log of time.

While formaldehyde emission rates decrease over time, emission rates increase as temperature and/or humidity increase. It is estimated that emission rates double with an increase of 12 F°. The concentration of formaldehyde that results from particleboard emissions depends on a number of factors other than the age of the particleboard and temperature and/or humidity of the space in which it is installed, including the formulation of the resin, whether the particleboard has been sealed or is behind another finish that would inhibit the emissions, and the size and ventilation rates of the space.[35]

While the primary concern that use of particleboard raises is with formaldehyde emissions, studies have indicated that particleboard may emit other VOCs. One draft study reported emissions of acetone

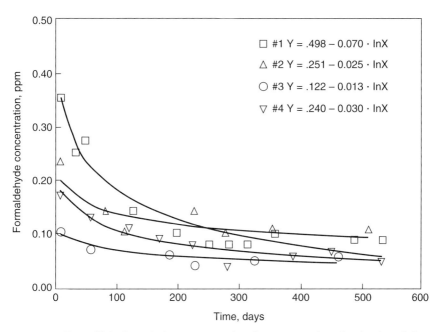

Figure 4.1 Formaldehyde emission concentration data versus time for site A and the corresponding models of the emission decay relationship. (*From "Long-Term Study of Formaldehyde Emission Decay from Particleboard," Terry W. Zinn, Dennis Cline, and William F. Lehmann, Forest Products Journal, vol. 40, no. 6, June 1990, p. 16.*)

(0.037 mg/m²/h from 8-month old particleboard) and hexanol (0.024 mg/m²/h from 8-month old particleboard.)[36] Another study examined three types of UF particleboard and reported that one emitted 11 VOCs, of which 6 are suspected carcinogens.[37] Some of these emissions are derived from the resin and some, such as pinene, come from the wood itself.[38]

Manufacturers continue to experiment with alternative adhesives, as well as with using additives to obtain special characteristics such as fire resistance. The specifier of particleboard should be aware of the potential for other problem-causing substances which can be added.

Use low-emitting UF-bonded particleboard when possible. Avoid using UF in areas of high humidity or where condensation could be a problem because the higher the humidity, the greater the increase of emission rates. Consider limiting the amount of particleboard that will be in a given space. If that is not an alternative, ensure that extra ventilation capacity is available for vapor exhaust and contaminant dilution. Continue this process until the emission rate has diminished significantly.

Whenever possible, try to seal large amounts of unfinished materials, such as floor underlayment, or use particleboard made with PF adhesives. Be sure to check the impact of VOCs emitted by the sealer.

Currently, the regulations involving formaldehyde are limited. The standard established by The American National Standards Institute, ANSI A208.1-1989, is a 0.30 ppm maximum emissions for all grades of particleboard.[39] Product loading ratio, the square footage of particleboard per cubic foot of space, used in formaldehyde testing typically reflects actual end-use loading and varies per grade of particleboard. The NPA has established a voluntary standard of 0.20 ppm (NPA 10-92).[40] Currently, the ANSI standard is undergoing revision to incorporate the NPA reduced emission limit.[41]

Some states are establishing regulations covering formaldehyde. Minnesota has adopted HUD regulations as a standard for all construction, and California's Proposition 65 requires manufacturers to provide warnings if a product provides exposure above "no significant risk" level.

Emissions from particleboard used for manufactured homes are regulated by HUD. These regulations can serve as a guideline when specifying particleboard for commercial use.

4.2.5 Plywood

Plywood consists of several thin layers or plies of wood which are permanently bonded by an adhesive. The outside plies are referred to as faces and the inside plies are known as the core.

Plywood has several characteristics which make it a beneficial material in the construction industry. In its fabrication, plies of wood are stacked with the wood grains alternating at 90°, giving the composite board equal strength in both length and width, less dimensional change in moisture content, and less susceptibility to splitting. For interior finishes, plywood veneer paneling offers an economical alternative to more expensive native and tropical solid woods.

Plywood is generally classified as either softwood or hardwood. Approximately 80 percent of all softwood plywood is used as wall and roof sheathing, siding, concrete framework, roof decking, and subflooring. Hardwood plywood is used for building furniture, cabinets, shelving, and interior paneling. Paneling, which represents 40 percent of the hardwood market, is made from a plywood core, which receives a finished wood face veneer.[42]

The IAQ effects of softwood and hardwood plywoods vary with the adhesive used to bond the plies, as well as the proportion of the material surface area to the volume of the area in which it is installed. Softwood plywood, for exterior use, is adhered with PF resins, which have very low formaldehyde emissions and excellent resistance to moisture, heat, and cold. PF resins are made synthetically from petroleum or coal tar. Hardwood plywood and interior-grade softwood plywood are typically bonded with UF resins. (The health effects of formaldehyde are discussed in Sec. 2.3.) The number of emissions from UF resins has diminished by 70 to 95 percent in the last decade, according to the Hardwood Plywood Manufacturers Association,[43] but some IAQ concerns still exists. The potential hazard from interior plywood relates to its usage in large amounts in the interior of buildings (e.g., paneling and millwork). Building occupants must rely on ventilation systems to exhaust the emissions to alleviate adverse effects. It should be noted that off-gassing of UF may be compounded by sources other than plywood within the building.

Varying theories exist regarding the permissible UF exposure levels for building occupants. The range at which eye irritation becomes evident has been cited at between 0.05 and 0.5 ppm.[44] HUD has set a standard for manufactured housing of 0.2 ppm for hardwood plywood paneling and 0.3 ppm for industrial hardwood plywood.[45] ASHRAE Standard 62-1989 (App. C) lists a level of 0.1 ppm as a level of concern and 0.4 ppm as a maximum background level for manufactured homes.[46]

Various factors affect the concentration of emissions generated from plywood formaldehyde, including the size, temperature, and humidity of a space and the surface area and finish of the plywood. As noted in Sec. 4.2.4, emissions double with an increase of 12 F°. Several different studies show that a 2-mil vinyl overlay finish on a wall panel reduced formaldehyde emissions by 90 to 95 percent,[47] while decorative cuts into wall panels increased emissions by 30 to 40 percent.[48] In the first case, the relatively small amount of emissions from vinyl overlay should be considered in evaluating the TVOCs of a space.

Another factor for consideration is the compounding effect of other materials inside a building that also emit formaldehyde. These include such items as permanent press fabrics, cosmetics, paint, and unvented kerosene heaters.[49] All potential sources must be considered when analyzing the IAQ in a specific study. This will be further discussed in Sec. 4.2.12.

When specifying plywood, the architect should evaluate all potential sources of exposure to formaldehyde, particularly cabinetry and furniture, and consider precautionary measures to diminish adverse effects. For hardwood paneling installation, consider an alternative adhesive called polyvinyl acetate, which contains very low amounts of formaldehyde. Installation in areas of high temperatures and/or humidity should be avoided.[50] Elimination of unsealed openings in the exposed surfaces of the plywood can reduce emissions. Encapsulation with vinyl coating is recommended whenever possible, with periodic inspection and proper maintenance of the encapsulant. Provide ventilation systems with rates that exceed the minimum requirements of ASHRAE Standard 62-1989, particularly shortly after installation when the off-gassing is the highest.

4.2.6 Carpets

Of all of the materials currently classified or being evaluated for effects on IAQ, carpet systems have generated the most debate regarding the identification of specific causes and degree of health hazard. Variables within the composition of a carpet system are fiber, backing, adhesive, and, in residential applications, a carpet pad, as shown in Fig. 4.2. The specifier or purchaser must be aware of each of these components individually and consider them collectively in order to properly evaluate the IAQ effects of the carpet system.

Fiber. Today's carpet consists of five basic fiber materials. The natural fiber wool comprises only 1 percent of today's market. The four synthetic fibers include nylon, olefin, polyester, and polyethylene terephthalate (PET), which is generated by recycling plastic containers. Derived from petrochemicals, synthetic fibers have captured the market with higher strength, more resistance to abrasion, and more overall durability than the previous dominator, wool.[51] Table 4.7 lists these fibers and their specific characteristics.

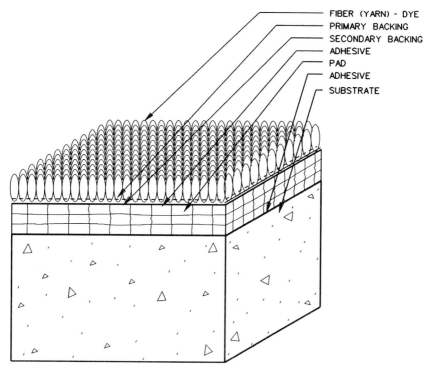

FIBER (YARN) - DYE
PRIMARY BACKING
SECONDARY BACKING
ADHESIVE
PAD
ADHESIVE
SUBSTRATE

Figure 4.2 Components of the carpet systems. (*Used with permission of Gobbell Hays Partners, Inc., Nashville, Tenn.*)

Another beneficial characteristic of certain synthetic fibers is that they are continuous filament fibers, defined by the CRI as continuous strands of synthetic fibers extruded in yarn form without the need for spinning, which natural fibers and synthetic staple fibers require for yarn formation. Due to this process, synthetic fibers seem less likely than wool to release small particles into the air, which can contribute to pulmonary irritation.

Dye.   A carpet system includes not only specific fibers but also the dye used in manufacturing carpet. While the type of dye and its manufacturing process have an impact on the environment in terms of waste management, at present there is no known link between dyes and IAQ.[52]

Adhesives.   Adhesives in the carpet systems can be used in two applications: to glue the fiber to the backing and/or to glue the carpet system to the substrate (see Sec. 4.2.1 for a discussion of adhesives).

TABLE 4.7   Carpet Fibers and Their Specific Characteristics

Wool	Very resilient with excellent texture; more expensive and less durable than synthetics and generates static electricity in dry climate. Wool is a natural fiber. Primary application: residential
Nylon (most recent generation)	Has the reputation of being the strongest and the most resistant to stains and abrasion but generates static electricity, is subject to fading, and is vulnerable to mineral acids. Primary application: commercial
Olefin (polypropylene)	Is an equal to nylon for strength, durability, and abrasion; resists stains, chemicals, and fading, but is not receptive to dye and is not resilient; loses texture over time. Primary application: commercial and institutional
Polyester	Current fiber makeup has excellent texture, receives color very well, hides soil and resists stains but is less durable than nylon and olefin. Primary application: residential and light commercial
Polyethylene terephthalate	A polyester often attained from recycled plastic which is processed, melted then extruded into fibers that are made into yarn. Primary application: residential and light commercial.

SOURCE: Based on information from *Environmental Resource Guide Subscription,* American Institute of Architects, Washington, D.C., July 1992, Topic. I-9681.

Many U.S. adhesive manufacturers now provide low-emitting adhesives with synthetic polymers and resins in a water base, thereby minimizing VOCs.[53] However, some adhesive manufacturers still use styrene butadiene latex as a binder to obtain the desired degree of elasticity. This latex contains 4-phenylcyclohexene (4-PC), a material suspected as a possible source for occupant complaints of illness.[53a] It is important to note that all water-based adhesives are not necessarily low-emitting. The overall composition is the final determinant.

Backing.   The carpet backing is used to keep fibers in place, to strengthen dimensional stability, and for resilience and user comfort. Often two carpet backings are incorporated into a carpet system. The *primary backing* keeps fibers in place. It most frequently consists of polypropylene, which is resistant to acid and abrasion. The *secondary backing,* used to add strength and stability, is made from fabric, jute, or polypropylene bonded by either SBR latex or a polymer coating such as synthetic latex. The chemicals styrene and butadiene in SBR latex are known irritants to mucous membranes and skin. In addition, the SBR latex adhesives found in both primary and secondary backing emit low but steady amounts of the by-product 4-PC, which causes the "new carpet" odor. Tests documented for EPA indicated that 4-PC emissions over a period of 1248 h averaged 113 mg/m^2/h.[54]

Pads. Carpet pads or cushions, an optional portion of the carpet system, are used for softness and sound absorption and generally are not major contributors to IAQ problems. Carpet pads may be installed separately or may be fixed to part of the backing. Five general types of pads are bonded urethane, prime polyurethane, sponge rubber, synthetic fiber, and rubberized jute. Table 4.8 shows the market percentage of these cushions.[55]

TABLE 4.8 Carpet Pads

Type	% of market sold	Primary materials	IAQ impact
Bonded urethane	56	90% scrap polyurethane blended with polyether and toluene diisocyanate.	The average 24-h emission factor for carpet cushion is 1.24 mg/m^2/h. The average 24-h emission factor for carpets is 0.15 mg/m^2/h for TVOC and 0.064 mg/m^2/h for 4-PC. These emissions decrease to barely detectable levels at the end of one exposure week.
Prime polyurethane	33	Manufactured by the reaction of polyether, toluene diisocyanate, and water.	
Sponge rubber	6	Synthetic styrene butadiene latex or natural rubber.	
Synthetic fiber	3	90% scrap made from waste fibers and woven polypropylene.	
Rubberized jute	2	Made from finely cut carpet strips, natural jute fibers, burlap bags, polypropylene mesh, and 10–15% SB latex.	

SOURCE: Based on information from the Carpet Policy Dialogue Report, September 27, 1991, and *Environmental Resource Guide Subscription,* American Institute of Architects, Washington, D.C., July 1992, Topic. I-9681.

One of the initial carpet controversies with regard to IAQ resulted from grievances filed by EPA employees in three EPA buildings in Washington. These employees reported occurrences of symptoms such as nausea, headaches, skin rashes, eye irritations, and respiratory problems. These symptoms corresponded to those commonly identified with VOC exposure. The EPA conducted repeated tests for emissions of VOCs, including 4-PC, formaldehyde, and carbon dioxide, as well as temperature and relative humidity. Test results reported low emission levels of several VOCs, including 4-PC. The first day, 4-PC was monitored in one room with a result of 6.6 parts per billion (ppb); the next day the same room tested at 4 ppb. Complaints continued, however, and the same room was retested 6 months later. This time, 4-PC levels measured 0.12 ppb.[56]

Since the findings were inconclusive, the EPA employee grievances were not upheld. However, the publicity raised many questions and, in response, the CRI and the EPA generated the Carpet Policy Dialogue. The Carpet Policy Dialogue stipulated that a private laboratory carry out testing, while comparison studies were performed by the EPA. The results of these studies were reasonably similar to those of the contracted laboratory.[57]

Nineteen latex-backed carpets, three carpet cushions, and four adhesives (including one low-emission adhesive) were tested by the CRI, with the following observations:[58]

1. Emissions from carpets were very low when compared to the emissions of other building materials influencing IAQ.

2. Fiber, dye process, and topical treatments did not considerably raise the VOC emissions of the carpets. TVOCs in an average 24-h time frame yielded emissions of 0.15 mg/m^2/h for carpet and 0.064 mg/m^2/h for the 4-PC in the carpet backing, or potential concentrations of 0.061 mg/m^3 for TVOC and 0.026 mg/m^3 of 4-PC. These emissions dissipated to negligible levels within 1 week.

3. Results indicated that the TVOC emission rate from adhesives was high, taking 6 weeks to decrease to the suggested EPA standard of 0.6 mg/m^2/h. The comparison of low-emitting adhesives to traditional adhesives resulted in means of 0.7 mg/m^2/h to 88.5 mg/m^2/h, respectively. In addition, a double glue-down application increased the emission rate by 25 percent, from 40 mg/m^2/h to 60/m^2/h.

Additional confusion and contradiction regarding the effects of carpet systems resulted from a series of tests performed and evaluated by Anderson Laboratories, Inc. (ALI) in Massachusetts. In this case, nine carpets were submitted to the laboratory from facilities in which individuals had experienced health problems. The symptoms included a combination of eye, nose, and/or throat irritations; breathing difficulty; headaches; memory loss; fatigue; and muscular pain and weakness.[59]

In the original tests by ALI, laboratory mice exposed to off-gassing from the specimen carpets manifested dramatic health effects including changes in breathing, loss of balance, convulsions, and in many cases death.[59] The results generated various questions from indoor air specialists and the carpet industry regarding such variables as the test conditions for the mice, temperature of the carpet specimens, and the testing chamber used.

Due to controversy, ALI and separate laboratories under the direction of the EPA and CRI tried to replicate the tests, but to date the results remain inconclusive. The CRI's tests, performed by the Graduate School of Public Health at the University of Pittsburgh, showed that the new carpet provided by the CRI caused mild sensory and pulmonary irritation but no toxicity or death in the mice.[60]

In further EPA testing, carpet samples were provided by the CPSC and tested by both ALI and the EPA. The results from ALI were similar to results it had reported earlier, but according to Robert Dyer of EPA's Health Effects Research Laboratory, the EPA tests produced no difference in the study mice exposed to the new carpet and the control mice which were not exposed.[61] Furthermore, a recent EPA conference reported that although the agency has conducted more than 50 studies on the toxic effects of carpet, it has failed to find any toxicity.[62] However, other laboratory tests have introduced a new concern regarding the relationship of carpet fibers and backing to ozone emissions. In tests of four carpet samples, it was observed that ozone emitted from office equipment reacted with carpet fibers and backing, changing the mix of some VOCs. Levels of 4-PC emissions decreased when mixed with ozone and increased once the ozone had decayed. Conversely, formaldehyde emissions increased when the samples were exposed to ozone. Significant levels of other aldehydes which had not been detected earlier were measured when ozone was introduced in the testing chamber.[63]

Additional IAQ concerns are based on inconsistent production by manufacturers, which contributes to further confusion of the carpet issue. Recent testing performed for the CRI showed that one of seven batches of the same carpet did not meet the manufacturer's standards for emissions of 4-PC and TVOCs.[64] These figures would indicate that in a large building project, the same type carpet might produce irritation in some areas and not in others. More research is needed.

Another consideration is the carpet's sink factor, which is the ability of a material to adsorb chemicals and pollutants emitted from other materials and release them into the air later. The higher the accessible surface area to unit mass, the more VOCs may be adsorbed, although various chemicals have varying rates of adsorption and desorption.[65] One study suggests that natural fibers such as wool and cotton adsorb more VOCs than synthetic fibers.[66]

To date there are more questions than answers to IAQ carpet concerns. Specifiers and purchasers should follow developments in this area closely, using the resources cited in the appendixes of this book, until more definitive information is available.

At this time only voluntary standards exist through the CRI. In September of 1992, a testing/certification program began, established as part of the Carpet Policy Dialogue. Under this program, carpets are laboratory tested to see if they meet the following emission rates:[67]

- TVOCs 0.6 mg/m^2/h

- Styrene 0.4 mg/m^2/h

- 4-PC 0.1 mg/m^2/h

- Formaldehyde 0.05 mg/m^2/h

If the carpet passes, it receives a green label indicating its participation and is tested on a yearly basis to verify compliance. However, the attorneys general from New York, Vermont, Connecticut, and Oregon have challenged the program, stating that the testing protocols are "misleading and unscientific."[68] But the CRI stipulates that the label is "not a guarantee that the carpet will not cause health problems."[69] As of January 1, 1994, the carpet labeling program has been modified to include health warning labels, installation guidelines, and a statement of participation.[70]

Even with the manufacturers' voluntary efforts to lower emissions, until the specific causes of health hazards from carpet are identified and remedied, several precautions are recommended. Carpet covers a large surface area; therefore, VOC emission potential is a concern. In addition, the potential for carpet to act as a sink is significant. Specify low VOC-emitting carpet systems, and, when possible, avoid systems that release 4-PC and formaldehyde or increase ventilation to dilute these emissions. This information may be obtained from manufacturer's literature. Comply with the CRI guidelines for installation. Spaces containing carpet should be ventilated for a period after installation, with a ventilation program equal to the EPA recommendation of 72 h,[71] or longer, when appropriate.

4.2.7 Resilient flooring

Resilient flooring is a pliable or flexible flooring. Tile and sheet are the two basic forms, both of which are attached to a substrate by adhesives (see Sec. 4.2.1). The various compositions of resilient flooring include vinyl, rubber, and linoleum.

Tile flooring. Vinyl tile is manufactured as homogeneous vinyl and vinyl-composition tile. Both are made primarily of polyvinyl chloride resins (often referred to as PVC), plasticizers to provide flexibility, fillers, and pigments for color. A major distinction between homogeneous vinyl and vinyl-composition tile is the percentage of filler in the products. Vinyl composition tile normally contains over 80 percent filler (typically limestone).

Rubber tile comes in two forms, smooth surface and molded. Rubber tile is made from a combination of synthetic rubber (styrene butadiene), nonfading organic pigments, extenders, oil plasticizers, and mineral fillers.

Linoleum, first produced in the mid-1800s, is a natural, organic, and biodegradable product. The key components are linseed oil, rosin, wood flour, cork powder, pigments, driers, and natural mildew inhibitors. Linoleum tiles are very durable, greaseproof, and water and burn resistant. Due to the oxidation of the linseed oil, linoleum is naturally antibacterial and termite resistant.[72]

Sheet flooring. Sheet flooring is available in solid vinyl and rubber, and as an organic linoleum. The compositions of the vinyl, rubber, and linoleum sheet floorings are the same as tile. Sheets of flooring are generally available in 6- and 12-ft widths.

Vinyl flooring is often found in residential areas (kitchens, baths, play rooms) and commercial buildings (schools and hospitals) requiring easy maintenance and long-lasting materials. Rubber flooring is used in both interior and exterior conditions, for walk-off mats at building entrances, floors that get cleat and spike traffic in sports facilities, and ramps where traction is important. Linoleum typically is used for flooring but may also be used on countertops and desk tops.

Typically no individual compound in resilient flooring has high VOC emissions. In one study, a sample of vinyl tile flooring consisted of 20 chemicals, all with individually low levels of emissions, and had a TVOC emission rate of only 0.045 mg/m^2/h.[73] The composition of the different types of sheet flooring vary greatly, and thus, the VOC emission rates from sheet floors can vary. In a European study, emissions from *solid vinyl* flooring amounted to 2.3 mg/m^2/h.[74] Another European study evaluated seven samples of both used and new vinyl flooring for emissions. Some of the used samples came from flooring that had received health complaints from their users. The TVOC emissions for new PVC, or vinyl, flooring varied from 1.122 to 2.192 mg/m^2/h. Emissions from the old PVC which had been the cause of complaints ranged from 0.910 to 7.034 mg/m^2/h. In all PVC samples taken, the specific plasticizer 2,2,4-trimethyl-1,3-pentanediol-diisobutyrate (TXIB) which emits low amounts of VOCs for years, was responsible for 50 percent of the emissions.[75]

Another form of resilient flooring is linoleum, a product used frequently in the United States prior to the introduction of sheet vinyl products. Studies of VOC emissions from linoleum show very low emissions.[76] The driers used in linoleum are typically lead monoxide or red lead, both of which are poisonous. Some pigments in linoleum include titanium dioxide, which was listed as a potential human carcinogen by NIOSH in 1990, although other organizations still list it as a "nuisance dust."[77] Linoleum can emit an unpleasant odor, which is caused by the oxidation of fatty acids.[76]

Due to the typically large ratio of surface areas of vinyl and linoleum flooring to spatial volume, these products should not be installed without adequate ventilation.[75] Note that low emission levels can continue for an extended period of time, but VOC concentrations decrease substantially after 24 h. Since the plasticizer is the main emissions culprit, the more rigid, less plastic vinyl tile is recommended over sheet vinyl to avoid potential hazards. However, even low-emitting flooring materials may be glued with high-emission adhesives.

4.2.8 Wallcoverings

Wallcoverings are one of the most popular alternatives to paint for decorative and durable treatment of walls. The three basic categories of wallcoverings are paper, vinyl, and fabric. Traditional wallcovering is paper, which is found in residential applications more frequently than in commercial ones. A fabric wallcovering may be specified by architects and interior designers as sound absorbers in areas where noise reduction is desirable. Vinyl wallcovering is found most frequently in commercial applications that require resistance to wear and moisture. In all cases, the installation of the selected material requires adhesives to secure the wallcovering to the substrate. It is the combination of the adhesive and the wallcovering that causes the IAQ concern. (Refer to Sec. 4.2.1 for further information on adhesives.)

Paper. Paper wallcovering is not known to present significant IAQ problems, although modest amounts of formaldehyde may be found in the adhesives which bind the paper fibers. The adhesives used for installation of paper wallcovering are generally 100 percent water-based pastes and natural starches,[78] which do not emit high levels of VOCs. One study of wallpaper glued to sheetrock revealed small amounts of 1,1,1-trichloroethane and o-xylene, but the source of the emissions was not specified.[79]

Fabric. The primary IAQ concern in the use of fabric wallcovering is the possible content of formaldehyde, which is sometimes used in fabrics to improve the color-fastness of dyes and the water resistance of the fabric. (The health effects of formaldehyde are discussed in Sec. 2.3.) Another consideration is the sink factor of the fabric, or its ability to absorb extraneous VOCs within a building and reemit them into a space.

Vinyl. Vinyl-coated wallpaper has been known to emit the following VOCs: amines, n-decane, formaldehyde, 1,2,4-trimethylbenzene, and xylenes.[80] With more and more awareness of IAQ issues, the vinyl wallcovering manufacturers are doing more research in response to questions from architects, specifiers, and users. The new vinyl wallcovering may emit odors due to the printing and finishing solvents used during manufacturing. Manufacturers estimate that the odors take 1 to 2 weeks to diminish during normal heating and ventilation conditions. It should be noted that research is continuing, as indicated by one company's goal to phase out most solvents used in the printing and finishing of the vinyl wallcovering by 1996.[81]

A major concern with vinyl wallcovering is the environmental conditions of the project location and the construction of the walls receiving the finish. Particularly in temperate climates where there is no season during which moisture can evaporate, construction oversights during sheetrock installation can lead to problems from biological sources of indoor air pollutants. Hotel owners report that almost $68 million was spent in 1990 due to mold and mildew, and 12 new hotels were unable to open due to resultant stains and odors. The overall solution is to remove one of the environmental conditions that promotes fungal growth: moisture, heat, fungi spores, or a food source. In humid climates, storage of gypsum board and a proper construction sequence are critical. The exterior envelope of the building must be completed, and the HVAC system must be turned on prior to installation of gypsum board and wallcovering.[82] Biological factors in building construction are further discussed in Sec. 4.3.

Currently there are no known regulations for wallcoverings, although ASTM G21 standard addresses the "Practice for Determining Resistance of Synthetic Polymeric Materials to Fungi" through testing of samples and establishing a rating system of 0 to 4. The standard for vinyl wallcovering is a ranking of 0 to 1, which represents no fungal growth to a trace of growth on less than 10 percent of the area.[83]

Alternatives to vinyl wallcovering are perforated vinyl wallcoverings, textured fiberglass sheets which are painted with latex paint that allows the finish to "breathe," and other materials that allow the substrate to breathe. If vinyl wallcoverings are used, the specifier or purchaser should require either that the spaces receiving the new finish be allowed to ventilate prior to occupancy or provide increased ventilation during occupancy.

A wide variety of products and finishes are used in wallcovering. Since limited data on emissions are available, each wallcovering must be evaluated individually to determine the potential VOC emissions. Low-emitting adhesives are recommended. Large surface areas, generally associated with wallcovering, dictate budgeting an appropriate flushout period. (Refer to Sec. 4.7 for further discussion on new construction.)

4.2.9   Insulation

Insulation is a material that separates a surface from the surrounding air or one surface from another to prevent or reduce the transfer of heat, sound, or electricity. Most insulation is made of fiberglass, mineral wool, and cellulose (made from recycled wood). The mineral asbestos was used extensively as an additive to insulation material until the late 1970s (see Sec. 4.3).

Thermal insulation is the most common insulation type, and it decreases heat transfer to or from a surface. As a building insulator, it is found most frequently in two forms: batt and rigid foam. Batt insulation is placed within the cavity of exterior or interior walls; rigid foam board is typically applied to the exterior face of a building. Another major application for thermal insulation is for piping and ductwork. Generally, premolded fiberglass is the most common pipe and duct insulation.

Acoustical insulation, sometimes referred to as *sound batts,* works to reduce noise transmission from one space to another. It is frequently used in hospital patient rooms, around restrooms, and to isolate conference rooms. Sound batts are generally made of fiberglass and are similar to fiberglass batts used for thermal insulation.

Fireproofing is another form of insulation. Its purpose is to help a structural steel system maintain its integrity by shielding the system from the fire's heat, thus allowing firefighters additional time to combat the blaze. This type of material can also be used as a thermal insulation for the building envelope when applied to the exterior skin, as in the Astrodome. Generally, fireproof insulation is a cellulose or mineral wool material field-mixed with water and spray-applied to its substrate. Figure 4.3 shows spray-applied fireproofing covering structural steel beams, columns, and decking.

Figure 4.3 Fireproofing on structural beams, column, and deck-ing. (*Used with permission of Gobbell Hays Partners, Inc., Nashville, Tenn.*)

Miscellaneous insulation is used in a variety of locations where heat and sound transfer is undesirable. A batt-type as well as a foamed insulation known as fire-safing exists within this category of insulation/fire-proofing. This insulation is used to prevent fire, smoke, and toxic fumes from infiltrating small penetrations in the floor or ceiling of a multilevel building.

These insulation types and materials potentially affect the quality of indoor air either through the release of particulates into the air, the emission of VOCs, or the growth and amplification of biological contaminants due to exposure to moisture. The latter category is discussed in Sec. 4.3.

Fiberglass and mineral wool have raised IAQ concerns because of the small fibers produced when the material is disturbed. In lab tests during the late 1980s, cancer tumors resulted when fiberglass fibers were implanted in test animals. Shortly after these results were announced, the International Agency for Research for Cancer classified fiberglass as a possible carcinogen.[84] The tests were questioned by some who felt that no particles as large as those implanted could be inhaled.[85] Research by the University of Pittsburgh School of Public

Health indicated a "small but statistically significant" excess of lung disease in workers in a fiberglass plant.[85] As with the previous test, the results were questioned, citing that the factory in which the workers had been employed was contaminated by asbestos, a known carcinogen.[86]

Cellulose insulation, generally spray-applied, is considered a nontoxic material. However, one test indicated that particulate amounts caused death in animals, probably due to the lung's inability to expel or dissolve the material.[87] OSHA has classified cellulose dust as a nuisance dust and established a PEL for nuisance dust of 15 mg/m^3 total dust and 5 mg/m^3 respirable dust.[88]

Foam insulation has received most of its attention for its impact on the environment rather than its contribution to IAQ problems. However, VOCs are emitted from synthetic foam insulation during the polymerization process.[89] This process is a chemical reaction where simple molecules of a compound, the monomer, are linked together to generate a larger and heavier molecule.[90] This process can occur during manufacturing or while using spray foam. Polystyrene foam boards are frequently used in construction, and these boards are known to emit chlorobenzene and p-dichlorobenzene.[91] Spray foams are known to emit acetone, chlorobenzene, xylenes, cyclohexane, and dichlorobenzenes. Polyurethane foam board emits dichloromethane, chloroform, acetone, chlorobenzene, and dichlorobenzene.[91]

The only regulation regarding current insulation material is OSHA's requirement that warning labels and MSDSs be provided on fiberglass material, due to its being listed as a possible carcinogen. In 1992, OSHA was in the process of determining permissible exposure limits for both fiberglass and mineral wool. In June of 1992, however, the courts overturned OSHA's proposal for PELs on various air contaminants.[92]

Specifiers and purchasers should be aware of VOC content in insulations in order to evaluate the total volatile compounds in a building. In addition, precautions during installation of fiberglass and mineral wool products need to be understood and complied with if those materials are being used on a particular project.

In conclusion, be sure to keep insulation materials dry since they are an excellent habitat for microbial growth. Furthermore, because insulation material has a large surface area, use it cautiously in areas that are part of pollutant pathways or the HVAC airstream (see Secs. 3.3 and 4.4).

4.2.10 Acoustical ceiling tile

One of the most common ceilings found in offices today is the suspended acoustical ceiling. This ceiling is made up of lightweight ceiling tiles placed into a metal grid system, which is suspended from the building structure. This suspended system provides access to above ceiling systems and supports items such as fluorescent light fixtures and HVAC diffusers. In today's office environment, the space above the typical suspended ceiling has become a major utility corridor.

Most acoustical ceiling tile (ACT) is made from mineral or wood fibers which are wetted, compressed to the desired thickness, panel size, and pattern, and factory-coated with a latex paint. Typically, these contain starch, perlite, and clay. Another common configuration is a fiberglass board with a vinyl face. The criteria used for selection of acoustical tile vary significantly, based on acoustic requirements, moisture resistance (specifically humidity levels), durability standards, fire resistance, and aesthetic preferences. The textured surface provides better acoustical characteristics than harder surfaces such as smooth, dense plaster or gypsum board finished with a high-gloss paint.

One IAQ concern regarding ACTs is the occurrence of microbial growth on either mineral fiber or fiberglass tile that is exposed to moisture.[93] This moisture may result from things such as high humidity, as is found in a kitchen, or leaks. Another concern has been that a small percentage of ceiling tiles contained asbestos (see Sec. 4.3). Currently, however, no U.S. manufacturer is producing asbestos-containing ceiling tile. Information has not shown significant VOC emissions from ceiling tile. However, formaldehyde has been indicated as a potential VOC emitted by ceiling tile.[94] A further consideration is that porous ceiling tiles can absorb VOCs emitted into a space and gradually reemit those VOCs. In spaces exposed to high levels of VOCs, consider the sink factor of the tiles and provide appropriate ventilation. Finally, if this material is damaged, there is a potential for particle release of either mineral wool or fiberglass.

Due to the large surface areas common in the use of ceiling tile, consider the likely impact in a new application. Perform maintenance activities to replace damp or water-damaged ceiling tiles to avoid mold formation. When the acoustical ceiling acts as part of the return air plenum, care should be given in selecting the ceiling tile system so that it accommodates the requirements of the return air plenum (see Chap. 3). When selecting ceiling tiles for areas of high humidity, specify a material appropriate for such application.

4.2.11 Furnishings

IAQ is affected not only by building materials used in constructing the building but by the building's furnishings, as well. Included in this section are items such as prefabricated movable partitions, prefabricated workstations, and standard office furniture such as chairs, desks, and credenzas. Both movable partitions and the workstations which often accompany the partitions are used in many offices which require flexibility or an open spatial plan. Movable partitions have potential for high impact on the TVOCs due to the high square footage of material area compared to the actual room volume and the actual emissions from these materials. In addition to the furnishings discussed, there are IAQ concerns regarding office equipment, specifically photocopiers and the carbon-based toner used in their operation. See Sec. 4.3 for an analysis of emissions from office equipment and supplies.

Case study

In the 1980s, IAQ was becoming a notable concern for building occupants, owners, architects, and engineers. In 1982, an office building owned by the state of Washington received numerous reports of indoor air quality complaints. In 1989, a state IAQ task force was established to generate policies and procedures for IAQ in state-owned buildings. A program management consultant was hired to assist the state in preparing a sample indoor air specification (now required to be incorporated into the specifications of any state-owned building project in Washington) to be implemented on two design/build office buildings known as the East Campus Plus (ECP) project.[95]

TABLE 4.9   Overall Emission Standards for Building Finishes: Washington State*

Material	Concentrations
Formaldehyde	0.05 ppm at anticipated loading within 30 days of installation
Total volatile organic compounds (TVOCs)	0.5 mg/m^3 at anticipated loading within 30 days of installation
4 Phenyl cyclohexene (4PC)	1 ppb at anticipated loading within 30 days of installation.

Primary or secondary outdoor air pollutants must meet standards promulgated by National Ambient Air Quality Standard (EPA, Code of Federal Regulations, Title 40, Part 50).

Pollutants not specifically mentioned must meet an emission rate that will not produce an air concentration level greater than one-tenth the threshold limit value of the industrial workplace standard (American Conference of Governmental Industrial Hygienists) at anticipated loading within 30 days of installation.

*Test calculations assume 900 ft^3 to workstation volume. All emission rate testing pursuant to this specification shall be completed according to the dynamic environmental chamber technology as prescribed by EPA-600/8-89-074.

SOURCE: Used with permission of the Department of General Administration, State of Washington, Olympia, Wash. From *Indoor Air Quality: A Model Project,* December 1992.

The state found that inadequate information on emissions from office furniture and movable partitions existed, although these furnishings were suspected contributors of indoor air pollutants due to their components, such as plywood or particleboard, fabrics, adhesives, and plastics.

Because of Washington's commitment to generating a model project intended to set an example in the construction industry, no manufacturer was allowed to bid on the project without submission of test results on specific product emissions. Ultimately all competing manufacturers produced existing data or conducted tests and produced the data requested, in many cases providing architects and specifiers with previously unavailable data on furniture emissions.[96]

The resulting standards for systems furniture generated by the Washington State Department of Labor and Industries, Industrial Safety and Health Division, are shown in Table 4.9. Tables 4.10, 4.11, and 4.12 are based on information presented at ASHRAE's IAQ '91 and list the specific components and test results of one manufacturer for a high-backed office chair with arms, a movable partition system, and a modular workstation.

TABLE 4.10   Prefabricated Movable Partition Construction and Emissions

Construction	
Component	Material
Tackable panel fabric	Fabric without coating
Sound absorption material	Molded fiberglass blankets with phenol-formaldehyde resin
Septum barrier	Untreated/uncoated paper chipboard
Steel frame and trim	Steel with polyester baking enamel coating
Reveal strip	Extruded PVC plastic
Connection hinges	Extruded polypropylene plastic

Emissions			
Contaminant	Emission rate $(mg/m^2/h)$	Exposure time (h)	Air concentration
Formaldehyde:			
Maximum	0.158	1	42.0 ppb
Minimum (steady-state)	0.037	48	9.8 ppb
Particles	Undetected	1–1007	Undetected
Total VOCs			
Maximum	0.0076	2.5	0.024 mg/m^3
Minimum	0.0060	581.0	0.002 mg/m^3

SOURCE: Based on information from "Volatile Organic Compounds and Particle Emission Rates and Predicted Air Concentrations Related to Movable Partitions and Office Furniture," by James R. Strobridge, CIH, and Marilyn S. Black, PhD, 1991. Used with permission.

TABLE 4.11   Prefabricated Workstation System Construction and Emissions

Construction	
Component	Material
Steel components	Steel with polyester baking enamel coating
Plastic laminate finish	Paper saturated with melamine and phenolic resins, cured and bonded by pressure and heat
Laminate adhesive	Neoprene rubber contact adhesive to bond laminate to steel structure
Countertops	Medium-density fiberboard covered with plastic laminate

Emissions			
Contaminant	Emission rate $(mg/m^2/h)$	Exposure time (h)	Air concentration
Formaldehyde			
Maximum	1.47	48	15 ppb
Minimum (steady-state)	0.83	336	9 ppb
Particles			
Maximum	0.18	1–912	0.002 mg/m^3
Minimum	0.085		Undetected
Total VOCs			
Maximum	32.0	1	0.403 mg/m^3
Minimum	0.01	912	0.002 mg/m^3

SOURCE: Based on information from "Volatile Organic Compounds and Particle Emission Rates and Predicted Air Concentrations Related to Movable Partitions and Office Furniture," by James S. Strobridge, CIH, and Marilyn S. Black, PhD, 1991. Used with permission.

Note that the workstation tests were set up with ventilation standards based on a new building system as required by the state of Washington. The movable partitions and office chair were analyzed based on ventilation standards set by ASHRAE Standard 62-1989.[97] Obviously, the effects of these same furnishings would be dramatically altered if the ASHRAE ventilation standards were not implemented. See Fig. 4.4 for the specific components of the partition system and workstation tested.

Presently, there are few national and state regulations regarding emissions from building furnishings and equipment. The permissible airborne concentration of formaldehyde is 0.75 ppm as an 8-h TWA.[98] Some states are developing notification and construction standards for use with their own facilities.

The variety of emissions that may be released by office furniture systems can generate a complex and interactive environment for VOCs. Often these systems are installed where they would have a high-surface-area-to-room volume ratio. Provide adequate ventilation for an appropriate amount of time to avoid a high buildup of TVOCs within a given space.

TABLE 4.12   **Office Chair System Construction and Emissions**

Construction	
Component	Material
Cover fabric	Fabric of wool, nylon, or blend of wool and nylon
Other fabric	Polyester in cushion
Cushion	100% flexible polyurethane foam
Cushioning adhesives	Hot melt powder: nylon resin
	Contact: polyurethane resin based
	Contact: synthetic elastomer based
Structure	Injection-molded polypropylene
Casters	Injection-molded nylon resin
Control handle	Thermoplastic rubber
Arms	Integral-skin polyurethane
Steel components	Steel with polyester baking enamel coating

Emissions			
Contaminant	Emission rate $(mg/m^2/h)$	Exposure time (h)	Air concentration
Formaldehyde	Undetected	1–981	Undetected
Particles	Undetected	1–981	Undetected
Total VOCs			
Maximum	1.06	1	0.076 mg/m^3
Minimum	0.10	981	0.0073 mg/m^3

SOURCE: Based on information from "Volatile Organic Compounds and Particle Emission Rates and Predicted Air Concentrations Related to Movable Partitions and Office Furniture," by James R. Strobridge, CIH, and Marilyn S. Black, PhD, 1991. Used with permission.

Research and standardization of testing protocols are proceeding, and information is available from systems manufacturers. Due to the large number of materials that comprise a furnishing system, MSDSs may not be available on the assembled items.

4.2.12   Summary

Over the last decade, both governmental agencies and the construction industry have become increasingly aware of the issues of IAQ, often due to mounting public concern. Many health complaints have been linked to new materials installed in new or renovated structures. As a result, the VOCs emitted by construction materials are a topic of debate and, in some cases, litigation. Consequently, both public agencies and private industry are promoting the use of low-emit-

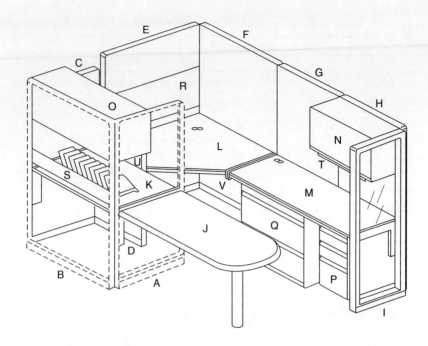

A	65 × 30 nontackable panel	M	70 × 25 worksurface, cableway left
B	65 × 45 tackable acoustic panel	N	35-in binder bin
C	61 × 30 tackable acoustic panel	O	45-in binder bin
D	24 × 42 fabric/steel panel	P	25-in box-box file ped and
E	65 × 45 energy mgmt. power panel		convenience try (in pedestal)
F	65 × 45 tackable acoustic power panel	Q	35-in 2-drawer lateral file
G, H	65 × 35 nontackable panel	R	45-in tackboard
I	65 × 25 glazed panel	S	Paperflo back, supports, and trays
J	60 × 30 panel mount table	T	20-W task light (cord left)
K	45 × 30 worksurface, cableway	U	40-W task light
	left, cableway right	V	Duplex receptable
L	45 × 25 corner worksurface,		
	cableway center		

Figure 4.4 Workstation. (*From "Volatile Organic Compounds, and Particle Emission Rates and Predicted Air Concentrations Related to Movable Partitions and Office Furniture," by James R. Strobridge, CIH, and Marilyn S. Black, PhD, 1991. Used with permission.*)

ting building materials. Certain public agencies, particularly the EPA, are active in the development of recommendations and regulations for architects and engineers, as well as for contractors and building owners. In response to both public and governmental pressures, some private industries are now initiating product testing for pollutants such as VOCs. These test results provide architects and engineers with a means of evaluating the impact of individual products specified in a new building in relation to the total VOCs generated in individual spaces. Understanding the effects that products have on the indoor air in a building assists the architect and building owner in avoiding potential IAQ problems and the resultant economic impact. The use of hazardous materials can be minimized, proper ventilation can be provided to avoid detrimental effects of particular products, and preventative maintenance procedures can be enacted.

On a national level, certain standards organizations and agencies play primary roles in making recommendations and regulations regarding emissions from building materials. The primary national agencies involved in such actions are:

1. ANSI sets standards for products such as particleboard.

2. The CPSC sponsors research and makes recommendations for potentially hazardous building materials such as carpet systems, paints, and adhesives.

3. HUD sets standards for federal housing and has issued regulations such as the limit on formaldehyde emissions in the Manufactured Home Construction and Safety Standard.

4. The EPA has been a catalyst in the early research of emissions, developing a classification of materials considered to be low-emission materials. In addition, the EPA has worked with various industry organizations to develop voluntary guidelines for emission control. Table 4.13 is provided by the EPA. The EPA is currently developing the publication *Designing for Good Indoor Air Quality: An Introduction for Design Professionals,* which should be available before the end of 1994. It will provide general guidance to design professionals such as architects, engineers, and interior designers, directing them through a decision-making process to optimize IAQ.

5. ASHRAE has established standards for ventilation (see Chap. 3). Appendix C of Standard 62-1989 reviews criteria for the indoor environment.

6. The ACGIH has developed TLVs which, like OSHA standards, are intended for the industrial environment. ASHRAE recommends that where standards or guidelines have not been established, a concentration of 1/10 TLV would not produce complaints in a nonindustrial facility (school, office, or residence).[99]

7. OSHA, which was established under the U.S. Department of Labor, issues regulations concerning health and safety hazards in the workplace. It has been responsible for establishing regulations

TABLE 4.13   A Classification of Low-Emitting Materials and Products*
Based on emissions of total organic vapors, except as noted

Material or product	Maximum emissions[†]
Flooring materials	0.6 mg/m²/h
Floor coatings	0.6 mg/m²/h‡
Wall materials	0.4 mg/m²/h
Wall coatings	0.4 mg/m²/h‡
Movable partitions	0.4 mg/m²/h
Office furniture	2.5 mg/workstation/h
Office machines (central) Ozone emissions	0.25 mg/m³ of space/h 0.01 mg/m³ of space/h
Office machines (personal) Ozone emissions	2.5 mg/workstation/h 0.1 mg/workstation/h

*Basic Assumptions: Indoor air is well mixed, ventilation rate is 0.5 exchange of outdoor air per hour, maximum prudent increment in indoor concentration of organic vapors from any single source type is 0.5 mg/m³, maximum prudent increment of ozone is 0.02 mg/m³ (0.01 ppm), and volume of concern for dispersion of emissions from furniture and machines at workstations is 10 m³.

†This column lists default values for use where predictive modeling of IAQ impacts is not done. For specific indoor situations, modeling is generally preferable to using these defaults and may yield very different values for maximum emissions. Values for particularly noxious compounds will also be lower than those shown.

‡Many varnishes, paints, waxes, and other wet coatings have emission factors substantially higher than this, immediately after application. These coatings might still be considered "low-emitting" if their emission factors drop below this level within several hours. However, the presence of other surfaces that adsorb coating vapors and subsequently reemit them complicates the classification of coatings.

SOURCE: W. Gene Tucker, EPA, "Building with Low-Emitting Materials and Products: Where Do We Stand?" presented at Indoor Air '90, Toronto, July/August 1990.

for permissible air concentrations of certain materials, referred to as PELs. These standards were developed for the industrial setting, and even approaching these levels would be problematic to the IAQ of a typical office environment. OSHA requires warning labels and MSDSs for any hazardous materials. These MSDSs can be a useful tool for analyzing the potentially hazardous ingredients contained in a product. Refer to Fig. 4.5 for an example MSDS.

Several states have actively addressed the issue of building contamination through building construction. California has enacted the Safe Drinking Water and Toxic Enforcement Act of 1986, known as Proposition 65. This act lists hazardous materials, requiring manufacturers to notify the state of hazardous materials used in their products. However, Proposition 65 does not set standards for emissions.

The most comprehensive approach to controlling the emissions of building materials and furnishings has been taken by the state of Washington, as discussed in Sec. 4.2.11. In 1982, complaints were registered from occupants of a state-owned office building. Multiple investigations resulted with no resolution to the sources of irritation. Ultimately the building was "abandoned as a suitable place for office workers."[100] The building was made into a warehouse.

In 1989, Washington took advantage of a planned project for an office building complex known as the ECP project to make a standard regarding IAQ and new construction. The $237.4 million expansion involved four office buildings totalling 1,010,700 usable square feet. Emissions testing was required for building materials and furnishings to comply with overall emission standards for building finishes as noted in Table 4.9.

Several factors must be considered in the final comprehensive analysis of building materials' impact on a building: the total VOCs within a space (including the materials that act as sinks) the volume of the space, the anticipated duration of the emissions, and the ventilation capacity of the HVAC system. Individual products such as adhesives and paints may emit initially high levels of VOCs, yet when considered as the only source of pollution, they may not exceed recommended air concentrations. More important are the total emissions from various materials in a building, which must be evaluated and dealt with as a whole, using information available in MSDSs, to avoid health risks to both building construction workers and building occupants.

With data on total amounts and duration of emissions in project materials, as well as the spatial design of the building, the design team can better determine when a building is acceptable to occupy and what ventilation systems need to be in place to avoid exposure to potentially harmful off-gassing.

In order to determine TVOCs in a building, one must first have product emission data achieved through air sampling. The state of Washington found during the ECP project that few tests on furniture were available. Subsequently in the project's requests for proposals from furniture vendors, emission test results were required. Not all projects are of the scope that can demand such costly data, but manufacturers are beginning to realize the economic and public relations benefits that can come from selling a material emitting low VOCs. Such was the case of a predominate movable wall panel manufacturer who bid on the ECP project.[101]

Within a product test report, the architect should look for the following items:[97]

DATE: October 1, 1993
REPLACES: July 11, 1993

Armstrong World Industries, Inc.
Human Resources Department
313 W. Liberty St.
P.O. Box 3001
Lancaster, PA 17604

Telephone 717 396-2328 or 396-2935

S-172 Floor Patch/ Skim Coat

Material Safety Data Sheet

DIVISION:	ISSUED BY:
Floor Products	Safety, Health and Industrial Hygiene Department

NFPA 704 (0 = no hazard; 4 = severe hazard):

HEALTH = 1   FIRE = 0   REACTIVITY = 0

DEPT. OF TRANSPORTATION INFORMATION:

SHIPPING NAME: Not classified. HAZARD CLASS: N/A. ID#: N/A.

I. PRODUCT INFORMATION:

PRODUCT NAME: S-172 Floor Patch/Skim Coat. CHEMICAL NAME AND SYNONYMS: N/A. CHEMICAL OR PRODUCT FAMILY: Gypsum (Plaster of Paris).

II. INGREDIENT INFORMATION:

HAZARDOUS COMPONENTS (Chemical Identity; Common Name)	C.A.S. NO.	%	OSHA PEL	ACGIH TLV
CALCIUM SULFATE	7778-18-9	99	total dust: 15 mg/m³	10 mg/m³
			respirable dust: 5 mg/m³	N/A

This product formulation does **NOT** contain asbestos.

III. PHYSICAL DATA:

APPEARANCE AND COLOR: Pink powder. BOILING POINT (degrees F): N/A. VAPOR PRESSURE (mm Hg 20 degrees C): N/A. VAPOR DENSITY (Air = 1): N/A. SOLUBILITY IN WATER: N/K. SPECIFIC GRAVITY (H_2O = 1): N/K. PERCENT VOLATILE BY WEIGHT (30 min. @ 275 degrees F): N/A. EVAPORATION RATE (Butyl Acetate = 1): N/A. pH: N/A.

IV. FIRE AND EXPLOSION DATA:

FLASH POINT: N/A. FLAMMABLE LIMITS: LEL = N/A; UEL = N/A. EXTINGUISHING MEDIA: N/A. SPECIAL FIRE FIGHTING PROCEDURES: None. UNUSUAL FIRE AND EXPLOSION HAZARDS: None.

Figure 4.5   Material safety data sheet. (*Used with permission of Armstrong World Industries, Inc., Lancaster, Pa.*)

S-172 Floor Patch/Skim Coat (cont'd)

V. HEALTH DATA:

PRIMARY ROUTE(S) OF ENTRY: Inhalation and direct dermal exposure. **TARGET ORGANS:** Upper respiratory tract, skin and eyes. **EFFECTS OF OVEREXPOSURE:** SKIN AND EYES: Prolonged or repeated overexposure to dust may cause skin and eye irritation. Prolonged contact with product mixed with water or S-173 Latex may cause severe irritation or burns to the skin. INHALATION: Prolonged or repeated overexposure to dust may cause nose and throat irritation. **CARCINOGENICITY:** NTP: No; IARC Monographs: No; OSHA Regulated: No. **MEDICAL CONDITIONS GENERALLY AGGRAVATED BY EXPOSURE:** Existing skin conditions. Preexisting upper respiratory and lung disease such as, but not limited to bronchitis, emphysema, and asthma. **FIRST AID PROCEDURES:** SKIN AND EYES: In case of eye contact, flush eyes with plenty of water continuously for at least fifteen (15) minutes. Call physician immediately. Additionally with skin contact, thoroughly wash with soap and water or hand cleaner. Refer to physician if irritation or symptoms persist. INHALATION: Remove to fresh air.

VI. REACTIVITY DATA:

STABILITY: Stable. **INCOMPATIBILITY:** N/K. **HAZARDOUS DECOMPOSITION PRODUCTS:** N/K. **HAZARDOUS POLYMERIZATION:** Will not occur.

VII. SPILL OR LEAK PROCEDURES:

STEPS TO BE TAKEN IF MATERIAL IS RELEASED OR SPILLED: Avoid raising excessive dust. When sweeping up, use water mist or vacuum. **WASTE DISPOSAL METHOD:** Do not reuse container. Dispose of container and any unused contents in accordance with Federal, State, and Local Waste Disposal Regulations. Do not flush unused contents or residue down drains.

VIII. SPECIAL PROTECTION INFORMATION:

VENTILATION: Normal, ambient air circulation or ventilation should be adequate. **RESPIRATORY PROTECTION:** Should not be required. If work process generates excessive quantities of dust, wear respirator approved for nuisance dusts. **SKIN AND EYE PROTECTION:** Wear gloves to avoid direct skin contact. When mixing with water or latex, wear safety goggles to avoid splashing in eyes.

IX. SPECIAL PRECAUTIONS:

PRECAUTIONS TO BE TAKEN IN HANDLING AND STORAGE: When mixed with water or S-173 Latex, this material hardens and then slowly becomes hot. Do not attempt to make a cast enclosing any part of the body. **OTHER PRECAUTIONS:** None.

The information presented herein is supplied as a guide to those who handle or use this product. Safe work practices must be employed when working with any materials. It is important that the end user makes a determination regarding the adequacy of the safety procedures employed during the use of this product.

N/A = Not Applicable or Not Available
N/K = None Known or Not Known

Form 47494 10/93J

Figure 4.5 *(Continued)*

1. *Summary.*   Identification of products to be evaluated, system components if applicable, specific emissions identified, as well as general type of testing performed (e.g., large or small environmental chamber testing).

2. *Testing procedures.*   Explanation of specific test protocol (ASTM, EPA, or other) equipment, environmental conditions (such as humidity levels), duration of testing, monitoring techniques, and sampling protocols.

3. *Analytical measurements.*   Summary of analytical methodology.

4. *Quality assurance and control.*   Description of measures taken to ensure the integrity of the testing procedures, such as handling of the samples and the status of the environmental chamber. The report should show evidence that the materials tested are representative of the materials that will actually be used in the facility.

5. *Air concentration calculations.*   Calculation of emission rates and resulting air concentration of any suspect contaminant and assumptions used in the calculations.

6. *Discussion.*   Evaluation of test results as they compare to recommended guidelines and the specific building configuration where the material is to be used.

7. *Conclusion.*   Summary of data and subsequent findings.

One difficult task facing professionals involved with IAQ is overcoming skepticism about the causes and effects of contaminants in the indoor environment. The more information available on individual building materials, the better we understand the total building and how to best minimize effects of VOC emissions.

Failure to consider sources of building pollutants for new building designers and their consultants can have serious ramifications. In 1990, children in an elementary school in Texas experienced health problems, the most serious of which was one case of the equivalent of "cocaine nose," which resulted in possible permanent damage. The subsequent $4.6 billion lawsuit filed by parents implicated 29 people, from architects and contractors to product manufacturers and product suppliers.[102] In order to avoid such tragedies and legal actions, the construction industry must understand and respond to the growing concern regarding building products and their potential impact on IAQ.

Building materials release VOCs, and while guidelines exist in some cases, the combined, complicated effects of VOCs are the subject of much debate. It will be the role of the specifier or purchaser to understand that the impact of a building material with higher emissions may be controlled by increased ventilation and flushout periods, as discussed in Sec. 4.7. However, when building materials have a high-surface-area-to-room-volume ratio, every effort should be made to specify low-emitting products to avoid potentially harmful effects on building occupants. Table 4.14 is a list of specific emissions from various building materials and furnishings.

TABLE 4.14   Specific Emissions from Building Materials and Furnishings

Note: Where emission rates are not available, the category is blank.

Material	Typical chemicals emitted	Emission rate (illustrative)
Adhesives	Alcohols	
	Amines	
	Benzene	
	Decane	
	Dimethylbenzene	
	Ethylbenzene	
	Formaldehyde	
	Limonene	
	Nonane	
	Octane	
	Terpene	
	Toluene	
	Xylenes	
	Other VOCs	
Sealants	Alcohols	
	Alkanes	
	Amines	
	Benzene	
	Diethylbenzene	
	Ethylbenzene	
	Formaldehyde	
	n-Propylbenzene	
	Methylethylketone	
	Xylenes	
	Other VOCs	
Architectural coatings		
Paints	C4-benzene	
	2-Ethoxyethanol	
	2-Ethoxyethylacetate	
	Isopropylbenzene	
	Limonene	
	n-Propylbenzene	
	Toluene	
Stains and varnishes	Amines	
	Benzene	
	Decane	
	Dodecane	
	Formaldehyde	
	n-Heptane	

TABLE 4.14   Specific Emissions from Building Materials and Furnishings (*Continued*)

Note: Where emission rates are not available, the category is blank.

Material	Typical chemicals emitted	Emission rate (illustrative)
Particleboard/chipboard (plywood similar)	Amines 3-Carene Ethylbenzene	
	Formaldehyde	0.2–2 mg/m^2/h 95–230 μg/m^2/h (particleboard) 1 mg/m^2/h (plywood)
	n-Hexane	15–26 μg/m^2/h (particleboard)
	Hexanol Limonene n-Pentanol n-Propanol	
	2-Propanone (Acetone)	37–41 μg/m^2/h (particleboard)
	n-Propylbenzene Terpene Toluene	
	TVOCs	0.1 mg/m^2/h (chipboard)
Carpeting	n-Dodecane 2-Ethylhexanol Formaldehyde 4-Methylethylbenzene	
	4-Phenylcyclohexene	0.1 mg/m^2/h (latex backed carpet)
	n-Propylbenzene Styrene 1,2,4-Trimethylbenzene n-Undecane Other VOC	
Resilient flooring General	Amines Alkanes C3-benzene C4-benzene n-Butanol 2-Butanone Diethylbenzene Ethylacetate Formaldehyde Isopropylbenzene Methyl styrene Xylenes Other VOC	
Linoleum	Trichloroethylene	3.6 μg/m^2/h

TABLE 4.14   Specific Emissions from Building Materials and Furnishings (*Continued*)

Note: Where emission rates are not available, the category is blank.

Material	Typical chemicals emitted	Emission rate (illustrative)
Wall coverings		
Wall paper	TVOCs	0.1 mg/m²/h
General wall coverings	Amines	
	Alkanes	
	C3-benzene	
	C4-benzene	
	n-Butanol	
	2-Butanone	
	Diethylbenzene	
	Ethylacetate	
	Formaldehyde	
	Isopropylbenzene	
	Methyl styrene	
	Xylenes	
	Other VOC	
Vinyl-coated wallpaper	Amines	
	Formaldehyde	
	n-Decane	
	1,2,4-Trimethylbenzene	
	Xylenes	
Floor adhesives	TOV	100–1700 mg/m²/h
Insulation		
Polyurethane spray foam	Acetone	ND–0.02 mg/m²/h
	Chlorobenzene	0.1–0.2 mg/m²/h
	Xylenes	0.03 mg/m²/h
	Cyclohexane	ND–0.03 mg/m²/h
	Dichlorobenzenes	ND–0.03 mg/m²/h
Polyurethane foam board	Dichloromethane	0.01–0.08 mg/m²/h
	Chloroform	ND–0.002 mg/m²/h
	Acetone	ND–0.03 mg/m²/h
	Chlorobenzene	0.2–0.3 mg/m²/h
	Dichlorobenzenes	ND–0.04 mg/m²/h
Polystyrene foam	Chlorobenzene	0.5 μg/m²/h
	p-Dichlorobenzene	0.7 μg/m²/h
Acoustical ceiling tiles	Formaldehyde	
Furnishings		
Upholstery	Formaldehyde	
Drapery	Toluene	
	Formaldehyde	
Fabric protector	1,1,1-Trichloromethane	
	Propane, petroleum distillates	

SOURCE: Based on information from *Understanding Indoor Air Quality*, Bradford Brooks and William Davis, CRC Press, 1991, and *Gaseous Pollutants*, Jerome O. Nriagu, ed., John Wiley, New York, 1992.

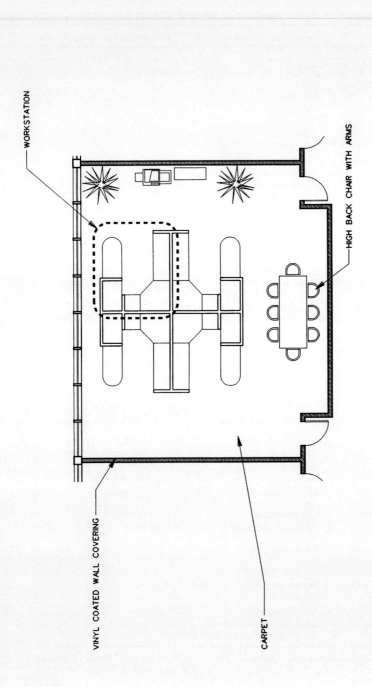

WORKSTATION

HIGH BACK CHAIR WITH ARMS

VINYL COATED WALL COVERING

CARPET

0' 2' 4'   8'   16'   24'

Figure 4.6 Floor plan. (*Used with permission of Gobbell Hays Partners, Inc., Nashville, Tenn.*)

Figure 4.6 is a floor plan showing emissions data on furnishings and finishes found in a typical office. The following are examples of emissions from specific products (data specific to product brands) in Fig. 4.6:

Workstation.[97]   (Emission rates were measured using EPA and ASTM guidelines).

Formaldehyde
  Maximum emission rate (after 48 h) = 1.47 mg/m^2/h
  Minimum emission rate (after 336 h) = 0.83 mg/m^2/h

Particles
  Maximum emission rate (after 1 h) = 0.18 mg/m^2/h
  Minimum emission rate (after 912 h) = 0.085 mg/m^2/h

Total VOCs
  Maximum emission rate (after 1 h) = 32 mg/m^2/h
  Minimum emission rate (after 912 h) = 0.01 mg/m^2/h

High-back chair with arms.[97]   (Emission rates were measured using EPA and ASTM guidelines).

Formaldehyde
  None detected after 1 h or after 981 h

Particles
  None detected after 1 h or after 981 h

Total VOCs
  Maximum emission rate (after 1 h) = 1.06 mg/m^2/h
  Minimum emission rate (after 981 h) = 0.10 mg/m^2/h

Vinyl-coated wallcovering[103]

Formaldehyde
  Average emission rate over 24 h = 15 μg/m^2/h

Toluene
  Emission rate after 1 h = 5 μg/m^2/h
  Emission rate after 24 h = 50 μg/m^2/h
  Average emission rate over 24 h = 21.7 μg/m^2/h

Chlorinated hydrocarbons

Emission rate after 1 h = 10 $\mu g/m^2/h$

Emission rate after 24 h = 20 $\mu g/m^2/h$

Average emission rate over 24 h = 13.3 $\mu g/m^2/h$

Other aromatic hydrocarbons

Emission rate after 1 h = 5 $\mu g/m^2/h$

Emission rate after 24 h = 15 $\mu g/m^2/h$

Average emission rate over 24 h = 10 $\mu g/m^2/h$

Carpet.[103]   Nylon carpet, polypropylene primary and secondary backing; polyurethane secondary backing.

Total VOCs

Emission rate after 1 h = 71 $\mu g/m^2/h$

Emission rate after 144 h = 779 $\mu g/m^2/h$

Average emission rate over 144 h = 425 $\mu g/m^2/h$

Figure 4.7 is an interior perspective suggesting ventilation treatments of a typical office.

4.3   Other Sources of Building Contamination

This section addresses asbestos, lead, radon, PCBs, pest control, and operational and construction activities, all of which can have an impact on air quality. Pollutant pathways, other than HVAC systems, and uncontrolled moisture are also discussed. Moist building materials act as hosts for a variety of biological contaminants. Maintenance and construction activities, in and of themselves, can create by-products that will harm the indoor environment.

Over the last several years, asbestos, lead, radon, and PCBs have been classified as hazardous. Asbestos, lead, and PCBs have the potential to be released from products within a facility and can result in exposure to the building occupants. Radon, a naturally occurring gas, finds its way into buildings through soil and rock formations and is generally more of a problem in poorly ventilated spaces below grade.

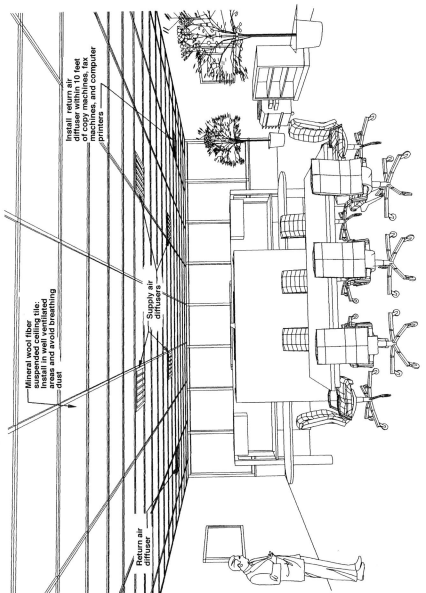

Mineral wool fiber
suspended ceiling tile:
Install in well ventilated
areas and avoid breathing
dust

Install return air
diffuser within 10 feet
of copy machines, fax
machines, and computer
printers

Supply air
diffusers

Return air
diffuser

Figure 4.7 Interior perspective. (*Used with permission of Gobbell Hays Partners, Inc., Nashville, Tenn.*)

4.3.1 Moisture

Moisture in the wrong places can affect the quality of the indoor environment. Damp materials can deteriorate and can provide a breeding ground for microbes and pests.

Vapor retarders.   Inadequate vapor retarders are a major cause of microbial buildup and contribute to a significant portion of IAQ complaints. It is important to understand the need for adequate vapor retarders and where they should be located to prevent a moisture buildup in building materials. Air contains moisture, and the warmer

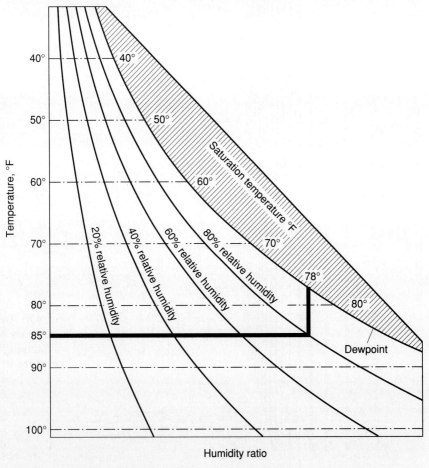

Figure 4.8 Schematic psychrometric chart. (*Based on ASHRAE Psychrometric Chart No. 1 in* 1993 ASHRAE Handbook: Fundamentals, *I-P ed., American Society of Heating, Refrigerating and Air-Conditioning Engineers, Inc., Atlanta, GA, 1993, p. 6.15.*)

the air, the more water vapor the air can contain. However, when air with a high moisture content drops in temperature to a point at which condensation occurs, vapor converts to water droplets. This point is called the dewpoint. Figure 4.8 shows how to use a psychrometric chart to find the dewpoint.

One can observe the effects of condensation by putting ice into a glass on a hot, humid day and watching water droplets appear on the outside of the glass. Furthermore, if the glass is sitting on a napkin, the napkin also becomes damp. In the same way, due to a difference in temperatures, moisture can build up on a building material and affect other surrounding materials.

In buildings, condensation may occur when there is a difference in temperature between the inside and outside. The warmer side generally will have a higher moisture content than the cooler side. In regions of high humidity, where the inside temperature may be below the dewpoint, moisture problems occur primarily in the summer. The outside dewpoint temperature will rise above the inside temperature, thereby creating the potential for condensation. A vapor retarder is used to block the moisture penetration into the building skin so that the water vapor does not reach the point at which it would convert to water droplets.

Air containing water vapor is a gas and can penetrate cracks and crevices and even building materials. While a vapor retarder will not block 100 percent of the moisture, if it is made of an impervious material such as polyethylene, it is highly effective in reducing moisture-associated problems. The term *vapor barrier* is often used synonymously with the term *vapor retarder*.

Sample calculation

In a building in the Southeastern part of the United States, the outside temperature is 80°F with 80 percent humidity. The inside in the air-conditioned structure is 70°F. Calculate the dewpoint, and estimate the location within the wall where water droplets will occur (use Fig. 4.8). To determine the dewpoint from Fig. 4.8, find the temperature in degrees Fahrenheit, project that line to where it intersects the relative humidity line, and then project perpendicularly to the saturation temperature in degrees Fahrenheit.

Solution:

The dewpoint is 78°F. If the vapor retarder is on the inside wall, the vapor can penetrate from the exterior to the point in the wall system where the temperature is 78° and then turn to water droplets. In this case, the dewpoint would occur within the building insulation. If the vapor retarder is along the outside wall, the water vapor will be blocked prior to reaching the dewpoint.

Figure 4.9 shows a wall construction without a vapor retarder and subsequent moisture buildup. Figure 4.10 shows a vapor retarder in the proper location.

Generally, the vapor retarder should be located on the warmer side of a wall (this applies to other exterior building surfaces, such as roofs and floors). In cold climates, the vapor retarder would be located just outside the interior finish of the exterior wall. In warmer, more humid climates, the vapor retarder should be just inside the outside finish of the exterior wall. Use caution to avoid creating totally air-tight areas, since existing moisture may become trapped and condense with temperature changes.

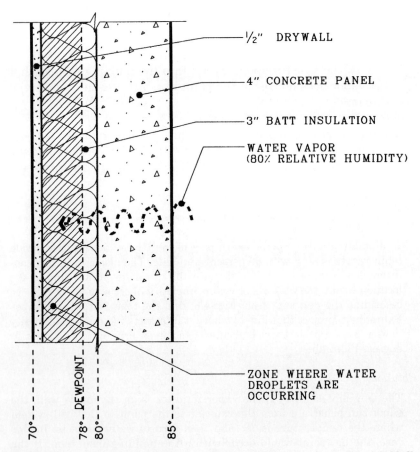

Figure 4.9 Wall section without vapor retarder. (*Used with permission of Gobbell Hays Partners, Inc., Nashville, Tenn.*)

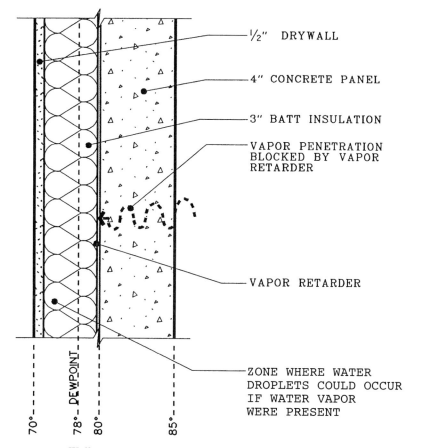

- 1/2" DRYWALL

- 4" CONCRETE PANEL

- 3" BATT INSULATION

- VAPOR PENETRATION BLOCKED BY VAPOR RETARDER

- VAPOR RETARDER

- ZONE WHERE WATER DROPLETS COULD OCCUR IF WATER VAPOR WERE PRESENT

Figure 4.10 Wall section with vapor retarder. (*Used with permission of Gobbell Hays Partners, Inc., Nashville, Tenn.*)

High-humidity areas within a building, such as kitchens, shower rooms or showers, exercise areas, indoor swimming pools, and hot tubs, can cause condensation. As an example, in a 1990 survey, the American Hotel and Motel Association (AH & MA) estimated $68 million in damage caused by mold and mildew in areas where the vinyl wallcovering acted as an improperly located vapor retarder.[104]

Case study

In another case, a hospital used foil backing on drywall as a vapor retarder for prototypical facilities. The concept worked well in northern climates, but with the high humidity of southern climates, the condensate buildup in the walls along the foil back caused wet insulation, carpet, and drywall to the point that the drywall started to crumble, and mold and mildew became evident. The problem was solved by replacing the drywall on exterior walls with a non-foil-backed product.

Another problem is moisture trapped within construction materials that is not allowed to migrate out. Take care to avoid sealing materials when there is high humidity or if the material has a high moisture content. High-humidity areas within a building can create condensate. For example, when structural members are not insulated from the outside, they become colder than the dewpoint for interior conditions, thus causing condensate to form.

Case study

Within a tennis facility, the steel roof purlins touch the exterior skin and are not insulated. The roof deck between purlins is insulated. During winter months, it is common for the temperature of the uninsulated purlins to drop below the dewpoint and cause condensate to form on the steel purlin, wetting surrounding insulation in sufficient quantities to create visible stain lines and to drip on the tennis courts. The resolution is to insulate the purlins so that the temperature of the steel does not reach the interior dewpoint.

Leaks.   The most common cause of moisture within a building is leaks—either from the roof, through walls, or through floors.

Roof leaks are caused by failure of the roofing membrane or by roof penetrations that are not watertight, either because of improper sealing or deterioration. A few examples of roof penetrations are plumbing vents, HVAC equipment, and parapet walls. Water also penetrates through walls above grade due to improper flashing or porous construction. Penetrations such as windows, doors, and louvers can exacerbate the problem. Leaks below grade are generally caused by hydrostatic pressure of ground water, forcing water either through walls or floors.

Large leaks are obvious and generally receive immediate repair. Unfortunately, it is not uncommon for building maintenance personnel to replace only visibly water-damaged materials without attending to moist materials that may not be visible to the general public. An example would be the repair of a plaster wall, without replacing or drying the fiberglass insulation behind the wall. Leaks in service areas such as mechanical rooms, utility chases, crawl spaces, and basements are often allowed to continue if they are not causing structural damage. And small leaks, where visible damage is minor, are often ignored. The result is that materials remain damp longer, allowing microbials to breed.

Equipment and plumbing can also generate similar kinds of moisture problems. Equipment itself may leak either water or some other liquid that can cause a potential problem. Condensate on chilled water lines for the HVAC system can also generate moisture problems.

In conclusion, the IAQ is directly affected by microorganisms and pests that are promoted by moist materials in a building (see the discussion of pest control in Sec. 4.3). Exercise care to repair moist building materials. Eliminate or correct the source of the moisture. Allow wet materials to dry or replace them prior to sealing them. Finally, note that while a moist area may not appear to be damaging materials and may be located away from the building occupants, contamination of occupied spaces can occur through pollutant pathways (see Sec. 4.3.5).

4.3.2 Operational activities

Proper operation of a facility is essential in optimizing the quality of the indoor air environment. Inadequate maintenance or housekeeping that allows dust or particulate buildup ultimately leads to potential contamination of the air. Animal feces, dust mites, and dust particles are well-documented as human irritants or health hazards (see Sec. 2.3). Most of these problems are associated with high concentrations of a contaminant that can be minimized by routine cleaning.

Routine cleaning involves normal vacuuming and dusting but, depending upon the configuration of the facility, may need to go beyond the publicly visible areas. Depending on how the HVAC system works, routine cleaning may need to occur in mechanical rooms and other spaces that are part of the airstream. Unsanitary conditions promote IAQ problems. Special attention should be given to areas in which food products are consumed or prepared, such as break rooms and kitchens. Because emissions from stored trash occur, monitor trash storage and trash removal schedules. Pay special attention to areas such as restrooms and kitchens. Set and maintain cleaning schedules appropriate for the activities that occur in the particular facility.

Cleaning and maintenance chemicals. While cleaning activities are necessary and generally promote good IAQ, exercise caution to monitor and minimize the VOCs that may be emitted by cleaning products or processes. In a typical office space, a variety of cleaning compounds can be found that emit VOCs, as shown in Table 4.15.

Most of the information concerning specific chemicals in cleaning compounds can be obtained from MSDSs. When purchasing cleaning products, review MSDSs and select the safest products that will do

TABLE 4.15   Sources of Contaminants in Cleaning Products

Sources	Contaminants*
Cleaners and waxes	Particulates
Aerosol bathroom cleaner	Nonmetals (phosphates, other
Unpressurized aerosol window cleaner	inert powders)
Liquid all-purpose cleaner	VOCs
Powdered abrasive cleaner	Aromatic hydrocarbons (toluene,
Dishwashing detergent	p-dichlorobenzene)
Concentrated spot remover	Halogenated hydrocarbons (per-
Liquid floor wax	chloroethylene; methylene chlo-
Aerosol furniture wax	ride; 1,1,1-trichloroethane)
Aerosol and solid room deodorants	Alcohols
Paste furniture wax	Ketones (acetone, methyl ethyl
Oven cleaners	ketone)
	Aldehydes (formaldehyde)
	Esters (alkyl ethoxylate)
	Ethers

*The reader should not attempt to match specific contaminants with specific products.

SOURCE: EPA *Introduction to Indoor Air Quality: A Reference Manual,* U.S. Environmental Protection Agency, U.S. Public Health Service, and National Environmental Health Association, EPA/400/3-91/003, July 1991, p. 21.

the job. Try to avoid high-VOC products, such as floor wax, for use in large areas. Note that the use of deodorizers and fragrances is a factor in IAQ. The use of cleaning products that introduce strong odors or contaminants may need to be scheduled for unoccupied periods and used with additional ventilation. Many products have very high emissions initially, followed by a low-level steady emission rate. For example, according to EPA research, floor wax emissions decrease from 10,000 μg/cm^2 to approximately 500 μg/cm^2 in about 1 h and drop below 10 μg/cm^2 in about 10 h.[105]

When they are not in use, store cleaning products according to the manufacturers' directions and in proper containers. Maintain the storage area under negative pressure, with local exhaust to the outside properly designed and maintained.

Office equipment operation and maintenance. Office equipment, such as wet- and dry-copying machines, computers, and laser printers, emit a number of VOCs during operation. The equipment may also require chemicals for maintenance and cleaning that are potential sources of hazardous emissions. Table 4.16 lists types of equipment and supplies commonly used in offices and the associated pollutants.

TABLE 4.16   **Emissions from Office Equipment and Supplies**

Equipment or supply	Typical pollutant emissions
Carbonless copy paper	Chlorobiphenyl Cyclohexane Dibutylphthalate Formaldehyde Paratoluene sulfinate (Michler's hydrol)
Computers/VDTs	2,6,-Bis(1,1-dimethyl)-4-methyl phenol n-Butanol 2-Butanone 2-Butoxyethanol Butyl 2-methylpropyl phthalate Caprolactam Cresol Decamethyl cyclopentasiloxane Diiosoctyl phthalate Dimethylbenzene Dodecamethyl cyclohexasiloxane 2-Ethoxyethyl acetate Ethylbenzene Heptadecane Hexanedioic acid 4-Hydroxy benzaldehyde 3-Methylene-2-pentanone 2-Methyl-2-propenoic acid Ozone Phenol Phosphoric acid 2-$tert$-Butylazo-2-methoxy-4-methyl-pentane Toluene Xylene
Duplicating machines	Ethanol Methanol 1,1,1-Trichloroethane Trichloroethylene
Electrophotographic printers photocopier supplies	Ammonia Benzaldehyde Benzene Butyl methacrylate Carbon black Cyclotrisiloxane Ethylbenzene Isopropanol Methylmethacrylate Nonanal Ozone Styrene Terpene

TABLE 4.16   Emissions from Office Equipment and Supplies

Equipment or supply	Typical pollutant emissions
Electrophotographic printers photocopier supplies	Toluene 1,1,1-Trichloroethane Trichloroethylene o-, m-, p-Xylene Zinc stearate combustion products
Microfiche developers and blueprint machines	Ammonia
Preprinted paper forms*	Acetaldehyde Acetic acid Acetone Acrolein Benzaldehyde Butanal 1,5-Dimethylcyclopentene 2-Ethyl furan Heptane Hexamethyl cyclosiloxane Hexanal 4-Hydroxy-4-methyl pentanone Isopropanol Paper dust Pentanal 2-Pentyl furan Propionaldehyde 1,1,1-Trichloroethane
Rubber cement	Naphtha Toluene
Typewriter correction fluid	Acetone 1,1,1-Trichloroethane

*Volatile emissions detected at 180°C (operating temperature of hot roll in typical electrophotographic equipment).

SOURCE: Reprinted with permission from *Understanding Indoor Air Quality* (p. 26–27). Copyright CRC Press, Boca Raton, Fla.

Several general observations have been made by researchers and IAQ investigators who conducted chamber testing and case studies of office equipment emissions:[106]

1. Wet-process photocopiers emit small amounts of a number of VOCs from solvents with each copy. In areas in which many copying machines are located, photocopiers may contribute up to 90 percent of the TVOC concentration.

2. Computer terminals, printers, and fax machines also release a number of VOCs.

3. Office machinery is the most significant indoor source of ozone in office buildings. Elevated ozone levels may be created in areas that have a high density of office equipment or deficiencies in the ventilation systems.

Equipment emissions are not regulated. However, the EPA has recommended the following standards as guidelines:[106]

For centrally located office machines

0.25 mg of VOCs/h/m³ of workspace

0.01 mg of ozone/h/m³ of workspace

For personal-use office machines

2.5 mg of VOCs/h/workstation

0.1 mg of ozone/h/workstation

To minimize equipment emissions, building owners and managers should consider purchasing lower-emitting equipment and requesting emissions data from manufacturers. Some manufacturers are including replaceable ozone filters in new equipment and providing ozone emissions information in their product manuals.

Whenever possible, turn off machines that are not in use or schedule large copying or printing jobs for unoccupied times. Locate equipment in well-ventilated spaces and use additional exhaust systems when necessary.

Ensure that equipment is used and maintained properly. Monitor maintenance chemicals in a similar manner as cleaning products, including provisions for storage. Use them according to the manufacturers' directions. Even when maintenance contracts are in effect, the building owner or manager should monitor schedules and processes to ascertain that precautions are taken to minimize VOCs.

Pest control. Pest infestation is well known to have detrimental effects on the indoor environment. Organisms are considered pests whenever they unfavorably affect human life and activities by presenting health risks, destroying property, which results in economic losses, or merely being unsightly. Pests enter buildings, make their homes, and multiply because conditions are suitable for habitation. Pests need air, food, moisture, warmth, and shelter. Building construction, maintenance practices, and occupant activities that create access for pests and provide their basic life needs invite pests and promote pest infestation.

In today's commercial buildings, routine use of pesticides is common. Pesticides, by their nature, are inherently toxic, and use of the

TABLE 4.17 Pesticides as a Source of Indoor Air Contaminants

Sources	Contaminants*
Pesticides	Particulates
Termite treatment of homes	Nonmetals (sulfur, lime)
Aerosol all-purpose household pesticides	VOCs
Roach killer (powder, liquid, spray)	Aliphatic hydrocarbons (kerosene)
Flea killer (powder, liquid dip, aerosol)	Aromatic hydrocarbons (xylene)
Mold and mildew inhibitors	Halogenated hydrocarbons (chlordane, p-dichloroben-zene, heptachlor, chloropyri-fos, diazinon)
Houseplant insecticides	
Moth repellents	
Rodenticides (rat or mouse killer)	
Fungicides (household disinfectants)	Ketones (methyl isobutyl ketone)
	Organic sulfur/phosphorous compounds (malathion)

*The reader should not attempt to match specific contaminants with specific products.

SOURCE: EPA *Introduction to Indoor Air Quality: A Reference Manual,* U.S. Environmental Protection Agency, U.S. Public Health Service, and National Environmental Health Association, EPA/400/3-91/003, July 1991, p. 21–22.

pesticides introduces into the indoor environment toxic substances designed to eliminate the pests. These substances that have the potential to cause harm to humans who are sufficiently exposed.[107] Table 4.17 lists contaminants that can be found in a variety of pesticides.

In recent years, there has been a movement to reduce the amount of pesticides introduced into schools. This approach is called Integrated Pest Management (IPM). While specific guidance documents are oriented toward educational facilities, it is feasible to use the IPM concept in other types of facilities. The IPM program is based on understanding pest behavior and biology. The goal of the program is to control pests effectively while reducing the use of pesticides. The IPM program utilizes a combination of methods, many of which are low-cost, aimed at eliminating conditions that provide attractive pest habitats.[108] The following guidelines incorporate the IPM strategies for a comprehensive program of pest management:

1. *Control pest entry.* Caulk or seal cracks, crevices, or holes to prevent infestation. Use weatherstripping on doors. Install or repair screens.

2. *Modify pests' habitats.*   Practice good general sanitation. Allow food and beverages only in designated areas. Keep food preparation and service areas clean and free of crumbs. Store food and waste in containers inaccessible to pests. Remove waste at the end of each day. Keep areas dry. In order to eliminate harborage for pests, do not store paper products or cardboard boxes near moist areas, directly on the floor, or against the wall. This also facilitates inspection.

3. *Identify pests of concern.*   General spraying may not be necessary. Rodents, for example, may be controlled by the use of snap or glue traps. Correctly identify the pest in question, and monitor pests and infestation levels. Pheromone traps may be used to determine the presence and activity periods of certain pests.

4. *Use pesticides judiciously.*   Select pesticides that are species-specific, and know the hazards and safety precautions of the specific pesticides used. Contractors or vendors should be able to provide EPA labels and MSDSs. Limit the use of sprays, foggers, or volatile formulations. Use baits or traps and place them at or near cracks and crevices. Be certain that the pesticide is applied as directed in targeted locations. Schedule pesticide applications for unoccupied periods, if possible, and introduce additional ventilation during and after the application. Be certain that the HVAC system does not distribute pesticides into occupied areas. Consider using temporary exhaust systems during the pest control activities.

5. *Store pesticides properly.*   Pesticides should be stored off site, if possible. If stored on site, they should be stored in a locked area that is properly ventilated to the outside. Refer to EPA labels for instructions and requirements for proper storage. All containers should be tightly closed.

6. *Maintain good records.*   Keep copies of the pesticide labels and MSDSs. Records on monitoring and results can show whether pest populations increase or decrease, thus indicating what further actions are required.

For optimum results, the IPM program should integrate pest management planning with preventive maintenance, housekeeping practices, occupant education, and staff training.[109]

EPA's *Introduction to Indoor Air Quality: A Reference Manual* provides further information regarding the use of pesticides, including examples of biological control of pesticides, guidelines for cleaning pesticide spills and residues, first aid guidelines for pesticide poisonings, and guidelines for safe application and disposal of pesticides.[110]

4.3.3 Construction activities in occupied buildings

Renovations of commercial buildings are a cost-effective solution for many building owners in the 1990s. This was not so in the 1960s when older buildings with inadequate elevator and restroom capacities and a shortage of fire exits were not easily adaptable to new functions. Today's 30-year-old buildings generally contain all the basic elements for current needs, so upgrading HVAC systems and applying new finishes and even new exterior skins become economically feasible. With the infrastructure of the modern building allowing for a longer lifespan, more and more renovations of commercial buildings can be expected during the next decade, particularly small-scale partial renovations which do not involve relocation of building occupants.[111]

Certain construction activities that occur during a renovation can cause significant IAQ problems, especially in occupied spaces. Good IAQ management during construction includes proper containment of the work area; selection of products, materials, and furnishings with low VOC emissions; attention to scheduling; and control of storage and routine housekeeping activities.

Proper containment protects the occupants from dust and particulates, vapors, and noise. A barrier that isolates the work area visually does not necessarily keep vapors and dust out of the occupant spaces. Contaminants can recirculate through the HVAC system from the work area into occupied areas. Some processes that occur during renovation, such as refinishing, generate harmful and combustible vapors that require additional ventilation in the work area.

It is not uncommon for occupants in spaces some distance away from the construction to complain of nausea, headaches, and other symptoms of discomfort. Figure 4.11 illustrates how contaminants may be transported.

Generally, the appropriate precautions are to shut off the HVAC, seal the air grilles, and install a temporary exhaust system to ventilate the construction area. Whenever temporary barriers are constructed, always maintain required fire exits and exitways. New materials and furnishings introduced into a renovated area can be extremely high in VOCs, particularly when new and initially installed. In addition to specifying building materials and furnishings that have a low potential for toxic vapor emissions, request installation procedures that limit emissions of contaminants to maintain good IAQ during a renovation. Store new materials and furnishings in a clean, dry, well-ventilated area until chemical emissions have diminished, and flush the renovated area with fresh air to dilute emissions after installation of the new components. Be aware of cer-

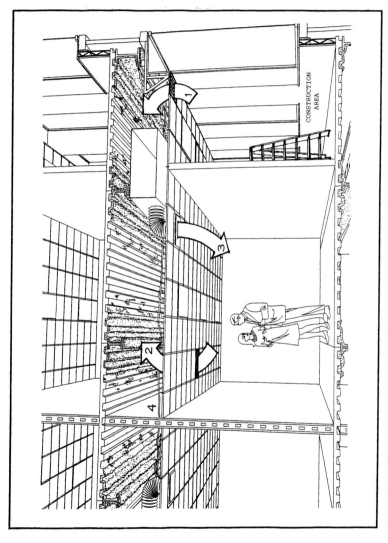

Figure 4.11 Contaminant transport. Contaminants from construction area enter above ceiling plenum (1), mix with return air from occupied space (2), and are supplied into occupied space (3) through ceiling diffusers. The above ceiling partition (4) prevents distribution of contaminants to other areas by isolating the return air plenum area. *(From "IAQ and Renovation: What Building Managers Should Know," by Ronald V. Gobbell, in Indoor Air Review, IAQ Publications, Chevy Chase, MD, Copyright 1994.)*

TABLE 4.18   Trade Groups and Potential Hazardous Materials and Operations

Trade	Hazardous material or operation	Hazard
Carpenter	Wood preservatives	Aniline, creosol
	Protective finishes, glues	Alkyls, amines
	Wood sealers and glues	Anhydrides, phenol, naphthalenes, ethylenediamine formaldehyde
	Form release oils or agents	Kerosene, mineral oil
	Putty	Coal tar pitch, gums, resins, linseed oil, lead, sodium silicate, solvents
	Sandpaper	Glass fibers, flint, corundum, glue
Carpet, linoleum, soft-tile layer	Solvents	Acetone, aliphatic hydrocarbons, ammonia, aromatic hydrocarbons, ketones, petroleum naphtha, toluene, tetrachloroethene
	Adhesives	Chlorinated diphenyls and naphthalenes, curing agents, ethylenediamine, isocyanates, petroleum distillates, solvents
Electrician	Soldering	Metals
	Fluves	Acids (hydrochloric, hydrofluoric, sulfuric)
	"Bright" dip	Sulfuric acid
	Cable joints and coatings	Amines, anhydrides, chlorinated diphenyl and naphthalenes, ethylenediamine, resins, solvents
	Wire coverings, transformers	Amines, isocyanates, resins, solvents
Glazier	Putty	Coal tar pitch, gums, resins, sodium silicate, solvents
Hod carrier	Building materials	Gypsum, hydrochloric acid, calcium oxide, sulfuric acid, silica, silicates, trace metals
Iron worker	Welding	Metals, carbon monoxide
	Electrodes	Manganese
	Oxy-acetylene welding	Acetylene, arsine, phosphine
	Fluxes	Acids (hydrochloric, hydrofluoric, sulfuric), zinc chloride
	Scraping	Metals, coatings
Operating engineer	Cleaning, degreasing	Gasoline, solvents
Painters, wallpaper hangers	Paints, varnishes, lacquers solvents	Acetates, benzene, creosol, cycloparaffins, ketones, isopropyl alcohol, methylene chloride, phenol, xylene tetrachloroethylene, turpentine, petroleum distillate pigments, metals
	Flame-retardant paints	Antimony oxide
	Impermeable paints and coatings	Anhydrides, resins, solvents, ethylenediamine, naphthalenes, chlorinated diphenyls
	Putty	Antimony, sulfide, calcium oxide, glycerin, solvents, sodium silicate
	Wallpaper dyes	Analine compounds
	Material being removed, cleared	Cement, paint, wood, surface coatings

TABLE 4.18   Trade Groups and Potential Hazardous Materials and Operations (*Continued*)

Trade	Hazardous material or operation	Hazard
Plumbers, pipefitters	Soldering	Carbon monoxide, metals
	Fluxes	Acids (hydrochloric, hydrofluoric, sulfuric)
	"Bright" dip	Sulfuric acid, nitric acid
	Pipe cements (polyurethane resins)	Amines, isocyanates, solvents
	Plastic pipe cements	Amyl acetate, butadiene
	Refrigeration, air-conditioning	Ammonia, freon
Roofers	Asphalt	Gasoline, kerosene
	Coal tar pitch	Acridine, creosol, phenol, solvents
	Coal tar roofing	Acridine, creosol, phenol, solvents
Sheet metal workers	Welding, soldering	Zinc
	Metal cleaners	Solvents

SOURCE: Reprinted with permission of the Construction Specifications Institute from *The Construction Specifier,* September 1993, p. 88.

tain procedures used strictly for the construction process that result in high concentrations of contaminant emissions. Dust from sanding drywall, fumes generated by welding and cutting torches, or vapors from cleaning solvents are a few common examples. Table 4.18 lists hazardous materials and operations which are part of the construction process. Understanding the materials used in the process and the process itself is critical for controlling air quality during a renovation.

In an occupied building, the careful scheduling of construction activities is another key element for good IAQ management. If at all possible, the containment should be constructed while the space is unoccupied, as should any activities that produce dust, odors, and chemical emissions. Buildings with round-the-clock operations, such as hospitals, require more careful scheduling and may call for some relocation of occupants for periods of time, even for minor renovation activities. Determine whether sound isolation is possible; if it is not, schedule noisy construction activities accordingly.

Potentially hazardous products such as paints, solvents, and adhesives are used in all construction projects. The safe storage of such products is always important, particularly when used in an occupied building. Proper containment is critical and, when possible, a chemical storage room should be maintained under negative pressure.

Routine activities such as sweeping and vacuuming can cause particulates in the work area to become airborne. The use of portable HEPA vacuums instead of low-efficiency paper-bag collectors reduces contaminants in the airstream. Any efforts to keep the construction area clean—even controlling where workers eat, smoke, and dispose of garbage—improve the quality of the indoor environment. Prior to enclosing spaces such as plumbing chases, air shafts, and return air plenums, check for cleanliness because contaminants in such hard-to-access spaces may eventually find their way into the building airstream.

4.3.4 Hazardous materials

Over the past 30 years, health issues have arisen over building materials that contain asbestos, electrical equipment that contains PCBs, paint, water, or soil that contains lead, and radon, a naturally occurring gas that can seep into occupied buildings. Since a direct link exists between these substances and diseases, efforts have been initiated to abate the hazard of each particular substance, although these efforts fail to address other environmental issues essential to a healthy building. The following section outlines the material-specific issues for each substance and then addresses them in the context of the total air quality.

Asbestos. Asbestos, a naturally occurring fibrous mineral found in certain types of rock formations, was considered a "miracle mineral" by the Greeks who recognized its inherent properties of softness, pliability, and resistance to heat. Its fibrous characteristics allowed it to be both spun and woven to produce cloths, and it was used in religious services as wicks in sacred lamps and for table cloths which could be cleaned by being placed in a fire.[112]

From 100 A.D. to the late 1800s, asbestos materials were viewed with fascination, but the use of asbestos became widespread with the discovery of large quantities of the mineral in Canada. At that time, the mining of asbestos was developed commercially. With additional deposits discovered in the United States, South Africa, and Russia, asbestos fibers became a plentiful, inexpensive filler which resulted in very workable, strong, and noncombustible materials. The properties of asbestos made it largely impervious to chemical corrosion and a poor conductor for electricity. The many ways to process asbestos, from crushing it into tiny fibers to weaving it into fabric as the Greeks did, ultimately led to the use of asbestos in hundreds of products.[113] Table 4.19 lists several of these most common materials. This table lists asbestos-containing materials (ACMs) in the three categories established by the EPA: surfacing material, thermal system insulation, and miscellaneous.

TABLE 4.19   Summary of Asbestos-Containing Materials

Surfacing

Walls and ceilings
  Spray-applied fireproofing (generally above ceiling)
  Spray-applied coating (for acoustical control)
  Trowel-applied coating (decorative)

Thermal Systems Insulation

Mechanical rooms, attics, crawlspaces
  Preformed pipe and pipe joint covering (made with magnesium carbonate or calcium silicate)
  Insulation board
  Boiler insulation (tank insulation and flue insulation)
  Pipe wrap (used to protect underground pipes, particularly gas and oil lines)
  Ductwork insulation
  Paper products
    Cardboard air-cell insulation
    Corrugated paper wrap
    Gaskets (used at various joints) and packings

Miscellaneous

Throughout
  Paper products
    Millboard (used on ceilings and walls)
  Flooring products
    Vinyl asbestos tile
    Asphalt/asbestos tile
    Floor sheeting
  Roofing products
    Roofing felt (used on built-up roofing) and base flashings
    Roofing shingles
    Roofing asphalt
    Roof putty
    Asphalt roofing tile cement
  Compounds
    Mastic (floor tile, floor base and sink pipe joints)
    Drywall joint compound or "mud" (interior walls)
    Pipe joint compound or "seam paste" (elbows, fittings, and joints)
    Caulking putties (window glazing)
    Spackling compound (wall patching)
    Cold-applied adhesive

TABLE 4.19 Summary of Asbestos-Containing Materials (*Continued*)

Miscellaneous (*Continued*)

Cementitious

Piping (storm drains, water, sewer, and industrial process piping; used due to resistance to damage from termites, rodents, water, soils, and/or sewage)

Interior and exterior extrusion panels (corrugated, flat, laminated, or flexible sheets; used where durability, fire, water, and/or chemical resistance was desired)

Exterior finishes (clapboard or shingle siding; roof shingles)

Chalkboards

Acoustical panels

Electrical and telephone conduit and ducts

Asbestos cement board and sheet (exterior roofing and siding; interior and exterior soffits, walls, ceilings; areas requiring fire resistance, fume hoods, laboratory countertops, cooling tower panels)

Fire protection

Fire doors (asbestos fibers in interior core of door)

Asbestos cement board and sheet

Textiles*

Fire curtains (often found in theaters and auditoriums)

Fire blankets, laboratory aprons, gloves, cords, curtains and ropes (often found in schools)

Flexible duct (often found at transitions from furnaces to ductwork)

Electrical wire insulation

*Textiles have high asbestos content but typically are coated or impregnated prior to assembly; consequently they are not always labeled as asbestos-containing materials.

SOURCE: Compiled from information provided by EPA *Asbestos Waste Management Guidance,* Office of Solid Waste, May 1985; Hornbostel, Caleb, *Construction Materials,* John Wiley, New York, 1978; EPA *Managing Asbestos in Place* (Green Book), 20T-2003, July 1990; and EPA *Guidance for Controlling Asbestos-Containing Materials in Buildings* (Purple Book), EPA 560/5-85-024, June 1985.

Serpentine and amphibole are the two mineral categories of asbestos. There are six separate minerals within these two groups:

1. Chrysotile, the only serpentine and the most frequently found in buildings in the United States; often referred to as "white" asbestos

2. Amosite, the second most frequently used in buildings in the United States; often known as "brown" asbestos

3. Crocidolite, used in high-temperature insulation applications; also known as "blue" asbestos

4. Anthophyllite

5. Tremolite

6. Actinolite

The latter three types of asbestos are rare and of little commercial value but are occasionally found as contaminants in materials containing one of the first three.[112]

A primary use of asbestos was as a fireproofing material, applied to structural steel members in multistory commercial buildings to attain proper fire protection. With its resistance to heat, asbestos was able to keep the building structure from bending and warping if exposed to fire. The amount of asbestos in fireproofing ranged from 5 to 95 percent. In addition, asbestos was used to strengthen materials such as cement products (exterior siding and roofing) and miscellaneous materials (floor tile, joint compounds, and adhesives, sometimes referred to as *mastics*).[114]

Asbestos was also used in thermal insulation and acoustical materials. Acoustical materials were usually sprayed on or applied with a trowel. Thermal insulation could be premolded and field installed or could be factory installed on or within equipment. Asbestos was used as an enhancer of strength when added to cementitious products such as cement shingles, cement siding, and flat sheets used as a wall finish.[114]

After widespread use of asbestos over a 15- to 25-year time span, a pattern of illnesses—specifically diseases of the lung—gradually began to occur in asbestos workers. It was determined that if ACMs were or became friable, or capable of being crushed by hand pressure, fibers could be inhaled and cause diseases which disrupt the normal functioning of the lungs. Three diseases linked to asbestos exposure are asbestosis, a fibrous scarring of the lungs, lung cancer, and mesothelioma, a cancer of the lining of the chest or abdominal cavity. Symptoms of these diseases may not appear for 20 years or more after inhalation.[115] (See Sec. 2.3 for further discussion of the health effects and hazards of asbestos.)

Because the risk of exposure to asbestos fibers relates to friability of the product, it is important to evaluate the cohesiveness of the material containing asbestos (i.e., loose sprayed-on fireproofing versus resilient floor tile), its condition, and its location. ACM which has been damaged or disturbed or has deteriorated poses the greatest risk because it can release fibers into the building air, and these fibers can be inhaled.

In response to these concerns, OSHA and the EPA began to establish regulations to protect those who work with asbestos and to control the use of asbestos. Regulations began to go into effect in 1971 when the EPA listed asbestos as a hazardous indoor air pollutant.[116] OSHA set its original "occupational" limit of exposure for workers and has revised the standard several times. New OSHA regulations provide for a permissible exposure limit of 0.1 f/cm^3 for an 8-h TWA and an excursion limit of 1.0 f/cm^3 for any 30-min sampling period.[117]

It is important to note that while asbestos is now rarely used in new construction materials in the United States, it is still used elsewhere in the world and is mined in Canada, South Africa, Russia, and the United States. Hundreds of thousands of older buildings in the United States still have ACMs.

If a building owner suspects that a building has ACMs, the EPA's reference publication, *Guidance for Controlling Asbestos-Containing Materials in Buildings,* commonly referred to as the Purple Book, is a useful guide.[118]

The first step in controlling the potential hazard is a general building inspection to determine the types and quantities of asbestos-containing material and to document their locations and conditions. Take samples and have them analyzed by a qualified laboratory. If a sample's content is higher than 1 percent asbestos, it is considered to be an ACM and should be controlled in some manner to protect building occupants. During the inspection and sampling time, review the original construction documents (if available) for confirmation that the ACM originally specified was actually installed and still remains.

The next step, once an ACM is identified, is the development of a management plan, which identifies the management team and the asbestos program manager. The management plan defines appropriate response actions and includes a plan for managing asbestos in-place, known as an O&M program. There are four basic response actions, depending on the location and condition of the ACM. These methods are encapsulation, enclosure, removal, and O&M. Encapsulation, enclosure, and removal have common requirements:[119]

1. Full assessment of the area in which the ACM is located

2. Worker protection during the abatement activities

3. Proper work area containment

4. Thorough postabatement cleanup

The EPA defines encapsulation as "the spraying of ACM with a sealant...[to] bind together the asbestos fibers and other material components and offer some resistance to damage from impact."[120] This technique is recommended for materials which are in good condition, showing no delamination or deterioration,[121] and in areas inaccessible to the public.

Enclosure is another option for controlling asbestos. This method is the construction of a virtually airtight enclosure around the ACM.[121] This technique works well with vertical surfaces, such as a wall with asbestos-containing plaster as its finish, where a new wall is simply constructed in front of the existing one without disturbing the ACM. This approach may also be taken in small horizontal applications, such as an insulated pipe along the perimeter wall of a room. However, large horizontal spans to enclose a surfacing material, such as fireproofing or acoustical plaster, may be impractical due to the cost of the enclosure system. The necessity for frequent supports contacting the ACM may result in damage to the ACM. Joints between walls and ceilings should be caulked. Materials approved by the EPA as acceptable enclosures are gypsum boards with taped seams, tongue and groove wooden boards, and boards with spline joints. Suspended acoustical tile ceilings are unacceptable.[121]

A design for asbestos removal should specify techniques for full containment of the work area during removal or localized containment bag removal, whichever is most appropriate based on the type, location, and condition of the ACM. For example, in mechanical rooms or in industrial settings, containment bags, referred to as glovebags, may be used instead of construction of a full containment area. These bags are made of polyethylene or PVC and can be taped around the area to be removed. Figure 4.12 illustrates a glovebag configuration for pipe insulation removal.

The glovebag has lined sleeves with gloves, into which the worker's arms are inserted, allowing the worker to remove the ACM and drop it into the bag for disposal. This method is used primarily for removal of pipe insulation. When full containment is required, an abatement design should be generated, including specifications and drawings.

A valuable source for abatement specifications' content and format is the National Institute of Building Sciences' publication, *Asbestos Abatement & Management in Buildings: Model Guide Specifications.*[122] The abatement drawings should indicate such items as:

1. The boundaries of the abatement containment.

2. The number of negative air pressure machines required during abatement. (These machines maintain negative air pressure in the containment area to ensure that contaminated air is not escaping from the work area.)

3. The location of the decontamination area(s) where workers prepare to enter and exit the work area and shower prior to exiting to remove asbestos fibers from skin, clothes, shoes, and hair.

As part of the management plan an O&M program must be developed to protect and maintain any remaining ACMs, to provide precautionary measures to avoid damage to ACMs and to train workers

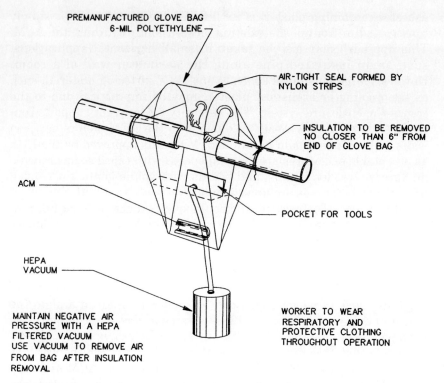

PREMANUFACTURED GLOVE BAG
6-MIL POLYETHYLENE

AIR-TIGHT SEAL FORMED BY
NYLON STRIPS

INSULATION TO BE REMOVED
NO CLOSER THAN 6" FROM
END OF GLOVE BAG

ACM

POCKET FOR TOOLS

HEPA
VACUUM

MAINTAIN NEGATIVE AIR
PRESSURE WITH A HEPA
FILTERED VACUUM
USE VACUUM TO REMOVE AIR
FROM BAG AFTER INSULATION
REMOVAL

WORKER TO WEAR
RESPIRATORY AND
PROTECTIVE CLOTHING
THROUGHOUT OPERATION

Figure 4.12 Glovebag detail (not to scale). (*Used with permission of Gobbell Hays Partners, Inc., Nashville, Tenn.*)

regarding the appropriate response to any release of asbestos that occurs during daily building operations. Records documenting worker protection actions are important for the building owner. Additionally, the O&M program informs building occupants and workers of the location of asbestos. Workers are given information on the proper ways to handle each type of ACM, how to conduct periodic checks of the ACM to detect deterioration and damage, and the need for medical surveillance.[123] An O&M program allows a building owner to phase asbestos abatement over a longer period of time in coordination with building renovations and tenant changes. It is important to note that the building owner's commitment is the primary factor in the success of an O&M program.[124]

EPA's *Managing Asbestos in Place: A Building Owner's Guide to Operations and Maintenance Programs for Asbestos-Containing Materials* provides further information on O&M programs.

The EPA divides O&M activities into three types: unlikely to involve direct contact with ACM, accidental disturbance of ACM, and small-scale, short-duration maintenance or repair activity, which may involve intentional disturbance of ACM.[125]

National regulations for asbestos have been generated through the EPA, OSHA, and/or the CPSC. Individual states and local agencies may have adopted additional regulations.[126] OSHA and the EPA have established regulations for workers' protection, OSHA relating to private sector employees and the EPA relating to public sector employees. OSHA set PELs for exposure to airborne asbestos fibers. The use of respirators and protective clothing and monitoring both the levels of fibers in the air and the medical status of all workers are required if the PEL is exceeded.

In 1984, the EPA issued rules regarding National Emission Standards for Hazardous Air Pollutants (NESHAP) for demolition and renovation projects. Amended rules require notification of the EPA or the responsible state agency designated under NESHAP prior to beginning the demolition and renovation involving more than 160 ft^2 of friable ACM, 260 linear feet of friable ACM on piping over a 1-year period, or 35 ft^3 of ACM removed from facility components where the length or area could not be measured previously.[127] NESHAP also issues rules for disposal and shipment of asbestos waste[128] which track the materials from the waste generator to the transporter and the waste disposal site, where quantities measured by the generator are checked against quantities received. Records are to be kept by all parties, but the owner of the building is held responsible for the waste in perpetuity.

In 1990, the EPA enacted an Asbestos Ban and Phase Out rule prohibiting importation, manufacture, and processing of 94 percent of all remaining asbestos products in the United States by the end of 1997.[128] This regulation was challenged by asbestos product manufacturers and was remanded by the U.S. Court of Appeals. The EPA is currently evaluating the ban.

A history and summary of significant federal actions regulating asbestos are given in Table 4.20.

Lead. Lead, a heavy, soft, malleable metal, has been used in construction since the Greek and Roman civilizations. One theory suggests that the fall of the Roman Empire was due in part to lead poisoning dispersed by lead used to line the aqueducts bringing water to the city. The Romans reportedly noticed that servants who worked with lead for long periods suffered convulsions, and even death.[129] Since then, lead has been used in paint, utensils and pottery, plumbing pipes and fittings, and gasoline additives. It is estimated that there are 3.8 million homes in the United States with peeling lead paint or lead dust, where children under the age of 7 live.[130]

TABLE 4.20   Regulatory Requirements

	Chronology of Major Federal Actions on Asbestos
March 1971	EPA listed asbestos as a hazardous air pollutant.
July 1972	"Permanent standard" for the occupational exposure level to airborne asbestos 5.0 f/cm^3.
April 1973	EPA prohibited spray application of materials containing more than 1 percent asbestos. EPA passed the "no visible emissions" standards for demolition of buildings.
October 1975	EPA added waste collection and disposal to the "no visible emissions" standard. OSHA proposed lowering the occupational exposure standard to 0.5 f/cm^3.
July 1976	OSHA occupational exposure standard of 2.0 f/cm^3 became effective.
December 1976	NIOSH recommended that OSHA lower the occupational exposure standard to 0.1 f/cm^3.
August 1979	Department of Transportation issued a rule requiring controls during transportation of friable asbestos.
May 1980	EPA listed asbestos as a hazardous waste for disposal purposes.
May 1982	EPA issued a final rule requiring schools to identify friable asbestos-containing materials and notify staff and parent-teacher associations.
April 1984	EPA issued NESHAP standard for demolition, renovation, and disposal, 40 CFR 61, Subpart M.
August 1984	Asbestos School Hazard Abatement Act (ASHAA) was signed into law. EPA provided assistance in the form of loans and/or grants to schools for the abatement of serious asbestos hazards.
June 1986	OSHA issued a revised general industry standard and construction standard (29 CFR 1910 and 1926). Both standards established an action level of 0.1 f/cm^3 as an 8-h TWA and a permissible exposure limit of 0.2 f/cm^3 as an 8-h TWA.
October 1986	Asbestos Hazard Emergency Response Act (AHERA) was signed into law. The act required EPA to promulgate rules regarding inspection of all public and private school buildings, development of comprehensive management plans, and description and implementation of response actions to deal with asbestos hazards.
November 1986	Department of Transportation promulgated regulations pursuant to the disposal of asbestos wastes.
October 1987	EPA issued final regulations to carry out AHERA.
September 1988	OSHA issued an amendment to 29 CFR 1910 and 1926, establishing an excursion limit of 1.0 f/cm^3 as averaged over a 30-min sampling period.
November 1990	EPA amended NESHAP rule 40 CFR 61, Subpart M, governing asbestos demolition and renovation projects, requiring inspection of all facilities for asbestos prior to renovation or demolition, changing notification period to 10 working days, and providing definitions for Category I and II ACM.
1992	Asbestos School Hazard Abatement Reauthorization Act (ASHARA) required all persons inspecting for asbestos or designing or conducting asbestos response actions in public and commercial buildings to be accredited in accordance with the Model Accreditation Plan.

Lead poisoning effects range from sluggishness to death. Children, fetuses, and pregnant women are the most susceptible to poisoning. Lead poisoning effects in children include attention span deficiencies, impaired hearing, reading and learning disabilities, delayed cognitive development, reduced I.Q. scores, mental retardation, seizures, convulsions, coma, and even death.[129] Small exposures over weeks or years can cause lead poisoning because it bioaccumulates, or builds up in the body tissues.[129] The symptoms of lead poisoning are listed in Table 4.21.[131] See Sec. 2.3 for a discussion of the health effects of lead poisoning.

Potential sources of lead exposure include lead-based paint, lead dust in the soil, air, or drinking water, and lead materials in use in the workplace.[129] Exposure can also occur from uncontrolled lead removal activities. Work on or around surfaces previously coated with lead-based paint (such as bridge repair) and lead-based paint abatement projects (such as building renovation) are two of the many sources of potential lead exposure. Lead exposure may occur in the following operations:[132]

Operations generating lead dust and fumes:

1. Flame-torch cutting, welding, and grinding of lead-painted surfaces in repair, reconstruction, dismantling, and demolition work
2. Abrasive blasting of bridges and other steel structures that contain lead-based paints
3. Using torches, heat guns, and sanding machines on lead-based paint
4. Maintaining industrial process equipment or exhaust ductwork

TABLE 4.21   **Symptoms of Lead Poisoning**

Headache	Sleeplessness
Poor appetite	Hyperactivity
Dizziness	Weakness
Irritability/anxiety	Reproductive difficulties
Constipation	Nausea
Pallor	Fine tremors
Excessive tiredness	Insomnia
Numbness	"Lead line" on the gums
Metallic taste in the mouth	"Wrist drop" (weakness of extensor muscles)
Muscle and joint pain or soreness	

SOURCE: "Working with Lead in the Construction Industry," U.S. Department of Labor, OSHA, U.S. Dept. of Health and Human Services, NIOSH, OSHA 3126, April 1991, p. 2.

Operations involving exposure to lead-containing products:

1. Spray-painting bridges and other structures with lead-based paints and primers
2. Using solder in plumbing and electrical work

"Pathways" of lead from the environment to the body are illustrated in Fig. 4.13.[133]

The Centers for Disease Control's (CDC's) advisory committee on lead recommends testing for lead exposure or poisoning in children unless they are from areas where widespread screening has indicated no problem. The CDC recommends screening at 12 months and then again at 24 months, and high-risk children (from older run-down homes) should be tested earlier and more often.[134]

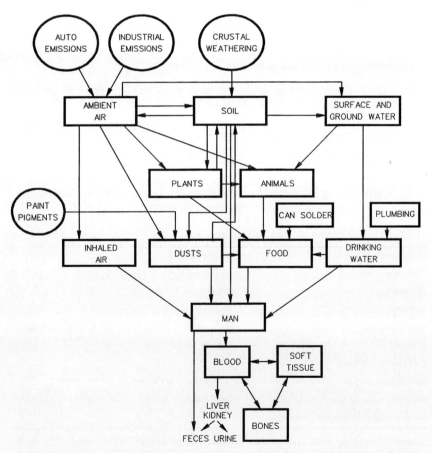

Figure 4.13 Pathways of lead from the environment to a person and the body disposition of lead. (*Adapted from EPA, 1986.*)

The EPA estimates that approximately 5 to 10 percent of U.S. children under age 6 have blood levels greater than 10 micrograms per deciliter (μg/dl), which is the CDC's current threshold of concern.[135]

Lead dust can be controlled by various methods which include controls ranging from in-place management to lead dust removal projects. In-place management includes the proper cleaning of accumulated dust on a periodic basis. Cleaning should be performed by trained individuals using *wet* mops or cloths soaked in a solution of trisodium phosphate (TSP) or phosphate-containing powdered dishwasher detergent and warm water. Most multipurpose household cleaners are not effective in cleaning up lead dust. Use two buckets, one for TSP water and one for rinsing, and avoid mixing cloths or wash and rinse water. Rinse thoroughly and repeat the process.[136] Do not sweep or vacuum with household vacuum cleaners since these methods disperse lead dust.

Lead-based paint abatement techniques include building component or "part" replacement, the permanent covering of the lead-based painted surface by encapsulation or enclosure, and paint removal methods. Replacement of components provides the most reliable method of the lead dust source removal, although feasibility depends on the item to be removed. A steel handrail, for example, may be successfully unbolted and disposed of properly, while a historic, elaborate crown molding may not be easily or aesthetically removed and replaced. Encapsulation of flat surfaces, such as drywall or plaster walls, may be a feasible solution to a particular lead paint problem. Many products have been introduced to the market for coating surfaces, curved and flat, to seal the lead surface inside a thick, continuous coating. Maintain caution since the lead material is still present; the coating may somehow be broken and dust released again. The degree of success of paint removal techniques depends on the process used. Consistently use and monitor polyethylene floor coverings that are turned up on the walls and taped, HEPA-filtered vacuum cleaners, wet cleaning methods, and careful lead removal techniques for a thorough lead abatement project.

"Clearance levels" of lead dust or acceptable amounts present after abatement activities have been defined by HUD in their "Lead-Based Paint: Interim Guidelines for Hazard Identification and Abatement in Public and Indian Housing." It is currently the most widely accepted document providing a guideline recommendation for lead management and abatement. The protocol was designed to determine residual levels of lead dust after abatement cleanup procedures but can also be used effectively as a risk assessment tool. The procedure is easy to learn and requires inexpensive equipment and supplies.

Interior dust samples from a dwelling usually consist of samples from several areas and from various surfaces within each area, such as floors and window troughs. The clearance levels acceptable on all HUD-sponsored lead-based paint abatement projects assume that windows are a major lead dust source. HUD clearance standards are as follows:[135]

Floors	200 μg lead/ft^2
Interior window sills	500 μg lead/ft^2
Window troughs and exterior concrete or other rough surfaces	800 μg lead/ft^2

These standards should be used unless EPA regulations establish different clearance levels. According to HUD guidelines, lead dust levels present a minimal risk below these values.[137]

These levels are apparently based on evidence that children exposed to lead levels below several hundred micrograms per square foot have shown no adverse effects, while exposures to lead dust of several thousand micrograms per square foot have resulted in symptoms. These limits remain controversial, and further research should yield information to refine or replace them.[137]

Lead paint regulation began in 1971, with the passage of the Lead-Based Paint Poisoning Prevention Act (LBPPPA). Under this law, the CPSC was directed to conduct research on multiple layers of dried paint film to determine the safe level of lead in residential paint products. In addition, the Secretary of HUD was directed to determine the nature and extent of the problem of lead-based paint poisoning and to identify methods for removing lead-based paint from surfaces in residential housing, where many children are exposed.[138]

Currently, the National Institute of Building Sciences (NIBS) is preparing two documents which address operations and maintenance practices that involves lead-based paint and testing and abatement of lead-based paint: *Work Practices Manual for Managing Lead-Based Paint Hazards in Residential and Commercial Buildings* and *Guide Specifications for Reducing Lead-Based Paint Hazards.*

Radon.   Radon is one of seven decay products that begin with uranium 238. In the decay chain, radon comes directly from radium-226. Uranium-238 is found in soils and bedrock; it undergoes radioactive decay, producing radium-226, radon-222, polonium-218, lead-214, bismuth-214, polonium-214, and lead-210. Varying amounts of radium exist in certain soils and bedrock. The important distinction between radon and the other by-products of uranium-238 is that radon is the only *gaseous* by-product and as such can enter a residence through cracks and openings in walls and concrete slabs.[139]

Radon exists in various types of soil and bedrock. Some types of granite and high-grade metamorphic rocks, phosphate rocks, marine black shales, and mineralized veins and fracture zones have elevated levels of radium.[140] Table 4.22 shows states categorized by radon measurements. When air pressure inside a building is lower than the gas pressure in the surrounding soil, the odorless radon can be suctioned into adjacent building walls.[141] While most publications on radon address air concentrations in residences, recent studies have raised

TABLE 4.22   Preliminary Categorization of States into Three Groupings*

States above 4 pCi/L	States between 2 pCi/L to 4 pCi/L	States below 2 pCi/L
Colorado	Connecticut	Alabama
Iowa	District of Columbia	Alaska
Maine	Idaho	Arizona
Minnesota	Illinois	Arkansas
Montana	Indiana	California
Nebraska	Kansas	Delaware
New Hampshire	Kentucky	Florida
New Jersey	Maryland	Georgia
North Dakota	Massachusetts	Hawaii
Ohio	Michigan	Louisiana
Pennsylvania	Missouri	Mississippi
South Dakota	Nevada	North Carolina
	New Mexico	Oklahoma
	New York	South Carolina
	Oregon	Texas
	Rhode Island	Washington
	Tennessee	
	Utah	
	Vermont	
	Virginia	
	West Virginia	
	Wisconsin	
	Wyoming	

*States are broken into three groups: (1) States that have short-term measurement average for the lowest livable space in existing homes that is *above 4 pCi/L,* (2) states that have short-term measurement average for the lowest livable space in existing homes that is *between 2 pCi/L to 4 pCi/L,* and (3) states that have short-term measurement average for the lowest livable space in existing homes that is *below 2 pCi/L.*

SOURCE: *Analysis of Options for EPA's Model Standards for Controlling Radon in New Homes,* prepared for EPA Office of Radiation Programs, Radon Division, Washington, D.C., by ICF Incorporated/Camroden Associates, Incorporated, July 1992.

concerns regarding radon in schools. In a National School Radon Survey based on random surveys of ground-contact schoolrooms, short-term test results indicated approximately 3 percent of the classrooms had levels above the EPA guidelines of 4 picocuries per liter (pCi/L). Long-term tests of 2832 classrooms showed 1.5 percent of the levels above 4 pCi/L.[142]

Radon has a very short half-life of 3.8 days, meaning that if a pound of radon was put into a container, 3.8 days later only $\frac{1}{2}$ lb would be in the jar, while the other half pound would have decayed into the short-lived decay products polonium, bismuth, and lead; 3.8 days after that, $\frac{1}{4}$ lb would be in the jar, and so on. In contrast uranium-238 has a half-life of 4.47 billion years and radium has one of 1620 years.[139] One decay of a radioactive atom is known as a disintegration. The shorter the half-life of a radioactive element, the more disintegrations of atoms occur, emitting more radiation per unit of time.[143] Of all seven uranium decay products, radon has the shortest half-life.

Radon's health hazard results from its decay into radioactive particles. These particles, referred to as *radon progeny,* are inhaled and lodged in the lungs where they "bombard" tissue with radiation. This exposure to radon leads to an increased risk of lung cancer.[141] Some EPA documents estimate that five to twenty thousand deaths occur per year in the United States due to radon.[139]

Radon levels are measured by picocuries of radon per liter of air. At present, the EPA recommends remedial action if average annual radon levels exceed 4 pCi/L or when radon progeny exceeds approximately 0.02 working levels (WL).[141] The working level is a unit of measurement derived to measure human exposure to radon and radon progeny.[144] The first step in addressing concerns about radon is to measure for the presence of radon in the building. The simplest test methods are "passive" tests, which are generally used as initial testing and evaluation. These tests involve the placement and exposure of sampling canisters for a specified amount of time, then submitting them to a laboratory for analysis.[145] Passive detectors are inexpensive and generally available at hardware stores. Some states, however, have special restrictions on test kit manufacturers and analytical labs. Contact the local EPA for recommendations prior to purchasing these materials in your state.

The second type of testing is called "active." Active testing is beneficial in determining source points within a building as well as in the mitigation and reduction of radon. This generally requires a building inspection and specialized test equipment, thus making these tests cost more than passive methods. Active testing may be used if passive testing indicated elevated levels of radon. A building inspection can identify soil gas entry points, existing building features that make the building susceptible, and structural considerations that might influence selection of reduction techniques. Special testing allows measurement of gaseous movement under a concrete slab, as well as infiltration routes of radon into the building. The information provided by these methods is crucial to the design of a radon reduction system.[146]

Radon mitigation involves prevention of radon entry into the building where possible and removal of radon that does enter the building. The EPA advises that the effectiveness of a removal system cannot be foreseen prior to installation.[141] The following summarizes alternative radon reduction techniques recommended by the EPA.[147]

Ventilation

Natural.   Increase movement of fresh outdoor air into the building without the use of fans. This process can reduce radon entering by convective and diffusive movement and dilute the radon that enters the building or crawlspace.

Forced air.   Increase movement of fresh air into the building crawl space with the use of fans.

Forced air with heat recovery.   Increase movement of fresh outdoor air into the building, exhaust a similar amount of building air, with transfer of heat from the exhausted building air to the incoming fresh air. This process dilutes radon levels in the building.

Sealing of soil gas entry routes.   Reduce or eliminate convective and diffusive radon movement into the building by sealing openings between the building and the soil.

Active soil ventilation

Drain tile ventilation.   Use a fan to draw suction on the perforated footing drain tiles that surround some buildings for water drainage. This process uses the tiles to maintain a low-pressure field in the soil or aggregate under and around the building, drawing soil gas into the tiles and exhausting it outdoors, preventing it from entering the building.

Subslab ventilation.   Use a fan to establish a low-pressure field under the slab, by drawing a suction on pipes inserted into the aggregate under the slab.

Block-wall ventilation.   Use a fan to draw suction on, or to blow outdoor air into, the void network inside hollow-block foundation walls. Intake should be as remote from the soil as is feasible. In this manner, use the void network as a collector for soil gas (to establish a low-pressure field, drawing soil gas from entry routes into the building) or as plenum to distribute air under pressure (to force soil gas away).

Isolation and venting of entry routes.   Install an enclosure over a floor or around a wall which is an entry route; use a fan to ventilate the enclosure.

Passive soil ventilation.   Use systems similar to the active soil ventilation systems above, but rely on natural phenomena to draw the suction (such as depressurization caused by wind near roofline, or thermal stack effect). This method avoids the maintenance requirements, noise, and operating cost of a fan.

Building pressure adjustments

Reduce depressurization.   Take steps to reduce the degree to which a building becomes depressurized relative to soil gas pressure in an effort to reduce soil gas influx. Or, for a given degree of depressurization, take steps to reduce air movement out of the facility in order to reduce soil gas influx.

Building pressurization.   If reducing depressurization is not adequate, maintain that part of the building which is in contact with the soil at a pressure higher than the soil gas so that soil gas cannot enter.

Air cleaning.   Remove the particulate decay products of radon from the indoor air by continuously circulating building air through a particle removal device.

Removal from water.   With the use of a granular activated carbon treatment unit, remove dissolved radon gas from well water before the water is used in the building, thus preventing the dissolved radon from being released into the air.

There are no current national regulations regarding radon, although the EPA has established guidelines. Some states have instigated varying degrees of regulations, most of which are directed toward residential construction.

Polychlorinated biphenyls.   PCBs are normally not associated with IAQ issues but, like asbestos, radon, and lead, PCBs pose a threat to the total environmental quality of buildings. Although found largely in industrial settings, PCBs may also be found in older office buildings.

PCBs, organic compounds from the family of chlorinated hydrocarbons, were produced in the United States between 1929 and 1977.

The characteristics of PCBs, like most other chlorinated hydrocarbons, include a high boiling point, low flammability, low electrical conductivity, and a high degree of chemical stability. These characteristics made PCBs ideal for use in electrical transformers and capacitors such as those found in light fixture ballasts. PCBs were also found in the coolant oil for the transformers. Other applications of PCBs included hydraulic fluids (elevators), dye carriers (carbonless copy paper), and construction-related materials such as paint, adhesives, and caulking compounds. But toward the end of the 1970s, public health concerns caused many manufacturers of PCBs to reduce or discontinue the production of PCBs on a voluntary basis. Yet, even today, with all of the regulations of PCBs, this material is being inadvertently produced as by-products during the manufacture of certain organic chemicals.[148]

The risk associated with PCBs occurs primarily in cases of leaks and fires, at which time contamination of air and surfaces can occur. Once PCB molecules are released into the environment, they tend to keep their integrity and not react with other substances. If PCBs enter the body, they can remain there for a long period of time (sometimes years) by being stored in body fat and ultimately released into the bloodstream. The concentration of PCBs can increase with time, even though exposure levels may be low.

PCBs can enter the body through inhalation or ingestion or by skin contact and can create long-term health effects by causing reproductive and gastric disorders and sometimes cancerous tumors. Short-term exposure to the vapor can result in irritation to the eyes, nose, and throat.[149]

The health concerns related to PCBs are supported by several serious incidents worldwide. The most tragic and famous incident occurred in Japan in 1969. Cooking oil somehow became contaminated from a leaking PCB transformer which resulted in death, central nervous system damage, stomach and liver disorders, and possible cancer.[150]

As with exposure to any other hazardous chemicals, exposure to PCBs is best avoided by employing reasonable engineering controls. Establishing regulated areas, posting signs, local exhausts, and employee awareness should be part of these controls. In the event of a PCB exposure episode, use protective clothing, respirators, and other protective and remediation equipment and procedures. One control method for PCBs involves disposing of the ballast or transformer. Another requires pumping out the contaminated oil from the transformer, flushing the transformer, and replacing the oil with material free of PCBs. NIOSH has specific criteria on engineering controls and occupational exposure to PCBs.

The continual operation of existing electrical equipment containing PCBs and additional public pressure from the United States Congress forced the EPA to promulgate regulations dealing with PCBs. In October, 1976, as a part of the Toxic Substance Control Act (TSCA), section 6(e), Congress specifically directed the EPA to regulate PCBs. This was the only chemical substance specifically named in TSCA, which indicated that Congress believed PCBs posed a significant hazard to the environment. On May 31, 1979, the EPA issued regulations effective July 1, 1979, that banned the manufacturing, processing, distribution, and use of PCBs. It also included provisions to control the disposal of this chemical compound.

Due to several lawsuits and provisions from 1979 to 1983, the EPA issued rules and amendments to provide exceptions and set limits on PBC concentrations. One of these amendments allows the continued use of electrical equipment containing PCBs if certain use and maintenance procedures are followed. According to the EPA, the use of transformers and electromagnets containing 500 ppm or greater of PCBs requires inspections and maintenance for leaks. Later, the EPA prohibited the use of this type of equipment wherever it posed a risk to food or feed. Another provision in 1988 prohibited the use of capacitors containing more than 3 lb of dielectric fluid except when it is located in restricted access areas.

The amendment also allows inadvertent PCB production in industrial processes, but only if it is not released (closed process manufacturing) or if it is released but disposed of in the controlled waste process. Other amendments regulate PCB-containing transformers in the railroad industry.

Because PCBs might exist in different forms and states or in different concentrations as part of another chemical compound, the methods of testing vary greatly. Testing methods may include soil, water, and vegetation sampling and personal and area air sampling.

4.3.5 Pollutant pathways

Architectural and mechanical pathways may allow pollutants to move from one area of the building to another. This movement is caused by airflow, and the problem in the complaint area may be significantly greater than in the area where a pollutant is located. Identification of pollutant pathways and an understanding of air movement are necessary when investigating a particular complaint in a given space.

Pollutants are known to travel great distances from the source. Not only are vapors transported throughout a building but so are particles and fibers, such as asbestos. The most common way for a contaminant to move through a building is via the HVAC system (see Sec.

3.3). However, there is a significant amount of air movement in a typical commercial building that is not driven by the HVAC system. Air can move between building spaces through elevator shafts, crawl spaces, utility tunnels or chases, doors, operable windows, stairways, wall openings, and accidental openings such as cracks and holes.

The movement of an elevator creates positive shaft pressure by the end of the cab (top or bottom) that is leading the direction of movement and negative shaft pressure by the trailing end. This action is similar to the piston in a hand-operated bicycle pump. This movement may be significant enough to transport a contaminant up or down several floors in a multistory building. Other vertical shafts may generate an air movement created by the stack effect—hot air rising, creating a transfer from floor to floor—and the potential for spreading pollutants.

Crawl spaces are areas that are often damp and pest-infested. These spaces are also frequently the site of improperly stored materials. Pollutants from these sources can leak into occupied areas of a building through openings around pipes and utilities and through structural cracks. Also, chases are usually required by fire codes to be firestopped, but if the firestops are in a deteriorated condition, utility chases may act as pollutant pathways. See Fig. 4.14 for examples of pollutant pathways.

The airflow between spaces may be part of the design of the HVAC system. However, whether it is intentional or not, the result is the same. The movement of air will enter an occupied space with the potential of carrying a pollutant with it. This problem may not always be constant.

Case study

> A hotel used large exhaust fans to control the chlorine emissions from an indoor swimming pool. Without adequate makeup air, the exhaust fans caused the flues from the gas hot water heater to backflow. This resulted in a buildup of carbon monoxide. The carbon monoxide migrated into a guest room, causing the death of an occupant.

Building areas that contain contaminant sources, such as bathrooms, food preparation areas, chemical storage areas, smoking lounges, or print rooms, should be maintained under negative pressure and exhausted to the outside. Spaces that need to be protected from contaminant entry, such as computer rooms and lobbies, should be maintained under positive pressure relative to surrounding areas and also relative to the outdoors.[151] Care should be given to avoid the spread of pollutants from the positive pressure spaces to adjacent areas.

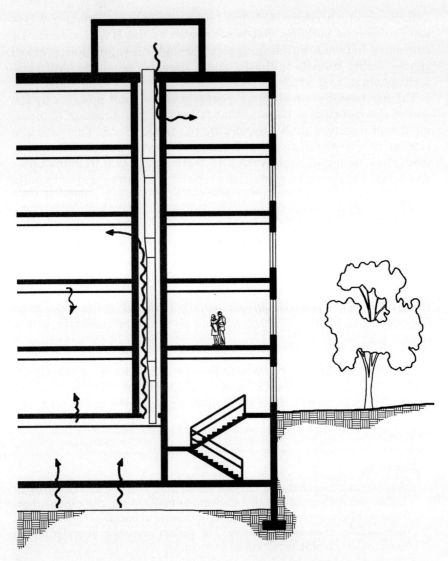

Figure 4.14 Building section. (*Used with permission of Gobbell Hays Partners, Inc., Nashville, Tenn.*)

When examining the direction of airflow, the IAQ investigator may need to make observations under different conditions since various factors such as weather, wind direction and velocity, and interior traffic patterns can change direction of air movement.

TABLE 4.23   VOCs in Cosmetics and Personal Care Products

Sources	Contaminants*
Cosmetic/personal care products	VOCs
Perfume	Alcohols (propylene glycol, ethyl alcohol,
Personal deodorants	isopropyl alcohol)
(aerosols, solids)	Ketones (acetone)
Body powder (talc)	Aldehydes (formaldehyde, acetaldehyde)
Shampoo and body soaps	Esters
Rubbing alcohol	Ethers (methyl ether, ethyl ether, butyl ether)
Hair sprays	

*The reader should not attempt to match specific contaminants with specific products.

SOURCE: EPA, *Introduction to Indoor Air Quality: A Reference Manual,* U.S. Environmental Protection Agency, U.S. Public Health Service, and National Environmental Health Association, EPA/400/3-91/003, July 1991, p. 22.

4.4   Building Functional and Occupant Loads

Occupant loads and the functional uses of a space have a direct impact on the IAQ of that space. (Chapter 3 addresses ventilation requirements of a space based on the function and occupancy.) Humans are polluters because their activities emit heat, odors, water vapor, and VOCs. As part of any IAQ evaluation, the occupant load and related functions of a given space are critical considerations. Table 4.23 is a list of VOCs found in cosmetics and personal care products.

Changes in the use of buildings or of specific building areas are common in today's workplace. Tenants, programs, and technology change, and modifications are required to meet building codes, such as those affecting the handicapped. Yet, all too often, corresponding adjustments in related systems do not reflect current usage. Consider any of the following spatial changes as possible reasons for, or contributors to, IAQ problems:

1. *Change in occupant load.*   Increased occupant density results in additional heat, humidity, and VOCs. The conversion of an executive office to a clerical office occurs frequently, increasing the occupant population from one to several, and the quality of the air is immediately affected. Severe reductions in occupant loads can also be a problem that affects air distribution and changes thermal comfort requirements.

2. *Change in occupants' activities.*   General office space modified for use as an aerobics class introduces an activity which is more physical, thus affecting temperature and humidity.

3. *Change in equipment load.*   Addition of equipment such as copiers and personal computers significantly increases heat and VOC emissions. Adding new equipment often taxes the capacity of related systems to accommodate the new operations within a given space. Local exhaust may be required for point sources to remove contaminants.

4. *Change to a special-use area.*   General office space converted to a break room, print shop, smoking lounge, copy center, or laboratory necessitates alterations to the electrical or lighting systems and the addition of specialized equipment. Pressure relationships between the special-use areas and surrounding areas may be affected. Local exhaust or additional ventilation capacity may be required. In addition, architectural barriers such as doors or walls can minimize the impact on the air quality of surrounding areas.

5. *Change in interior layout.*   Rearrangement of workstations, particularly when requiring relocations of partitions, may change air-distribution requirements. Partitions must not block grilles or diffusers.

An important issue is how the building space was originally intended to function. In many buildings, the quality of the original design may have been inadequate in terms of IAQ. If the function has changed without the proper corresponding modifications, IAQ will be affected. Often the total occupant load and specific functions of a given space are not known when buildings are designed, especially when the design is speculative. As tenants evaluate the use of these spaces, they will need to determine whether the infrastructure will in fact support the occupant and functional characteristics of the space. IAQ problems have been documented in spaces which were designed and built for general offices, based on number of occupants per square feet, and subsequently leased to computer software companies with twice the number of occupants per square feet, all with their own computer terminals.

Case study

A standard office of 25,000 ft^2 was converted into an airline reservation center. In one specific area, approximately 7000 ft^2, the occupant load increased from 70 to 150. The number of computer terminals increased from 35 to 150. The existing energy-efficient HVAC system could not handle the 3000 cfm recommended by ASHRAE 62-1989. An entire rework of the existing system and the addition of a new system were required.

TABLE 4.24   Occupancy Load Standards Comparison

| Application | Occupant load (ft²/person) | |
	ASHRAE*	Architectural standard†
Food establishment		
Dining room	14	13–16
Cafeteria	10	12–15
Hotel		
Lobbies	33	20
Banquet/assembly	8	10–20
Educational		
Classroom	20	26
Auditorium	7	7
Libraries	50	30–35
Hospitals		
Patient rooms	100	100
Correctional facility		
Jail cell	50	48

*Based on information from ASHRAE *Standard 62-1989*

†Based on information from *Time Saver Standards,* 4th ed., McGraw-Hill, New York, 1966.

In designing spaces, architects use a variety of methods to calculate the size of a space needed for a certain function. Single-occupant offices may be sized to accommodate one person and his or her furnishings. Large assembly spaces may be sized based on square feet per each anticipated occupant. Engineering standards prescribe that the design be based on number of occupants anticipated for the area. Generally, the HVAC criteria are dictated by ASHRAE's recommended standards (see Table 4.24). Most of the standards are similar; however, there are times that the guide for the architect is substantially different from the guide for the engineer. The actual activities and operations that occur determine the criteria for evaluating IAQ.

4.5   Other Factors That Influence IAQ Perception

There is considerable evidence that health complaints and related symptoms associated with poor IAQ can be caused or complicated by stressors other than contaminated air. Some of the broad categories that should be considered in an evaluation of IAQ are physical conditions (temperature, humidity, noises, vibrations, and lighting), ergonomic conditions (physical attributes of workstations, including furniture and equipment), and psychological or social factors (including job-related or external stressors). Any of these factors may produce complaints that are similar to those resulting from poor IAQ, such as headaches, eye irritation, aching muscles, fatigue, and nausea. These related stressors can act independently or in combination with contaminated air.

4.5.1 Physical conditions

Temperature. Temperature within a building environment may rank first on the list of employee complaints regarding physical comfort. A temperature range of 68 to 79°F (20 to 26°C) is considered to be comfortable to most people,[152] although some studies have indicated adverse effects within that range. Reduced alertness has been observed in some employees when the temperature is above 75.2°F (24°C), and typical SBS symptoms have been experienced at temperatures above 71.6°F (22°C).[153,154] Temperatures higher than the 68 to 79°F (20 to 26°C) range may cause an increase in the initial VOC emissions from building materials and contribute to the sink effect,[155] which describes a material's ability to adsorb and re-release VOCs from other materials.

ASHRAE standard 55-1992 recommends an inside temperature range of 73 to 81°F in summer and 68 to 76°F in winter for human comfort.[156]

An ASHRAE research project in 1988 compared thermal conditions in offices to conditions recommended by ASHRAE standard 55. The study found that low air movement may present certain problems. Another conclusion from the study was that occupants are more satisfied with work area temperature when the degree of individual control increases.[157]

During a building walk-through, the IAQ investigator should note heat sources throughout the building. Computer areas, copy machines and other office equipment, overillumination, and high concentrations of electrical fixtures should be identified as possible sources of high temperature zones that may contribute to complaints.

Humidity. A significant factor in maintaining healthy air quality is the control of humidity levels inside buildings. Increased microbial growth has been associated with high humidity levels, while low humidity may result in dryness of the mucous membrane or skin.

ASHRAE recommends that relative humidity be kept between 30 and 60 percent in office environments to maintain occupant comfort levels.[156] Other research by E. M. Sterling in 1985 shows that for occupant comfort, humidity ranges should be between 40 to 60 percent RH, with 50 percent RH as the ideal level.[158] Dr. George Green of the University of Saskatchewan conducted studies which indicate that increasing indoor relative humidity from 20 to 30 percent will reduce absenteeism in the workplace by 15 percent.[159] Also in colder climates, humidity levels above 50 percent RH may cause condensation on windows or other building surfaces, resulting in moisture-related problems.

Noise. Noise is simply unwanted sound. Noise in office environments is considered a source of irritation or stress for many people. Such surroundings can make concentration difficult and often produce stress-related symptoms such as headaches. Furthermore, noises such as from a mechanical unit, from air moving through ductwork, or from other people in the building can produce symptoms similar to those associated with poor IAQ. When investigating building noise, consider the frequency, intensity, and duration of sound.

Sound is the sensation produced in the ear by vibrations transmitted through air. Frequency is the rate at which these vibrations (pressure oscillations) are produced. Frequency is measured in the unit hertz (Hz), one of which is equal to 1 cycle (oscillation) per second. Pitch is the subjective perception of frequency and is discussed in terms of hertz. A typical person's hearing range is from 20 to 20,000 Hz, and conversation among people is usually in the range of 300 to 6000 Hz.[160] Low ranges of pitch (0.1 to 20 Hz) are referred to as infrasound. Studies have shown that this frequency range can cause dizziness and nausea in some people if the intensity is above 120 decibels (dB), units which measure pressure levels. Other adverse symptoms may also be experienced in the 20 to 100 Hz range. This range of frequency is sometimes generated from HVAC equipment in a building.[161]

The loudness of sound or *intensity* is measured in sound wave pressure levels using decibels or as noise criteria (NC). The intensity of sound approximately doubles every 10 dB. Human perception of sound only occurs at particular frequency ranges, so typically noises are quantified in units of dBA where A represents the measurement of frequency. Loud sounds in the workplace can cause stress-related complaints. The level of intensity recommended by ASHRAE for private offices is NC-35.[162] NC curves are used in chart form for specifying design sound level, taking into account maximum permissible sound pressure levels in decibels for each frequency band in hertz.

Duration of sound is described as the length of time a particular sound continues. Sounds can vary or be constant. Constant sounds within a building generally do not cause as many problems as varying sounds. The human ear gets accustomed to constant sounds to the point where the sounds are no longer noticed. Therefore, irritation typically results from varying sounds rather than constant sounds in a building. Many offices introduce constant background sounds known as *white noise* to mask unwanted sounds, such as noisy chatter.

OSHA has set limits for daily sound exposure rates in industry, based on the duration of noise. The current permissible exposure level is 85 dBA over an 8-h period. As noise levels increase by 5 dBAs, the permissible exposure time is reduced by one-half.[163]

Noises have been linked with human stress, sleep disorder, loss of human efficiency, and stomach ulcers. Therefore, the IAQ investigator should be aware of complaints that can occur as a result of noises in the workplace. ASHRAE provides design criteria for attaining well-balanced sound for offices, schools, hospitals, and other facilities.[164] Additionally, standards regarding the level and quality of sound have been established by the International Organization for Standardization.[165]

Vibrations. Symptoms including irritability, dizziness, or nausea, often attributed to poor IAQ, can also be traced to low-frequency vibrations experienced in work spaces. Vibrations can be caused by nearby HVAC equipment and machinery or by movement of a highrise building. (Such movement has caused motion sickness in some people.)

Studies have shown that certain body organs, especially the eyes, have characteristic responses to low frequencies in the range of 1 to 20 Hz.[166] These frequencies often result from various vibrations within buildings, so there may be a correlation between building vibrations and employee complaints. Note that these vibrations are also measured in hertz, but these are vibrations of solid objects, while the discussion of noise was related to cycles of sound waves in the air, also measured in hertz.

Lighting. Inappropriate levels and poor lighting quality, flickering lights, and glare associated with computer screens are examples of lighting stressors in working environments. These conditions often result in complaints of eye irritation and headaches. In addition, too much artificial light and not enough natural sunlight can cause stress in the workplace, according to the EPA.

A minimum of 50 fc should be maintained in workstations. Some lighting consultants recommend a range of 50 to 70 fc, depending on the function of the space and the task being performed.[167] Lighting may be added if workstations are too dark, but doing so may increase the temperature in these spaces, possibly resulting in heat-related stress in some employees. Energy-efficient ballasts with return air and heat-removal capabilities should be considered in such cases.

The color or quality of light is also an important aspect of indoor lighting. Full-spectrum lamps with a high color rendition index can improve lighting quality. Poor light quality and incorrect placement of fixtures can also produce glare or shadows on work surfaces. Low-glare lenses can be installed on fluorescent fixtures to reduce excessive glare. Task lighting can be used to adjust the light quality and levels for specific tasks.

In today's office environments, light flicker is not reported as a significant problem, although this may occur in older lighting fixtures. Headaches and eye irritation often result from flickering lights. Solid-state high-frequency ballasts can be installed to reduce light flicker.

One of the most common lighting complaints in today's office environments is the indirect glare on video display terminals (VDTs). The VDT screen reflects background images while a person is working with an on-screen image. The user involuntarily focuses back and forth to the two images. Thus, as the eye shifts focus, fatigue and strain may result. The eighth edition of the *Illuminating Engineering Society of North America (IESNA) Lighting Handbook* is the current reference used by lighting consultants for lighting standards regarding quality and quantity of light in working environments.

4.5.2 Ergonomic stress

Ergonomic or physical elements of the work environment—such as employee workstations, chairs, desks, equipment, and computers—can create discomfort, irritability, and stress in employees. Workstations can be too crowded, chairs too high or too low for desks or computers, or the time spent in work spaces sitting or standing can cause undesirable symptoms. Ergonomic symptoms sometimes experienced by employees include pain in the neck and shoulders, upper and lower back, and hands and wrists, as well as fatigue and circulatory problems. The IAQ investigator should be aware of potential symptoms and stressors resulting from these uncomfortable physical conditions in the work environment and should realize that they may sometimes be easily remedied. A simple solution to this problem is to replace the office furniture that is causing ergonomic problems.

4.5.3 Psychological or psychosocial stress

Job stress and job dissatisfaction are considered to be possible causes of IAQ complaints, according to a 42-month study by Cornell University researcher Alan Hedge. The questionnaire-style study, conducted in 27 office buildings with a combined total of 4500 workers, showed that stress in the workplace may affect an individual's susceptibility to symptoms typically associated with poor IAQ. In addition, the study found that workers who stated that their jobs were stressful or those who expressed job dissatisfaction reported more symptoms than those who were not stressed or who rated their jobs as satisfactory.[168]

The IAQ investigator should consider psychological stressors in the workplace even when no evidence of poor IAQ is found. When poor IAQ is present, emotionally stressed and unhappy employees appear to be more susceptible to related symptoms than those who are positively challenged by, and satisfied with, their jobs.

4.6   Existing Buildings: Investigation and Corrective Strategies

There are a number of reasons for building investigations of IAQ. Such investigations may be implemented due to occupant complaints; however, many IAQ assessments are generated by a concern for the quality of the indoor environment, often prior to buying, leasing, or renovating a facility. To complete a thorough investigation, a good set of generic guidelines and procedures should be properly adapted to each specific facility. This section addresses the architectural, construction, and operational components of a building that may cause IAQ problems. (See Sec. 3.4 for HVAC systems analysis and Sec. 2.4 for occupant interviews and general interview strategies. All of these diagnostic tools should be integrated for a comprehensive building assessment.)

The investigative procedure is assisted by a checklist (see App. D). This checklist is a valuable part of the assessment process as a guide to determine elements of a building or facility operation that will have a negative impact on the indoor environment.

4.6.1   New materials

Note whether any building materials or furnishings installed within the last 12 months have a potential for releasing VOCs. If the answer is No, proceed to Sec. 4.6.2. If the answer is Yes, identify the specific materials that may be the source of the VOCs. Note the materials that have a large surface area relative to the total room volume. Quantify the materials to determine which have the potential for releasing VOCs in sufficient quantities to cause a problem. If possible, calculate the potential concentration in air of a VOC and determine if that level is approaching 1/10 TLV, as identified by ACGIH, or if the TVOCs are in excess of 0.5 mg/m^3. If estimated levels exceed these standards, consider increasing the ventilation rate, as identified in Chap. 3, or consider the possibility of removing the material(s).

4.6.2 Building contamination

In this portion of the checklist, the primary concern is to determine whether there is a potential for the presence of a contaminant and whether the contaminant can be transported to building occupants.

Moisture. Moisture in buildings is known to support biological growth and improve the habitat for pests. To determine if there is a probability for moist materials, first check for visible signs of water damage. Evidence of water penetration may be water stains on ceiling tile, deterioration of wall materials such as drywall or plaster, delamination of vinyl wallcovering, or stains on carpeting. Figure 4.15 shows stains caused by moisture on ceiling tile.

If water damage is visible, determine if it is the result of a new leak or one that has been repaired in the past. If possible, identify the source of the moisture causing the damage. The answer may not be obvious. Condensate on compressor lines may be the source, and moisture may occur only during periods of high humidity, although it has the appearance of a plumbing leak. The source of roof and wall leaks can be particularly perplexing since the water can migrate significant distances before staining interior materials. Knowing the source will not only assist in determining the corrective action required but will also help identify concealed materials that are damp as a result of the leak. Note that some materials may be moist and, therefore, problematic even though the finish surface may appear to be dry. Check moist materials for odor, pest infestation, slime, mold, mildew, or decay.

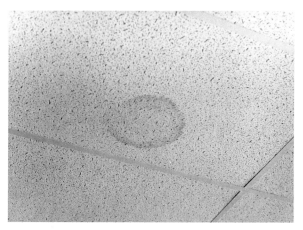

Figure 4.15 Stains on ceiling tile caused by moisture. (*Used with permission of Gobbell Hays Partners, Inc., Nashville, Tenn.*)

Roof leaks, one of the most common means of water migrating into the building, generally leave obvious marks; however, it is possible for roof leaks to enter into walls or migrate to other areas without damaging finish materials. Check for a history of roof leaks to locate concealed materials that may be damp. If material damage occurs, roof leaks must be stopped and the materials properly dried out or replaced.

The absence of visible signs does not entirely eliminate the concern for IAQ problems generated by moisture. Check to determine if vapor barriers are properly installed. If they are not, ascertain whether this is an immediate concern or a potential problem. The best way to make this determination is to check a wall section on the original architectural drawings that were used for construction. However, note that not all buildings are constructed as drawn. Figure 4.16 shows how a vapor retarder would be indicated on a wall section.

Should evidence indicate that the vapor retarders were designed correctly but vapor penetration may still be a problem, find an area and confirm the location of the vapor barrier. This process requires cutting into the wall system. Areas such as above drop ceilings and along outside walls, in mechanical rooms, or in storage closets may prove convenient and may minimize repairs. Pay attention to areas where wall irregularities cause the vapor barrier to be incomplete.

Locate mechanical equipment to determine if this may be a source for moisture inside the building envelope (see Sec. 3.4 for HVAC equipment). Investigate the potential of condensate forming on equipment or refrigerant lines. Check to see if plumbing lines may be leaking or if the equipment itself, such as ice makers or dishwashers, may generate activities which could lead to spills.

Moist building materials, except those designed for wet or damp conditions (in showers or commercial kitchens, for example) will lead to IAQ problems if unattended. It may be necessary to open walls or roof areas in order to dry out materials that have become wet.

Maintenance activities. Inadequate maintenance and custodial activities have a significant impact on the quality of the indoor air. Thorough inspections for dust buildup or other signs of poor housekeeping are necessary. Check storage rooms, mechanical equipment rooms, file rooms, and other areas where daily housekeeping should occur but may be overlooked. Check for areas where dust may get into the pollutant pathway. Determine if the quantity and type of dust is enough to create potential problems.

Pay careful attention to stored materials. Check to determine if they are stored correctly, whether any evidence of leaking exists, and why they are there. Some materials may not be worth keeping inside

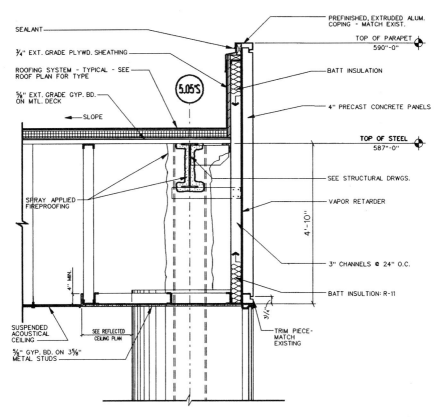

SEALANT

¾" EXT. GRADE PLYWD. SHEATHING

ROOFING SYSTEM - TYPICAL - SEE
ROOF PLAN FOR TYPE

⅝" EXT. GRADE GYP. BD.
ON MTL. DECK

←— SLOPE

5.05 S

SPRAY APPLIED
FIREPROOFING

4" MIN.

SUSPENDED
ACOUSTICAL
CEILING

SEE REFLECTED
CEILING PLAN

⅝" GYP. BD. ON 3⅝"
METAL STUDS

PREFINISHED, EXTRUDED ALUM.
COPING - MATCH EXIST.

TOP OF PARAPET
590"-0"

BATT INSULATION

4" PRECAST CONCRETE PANELS

TOP OF STEEL
587"-0"

SEE STRUCTURAL DRWGS.

VAPOR RETARDER

4'-10"

3" CHANNELS @ 24" O.C.

BATT INSULTION: R-11

3/4"

TRIM PIECE-
MATCH
EXISTING

Figure 4.16 Wall section. (*Used with permission of Gobbell Hays Partners, Inc., Nashville, Tenn.*)

the building if the frequency of use does not justify the risk. Check for evidence of past leaks. Review MSDSs to determine if any chemical or combination of chemicals should be of concern.

Determine if cleaning and maintenance chemicals are being used correctly. If possible, assess options that would reduce the amount of chemicals being used for the variety of cleaning tasks performed.

Evaluate the pesticide program to determine whether an Integrated Pest Management Program is in place or would be advisable for this specific application. Determine if there is evidence of insect or animal infestation, and check for evidence of previous infestation. Also check the potential for restricting pest access into the structure. Note any other habitat support elements, such as food or damp materials. Determine the amount of pesticides being used and whether they are being used properly for the specific problem pest.

Construction activities. If there is construction or renovation in the building, identify the particular activities and evaluate their environmental impact. Determine whether containment appropriate for the specific types of operations has been established. Check for proper ventilation of the work area and adjoining occupied spaces. Identify the chemicals in use and confirm that each is being used correctly. If the chemicals are stored on site, determine that they are stored properly. Note whether there have been any spills.

Make every effort to minimize contaminants inside the construction area and control any migration of pollutants into occupied areas of the building. Review scheduling to determine if more activities can occur during unoccupied periods.

Hazardous materials. The initial phase of an IAQ investigation does not involve testing for hazardous substances; however, the investigation may progress to sampling and analysis of certain materials. The IAQ investigator should determine whether there have been surveys for asbestos, lead, or PCBs or tests for radon. If so, the results may indicate that none of these materials is present in the facility. If these hazardous materials do exist, however, determine whether a management plan is in place. Make sure it outlines the response actions intended to control the material and establishes an O&M plan which allows building users to avoid the harmful effects of the hazardous material. Note whether a reinspection or testing program is in place to monitor the condition of the material as well as the success of the O&M program.

Pollutant pathways. If no pollutants have been identified, skip this section. If contaminants have been identified, however, determine where and how these pollutants can be transported throughout the building and determine the affected parts of the building. If the investigation is due to a complaint, clearly check pollutant pathways related to the complaint area and thoroughly investigate the spaces that those pathways serve. Check pathways such as elevator shafts, crawl spaces, utility tunnels or chases, doors, operable windows, stairways, and party walls. Remember that air movement can occur through accidental openings such as cracks and holes.

4.6.3 Building functional and occupant loads

Coordinate with the HVAC investigation to determine if the ventilation capacity is appropriate for the occupant load and building use. Note any special-use areas that could be problematic to IAQ, such as smoking areas. Pay particular attention to spatial changes that have increased occupant density or introduced a function into the space that is not compatible with the original design. Note whether workstations have been rearranged, and, if so, determine whether corresponding changes in air distribution have been made.

4.6.4 Other factors that influence IAQ perception

Determine if there are other related areas that may cause complaints or be a source of stress for the building users. Coordinate with the HVAC investigation for temperature and humidity items. Note any areas where excessive noise or vibrations may be a distraction to occupants. Review lighting to determine if the quantity and quality of light in a given space are appropriate for the specific tasks performed.

The checklist in App. D should act as a guide to corrective strategies required. IAQ investigators should be experienced and understand the relative importance of their findings. They should not rely on myopic conclusions without understanding the importance of their observations in the overall assessment.

4.7   New Construction

4.7.1   Planning

Planning and constructing new facilities involves a variety of issues, including budget concerns, spatial conflict, and resolution of technical problems. Rarely has the quality of the indoor air been a primary concern of the design and construction team. For this reason, 20 to 40 percent of buildings today are reported to have problems with IAQ.[169] However, with proper planning and an integrated team approach, the majority of reasons for indoor environmental concerns can be resolved without significant monetary or functional compromises.

The planning process must first define the goals for IAQ considerations in the new facility. Once the mission is defined, establish criteria that will yield the desired effect. As an example, the ASHRAE thermal comfort goal is 80 percent of the building occupants,[170] or four people out of five. As this translates, one person in five may be uncomfortable. Evaluate this goal to suit the specific circumstances of the building and its users. Established goals will serve as a benchmark for IAQ concerns.

The design process is a series of value judgments requiring creativity, innovation, and compromise. For example, it may not be practical to use low VOC-emitting materials, but it may be possible to control VOC buildup in the building by increasing the ventilation rate and extending the flushout period. It may be too costly in a cold climate to provide a high percentage of outside air during the winter months;

however, some of the more problematic areas may be controlled with a local exhaust system. Many of the IAQ problems that we currently address in existing buildings were created because of single-issue answers to the energy concerns of the 1970s and 1980s. IAQ must be integrated into the total building and must not be treated as either an afterthought or an override of other critical components without regard to cost or energy concerns.

4.7.2 Site

After the goals are articulated, the next step is the proposed facility site evaluation. Outdoor air and soil contamination surrounding a facility will have a direct impact on the quality of the indoor air. Soil can emit contaminants that may be tracked into a building. As is often the case where soil near major highways may have been contaminated by lead in gasoline, the soil shows high concentrations of lead particles that can be tracked into a facility.

Particle transport by air is another concern and can vary daily, depending on wind direction, velocity, and emissions from a contaminating source. The sources of contamination and the wind transport of these contaminants should be considered when placing a building on a site and locating outside air intakes as well as other openings.

4.7.3 Functional organization

Consideration should be given to the functional layout of the facility to control IAQ questions and to separate incompatible activities, such as a cafeteria and office space. Efforts should be made to compartmentalize the building so that the spillover of air from one space to another is minimal. The HVAC system should reflect this scheme, and care should be taken to avoid incidental contaminant transfer through pollutant pathways. Whenever possible, anticipate the variety of functions that may occur in a space and design a flexible system to accommodate the options considered.

4.7.4 Materials selection

A primary source for VOCs found in the interior of buildings is new building materials. When selecting new materials, make every effort to select low-VOC-emitting products (see Sec. 4.2). The primary source of information about building products is the material manufacturer, catalogs, Spec Data sheets, manufacturers' associations, and MSDSs. Figure 4.17 is an example of a Spec Data sheet. Currently there are no independent agencies or organizations analyzing the broad spectrum of building materials used in a modern building.

1. PRODUCT NAME

SEAL HARD, Concrete Sealer, Densifier, and Chemical Hardener

2. MANUFACTURER

L & M Construction Chemicals, Inc.
14851 Calhoun Road
Omaha, NE 68152
Phone: (402) 453-6600
FAX: (402) 453-0244

3. PRODUCT DESCRIPTION

SEAL HARD is a proprietary, colorless solution that penetrates concrete surfaces to seal, densify, harden, dustproof, and waterproof. It is VOC-compliant, environmentally safe, odorless and easy to apply. SEAL HARD treated floors are especially effective in protecting concrete floors subjected to heavy vehicle and foot traffic.

Through a chemical-ion exchange process, SEAL HARD develops internal bonds which densify the concrete substrate into a hardened, chemically-cured, homogeneous, concrete mass that resists abrasion, petroleum contamination, and water penetration. This chemical-ion exchange process begins immediately after treatment and becomes increasingly more effective during the initial six months after application. SEAL HARD creates an interpore molecular filter that protects concrete from carbonation and, at the same time, allows surfaces to breathe, permitting moisture vapor to transmit naturally into the air.

SEAL HARD is safe to use. Its odorless, VOC-compliant formula allows its use in employee-occupied areas without concern. It can be applied in the close proximity of foodstuffs without fear of contamination. SEAL HARD is also safe to own. The

deeply penetrating chemical action leaves no film and will not alter the natural non-slip texture of the concrete floor.

SEAL HARD treated floors provide a significant savings in maintenance costs over conventional acrylic, urethane, and epoxy sealers. SEAL HARD will not yellow, discolor, chip, peel, or show unsightly wear patterns with use. SEAL HARD will not show hard rubber tire marks. In fact, the more a SEAL HARD floor is used and the older it gets, the better it looks.

Basic Use: L & M has been a basic innovator of concrete chemicals for over 30 years. Experience supported by a rigid quality control program assures trouble-free chemical hardening, waterproofing, densifying, and dustproofing of concrete. SEAL HARD is particularly effective for use on concrete floors subjected to medium to heavy fork-lift and tow-motor traffic: warehouses, distribution centers, manufacturing plants, textile mills, bottling plants, coolers and freezers, food processing plants, canning factories, breweries, bakeries, meat and poultry processing plants, waste-to-energy transfer stations, service garages, grocery stores, discount retail stores, and hub transfer facilities.

Other uses include concrete surfaces subjected to heavy pedestrian traffic, such as: civic centers, sports arenas, stadiums, hospitals, airports, museums, and grocery stores; as well as areas subjected to mild chemical attack: parking decks, silage storage silos, sewage treatment plants, dairies, meat processing plants, refineries, and water treatment plants.

Protection from oil or water penetration may be unsatisfactory if concrete surface is too porous or if surface is exposed before maximum densification has been developed.

Limitations: Keep from freezing.

Apply when temperatures are above 40°F (4°C). Not effective on lightweight or extremely porous concrete. Broom out all puddles and flush all excess off surface. Avoid contact with glass, aluminum or highly polished surfaces.

Note: SEAL HARD is not a curing compound. Fresh, green concrete contains excess moisture that will inhibit the penetration of SEAL HARD into the concrete surface and its ultimate effectiveness. Therefore, under normal conditions, L & M recommends using SEAL HARD on concrete that is three or more days old.

4. TECHNICAL DATA

Active Ingredients:

- 100%
- Type: Siliconate
- Flash Point (F):   None
- Specific Gravity: $1.15 \pm .02$
- VOC (GMS/Liter): 0.0

Applicable Standards: Recommended for ACI 302, Class 1 through 4, concrete floors and Class 9, super flat floors

VOC-compliant, all Federal, State, and municipalities

USDA-approved, as coating for structural surfaces where there is a possibility of incidental food contact

ASTM E 303, Skid Resistance

ASTM E 96, Water Vapor Transmission

ASTM C 944, Abrasion Resistance Determination of Concrete

5. INSTALLATION

New Concrete Surfaces Preparation: After final troweling and surface water glaze has dissipated, apply nonresidual curing compound, such as, L & M CURE, or dissipating resin curing compound complying with ASTM C 309, such as L & M CURE R. Wet curing is also acceptable. Plastic sheeting should be used only if care is taken

09800

Figure 4.17   Spec Data sheet. (*Used by permission, Construction Specifications Institute, Alexandria, Va.*)

to prevent objectionable stains. Allow concrete to cure a minimum of three days in the case of L & M CURE, or until curing compound has dissipated, as in the case of a resin-based curing compound. Clean concrete of any dirt, debris, laitance or residual curing compound. If an acrylic or resin-based curing compound is used, remove with environmentally safe, L & M CITREX. Do not use wax-based curing compounds on surfaces scheduled to receive SEAL HARD.

Application: Spray-apply directly from container one undiluted, uniform coat at the rate of 150-200 ft.^{2}/gal. (5 m^2/L). Aggressively scrub into surfaces with an automatic mechanical scrubber or stiff-bristle broom. This scrubbing will help achieve maximum penetration and will begin to polish hard-troweled floors.

Keep surfaces wet with SEAL HARD for a minimum of 30 minutes and continue scrubbing and/or brooming. When product begins to thicken, sprinkle with water and scrub another 5-15 minutes. At this time, thoroughly flush excess SEAL HARD with clean water and remove all solution from the floor by squeegee and wet vacuum. This residue solution is non-toxic and can be emptied into a sanitary sewer. Normally, one coat is all that is required; however, on porous or rough-textured, broom-finished surfaces, a second application may be required. This second application can be installed 2-4 hours following the first and is recommended to assure maximum densification and positive protection from contaminant penetration. Floors are immediately available for occupancy after removal of the residue.

Warning: Failure to thoroughly wash and remove all excess material from floor surfaces may result in unsightly white stains.

Old (Existing) Concrete Surfaces Preparation: Surfaces must be clean and structurally sound. Remove all residue, oil, sealers, contaminants, and laitance in order to insure maximum penetration and chemical reaction. Repair all holes, cracks and deteriorated areas with L & M EVERJOINT and DURAPATCH. Avoid acid etch-

ing and mechanical abrasion if possible. Environmentally safe CITREX is recommended for heavy-duty cleaning and for the removal of resin-based or acrylic curing compound products and unsightly black tire rubber markings.

Note: SEAL HARD is a colorless solution that will not alter the appearance of the concrete surfaces. It will, therefore, not hide serious staining or repair excessive wear. For extremely porous, worn, or stained concrete surfaces, L & M DURATHANE or DURAGLOSS may be recommended in place of SEAL HARD. Contact a local L & M representative for assistance.

Application: Follow the same application procedures as found under New Concrete. Depending on surface porosity and temperature, application rate may range from 150-200 ft.^{2}/gal. (3.5-4 m^2/L). In addition, a second coat may be required in some situations due to porosity or extreme dusting.

Application Temperature Limitations: 38°F to 100°F (4°C to 40°C)

Drying Time: Two to four hours

Warning: Failure to thoroughly wash and remove all excess material from floor surfaces may result in unsightly white stains. In hot weather, pre-dampen surfaces with water to cool. After standing water dissipates, apply SEAL HARD. Immediately wash off over-spray from glass, aluminum, or highly-polished surfaces with water to avoid etching of these surfaces. Flush equipment with water to clean. Do not allow SEAL HARD to dry before flushing excess from surfaces. Preparation of SEAL HARD treated concrete prior to installation of coating may require chemical or physical etching. Test sample is recommended to insure best results.

6. AVAILABILITY AND COST

Container Sizes: SEAL HARD is readily available from a national network of stocking distributors in factory-sealed 5-gallon (20-liter) and 55-gallon (205-liter) containers. Each container is properly identified with product name and batch number.

Cost: Average material-only cost is

approximately $.10/ft.^{2}/coat ($1.05/m^2/coat). The cost of application and cleaning on a particular project is not included. Exact costing is available from your local distributor.

7. WARRANTY

L & M guarantees that, after an initial cure period of 90 days, properly prepared and treated surfaces are chemically hardened, densified and water resistant for a minimum of ten years. Should SEAL HARD fail to perform as specified, L & M will supply sufficient SEAL HARD to redo the failed area.

The information offered herein is believed to be true and accurate and is provided in good faith. However, L & M, its agents, and distributors assume no responsibility for risks or liability that may arise from the use or performance of this product since the conditions, application and installer's capabilities are beyond our control.

8. MAINTENANCE

Good housekeeping practices, such as regular and frequent mechanical scrubbing, washing, wet mopping with mild detergent and sweeping are to be followed in order to maximize densification and resulting polish of hard-troweled surfaces, as well as to assure maximum performance and life expectancy of the SEAL HARD-treated surfaces.

9. TECHNICAL SERVICES

L & M maintains technical sales personnel throughout the country who are available as required. For nationwide technical assistance call (800) 362-3331.

L & M distributors have local sales personnel trained by L & M technical staff.

L & M continually conducts technical sales schools throughout the country to retain a technical edge.

10. FILING SYSTEMS

SPEC-DATA® II
Sweets' General Building and Renovation, BuyLine 03010/LMC
Literature and test data are readily available through sales personnel, distributors, or upon request.

Figure 4.17   *(Continued)*

Since the requirements for reporting environmental impact vary by materials and application, the specifier will have to look beyond the face representation a given manufacturer will make. Whenever a standard is established, although it may be of a different building type (such as HUD's formaldehyde emission standards for particle board and plywood in manufactured homes), consider applying the concept to other building types.

The material quantity and location will have a direct impact on the total VOCs emitted. A small amount of high-emitting material may be acceptable if the location is in an area where high ventilation is practical and in order. Other codes and performance criteria to consider are:

1. Energy

2. Moisture protection

3. Maintenance and life-cycle cost

4.7.5 Commissioning

The commissioning process inaugurates a new structure. (Read also Sec. 3.5.3.) The process of commissioning starts during the design of the building.

During construction, perform adequate field observation to determine proper implementation of design criteria. This quality control process includes a review of the contractor's submittals and on-site field inspections. Review the submittals for completeness and compliance with specifications. Additionally, the review should confirm that building systems, where all components may not have been specified, do not introduce a material that may cause future problems. Note contractor compliance with specifications and confirm good housekeeping during construction. Areas such as plumbing chases, plenums, and wall cavities require inspection prior to being sealed to determine that the area is appropriately clean.

If a significant problem is anticipated with a building material or furnishing, it may be possible to specify that the material be set at another site with an adequate ventilation system to allow the material to off-gas prior to installation in the new structure. The commissioning process would then include the inspection of this off-site facility to determine if the desired goals are being met and to schedule the material relocation.

When the construction process is almost complete, establish a flushout period to accommodate the off-gassing of building products. The length of the flushout process will vary, depending on the emission loading of the space, the percentage of outside air, and the exchange rate of the air. Bakeouts, the process of increasing the heat in a building to accelerate the release of VOCs, have been used during the flushout process. The results of bakeouts have been mixed. It is well documented that an increase of 12 F° will double emission rates of formaldehyde from particleboard.[171] But one of the problems relating to bakeouts has been that in order to get the temperature to the desired level, the ratio of outside to inside air was minimized. This process, whether performed automatically or manually, allowed VOCs to build up on the interior of the building, only to be adsorbed into other materials acting as sinks. Raising the temperature inside a building may also damage building finishes.

Use caution during the flushout stage in order to prevent materials from acting as sinks. Equipment such as computers may have high emissions when initially operated. They should be operated for a period of at least 48 h prior to building occupancy as part of the flushout process.

Upon occupancy of the facility, the commissioning process should establish an IAQ management plan that would include the following: (1) training in the operation of HVAC equipment, use of chemicals for maintenance, and guidance in the inspection for IAQ concerns, (2) installation of a record keeping system to monitor complaints, chemicals stored on site, MSDSs, and major maintenance activities that effect the quality of the indoor air, and (3) a management plan for other hazardous materials, such as asbestos and lead.

References

1. Scott, Kristine A., and Stockton, Margie B., "Potential Indoor Air Contaminant from Adhesives and Sealants," paper presented at the 85th Annual Meeting & Exhibition, Air & Waste Management Association, Kansas City, Mo., June 21–26, 1992, p. 2.
2. Christiansson, J., Neretnicks, I., and Yu, J. W., "Compartment Modeling of Emission, Uptake, and Reemission of Volatile Air Pollutants in an Ventilated, Furnished, Room," presented at IAQ '92 Environments for People, San Francisco, Calif., October 19–21, 1992.
3. Hansen, Shirley, *Managing Indoor Air Quality,* The Fairmont Press, Inc., Lilburn, Ga., 1991, p. 64.
4. "Carpets and Indoor Air," *Indoor Air Bulletin,* H. Levin, ed., vol. 2, no. 6, p. 1.
5. *Environmental Resource Guide Subscription,* American Institute of Architects, Washington, D.C., July 1992, Topic. 1-9681, p. 8.
6. Nichols, M., W. F. Taylor Co. personal correspondence, October 29, 1993.
7. *Environmental Resource Guide,* July 1992, Topic. 1-7920, p. 2.
8. Skeist, I., *Handbook of Adhesives,* 3d ed., Van Nostrand Reinhold, New York, 1990.
9. Scott and Stockton, p. 5.
10. Scott and Stockton, pp. 2, 5.

11. *Environmental Resource Guide,* Topic. 1-7920, p. 4.
12. *Environmental Resource Guide,* July 1992, Topic. 1-9900, p. 9.
13. Storer, Ed, and Mowbray, Torin, "Emission Control," *The Construction Specifier,* August 1991, p. 115.
14. *Environmental Resource Guide,* Topic. I-9900, p. 11.
15. Wallace, Lance A., "Emission Rates of Volatile Organic Compounds from Building Materials and Surface Coatings," *Proceedings of the 1987 U.S. EPA/American Paint and Coating Association Symposium on Toxic and Related Air Pollutants,* Research Triangle Park, N.C., 1987 (as cited in *ERG,* Topic. I-9900, p. 11).
16. Holmberg, Krister, *High Solids Alkyd Resins,* Marcel Dekker, New York, 1987 (as cited in *ERG,* Topic. I-9900, p. 5).
16a. *Environmental Resource Guide,* Topic. I-9900, p. 5.
17. van Faassen, A., and Borm, P. J. A., "Indoor Air Pollution and Health Hazards by Waterborne Construction Paints," *Proceedings of the 5th International Conference on Indoor Quality and Climate,* Toronto, 1990 (as cited in *ERG,* Topic. I-9900, p. 11).
18. *Environmental Resource Guide Subscription,* Topic. I-9900, p. 5.
19. *Glycol Ethers—An Update,* National Paint Council of American Safety and Health Bulletin, 1982 (as cited in *ERG,* Topic. I-9900, p. 5).
20. *Environmental Resource Guide Subscription,* Topic. I-9900, p. 6.
21. *Environmental Resource Guide,* Topic. I-9900, pp. 6–7.
22. Holmberg (as cited in *ERG,* Topic. I-9900, p. 6).
23. *Environmental Resource Guide,* Topic. I-9900, p. 6.
24. Collier, Don, Porter Paints, personal correspondence, November 24, 1993.
25. *Environmental Resource Guide,* Topic. I-9900, p. 7.
26. *Coatings,* National Paint & Coating Association, vol. 45, no. 10, November 1993, p. 5.
27. Collier, Don, personal correspondence.
28. Ibid., November 29, 1993.
29. *Coatings,* p. 6.
30. *Environmental Resource Guide,* Topic. I-9900, p. 1.
31. *Environmental Resource Guide,* 1992, Topic. I-6124, p. 2.
32. National Institute of Environmental Health Sciences, *Sixth Annual Report on Carcinogens 1990,* vols. 1 and 2, U.S. Department of Health and Human Services, 1990 (as cited in *ERG,* Topic. I-6124, p. 4).
33. *Environmental Resource Guide,* Topic. I-6124, pp. 4, 6.
34. Zinn, T. W., Cline, D., and Letterman, W. F., "Long-Term Study of Formaldehyde Emission Decay from Particleboard," *Forest Products Journal,* vol. 40, no. 6, pp. 15–18.
35. *Environmental Resource Guide,* Topic. I-6124, p. 7.
36. Radian Corporation, *Draft of Classification of Indoor Air Pollution Sources,* U.S. EPA Contract, August 1990 (as cited in *ERG,* Topic. I-6124, p. 8).
37. Molhave, L., "Indoor Air Pollution Due to Organic Gases and Vapors of Solvents in Building Materials," *Environment International,* vol. 8, 1982 (as cited in *ERG,* Topic. I-6124, p. 8).
38. *Environmental Resource Guide,* Topic. I-6124, p. 8.
39. ANSI/A208.1-1989, *American National Standard/Wood Particleboard,* printed by National Particleboard Association, Gaithersburg, Md., approved February 1, 1989.
40. NPA 10-92, *Voluntary Standard for Formaldehyde Emissions from Urea-Formaldehyde Bonded Particleboard Flooring Products,* printed by National Particleboard Association, Gaithersburg, Md., approved May 19, 1992.
41. McCredie, William H., Executive Vice-President, National Particleboard Association, Gaithersburg, Md., January, 14, 1993, personal correspondence.
42. *Environmental Resource Guide,* January 1993, Topic. I-6118, p. 2.
43. Hardwood Plywood Manufacturers Association, "Formaldehyde Emission Characteristics of Hardwood Plywood June 1984–December 1989," 1989 (as cited in *ERG,* Topic. I-6118, p. 11).

44. National Research Council, Committee of Aldehydes, Board on Toxicology and Environmental Health Hazards, Assembly of Life Sciences, Formaldehyde and Other Aldehydes, National Academy Press, 1981 (as cited in *ERG,* Topic. I-6118, p. 11).

45. *Environmental Resource Guide,* Topic. I-6118, pp. 11–12.

46. ASHRAE Standard 62-1989, "Ventilation for Acceptable Indoor Air Quality," American Society of Heating, Refrigerating and Air-Conditioning Engineers, Atlanta, GA, 1989, App. C.

47. Groah, W. J., Gramp, G. D., and Trant, M., "Effect of a Decorative Vinyl Overlay on Formaldehyde Emissions," *Forest Products Journal,* vol. 34, no. 4.

48. Groah, W. J. *Formaldehyde Emissions: Hardwood Plywood and Certain Wood-Based Panel Products,* American Chemical Society, 1986 (as cited in *ERG,* Topic. I-6118, p. 12).

49. *Environmental Resource Guide,* Topic. I-6118, p. 13.

50. Ibid., p. 12.

51. *Environmental Resource Guide,* Topic. I-9681, p. 6.

52. Ibid., p. 10.

53. Ibid., p. 9.

53a. Ibid., p. 1.

54. *Catalog of Materials as Potential Sources of Indoor Air Emissions, vol. 1.,* Radian Corp., Research Triangle Park, N.C., prepared for EPA, June 93, pp. 4–19.

55. *Environmental Resource Guide,* Topic. I-9681, p. 12.

56. Ibid., p. 14.

57. Levin, Hal, "EPA Carpet Dialogue Concludes," *Indoor Air Bulletin,* September/October 1991 (as cited in *ERG,* Topic. I-9681, p. 15).

58. *Environmental Resource Guide,* Topic. I-9681, p. 15.

59. *Testimony Covering Carpet Studies,* Anderson Laboratories, Inc., presented to U.S. Senate Committee on Governmental Affairs, October 1, 1992.

60. *"Tests Commissioned by Carpet & Rug Institute Validate Carpet-Health Hazard Link," Indoor Air Review,* January 1993, p. 18.

61. "EPA Finds No Toxicity from Carpets, but Controversy Continues," *Indoor Air Quality Update,* vol. 6, no. 6, June 1993, p. 1.

62. "EPA Carpet Conference Hears More Research Results," *Indoor Air Quality Update,* October 1993, p. 12.

63. "Carpets and Ozone: Study Finds a New Wrinkle on an Old Problem," *Indoor Air Quality Update,* January 1993, pp. 6–7.

64. "Possible Explanations for the 'Deadly' Carpet," *Indoor Air Bulletin,* vol. 2, no. 6, p. 4.

65. Tichenor, Bruce A., "Evaluation of Indoor Air Pollutant Sinks for Vapor Phase Organic Compounds," *Proceedings of the 5th International Conference on Indoor Air Quality and Climate,* Toronto, 1990 (as cited in *ERG,* Topic. I-9681, p. 17).

66. Borazzo, John E. et al., "Sorption of Organic Vapors to Indoor Surfaces of Synthetic and Natural Fibrous Materials," *Proceedings of the 5th International Conference on Indoor Air Quality and Climate,* Toronto, 1990 (as cited in *ERG,* Topic. I-9681, p. 17).

67. Air Quality Sciences, Atlanta, Ga.

68. "Attorneys General Mount Latest Wave of 'Carpet Beaters'," *Indoor Air Review,* vol. III, no. 6, August 1993, p. 1.

69. Ibid., p. 8.

70. "Carpet Industry Unveils New Label Concerning Health Effects," *Indoor Air Quality Update,* vol. 6, no. 12, December 1993, pp. 12–14.

71. U.S. Environmental Protection Agency, *Indoor Air Quality and New Carpet: What You Should Know,* EPA/560/2-91-003, March 1992.

72. *Environmental Resource Guide,* April 1992, Topic. I-9651, pp. 2, 5.

73. U.S. Environmental Protection Agency, *Indoor Air Quality in Public Buildings,* vol. II, EPA, Washington, D.C., 1988 (as cited in *ERG,* Topic. I-9652, p. 6).

74. Molhave, L., "Indoor Air Pollution Due to Organic Gases and Vapors of Solvents in Building Materials," *Environment International,* vol. 8, 1982 (as cited in *ERG,* Topic. I-9652, p. 6).

75. Saarela, K., and Sandell, E., "Comparative Emission Studies of Flooring Materials with Reference to Nordic Guidelines," *Proceedings of IAQ '91,* ASHRAE/ICBR, Health Buildings Conference, Washington, D.C., 1991 (as cited in *ERG,* Topic. I-9652, pp. 6–7).
76. *Environmental Resource Guide,* Topic. I-9651, p. 1.
77. Ibid., p. 4.
78. Barden, Bruce, Gen Corp Polymer Products, Hackensack, NJ, personal correspondence, October 4, 1993.
79. *Catalog of Materials as Potential Sources of Indoor Air Emissions,* pp. 2–7.
80. Brooks, Bradford O., and Davis, William F., *Understanding Indoor Air Quality,* CRC Press, Boca Raton, Fla., 1992, p. 24.
81. Barden, Bruce, "Wallcovering Odors and Exposure," GenCorp Polymer Products, Hackensack, N.J., personal correspondence, October 1, 1993.
82. McGowan, M., "The Trouble with Vinyl," *The Construction Specifier,* March 1992, p. 54.
83. Ibid., p. 57.
84. "Insulation: An Update," *Custom Builder,* no. 10, 1987 (as cited in *ERG,* Topic. I-7200, p. 10).
85. Zipser, Andy, "Material Question—Is Fiberglass a Serious Health Hazard?" *Barron's,* September 7, 1992 (as cited in *ERG,* Topic. I-7200, p. 10).
86. *Environmental Resource Guide,* Topic. I-7200, p. 10.
87. Milton, D. K., et. al., "Toxicity of Intratracheally Instilled Cotton Dust, Cellulose, and Endotoxin," *American Review of Respiratory Disease,* vol. 142, pp. 184–192 (as cited in *ERG,* Topic. I-7200, p. 11).
88. *Environmental Resource Guide,* Topic. I-7200, p. 15.
89. *Environmental Resource Guide,* Topic. I-7200, p. 11.
90. Stein, J. Stewart, *Construction Glossary,* John Wiley, New York, 1980.
91. *Gaseous Pollutants,* Jerome O. Nriagu, ed., John Wiley, New York, 1992, p. 347.
92. Schuman, Loretta, Ph.D., Health Scientist, OSHA, personal correspondence, January 3, 1994.
93. *Indoor Air Bulletin,* vol. 2, no. 12, p. 8.
94. Brooks and Davis, p. 23.
95. Sadie, Shelley, *Indoor Air Quality: A Model Project,* Department of General Administration, State of Washington, December 1992.
96. Anderson, Ray, Energy Program Manager, State of Washington, personal correspondence, October 21, 1993.
97. Strobridge, James R., and Black, Marilyn S., "Volatile Organic Compounds and Particle Emission Rates and Predicted Air Concentrations Related to Movable Partitions and Office Furniture," presented at IAQ '91: Healthy Buildings, Washington, D.C., September 4–8, 1991.
98. OSHA 29 CFR Part 1910.1048 "Occupational Exposure to Formaldehyde Final Rule," May 27, 1992.
99. ASHRAE Standard 62:1989, p. 17.
100. Sadie, p. 2.
101. Ibid., pp. 1–2.
102. Sadie, p. 1.
103. *Catalog of Materials as Potential Sources of Indoor Air Emissions.*
104. McGowan, p. 52.
105. Hansen, p. 138.
106. "How Office Furnishings and Equipment Affect IAQ," *Indoor Air Quality Update,* vol. 5, no. 6, June 1992, p. 5.
107. U.S. Environmental Protection Agency, Office of Pesticides Programs, *Pest Control in Schools: Integrated Pest Management,* Washington, D.C., June 21, 1992, p. 3.
108. Ibid., pp. 1–22.
109. *Building Air Quality: A Guide for Building Owners and Facility Managers,* U.S. Environmental Protection Agency, U.S. Public Health Service, NIOSH, EPA/400/1-91/033, Washington, D.C., December 1991, p. 38.

110. *Introduction to Indoor Air Quality: A Reference Manual,* U.S. Environmental Protection Agency, U.S. Public Health Service, and National Environmental Health Association, EPA/400/3-91/003, Washington, D.C., July 1991.
111. Gobbell, Ronald V., "IAQ and Renovation: What Building Managers Should Know," Part I, *Indoor Air Review,* February 1993, p. 6.
112. *Asbestos in Buildings: Abatement Project Supervision,* The Environmental Institute, Atlanta, Ga., November 1988 (Revised July 1991), Sec. II, p. 2.
113. Ibid., pp. 2–3.
114. Ibid., p. 3.
115. *Managing Asbestos in Place: A Building Owner's Guide to Operations and Maintenance Programs for Asbestos-Containing Materials* (Green Book), U.S. Environmental Protection Agency, Pesticides and Toxic Substances (TS-799), Washington D.C., 20T-2003, July 1990, p. 2.
116. *Asbestos in Buildings: Abatement Project Supervision,* Sec. IV, p. 62.
117. *Federal Register,* vol. 59, no. 153, Wed., Aug. 10, 1994, Occupational Safety and Health Administration, U.S. Department of Labor, 1926.1101.
118. *Guidance for Controlling Asbestos-Containing Materials in Buildings* (Purple Book), U.S. Environmental Protection Agency, Office of Pesticides and Toxic Substances, Washington D.C., EPA 560-5-85-024, June 1985.
119. Ibid., pp. 5-1–5-3.
120. Ibid., p. 5-8.
121. Ibid., p. 5-6.
122. National Institute of Building Sciences, *Asbestos Abatement & Management in Buildings: Model Guide Specifications,* 2d ed., August 12, 1988.
123. *Managing Asbestos in Place,* pp. 12–22.
124. Ibid., p. 11.
125. Ibid., p. 6.
126. Ibid., p. 4.
127. *Code of Federal Regulations,* 40 CFF, Ch. 1 (7-1-91 ed.)
128. *Managing Asbestos in Place,* p. 28.
129. Rosmarin, Susan G., "The Regulatory Framework for Lead Abatement," *Environmental Choices,* July/August 1992, p. 14.
130. Waldman, Steven, "Lead and Your Kids," *Newsweek,* July 15, 1991, p. 48.
131. "Working with Lead in the Construction Industry," U.S. Department of Labor, OSHA, U.S. Department of Health and Human Services, NIOSH, OSHA 3126, April 1991, p. 2.
132. "Working with Lead in the Construction Industry." p. 20.
133. Environmental Protection Agency, 1986.
134. Waldman, p. 46.
135. *Guidelines for the Evaluation and Control of Lead-Based Paint Hazards in Housing,* prepared for HUD by The National Center for Lead-Safe Housing, March 15, 1994 (Draft).
136. "Home Repairs and Renovations: What You Should Know About Lead-Based Paint," National Lead Information Center, U.S. Department of Health and Human Services, Public Health Service, Centers for Disease Control, Atlanta, Ga., October, 1992.
137. Rosmarin, p. 18.
138. Ibid., p. 14.
139. Clarkin, Mike, and Brennan, Terry, *Radon-Resistant Construction Techniques for New Residential Construction*; U.S. Environmental Protection Agency, Office of Research and Development, Washington, D.C., EPA/625/2-91/032, February 1991, p. 3.
140. Krohe, T. L., *Technical Perspective on Indoor Radon: Sources and Occurrence,* EPA/State Conference on Indoor Air, USEPA report 904/9-87.
141. Henschel, Bruce, *Radon Reduction Techniques for Detached Houses,* Technical Guidance (2d ed.), U.S. Environmental Protection Agency, Office of Research and Development, Washington, D.C., and Air and Energy Engineering Research

Laboratory, Research Triangle Park, NC, EPA/625/5-87/019, Rev. January 1988, p. E-1.

142. Silverman, Jennifer, "EPA Study Finds Radon Problem in Schools Nationally," *Indoor Air Review,* January 1993, p. 23.

143. Papanicolopoulos, C. D., "Radon," *The Role of Environmental Audits and Site Assessments in Property Transfers,* Georgia Tech Research Institute, Atlanta, Ga., 1992.

144. Henschel, p. xvii.

145. Henschel, p. 12.

146. Ibid., p. E-3.

147. Henschel, pp. E-5–E-11.

148. U.S. Environmental Protection Agency, *Toxics Information Series: Polychlorinated Biphenyls,* EPA, Office of Toxic Substances, TSCA Assistance Office (TS-799), Washington, D.C., July 1983, p. 1.

149. "Hazardous Substance Fact Sheet," prepared by New Jersey Dept. of Health Right to Know Program, distributed by U.S. EPA Office of Toxic Substances, October 30, 1986, p. 2.

150. Miller, Marshall Lee, "Toxic Substances Control Act (TSCA)," *Environmental Law Handbook,* 10th ed., Government Institutes Inc. Publishers, Rockville, Md., 1989, pp. 341–345.

151. *Building Air Quality,* p. 175.

152. ASHRAE, *Standard 55-1981* "Thermal Conditions for Human Occupancy," American Society of Heating, Refrigerating and Air Conditioning Engineers, Atlanta, Ga., 1981, p. 4.

153. Wyon, D., "The Effects of Moderate Heat Stress on Typewriting Performance," *Ergonomics* Vol. 17, 1974, pp. 309–318.

154. Jaakkola, J., and Heinonen, O., "Mechanical Ventilation in an Office Building and Sick Building Syndrome, a Short-Term Trial," in *Indoor Air '87: Proceedings of the 4th International Conference on Indoor Air Quality and Climate,* vol. 2, Institute fuer Wasser-, Boden-, und Lufthygiene, Berlin, Germany, 1987, pp. 454–458.

155. Brooks and Davis, p. 34.

156. ASHRAE, *Standard 55-1992* "Thermal Environmental Conditions for Human Occupancy," American Society of Heating, Refrigerating and Air Conditioning Engineers, Atlanta, Ga., 1992, p. 5.

157. Schiller et al., "A Field Study of Thermal Environments and Comfort in Office Buildings," ASHRAE RP-462, 1988.

158. *Indoor Air Quality—An Overview,* The Steelcase Research Department, Steelcase, Inc., Grand Rapids, Mich., p. 19.

159. Duffy, Gordon, "Humidity Control's Changing Frontier," *Engineered Systems,* May 1992, p. 20.

160. "Noise: A Workplace Hazard," *Healthy Buildings International Magazine,* vol. 2, no. 1, pp. 4–5.

161. Molina, C., Pickering, C., Valbjorn, O., and DeBortoli, M., *Sick Building Syndrome: A Practical Guide,* Commission of European Communities, Directorate General for Science, Research and Development Joint Research Center, Institute for the Environment, Luxembourg, 1989, pp. 1–36.

162. ASHRAE, *1993 ASHRAE Handbook,* American Society of Heating, Refrigerating and Air-Conditioning Engineers, Inc., Atlanta, Ga., p. 7.9.

163. "Noise: A Workplace Hazard," p. 5.

164. American Society of Heating, Refrigerating and Air-Conditioning Engineers, Inc., *1987 ASHRAE Handbook,* ASHRAE, Atlanta, Ga., Chap. 52.

165. International Organization for Standardization, *Evaluation of Human Exposure to Whole-Body Vibration:* ISO 2631: 1-3, ISO, Geneva, Switzerland, 1985.

166. Hodgson, M., Permar, E., Squire, G., Cagney, W., Aller, A., and Parkinson, D., "Vibrations as a Cause of `Tight Building Syndrome' Symptoms," in *Indoor Air '87: Proceedings of the 4th International Conference on Indoor Air Quality and Climate,* vol. 2, 1990, pp. 449–453.

167. Gore, John, Power Management Group, Nashville, Tenn., personal correspondence, November 29, 1993.
168. "Job Stress Considered a Possible Marker for SBS Complaints," *Indoor Air Review,* January 1993, p. 3.
169. Hennessey, John F., III, "How to Solve Indoor Air Quality Problems," *Building Operating Management,* July 1992, p. 25.
170. *ASHRAE Standard 55-1992,* p. 4.
171. *Environmental Resource Guide,* Topic. 1-6124, p. 7.

5

Conclusion

5.1 IAQ Management

The issues of IAQ are complex and require an interdisciplinary team. A proactive approach by the building owner and consultant team is necessary to optimize the quality of the indoor air. To do this, the building owner should develop an IAQ profile, which will provide building management with an understanding of the current status of air quality in the building and baseline information on the factors that have a potential for causing problems in the future. The following steps are recommended by the EPA in developing an IAQ profile:[1]

1. *Collect and review existing records.* Review design, construction, and operating documents, check HVAC maintenance records against equipment lists, and review complaint records.

2. *Conduct a walkthrough inspection of the building.* Talk with staff and other occupants and look for IAQ problem indicators.

3. *Collect detailed information.* HVAC system condition and operation; pollutant pathways and pollutant sources; occupants.

As part of this process, most building owners need the technical support of IAQ consultants to supplement their existing staffs. The number IAQ firms increased by 25 percent between 1988 and 1992, according to an EPA survey of 1500 firms.[2] This growth parallels the growing public concern with IAQ issues. The survey indicated that in IAQ investigations, the following disciplines were used most often: industrial hygienist, mechanical engineer, chemist, air pollution scientist, microbiologist, architect, and medical doctor.[2]

5.2 Status of IAQ

Still, the IAQ industry is relatively young, as the survey indicated, with most firms reporting less than 10 years of experience in IAQ, and over half reporting less than 6 years.[2] This is an industry in which information and technology are changing rapidly and will continue to be refined as more data are collected. Technical innovations will most certainly occur. There will be better control of the HVAC system to make it more responsive to IAQ needs, utilizing continuous on-line monitors with computer integration into control of the HVAC system. Manufacturers are already moving to develop materials that are sensitive to the indoor environment, and we can anticipate this trend to continue with more complete product labeling.

The quality of the indoor air has been the subject of legislative activity for several years. In April of 1994 OSHA published a proposed rule for IAQ and environmental tobacco smoke. OSHA plans to set standards over the next 2 years. These IAQ provisions would affect more than 4.5 million nonindustrial worksites which include but are not limited to offices, schools and training centers, commercial establishments, health care facilities, cafeterias, and factory breakrooms. Environmental tobacco smoke provisions would apply to more than 6 million workplaces which are under OSHA's jurisdiction. Proposed compliance would, among other things, require employers to:

1. Develop and implement an IAQ compliance program to include such information as (a) a narrative and single-line drawings describing the building systems' equipment and areas they serve, (b) information on daily operation and management of the building systems, and (c) a written maintenance program for the building systems.

2. Assure that all building systems relating to IAQ are operating properly.

3. Demonstrate in good faith an effort to comply with provisions in cases where the employer does not control the ventilation system.

4. Implement controls for microbial contamination.

5. Manage the use of cleaning and maintenance chemicals, pesticides, and other hazardous chemicals in the workplace.

6. Assure appropriate controls during renovation and remodeling.

7. Provide employee information and training.

8. Provide designated nonworking smoking areas which are enclosed and exhausted directly to the outside if smoking is allowed in the building.

Legislative activity is only going to increase, with compliance becoming more burdensome. For example, radon legislation is currently being considered by the U. S. Congress. The next round of IAQ legislation will call for more research and data collection. This should interface with research currently under way by the EPA to determine the actual quality of the air in buildings where no complaints have been filed. There will be more legislation like Proposition 65 in California that addresses notification of occupants of the building. We can expect federal guidelines about actual standards, but we do not anticipate strict regulation or legislation setting limits for the typical nonindustrial facility.

Litigation is often going to be a part of a building that has IAQ problems. Workman's compensation claims have been filed, as well as suits against the building owners and architects. An example is the DuPage County Judicial Office Facility in Wheaton, Illinois, which was vacated shortly after construction so analysis and modifications could be made to improve IAQ. At least two sets of lawsuits have been filed. One of these sets was asking for indemnification against future employee-filed litigation. Named as defendants in these suits were the architect-engineer, civil engineer, general contractor, and the contractor's bonding company.[3] With any major dispute over the IAQ of a facility, litigation can be anticipated, and until the specific cause of the IAQ problem is clear, we can anticipate multiple defendants. It is in everybody's interest for proper due diligence to occur.

5.3   IAQ in Other Facilities

In evaluating a facility, a variety of functions are critical. For the purpose of this book, we have focused on office buildings, which is the most benign of all the occupancy types. Restaurants, where food storage, preparation, and consumption occur, have significantly different IAQ concerns than a laboratory where research is performed. Hospitals contain an exponential number of pollutant sources. IAQ evaluation in the hospital setting requires a detailed focus related to individual tasks being performed and the anticipated contaminants that may be encountered. Schools, with their variety of functions, heavy occupant load, and, often, poor maintenance, require special attention. Even an occupancy such as a retail clothing store has unique conditions, where products brought into the building for sale may be emitting VOCs such as tetrachloroethylene from dry cleaning.[4]

The authors of this book recommend that when analyzing IAQ, competent professionals be used who understand the building type and, by their training and experience, can focus on the critical elements of the specific occupancy type. In the fluid IAQ industry, it is critical to stay current with the most up-to-date information. In addition, there are many agencies and organizations who may be contacted for further assistance. A list is provided in App. E.

References

1. *Building Air Quality: A Guide to Building Owners and Facility Managers,* U.S. Environmental Protection Agency, NIOSH, EPA/400/1-91/003, Washington, D.C., December 1991, pp. 19–20.
2. "EPA Survey Indicates Strong Growth in US IAQ Companies," *Indoor Air Quality Update,* October 1993, p. 8.
3. McManamy, Rob, "Owner Files Suit in Illinois," *Engineering News-Record,* November 30, 1992, p. 12.
4. Nriagu, Jerome O., ed., *Gaseous Pollutants,* John Wiley, New York, 1992, p. 352.

Core Checklist

GENERAL
Name/Number of Building: _____

Address/Location: _____
Owner: _____ Facility Manager: _____
Tenants: _____
Nature of Business Conducted by Occupants: _____
Number of Occupants: _____ Number of Floors: _____ Hours of Operation: _____
Area of Building: _____ SF
Description of HVAC System(s): _____

Description of Maintenance Procedures: _____

Description of Housekeeping Procedures: _____

Description of Pest Control: _____
Description of Equipment Maintenance: _____
Date Building Built: _____
Date of Renovation(s): _____ _____ _____
Description of Renovations (Changes in Function/Occupancy/Equipment): _____
_____

SPECIAL USE AREAS	Yes	No
Cafeteria	___	___
Lab	___	___
Kitchen	___	___
Break Room (Cooking)	___	___
Printer Facilities	___	___
Equipment Room	___	___
Parking	___	___
Loading Docks	___	___
Medical Facilities	___	___

PLAN REVIEW		
Plans Available:	___	___
Specs Available:	___	___

SITE ANALYSIS
Description of Surrounding Property: _____
Pollutant Sources Nearby: _____
Other Facilities Nearby: _____
High Traffic Flow: _____
Contaminated Sites Nearby: _____

B

Occupant Health and Comfort Questionnaire*

---

*From *The Industrial Hygienist's Guide to Indoor Air Investigations,* Patrick J. Rafferty, ed., American Industrial Hygiene Association, Fairfax, VA, App. B pp. 57–60. Used with permission of AIHA.

(Optional)   Name:_____
              Job Title:_____
              Department:_____
              Phone:_____
Area or room where you spend the most time in the building: _____
Do any of your work activities produce dust or odor? ___Yes ___No
       Describe:
_____

Gender: ___Male ___Female
Age: ___Under 25 ___25-34 ___35-44 ___45-54 ___55 and over

Do you:
       Smoke?   ___Yes ___No
       Have hay fever/pollen allergies?   ___Yes ___No
       Have skin allergies/dermatitis?   ___Yes ___No
       Have a cold/flu?   ___Yes ___No
       Have sinus problems?   ___Yes ___No
       Have other allergies?   ___Yes ___No
       Wear contact lenses?   ___Yes ___No
       Operate video display terminals?   ___Yes ___No
       Operate photocopiers 10%, or more, of the time?   ___Yes ___No
       Use other special office machines?   ___Yes ___No
              Specify:_____
       Take medication currently?   ___Yes ___No
              Reason:_____

Office characteristics:
       ___ Number of persons sharing same room/work area
       ___ Number of windows in room/work area
              Do windows open? ___Yes ___No

       Please rate adequacy of work space per person
       Poor   Average   Excellent
       1   2   3   4   5

       Please rate room temperature
       Poor   Average   Excellent
       1   2   3   4   5
       Do others smoke in your work area? ___Yes ___No
How long have you worked:
       ___ In this room/area?   ___ In this building?

Symptoms: Select symptoms you have experienced in this building. This is a random
list - not all symptoms listed have been noted in this building.

Symptom	Occasionally	Frequently	Not related to building	Appeared after arrival	Increased after arrival
Difficulty in concentrating					
Aching joints					

Symptom	Occasionally	Frequently	Not related to building	Appeared after arrival	Increased after arrival
Difficulty in					
Muscle twitching					
Back pain					
Hearing problems					
Dizziness					
Dry, flaking skin					
Discolored skin					
Skin irritation					
Itching					
Heartburn					
Nausea					
Noticeable odors					
Sinus congestion					
Sneezing					
High stress levels					
Chest tightness					
Eye irritation					
Fainting					
Hyperventilation					
Problems with contacts					
Headache					
Fatigue/drowsiness					
Temperature too hot					
Temperature too cold					
Other (specify)					

Have you seen a doctor for any or all of these symptoms? ___Yes ___No
When do you experience relief from these symptoms?_____

When do these problems usually occur?
    TIME OF DAY   Morning   Afternoon   Evening
    DAY OF WEEK   S   M   T   W   TH   F   S
    MONTH   J F M A M J J A S O N D
    SEASON   Spring   Summer   Fall   Winter

Do symptoms disappear? ___Yes ___No When?_____

In your opinion, what is the cause of perceived indoor air quality problems? _____
_____

Comments: Please take this opportunity to comment on any factors you consider to be
important concerning the quality of your work environment. _____
_____

HVAC IAQ Investigation Checklist*

---

*Based on information from *Building Air Quality: A Guide for Building Owners and Facility Managers,* EPA/400/1-91/033, DHHS (NIOSH) Publication no. 91-114, December 1991.

Building: _____ File Number: _____

Completed by: _____ Title: _____ Date Checked: _____

Outside Conditions (DB/WB/%Rh) _____

Air Handling System No. _____ System Type:_____

Area Served:_____

Max. Zone Temp. (DB/WB)_____°F   Max Zone Rel Humidity _____%

Min. Zone Temp. (DB/WB)_____°F   Min Zone Rel Humidity _____%

Component	Yes	No	Remarks
Outside Air (O.A.) Intake/Plenum			
Are louvers obstructed?			
Standing water, bird droppings in vicinity of louvers?			
Odors from outdoors? (describe)			
Carryover of exhaust heat?			
Cooling tower within 25 feet?			
Exhaust outlet within 25 feet?			
Trash compactor within 25 feet?			
Near parking facility, busy road, loading dock?			
Bird Screen obstructed?			
O.A. Damper operation acceptable?			
Seal when closed?			
O.A. Damper motors operational?			
Outdoor Air (O.A.) Quantity *(Check against applicable codes and ASHRAE 62-1989).*			
Minimum % O.A. design			
Estimated % O.A. ------------ *Note day, time, HVAC operating mode above*			
Maximum % O.A. - design			
Is minimum O.A. a separate damper?			

Component	Yes	No	Remarks
For VAV systems: is O.A. maintained as total system air-flow is reduced?			
Mixing Plenum			
Clean?			
Floor drain trapped?			
Airtightness/Tight seal			
- of O.A. dampers?			
- of return air dampers?			
- of relief air dampers?			
All damper motors connected?			
All damper motors operational?			
Opposed blade dampers?			
Is mixing plenum under negative pressure? *Note: If it is under positive pressure, outdoor air may not be entering.*			
Filters			
Type _____			
Complete coverage? (i.e., no bypassing)			
Excessive air pressure drop?			
Debris/dirt visible?			
Odor noticeable?			
Moisture noticeable?			
How often changed?			
Cooling Coil/Condensate Pans			
Inspection access available?			
Water carryover into fan/ductwork?			
Any indication of condensation problems?			
Condensate pans accessible?			
Clean condensate pans?			

Component	Yes	No	Remarks
Standing water in condensate pans?			
Visible microbial growth in condensate pans?			
Condensate pan drains and traps clear?			
Evidence of water overflow?			
Auxiliary condensate drain pans installed?			
Are drain pans trapped properly?			
Are drains hard converted into sanitary sewer system?			
Supply Fans/Housing			
Location_____			
Fan blades clean?			
Proper belt tension?			
Excess vibration?			
Corrosion problems?			
Controls operational, calibrated?			
Leakage through supply fan housing?			
Are floor drains inside of fan housing?			
If floor drains present, are they trapped properly?			
Preheat/Heating/Reheat Coil			
Type of coil (gas, electric, water)			
Inspection access available			
Clean?			
Control sequence conforms to design/specifications? (describe changes)			
Evidence of moisture at water coils?			
Gas furnace ignition type?			
Gas furnace vent installed with no obstructions?			

Component	Yes	No	Remarks
Make up air for gas furnace?			
Steam Humidifier			
Humidifier type _____			
Treated boiler water?			
Standing water in ductwork?			
Visible microbial growth in ductwork?			
Duct liner within 12 feet? (If so, check for dirt, mold growth.)			
Straight length of ductwork on humidifier leaving air side?			
Supply Ductwork and Accessories			
Clean?			
Sealed, no leaks, tight connections?			
Fire dampers open?			
Access doors closed?			
Lined ducts?			
Flex duct connected, no tears?			
Light troffer supply?			
Balanced within 3-5 years?			
Balanced after recent renovations?			
Pressurized ceiling supply plenum?			
Return air plenums?			
Are plenum areas free of dirt, debris, moisture?			
Proper layout for air distribution?			
Supply diffusers open?			
Balancing capability?			
Noticeable flow of air?			
Short circuiting or other air distribution problems? *Note location(s) in "Comments"*			

Component	Yes	No	Remarks
Terminal unit controls working?			
Terminal unit filters in place?			
Terminal unit condensate pans clean, drain freely?			
VAV box minimum stops ___%			
Minimum outside air ___%			
HVAC Controls			
Type_____			
Evidence of overheating?			
Evidence of overcooling?			
Humidistat setpoints ___% RH			
Actual RH ___% in critical space			
Building Functions			
Supply and return each room?			
Signs of changed occupancy load?			
Signs of changed equipment loads?			
Signs of changed lighting loads?			
Pollutant Pathways			
Stairwell doors close and latch?			
Stairwell pressurization system?			
Return air plenum?			
Ceiling tile in place?			
Intentional openings in ceiling or walls?			
Return grilles?			
Balancing capability?			
Noticeable flow of air?			
Transfer grilles?			
Fire dampers open?			

Components	Yes	No	Remarks
Exhaust Fans			
Central?			
Distributed (locations)			
Operational?			
Control operational?			
Toilet exhaust only?			
Gravity relief?			
Total powered exhaust ___ cfm			
Make-up air sufficient?			
Special Use Areas:			
Toilets			
Fans working during occupied hours?			
Registers open, clear?			
Make-up air path adequate?			
Volume according to code?			
Floor drain traps wet or sealable?			
Bathrooms run slightly negative to building?			
Smoking Lounges Exhaust			
Room runs negative relative to building?			
Is air exhausted?			
Print Rooms Exhaust			
Room runs negative relative to building?			
Is air exhausted?			
Garages			
Operates according to codes?			
Fans, controls, dampers all operate?			

Component	Yes	No	Remarks
Garage slightly negative relative to building?			
Doors to building close tightly?			
Vestibule entrance to building from garage?			
Evidence of CO monitors?			
Mechanical Rooms			
General condition?			
Controls operational?			
Pneumatic controls:			
■ compressor operational?			
■ air dryer operational?			
Electronic controls? Operational?			
EMS (Emergency Management System) or DDC (Direct Digital Control):			
■ operator on site?			
■ controlled off-site			
■ are fans cycled "off" while building is occupied?			
■ is chiller reset to shed load?			
Preventive Maintenance			
Spare parts inventoried?			
Spare air filters?			
Control drawing posted?			
PM (Preventive Maintenance) schedule available?			
PM followed?			
Boilers			
Flues, breeching tight?			
Fuel system tight, no leaks?			
Combustion air: at least 1 square inch free area per 2000 Btu input.			

Component	Yes	No	Remarks
Cooing Tower			
Sump clean?			
No leaks, no overflow?			
Eliminators working, no carryover?			
No slime or algae?			
Biocide treatment working?			
Dirt separator working?			
Chillers			
No refrigerant leaks?			
Purge cycle normal?			
Waste oil, refrigerant properly disposed of and spare refrigerant properly stored?			
Condensation problems?			

Architecture Construction and Operations Checklist

NEW MATERIALS (Installed w/in the last 12 months)	YES	NO	S.F.	REMARKS (location, special conditions)
Sealants				
Adhesives				
Architectural Coatings				
Particle Board				
Carpet				
Resilient Flooring				
Wall Covering				
Insulation				
Furnishings/Equipment				
VOC's in Materials - Summary				
Figures/tables/photos/exercises				
Materials suspected of releasing VOC's				
TVOC's				
Materials suspected of exceeding VOC limit				

BUILDING CONTAMINATION	YES	NO	S.F.	REMARKS (location, special conditions)
Moisture				
Visible moisture present?				
Can source be identified?				
Odor present?				
Are there concealed absorbative materials?				
Slime?				
Current roof leaks?				
Past roof leaks?				
Is vapor barrier adequate?				
HVAC condensate leakage?				
Other equipment leakage?				
Plumbing leaks?				
History of plumbing overflows?				
Other sources of moisture in the building?				
Is there a need to perform destructive investigation?				

MAINTENANCE ACTIVITIES	YES	NO	S.F.	REMARKS (location, special conditions)
Chemicals being used in the building?				
Are MSDS's present?				
Are MSDS's stored properly?				
History of spills/leaks?				
Are MSDS sheets being used properly?				
Are there areas of excessive dust buildup?				
Pesticide program?				
Past pest infestation?				
Current pest infestation?				
Pest prevention?				
Food present?				
Damp materials?				
Access to building?				
Chemicals used?				
Are MSDS's present?				
Are chemicals appropriate for pests				

CONSTRUCTION ACTIVITIES	YES	NO	S.F.	REMARKS (location, special conditions)
Construction activities in building?				
Proper containment of work area?				
Proper ventilation of work area?				
Excessive noise?				

HAZARDOUS MATERIALS	YES	NO	S.F.	REMARKS (location, special conditions)
Asbestos				
Asbestos program required?				
Inspection report?				
Management plan in place?				
Management plan properly implemented?				
Lead				
Lead program required?				
Inspection report?				
Management plan in place?				
Management plan properly implemented?				

PCBs				
PCB program required?				
Inspection report?				
Management plan in place?				
Management plan properly implemented?				
Radon				
Radon test required?				
Remediation required?				

POLLUTANT PATHWAYS	YES	NO	S.F.	REMARKS (location, special conditions)
Contaminants identified?				
Is contamination spread through pathways?				
Are contaminated area boundaries defined?				

BUILDING FUNCTION AND OCCUPANT LOADS	YES	NO	S.F.	REMARKS (location, special conditions)
Is building function as intended?				
Are occupant loads as intended?				
Any other factors that may impact the IAQ of the facility?				
History of spills/leaks?				
Are MSDS sheets being used properly?				
Are there areas of excessive dust buildup?				
Pesticide program?				
Past pest infestation?				
Current pest infestation?				
Pest prevention?				
Food present?				
Damp materials?				
Access to building?				
Chemicals used?				
Are MSDS's present?				
Are chemicals appropriate for pests				

CONSTRUCTION ACTIVITIES	YES	NO	S.F.	REMARKS (location, special conditions)
Construction activities in building?				
Proper containment of work area?				
Proper ventilation of work area?				

Resources

Adhesive and Sealant Council
1627 K Street, NW, Suite 1000
Washington, D.C. 20006-1707
202/452-1500

Air and Waste Management Association
P.O. Box 2861
Pittsburgh, PA 15230
412/232-3444

American Conference of Governmental Industrial Hygienists (ACGIH)
6500 Glenway Avenue, Building D-7
Cincinnati, OH 45211
513/661-7881

American Consulting Engineers Council (ACEC)
1015 15th Street, NW, Suite 802
Washington, D.C. 20005
202/347-7474

American Floorcovering Association
13-154 Merchandise Mart
Chicago, IL 60654
312/644-1243

American Industrial Hygiene Association (AIHA)
2700 Prosperity Avenue
Suite 250
Fairfax, VA 22031
703/849-8888

American Institute of Architects (AIA)
1735 New York Avenue, NW
Washington, D.C. 20005-5209
202/626-7300

American National Standards Institute, Inc. (ANSI)
1430 Broadway
New York, NY 10018
212/354-3300

American Public Health Association (APHA)
1015 15th Street, NW
Washington, D.C. 20005
202/789-5600

American Society for Testing and Materials (ASTM)
1916 Race Street
Philadelphia, PA 19103
215/299-5571

American Society of Heating, Refrigerating, and Air-Conditioning Engineers
(ASHRAE)
1791 Tullie Circle, NE
Atlanta, GA 30329
404/636-8400

American Wood Council
1250 Connecticut Avenue NW, Suite 230
Washington, D.C. 20036-2603
202/833-1595

Asbestos Information Association
1745 Jefferson Davis Highway, Room 509
Arlington, VA 22202
703/979-1150

Association of Energy Engineers
4025 Pleasantdale Rd., Suite 420
Atlanta, GA 30340
404/447-5083

Association of the Wall & Ceiling Industries International
1600 Cameron St.
Alexandria, VA 22314-2705
703/684-2924

Building Owners and Managers Association International (BOMA)
1201 New York Ave., NW, Suite 300
Washington, D.C. 20005
202/408-2684

Carpet and Rug Institute (CRI)
310 Holiday Avenue
Dalton, GA 30720
404/278-3176

Construction Specification Institute (CSI)
601 Madison St.
Alexandria, VA 22314-1756
703/684-0300

Consumer Product Safety Commission (CPSC)
5401 Westbard Avenue
Bethesda, MD 20207
800/638-CPSC

General Services Administration (GSA)
18th and F Streets, NW
Washington, D.C. 20405
202/501-1464

National Institute for Occupational Safety and Health (NIOSH)
Hazard Evaluations and Technical Assistance Branch (R-9)
4676 Columbia Parkway
Cincinnati, OH 45226
513/841-4382

National Paint and Coatings Association
1500 Rhode Island Avenue, NW
Washington, D.C. 20005
202/462-6272

National Particleboard Association (NPA)
18928 Premiere Ct.
Gaithersburg, MD 20879
301/670-0604

National Pest Control Association
8100 Oak Street
Dunn Loring, VA 22027
703/573-8330

Occupational Safety and Health Administration (OSHA)
U.S. Department of Labor
200 Constitution Avenue, NW
Washington, D.C. 20001
202/523-9667

Thermal Insulation Manufacturers Association Technical Services
Air Handling Committee
1420 King Street
Alexandria, VA 22314
703/684-0474

U.S. Department of Health and Human Services
Office on Smoking and Health
National Center for Chronic Disease
Prevention and Health Promotion
Centers for Disease Control (CDC)
1600 Clifton Road, NE
Mail Stop K50
Atlanta, GA 30333
404/488-5705

U.S. Environmental Protection Agency (EPA)
Public Information Center
401 M Street, SW
Washington, D.C. 20460
202/260-2080

U.S. Environmental Protection Agency
National Pesticides Telecommunications
Network National toll-free number:
1/800 858-PEST
In Texas: 806/743-3091

World Health Organization (WHO)
525 23rd Street, NW
Washington, D.C. 20037
202/861-3200

Glossary

abatement Actions taken to lessen or reduce the risk associated with contaminants in buildings.

absorption A process in which gases are transferred into a liquid or solid medium in which they dissolve.

adiabatic process A humidification process in which no heat is added to or taken away from the supply air.

adsorption A method of collecting gases in which the gas is attracted to, concentrated in, and retained on a substrate.

aerosol Liquid droplets or solid particles, suspended in air, that are of fine enough particle size (0.01 to 100 μm) to remain so dispersed for a period of time.

air change rate Air exchange rate; rate of airflow moving through a space, usually expressed in terms of the room volume units per unit of time [i.e., (room) air changes per hour].

air circulation rate Air circulation ratio; the ratio of air circulating within a closed space per unit of time to the volume of the space.

air cleaner A device that actively removes impurities from the air, including forced air filtration systems and electronic air cleaners.

air-handling unit Part of the HVAC system responsible for moving air, which may also clean, heat, or cool the air.

air quality standard A government-mandated regulation which specifies the maximum contaminant concentration beyond which health risks are considered to be unacceptable.

aldehyde One of a group of highly reactive organic compounds that contain the common group CHO, such as formaldehyde (HCHO).

aliphatic hydrocarbons A class of organic chemicals in which the carbon atoms are attached to each other in a straight chain or branch chain. Some aliphatic compounds have been identified as either promoters or cocarcinogens.

alkane One of a group of saturated aliphatic hydrocarbons present in many waxes, polishes, and lubricants.

allergen   A substance that can trigger an immune response, resulting in an allergic reaction; also known as antigen.

allergy   An increased reactivity to an antigen as a result of previous exposure.

ambient air   Surrounding air; often refers to outdoor air.

amines   Chemical compounds added to steamboiler water to inhibit corrosion. Humidification systems using boiler steam may transfer these potentially dangerous chemicals to the airstream.

anemometer   Device to measure airflow rate.

antimicrobial   An agent that kills microbial growth.

aromatic hydrocarbons   A large class of highly volatile hydrocarbons containing a benzene ring, a class of organic chemicals including toluene, xylene, ethylbenzene, and styrene. Sources of aromatic compounds include paints, adhesives, and solvents.

bacteria   One-celled organisms which are members of the *Protista,* a biological classification.

bakeout   A technique for reducing emissions of new construction, in which the building temperature is raised (usually to at least 90°F) for several days to enhance emissions of volatile compounds from the new materials, while running the ventilation system at full capacity to exhaust the emissions. Factors to consider in planning bakeouts include achievement of adequate ventilation without lowering elevated temperature and the potential structural and material damage due to unanticipated climate stresses.

benzene (C_6H_6)   An aromatic hydrocarbon determined by occupational studies to be a confirmed human (Class A) carcinogen. The principal indoor source of benzene is environmental tobacco smoke. Other sources include petroleum products such as gasoline, oil, and certain petroleum-based solvents.

binder   A component of an adhesive composition that is primarily responsible for the adhesive forces which hold two bodies together.

bioaerosols   Airborne microbial contaminants, including viruses, bacteria, fungi, algae, and protozoa. The term also refers to the reproductive units, metabolites, and particulate material associated with these microorganisms.

biocontaminant   Contaminants which are either life forms (molds of the genera *Aspergillus*) or are derived from living things (rodent droppings).

breathing zone   Area of a room in which occupants breathe as they stand, sit, or lie down.

building envelope   The outer walls, windows, doors, roof, and floors of a building.

building-related illness (BRI)   A diagnosable illness with identifiable symptoms whose cause can be directly attributed to airborne pollutants within the building (e.g., Legionnaire's disease, hypersensitivity pneumonitis).

carbon dioxide (CO_2)   An odorless, colorless gas, which can, at high levels (above 1.5 percent, or 15,000 ppm), have physiological effects. Levels of 6 to 8 percent can cause stupor and death; the lowest detectable effects have been around 1 percent (10,000 ppm). In indoor environments, the main source of CO_2 is human respiration and its measured concentrations are used as an indication of ventilation conditions.

carbon monoxide (CO)   A colorless, odorless, tasteless, and fairly nonreactive gas that is the product of incomplete fuel combustion. It is a chemical asphyxiant; in the bloodstream it effectively prevents transport of oxygen to the body's tissues. CO exposure can affect the heart, lungs, and nervous system and can cause death. Sources include heating and cooking appliances, tobacco smoke, and entrained exhaust from parking garages and truck idling areas.

carcinogen   An agent suspected or known to cause cancer.

carrier   Water or organic solvents used in architectural coatings to provide fluidity for application and increase adhesion through evaporation.

ceiling plenum   The space between the suspended and structural ceiling, used as part of the air-distribution system. This space usually accommodates electrical, communications, and mechanical service connections as well.

chlorofluorocarbons (CFCs)   Compounds made of chlorine, fluorine, carbon, and hydrogen.

coil   A cooling or heating element; often including fins, through which treated gas or liquid is passed, exchanging thermal energy with air surrounding it for heating or cooling. The **cooling coil** is a heat-exchange component in air-handling units, usually consisting of a coil of chilled water or coolant, which cools and dehumidifies ventilation air.

comfort zone   The range of temperature and relative humidity in which 80 percent of the building occupants feel comfortable.

commissioning   The process for achieving, verifying, and documenting the performance of buildings to meet the operational needs of the building within the capabilities of the design and to meet the design documentation and the owner's functional criteria, including preparation of operator personnel.

concentration   The amount of a particular agent or contaminant in a given volume of air.

condenser   A heat-exchange device which condenses vapor by removing heat from the air.

conditioned air   Air that has been heated, cooled, humidified, or dehumidified to maintain an interior space; also known as tempered air.

contaminant   An unwanted constituent that may or may not be associated with adverse health or comfort effects.

convective movement   Air movement resulting from differences in air density caused by temperature differences.

cooling capacity   The maximum rate at which cooling equipment removes heat from airflow operating conditions (expressed in watts).

cooling tower   A heat-transfer device, which cools warm water using atmospheric air. In most designs, water passes through packing—a configuration of splash bars, vertical fins, or honeycombed assemblies—enhancing the exposure to the cooler outside air.

decay rate   The rate at which the concentration of a compound diminishes.

debris   Pieces of material that can be identified as to probable source by visual assessment of their color, texture, or composition.

dehumidifier   A device which removes water vapor from air.

dew point temperature   The temperature at which vapor condenses into liquid.

diffuser   A grille, or inlet; the room air-distribution fixture in HVAC systems that is usually composed of a series of fins that direct and/or mix airflow.

diffusive movement   Movement of a substance, such as radon, from air with a higher concentration of the substance into air with a lower concentration of the substance. The rate of diffusion is proportional to the concentrations of the substance and increases with temperature.

dilution   The reduction of airborne concentration of contaminants through an increase in outdoor air supply.

dirt   Any foul or filthy substance.

disinfectant   One of the three groups of antimicrobials registered by the EPA for public health uses. The EPA defines a disinfectant as an antimicrobial that destroys or irreversibly inactivates organisms, but not necessarily their spores. The EPA registers three types of disinfectant products based upon submitted efficacy data: limited, general, or broad spectrum and hospital disinfectant.

dose   The amount of a given agent that actually reaches the site in the body where it causes an effect.

draft   Local cooling of portions of the body, caused by poor air distribution.

drain pan   The metal trough located below cooling coil components in air-handling systems to collect water condensate.

duct   A tube or passage in an HVAC system for conveying air at low pressures. **Ductwork** refers to the system of ducts, including all branches (also known as trunking).

dust   Solid particles generated by handling, crushing, grinding, rapid impact, deterioration, and decrepitation of organic or inorganic materials, such as rock, ore, metal, coal, wood, and grain.

economizer   Any mechanical device that adjusts to variable conditions to maximize energy efficiency; a control option in ventilation systems that makes optimum use of outside air supply air, providing so called free cooling.

electromagnetic field (EMF)   The nonionizing electronic and magnetic radiation generated by electrical power lines and appliances.

electrostatic air cleaner   A device which uses an electrical charge to trap particles traveling in the airstream.

emission   The release of airborne contaminants from a source.

emission rate   A measure of the quantity of a chemical released into the air from a given quantity of a source during a given amount of time.

emission standard   A voluntary guideline or government regulation that specifies the maximum rate at which a contaminant can be released from a source; also called source emission standard.

encapsulant   A barrier used to prevent the release of contaminants from sources.

encapsulation   A mitigation technique which reduces or eliminates emissions from a source by sealing with an impenetrable barrier.

environmental tobacco smoke (ETS)   Combustion emissions (composed of over 3800 identifiable contaminants, including 43 known or suspected carcinogens) released either by burning tobacco or exhaled tobacco smoke.

ergonomics   The applied science that investigates the impacts of the physical environment on human stress, comfort, and health, considering such factors as climate control, lighting, furnishings, noise, and overcrowding.

exhaust air   Air removed from a space and discharged outdoors.

exhaust ventilation   Localized ventilation that removes pollutants, usually from a fixed source with known contaminants (e.g., equipment, bathrooms, and kitchens), and expels them outdoors.

exposure   The contact of a pollutant with the susceptible part of the body.

fan   A device with rotating blades that moves air; types of fans include an **axial fan:** one that propels airflow parallel to the axis; a **centrifugal fan:** one that draws air in axially, propelling it radially (roughly perpendicular to the axis); and a **tubeaxial fan:** an axial fan that is enclosed in a cylinder, such as a ducted fan.

fiberglass   A type of manufactured mineral fiber made from spun glass, often used to line HVAC ducts.

filter   A device or medium, such as a cartridge, used for removing either gases or particulates from the airstream.

flushout   A preoccupancy preventive procedure which involves running a ventilation system on its highest settings to remove the airborne emissions from newly installed furnishings and carpeting.

footcandle (fc)   A unit of illumination equal to 1 lumen per square foot.

formaldehyde (HCHO)   An odorous VOC that contains oxygen in addition to carbon and hydrogen which is usually in the form of a colorless gas at room temperature.

fresh air   Outdoor air; air from the outside that has not been previously circulated.

friable air   Capable of being crushed by hand pressure.

fume   Airborne particles formed by the evaporation of solid materials (e.g., metal fume emitted during welding); usually less than 1 μm in diameter.

fungi   Unicellular or multicellular eukaryotic organisms embracing a large group of microflora including molds, mildews, yeasts, mushrooms, rusts, and smuts.

gas   A state of matter in which the material has very low density and viscosity, can expand and contract greatly in response to changes in temperature and pressure, easily diffuses into other gases, and readily and uniformly distributes itself throughout any container.

grille (or grill)   A component of a ventilation system through which return air is collected.

halogenated hydrocarbon   An organic compound which has had one or more hydrogen atoms replaced by fluorine, chlorine, bromine, or iodine.

hazard   Something or a condition which has the capability of producing adverse health or safety consequences to humans.

heat   The thermal form of energy.

hertz (Hz)   One complete cycle in a sound wave which is propagated through air.

high-efficiency particulate air (HEPA) filter   A classification of high-efficiency filters.

house dust mite   Common microscopic household arachnid. Mites feed on shed skin scales and therefore tend to concentrate around mattresses and furniture. Humidity is a critical factor for dust mite populations, which require relative humidity levels greater than 45 percent for survival.

humidifier   A device that adds moisture to air.

humidifier fever   A form of pneumonitis attributed to allergic reactions of the alveolar walls to amoebae, bacteria, or fungi found in the humidifier reservoirs, as well as air conditioners and air-cooling equipment.

humidity   Water vapor in air.

HVAC   A heating, ventilation, and air-conditioning system.

hydrocarbons   The large class of organic compounds that contain both a carbon and hydrogen atom.

hypersensitivity disease   A type of disease characterized by allergic responses to antigens.

indoor air quality (IAQ)   The characteristics of the indoor climate of a building, including the gaseous composition, temperature, relative humidity, and airborne contaminant levels.

integrated pest management (IPM)   An alternative approach to pest control that minimizes the use of chemical pesticides, using a coordinated approach of sanitation, habitat control, nonchemical traps, and selective applications of pesticides when necessary.

isothermal process   A humidification process which adds moisture already converted to water vapor directly into the airstream.

latency period   The time elapsed between initial induction of effect and its detection; often used in context of carcinogenic effects.

Legionnaires' disease   One of two important diseases (the other being Pontiac fever) that are caused by *Legionella pneumophila* bacteria. The disease is a severe multisystemic illness that can affect not only the lungs but also the gastrointestinal tract, central nervous system, and kidneys.

load   A term referring to quantity of energy required per unit of time.

louver   A covering for an opening or inlet consisting of a series of sloped vanes to allow a flow of air while inhibiting the flow of rain or other elements.

materials safety data sheets (MSDSs)   OSHA-required documents supplied by manufacturers of potentially hazardous products. MSDSs contain information regarding potentially significant airborne contaminants, precautions for inspection, health effects, odor description, volatility, expected contaminants from combustion, reactivity, and procedures for spill cleanup.

mesothelioma   A type of cancer affecting the lung and chest cavity, often associated with asbestos exposure.

microbe   A microorganism that is pathogenic.

microorganisms   Life forms too small to be viewed with the unaided eye.

mildew   A superficial covering of organic surfaces with fungi under damp conditions.

mist   Suspended liquid droplets generated by condensation from the gaseous to the liquid or by breaking up a liquid into a dispersed state.

mitigation   A procedure or strategy aimed at reducing or eliminating an indoor air problem, either through source control, ventilation control, exposure reduction, or air cleaning.

mixing box   A compartment in an HVAC system in which airstreams from different sources are mixed and combined for release as a single airstream.

modifier   A chemically inert ingredient added to an adhesive formulation that changes its properties but does not react chemically with the binder.

mold   A fungal infestation that causes disintegration of a substance.

monitoring   The process of assessing exposure to specific pollutants.

multiple chemical sensitivities (MCS)   A medical condition affecting several organs in which a person reports sensitivity to very low doses of a variety of chemicals after an identifiable chemical exposure to one chemical.

National Ambient Air Quality Standard (NAAQS)   The U.S. outdoor air quality standards designed to protect public health. Pollutants covered by the NAAQS include ozone, sulfur dioxide, nitrogen dioxide, lead, respirable particulates, and carbon monoxide.

natural ventilation   The supply of outdoor air through passive flow from windows, chimneys, doors, and other infiltration.

occupied zone   The area in a room or building in which most human activity takes place, considered by ASHRAE to be between 3 and 72 in (75 and 1800 mm) from the floor and 2 ft (600 mm) from walls or fixed equipment.

odor   A chemical characteristic that is detected by the olfactory epithelium.

off-gassing   The release of gases, such as organic vapors, from a building material after the manufacturing process is complete.

operative temperature   The uniform temperature of an imaginary black enclosure in which an occupant would exchange the same amount of heat by radiation plus convection as in the actual nonuniform environment.

organism   A living thing, ranging from humans to single-cell bacteria, consisting of various parts, each specializing in a different function.

outdoor air   Atmospheric air drawn into a building that has not been previously circulated through the HVAC system.

ozone (O_3)   A highly reactive trivalent form of oxygen. Ozone exposure can result in mucous membrane irritation and potential pulmonary damage.

particulates   Small airborne particles found in the indoor environment that include fibrous material, solid-state semivolatile organic compounds such as polycyclic aromatic hydrocarbons (PAHs), trace metal, and biological materials.

passive sampler   A small device worn by an individual to measure personal exposure to specific contaminants.

PEL   Permissible exposure limit; air contaminant standards set by OSHA.

pesticide   A chemical used to kill or control living organisms. Pesticides include insecticides, herbicides, fungicides, rodenticides, antimicrobial agents, and plant growth regulators.

4-phenylcyclohexene (4-PC)   An odoriferous compound that is a by-product of the manufacture of styrenebutadiene latex backing of some carpets.

physical factors   Conditions other than indoor air contaminants that cause stress, comfort, and/or health problems (e.g., lighting, sound, and ergonomic factors).

plenum   An enclosure in HVAC systems that collects air at the origin or terminus of a duct system. Plenums may be above ceilings, below floors, or a shaft between walls.

pollutant   A contaminant that is known to cause illness; often used synonymously with contaminant.

pollutant pathway   A route of entry of an airborne contaminant from a source location into the occupant breathing zone through architectural or mechanical connections (e.g., through cracks in walls, vents, and open windows).

polychlorinated biphenyls (PCBs)   Compounds containing two benzene rings and at least two chlorine atoms. They are highly toxic.

polycyclic aromatic hydrocarbons (PAHs)   A group of complex organic substances with four or more ring structures, generally associated with certain combustion processes such as wood burning, tobacco smoking, and cooking; also known as polynuclear aromatic hydrocarbons or polynuclear hydrocarbons.

Pontiac fever   A form of legionellosis that is much milder than Legionnaires' disease. It has a short incubation period (2 to 3 days) and attacks 90 percent of those infected. Reports of Pontiac fever outbreaks are rare, possibly because of the similarity of the symptoms—fever, chills, headache, muscle ache—to the flu.

preventive maintenance   A program of building maintenance implemented to reduce the possibility of IAQ problems, usually through periodic inspection, cleaning, adjustment, calibration, and replacement of the functioning parts of the HVAC system, as well as good housekeeping practices to reduce the buildup of potential contaminants.

psychosocial factors   The individual psychological and group dynamic factors that cause or contribute to reported physical complaints, such as job stress, corporate organizational problems, interpersonal difficulties, and individual psychological factors.

psychrometer   An instrument for determining relative humidity by measuring both wet and and dry bulb temperatures.

radon   A colorless, odorless, radioactive gas emitted during the disintegration of radium. Radon can be a serious indoor air contaminant in building areas which are in contact with or are penetrated by gases emitted from radium-containing bedrock or building stones.

recirculated air   Return air that has been conditioned and returned to a given space.

relative humidity (RH)   The percentage of moisture in the air relative to the amount it could hold if saturated at the same temperature.

resin   A nonvolatile solid or semisolid organic material, usually of high molecular weight; obtained as gum from certain trees or manufactured synthetically; tends to flow when subjected to heat or stress; soluble in most organic solvents but not in water; the film-forming component of a paint or varnish; used in making plastics or adhesives.

respirable suspended particulates (RSP)   Inhalable particulate matter; particulates less than 10 μm in diameter.

return air   The air removed from an occupied space and returned to the air handler to be exhausted or recirculated.

risk   A statement, either quantitative via statistical expression or qualitative via subjected expression, of the probability or likelihood that harm will actually occur.

sanitizer   One of three groups of antimicrobials registered by the EPA for public health and, which reduces microbial colonies by 99.9 percent but does not necessarily eliminate all organisms on a treated surface.

sealant   Any material used to prevent the passage of liquid or gas across a joint or opening.

sealer   A liquid wood, plaster, etc., that prevents the surface from absorbing paint or varnish.

sick building   A building in which the IAQ is considered to be unacceptable to a substantial majority of occupants.

sick building syndrome (SBS)   A term used to refer to the condition in which a majority of building occupants experience a variety of health and/or comfort effects linked to time spent in a particular building, but where no specific illness or causative agent can be identified. Symptoms often include headaches, eye irritation, and respiratory irritation.

sink   A material with the property of adsorbing a chemical or pollutant with the potential of subsequent reemission; sometimes called a **sponge.**

smoke   A cloud of airborne particles, either solid, liquid, or both, produced by incomplete combustion of carbon-containing materials.

soil gases   Gases that enter a building from the surrounding ground (e.g., radon and volatile organics).

solvent   A liquid used to dissolve a solid (such as a paint resin) so that it is brushable; usually volatile; evaporates from the paint film after application.

source control   A preventive strategy for reducing airborne contaminant levels through the removal of the material or activity generating the pollutants.

stack effect   A condition resulting from the rise of heated air, which creates positive pressure near the top of the building and negative pressure toward the bottom. Stack-effect pressures have been known to overpower mechanical ventilation systems, disrupting proper circulation and contributing to the infiltration and stagnation of pollutants.

sterilizer   One of the EPA class of antimicrobial compounds that destroys or eliminates all forms of viruses, bacteria, fungi, and their spores; also known as a sporicide or sterilant.

stressor   Any biological, chemical, physical, psychological, or social factor that contributes to a complaint.

temperature   The thermal state of a substance, which determines its ability to exchange heat with adjacent substances.

threshold   The contaminant dose or exposure level below which there is no expected significant effect.

threshold limit value (TLV)   The ACGIH-recommended guideline for a contaminant exposure limit represented in terms of exposure over a work day (8 h) or work week (40 h).

threshold limit value-ceiling (TLV-C)   The contaminant concentration which should not be exceeded for any length of time during a work shift.

threshold limit value–short-term exposure limit (TLV-STEL)   The contaminant concentration to which research indicates workers can be exposed for a short time period without suffering from irritation, injury, or adverse health effects (assuming the TLV-TWA is not exceeded).

threshold limit value–time-weighted average (TLV-TWA)   The contaminant concentration to which research indicates workers can be exposed repeatedly over a specified time period without adverse effect.

total volatile organic compounds (TVOCs)   A measure representing the sum of all VOCs present in the air.

toxicity   The nature and degree of a given agent's adverse effects on living organisms.

tracer gas   An inert compound that is a rare constituent of indoor air, such as sulfur hexafluoride (SF_6), which is released into building air and monitored qualitatively and/or quantitatively to characterize airflow characteristics. Applications include contaminant pathway detection, infiltration, and ventilation efficiency measurements.

vapor   The gaseous forms of substances that are normally in the liquid or solid state (at room temperature and pressure).

variable air volume (VAV)   An HVAC system that modifies room temperature by varying the quantity of supply air rather than altering the supply air temperature.

ventilation air   The treated air leaving an air-handling unit, composed of both outdoor air and recirculated air.

ventilation standard   A specification for the minimum rate of input of outdoor air into indoor spaces.

volatile organic compound (VOC)   One of a class of chemical components that contain one or more carbon atoms and are volatile at room temperature and normal atmospheric pressure. In indoor air, VOCs are generated by such sources as tobacco smoke, building products, furnishings, cleaning materials, solvents, polishes, cosmetics, deodorizers, and office supplies.

zone   An area within a building conditioned by a single controlling device.

Symbols and Abbreviations

ABIH American Board of Industrial Hygiene

ABPA Allergic bronchopulmonary aspergillus

ACGIH American Council of Governmental Industrial Hygienists

ACM Asbestos-containing material

ACT Acoustical ceiling tile

AH & MA American Hotel and Motel Association

AIHA American Industrial Hygiene Association

AL Action limit

ALI Anderson Laboratories, Inc.

ANSI American National Standards Institute

ASHRAE American Society of Heating, Refrigerating, and Air-Conditioning Engineers

ASTM American Society for Testing and Materials

BEI Biological exposure indices

BRI Building-related illness

BTUH British thermal unit per hour

CDC Centers for Disease Control

CFC Chlorofluorocarbon

cfm Cubic feet per minute

CFU Colony-forming units

CIH Certified industrial hygienist

CIIT Chemical Industry Institute of Toxicology

CO Carbon monoxide

CO₂ Carbon dioxide

COHb Carboxyhemoglobin

CPSC Consumer Products Safety Commission

CRI Carpet and Rug Institute

dB Decibel

dBA A-weighted decibel

DDC Direct digital controls

EAT Entering air temperature

ECP East Campus Plus

EL Excursion limit

EMFs Electromagnetic fields

EPA U.S. Environmental Protection Agency

ETS Environmental tobacco smoke

fc Footcandles

FEP Free erythrocyte protoporphyrin

FIFRA Federal Insecticide, Fungicide and Rodenticide Act

f/cm³ Fibers per cubic centimeter

fpm Feet per minute

HCHO Formaldehyde

HEPA High-efficiency particulate air

HUD U.S. Department of Housing and Urban Development

HVAC Heating, ventilating, and air-conditioning

Hz Hertz

IAQ Indoor air quality

IESNA Illuminating Engineering Society of North America

IPM Integrated pest management

LBPPPA Lead-Based Paint Poisoning Prevention Act

LIL Lensed-direct lighting

LOD Limit of detection

LOQ Limit of quantification

MCS Multiple chemical sensitivity

MDD Medium density fiberboard

met-Hb Methemoglobin

mG Milligauss

mg/m³ Milligrams per cubic meter

mg/m² Milligrams per square meter

μg/dl Micrograms per deciliter

μg/cm² Micrograms per square centimeter

μg/ft² Micrograms per square foot

MSDS Material safety data sheet

MW Molecular weight

NAAQS National Ambient Air Quality Standards

NASA National Aeronautics and Space Administration

NBS National Bureau of Standards

NESHAP National Emission Standards for Hazardous Air Pollutants

NIOSH National Institute of Occupational Safety and Health

NIST National Institute of Standards and Technology

NO Nitric oxide

NO₂ Nitrogen dioxide

NOPES Non-occupational Pesticides Exposure Study

NPA National Particleboard Association

NPDES National Pollution Discharge Elimination System

O&M Operations and Maintenance

O₂ Oxygen

OHb Oxygemoglobin

OSHA Occupational Safety and Health Administration

OSHAct Occupational Safety and Health Act

PAH Polycyclic aromatic hydrocarbon

PBL   Parabolic louvers

4-PC   4-phenylcyclohexene

PCBs   Polychlorinated biphenyls

pCi/L   Picocuries per liter

PEL   Permissible exposure limit

PET   Polyethylene terepthalate

PF   Phenol formaldehyde

PNA   Polynuclear aromatic hydrocarbon

ppm   Parts per million

psi   Pounds per square inch

PVC   Polyvinyl chloride resins

QA   Quality assurance

RCRA   Resource Conservation and Recovery Act

RH   Relative humidity

RSP   Respirable particulate

s/cm³   Structures per cubic centimeter

SBR   Styrene butadiene rubber

SBS   Sick building syndrome

SF$_6$ Sulfur hexafluoride

SO$_2$ Sulfur dioxide

SVOCs   Semivolatile organic compounds

TEM   Transmission electron microscopy

TLV   Threshold limit value

TLV-C   Threshold limit value-ceiling

TLV-STEL   Threshold limit value-short-term exposure limit

TLV-TWA   Threshold limit value-time-weighted average

TSCA   Toxic Substance Control Act

TSI   Thermal systems insulation

TSP   Trisodium phosphate

TSS   Transitional steady-state

TVOCs   Total volatile organic compounds

TWA   Time-weighted average

UF   Urea formaldehyde

UFFI   Urea formaldehyde foam insulation

VAV   Variable air volume

VDT   Visual display terminal

VOCs   Volatile organic compounds

WHO   World Health Organization

Index

Index

ABOUT THE AUTHORS

STEVE M. HAYS, P.E., C.I.H. is a licensed chemical engineer and a certified industrial hygienist. A past president of the Environmental Information Association, he has also served on committees for the U.S. Environmental Protection Agency and the American Consulting Engineers Council. Currently he serves on committees for the National Institute of Building Sciences, the Amercian Society for Testing and Materials, the American Industrial Hygiene Association, and is a member of the Tennessee Air Pollution Control Board. Mr. Hays is a member of seminar faculties at the Georgia Tech Research Institute and The Environmental Institute and lectures frequently on environmental topics at conferences and universities throughout the United States. He is the author of many papers and articles on environmental issues.

RONALD V. GOBBELL, AIA has been a licensed architect in private practice for 20 years. He has served as advisor and consultant to the U.S. Environmental Protection Agency and has testified on environmental issues before the U.S. Senate and several state legislatures. He has conducted presentations for universities, government agencies, professional associations, and private organizations and has lectured internationally on environmental topics. Mr. Gobbell is a past chairman of Tennessee's Architectural, Engineering, Landscape Architects, and Interior Designers Registration Board and is a member of the National Council of Architectural Registration Boards. He is also the author of many papers and articles on environmental issues.

NICHOLAS R. GANICK, P.E. is a mechanical engineer with experience in the design and construction of HVAC systems in a variety of facilities throughout the United States. He is the author of many papers on the subject of indoor air quality and has performed numerous IAQ surveys.

The authors are member of Gobbell Hays Partners, Inc. (GHP), an architectural, engineering, and environmental consulting firm. The firm's practice is nationwide, with environmental projects at more than 6000 facililties from San Juan, Puerto Rico, to Anchorage, Alaska. The authors have had the opportunity to work together to test their solutions and strategies in the field.